GREAT
JEWISH
FAMILIES

ALSO BY DARRYL LYMAN

Civil War Wordbook
Dictionary of Animal Words and Phrases
Essential English
Fifty Golden Years of Oscar
Great Jews in Music
Great Jews on Stage and Screen
The Jewish Comedy Catalog
Jewish Heroes & Heroines

GREAT
JEWISH
FAMILIES

DARRYL LYMAN

 JONATHAN DAVID PUBLISHERS, INC.
Middle Village, New York 11379

GREAT JEWISH FAMILIES

Jonathan David Publishers, Inc.
68-22 Eliot Avenue
Middle Village, New York 11379

2   4   6   8   10   9   7   5   3   1

Library of Congress Cataloging-in-Publication Data

Lyman, Darryl, 1944–
  Great Jewish families / Darryl Lyman
         p. cm.
     Includes index.
     ISBN 0-8246-0400-8
     1. Jewish families—Biography. 2. Jews—Biography. I. Title.
  DS115.L95   1997
  920' .0092924—dc21

97–18940
CIP
r97

Design and composition by John Reinhardt Book Design

Printed in the United States of America

To Mom

ACKNOWLEDGMENTS

Thanks are due to the following individuals for supplying information and photographs for this book: Joan Adler of the Straus Historical Society, Joseph A. Koenigsberger of the Harry Frank Guggenheim Foundation, Kevin Proffitt of the American Jewish Archives, Howard M. Sachar, and Oscar S. Straus II of the Daniel and Florence Guggenheim Foundation. A special thank you goes to Fiorella deLima of Jonathan David Publishers for guiding the production of *Great Jewish Families*.

CONTENTS

INTRODUCTION

Great Jewish Families presents the stories of over eighty outstanding families of Jewish achievers. The families covered in these biographies were selected because of their tremendous impact on their fields of endeavor, on their eras, and on their nations and regions. These families made a difference in the human condition.

It is not surprising to find so many such families in the Jewish community. Ostracized and isolated for centuries by the outside world, Jews banded together in their own little units, especially the tightest, most natural unit—the family. Jews learned, by hard experience, that to succeed—indeed, to survive—they had to work harder than others. The lesson of diligence was passed down from generation to generation, and from those families with the strongest tradition of concentrated effort came the achievers who constitute the *Great Jewish Families*.

Business, philanthropy, religion, government, literature, theater—these and other fields of endeavor have been conquered by the great Jewish families. Staggering business success and philanthropy are represented by the Guggenheims, the Rothschilds, the Warburgs, and others. Among the great religious dynasties are the Hillels, the Maimons, and the Soloveichiks. The field of government service has the Begins, literature has the Singers, and the theater has the Adlers. In many cases, business success in early generations spawned the financial freedom for later generations to explore other fields, as with the Lehmans.

Great Jewish Families covers all eras. Examples include the Hasmoneans (or Maccabees) from the ancient world, Rashi and his descendants from the medieval period, and the Pritzkers from the modern age. The Abulafias produced a steady stream of outstanding members from the twelfth century to the twentieth, while the Schiffs have been prominent since the fourteenth.

Many of the great Jewish families have had a profound effect on their nations or regions. The Sassoons played a major role in the nineteenth-century commercial development of India and the Far East, helping to modernize that part of the world. Israel owes much of its contemporary spiritual, military, and political texture to the Dayans, the Herzogs, and the Netanyahus. In the United States, the Seligmans were the models and the pathbreakers for thousands of other Jewish immigrant families, being the first to achieve business and philanthropic prominence, the first to make the transition from merchants to bankers, and the first to attain high social distinction.

Great Jewish Families follows the most widely accepted definition of a Jew: anyone who was born of a Jewish mother or who converted to Judaism. Family members fitting this definition are included even if they did not practice Judaism or if they converted to another religion. Excluded by this definition are family members born of a Jewish father and non-Jewish mother. The Jewish financier August Belmont, for example, married a non-Jew and raised his children as Episcopalians, so that the famous family he founded was non-Jewish. The rare exception to the above rules is noted and explained in the text.

THE
ABULAFIAS

THE ABULAFIAS WERE A WIDESPREAD, influential family that produced celebrated rabbis, scholars, poets, statesmen, and community leaders. The name *Abulafia* (Arabic for "father of health") first appears in Jewish records of twelfth-century Spain.

The most important Spanish Abulafias, centered in Toledo from the 1100s, were Levites and usually surnamed Levi Abulafia. Todros ben Joseph ha-Levi Abulafia (died 1225) was a patron of literature and the father of the writer Joseph ben Todros ha-Levi Abulafia (fl. first half of thirteenth century), who participated in the controversy over the proper use of the writings of Maimonides, and the talmudist Meir ben Todros ha-Levi Abulafia (c. 1170–1244), the most renowned Spanish rabbi of his time. (At least one authority, however, believes that Meir's father was Tobias ben Meir Abulafia.)

Joseph ben Todros was the father of the talmudist and cabalist Todros ben Joseph ha-Levi Abulafia (c. 1220–83/98), one of the first Spanish Jews to follow the cabala. This Todros ben Joseph was the father of another Joseph ben Todros ha-Levi Abulafia (fl. late thirteenth and early fourteenth centuries), a cabalist who was an authority on the *Shem ha-Kotev*, one of the Divine Names.

Many other Spanish Abulafias made outstanding contributions.

Samuel ha-Levi Abulafia (fl. late thirteenth century), a scientist and engineer employed from 1252 to 1284 by King Alfonso X of Castile, constructed a water clock and perfected hoisting devices. Abraham ben Samuel Abulafia (1240–c. 1292) lived one of the most remarkable lives of the medieval period as an adventurous wanderer and as one of the most important early cabalists.

Todros ben Judah ha-Levi Abulafia (1247–after 1295) was one of the greatest medieval Hebrew poets. Samuel ben Meir ha-Levi Abulafia (c. 1320–c. 1360) served his Jewish community as a philanthropist and worked for the king of Castile as a treasurer, diplomat, and adviser.

After the expulsion of the Jews from Spain near the end of the fifteenth century, Abulafias established themselves elsewhere, notably in Palestine and Syria. Jacob ben Solomon Abulafia (c. 1550–c. 1622) served as rabbi of the Spanish congregation in Damascus, became an important halakic authority, and wrote responsa on the Pentateuch. Hayyim ben Jacob Abulafia (1580–1668), Jacob ben Solomon's son, was a Palestinian talmudist who settled in Jerusalem in 1628, later directed the yeshiva in Hebron, and, near the end of his life, returned to Jerusalem. A grandson of Hayyim ben Jacob was Hayyim ben David Abulafia (c. 1700–75), who was born either in Jerusalem or in Smyrna, lived in Greece for many years, served as rabbi of Smyrna (1761–75), produced many important halakic decisions, and wrote a number of works, including responsa.

One famous branch of the family was centered in the city of Tiberias, Palestine. Hayyim ben Moses (or Jacob) Abulafia (c. 1660–1744) served as rabbi in Smyrna, Safed, and, in old age, Tiberias, whose restoration he initiated; he was a prolific author of religious works. His son Isaac Abulafia (died 1764) succeeded his father as rabbi and community leader in Tiberias. Hayyim ben Moses' other son, Issachar Abulafia (fl. eighteenth century), became head of the talmudic academy in Sofia.

Later members of the family continued the rabbinic tradition in Tiberias. Joseph David Abulafia (died 1823) and his grandson of the same name (died 1898) were rabbis there. Hayyim Nissim ben Isaac Abulafia (1775–1861) succeeded his father as head of the Jews of Tiberias and late in life moved to Jerusalem, where in 1854 he was elected chief rabbi. Isaac ben Moses Abulafia (1824–1910) was born in Tiberias, served as rabbi of Damascus and Tyre, and died in Tiberias; a great halakic scholar, he wrote many published responsa.

Abulafias also settled in Italy, where the family name took such forms as Bolaffi and Bolaffio. Ezekiel (or Hezekiah) David ben Mordecai Abulafia (or Bolaffi) was an eighteenth-century Italian scholar and poet.

Meir ben Todros ha-Levi Abulafia

TALMUDIC COMMENTATOR

Meir ben Todros ha-Levi Abulafia was the most highly respected Spanish rabbi of the first half of the thirteenth century. A versatile man of learning, he produced a rich, varied body of literary works, notably his extensive commentary on the Talmud.

Meir was born in Burgos, Spain, probably in 1170. His father, Todros ben Joseph ha-Levi Abulafia, was greatly esteemed by the Jews of Castile because of his aristocratic background, his access to the court, and his generosity, especially his patronage of literature. Todros carried the honorary title of *nasi* ("prince"), which Meir inherited when his father died.

As a young man, Meir moved from Burgos to Toledo, Spain, where he remained for the rest of his life. He helped to organize the Jewish communities in Spain and to set up many religious regulations.

In his literary activities, Meir contributed to four categories: talmudic commentary, writings on the Masora (studies of the textual traditions of the Hebrew Old Testament), letters on the controversy over Moses Maimonides' opinion on the subject of resurrection, and Hebrew poetry. His commentary, covering about half the Talmud, summarized and concluded the talmudic school of the Spanish rabbis. Under the pseudonym Yad Ramah ("High Hand," a play on the abbreviation of his name), he wrote his commentary entirely in Aramaic in the book *Sefer peratei peratin* ("Book of Minute Details"), in which he went into the smallest details of each subject. He also wrote hundreds of responsa, of which about seventy became well known by being included in the collection *Or zaddikim* ("Light of the Righteous," published in 1799).

Meir's work *Masoret seyag la-Torah* ("Tradition Is the Fence of the Law"), presenting his research into the traditional text of the Scriptures, long influenced laws governing the writing of scrolls of the Torah. His textual studies also helped to establish the authenticity of the Aleppo Codex, a manuscript copy of the Bible.

Meir took a firm stand against the philosophical views of his older contemporary Moses Maimonides, especially the latter's doctrine of resurrection, which Meir believed to be heretical. He was the first European publicly to denounce Maimonides' ideas. Meir's arguments were mainly in the form of letters to the rabbis of southern France, especially those in Lunel, who held Maimonides in great esteem. However, though Meir disagreed with many of Maimonides' opinions, the younger man respected his elder's achievements. After Maimonides' death Meir wrote a long elegy on him.

He also authored a number of Hebrew poems. They show that he was acquainted with the poetry of earlier Spanish Jews and was influenced by Moses ibn Ezra in his meter, rhyme, and construction.

Meir's only son, Judah, died in 1226. But Meir also had daughters, who gave him grandchildren and great-grandchildren who lived in Toledo for a century after his death and were connected by marriage with the foremost families of the city.

Meir ben Todros ha-Levi Abulafia died in Toledo in 1244.

Todros ben Joseph ha-Levi Abulafia

Spiritual Leader of Jews in Castile

Rabbi, talmudist, and cabalist, the wealthy, learned Todros ben Joseph ha-Levi Abulafia was the spiritual leader of the Jewish community in the Castile region of Spain. He also had great influence at the court of King Alfonso X.

Todros was born in Burgos, Spain, in about 1220, son of the writer Joseph ben Todros ha-Levi Abulafia and nephew of the talmudist Meir ben Todros ha-Levi Abulafia. (Up to about 1930 Todros ben Joseph was confused with Todros ben Judah ha-Levi Abulafia, who, like Todros ben Joseph, was associated with the Toledo cabalists.)

From his uncle Meir, Todros inherited the honorary title of *nasi* ("prince") as well as a leading role in the spiritual life of Jews in Spain. He studied cabala under Moses ben Solomon ben Simeon and became one of the foremost cabalists of his generation. His teachings opposed the rationalistic doctrines of Maimonides.

Todros was the first to interpret the Haggadah (ancient Jewish lore) of the Talmud in the cabalistic (mystic) sense. His *Ozar ha-kavod* ("Treasury of Glory"), a cabalistic interpretation of Haggadoth in a number of talmudic tractates, combines the doctrines of the cabalistic schools in the Spanish regions of Castile and Gerona. Both it and his earlier work, *Sha'ar ha-razim* ("Gate of Secrets"), a commentary on Psalm 19, include quotations from the *Sefer ha-zohar* ("Book of Splendor") of Moses de León. He also wrote a commentary on the first chapter of Ezekiel.

Todros exerted secular influence as well, especially at the court of Alfonso X, who granted him estates during the distribution of lands in Seville (1253) and Jerez de la Frontera (1266). In 1275 he accompanied the king to France. In 1280–81 Alfonso ordered the arrest of all Jewish tax farmers, who were tortured in an attempt to make them convert. Todros pleaded for their release. However, he also criticized the Jewish community for mistakes that had precipitated the situation. In a sermon, he told his congregation to avoid gentile women and to carry out his imposed penances.

His son Joseph also became a noted cabalist in Toledo. Joseph was friendly with Moses de León and was among the first to receive a copy of the latter's *Sefer ha-zohar*, a seminal work in Jewish mysticism.

The date of Todros ben Joseph ha-Levi Abulafia's death is uncertain. He died in Toledo, probably in either 1283 or 1295.

Abraham ben Samuel Abulafia

CREATOR OF "PROPHETIC" CABALA

Abraham ben Samuel Abulafia fathered a new, "prophetic" kind of cabala, based on mystical doctrines that he claimed he obtained through inspired revelations. He lived a remarkable life full of travels and adventures, during which he produced a large, varied body of writing.

Abraham was born in Zaragoza, Spain, in 1240. In 1260 he traveled to Palestine in search of the mythical river Sambatyon and the remnants of the Lost Ten Tribes of Israel. Halted in his quest by the wars between Muslims and Christians, he returned to Europe through Greece, where he married, and Italy, where he studied the philosophy of Maimonides under Hillel ben Samuel of Verona and the cabala under Baruch Togarmi.

Back in Spain, Abraham intensified his cabala studies. Believing that he had attained prophetic inspiration, he began to develop his mystical doctrines and to cultivate a group of followers.

In 1273 he left Spain again, and throughout the rest of the 1270s he traveled in Italy, Sicily, and Greece. During those years, he wrote mystical essays expounding his new ideas.

In 1280 he was again in Spain, where he attracted a large following of young scholars. Some of them, confused by the apparent similarity between his prophetic revelations and Christian doctrine, accepted baptism.

Later that year Abraham went to Rome with the intention of converting Pope Nicholas III to Judaism or at least persuading him to help the Jews. Instead, the pope condemned the visionary to be burned at the stake. The pope's sudden death prevented the sentence from being carried out, and after a month in prison Abraham was released.

He went to Sicily, where he continued to write. During his stay there he predicted that the messianic era would begin in the Jewish year of 5050 (1290 C.E.). The number of his followers increased dramatically.

Many, however, opposed him vehemently. They accused him of claiming to be the Messiah and sought an opinion on him from the renowned rabbinic authority Solomon ben Abraham Adret of Barcelona. Adret called Abraham a charlatan. Abraham angrily replied that Adret and other talmudists mistakenly believed that the Talmud was the end of all wisdom.

To avoid the pressure from his opponents, Abraham fled to the desolate island of Comino, near Malta. There, in 1288, he finished writing *Sefer ha-ot* ("Book of the Sign"), his only "prophetic" writing still extant. He also wrote polemical works in defense of himself, a commentary on the Torah (1289), and *Imrei shefer* ("Words of Beauty," 1291), which embraces all his teachings.

Living during the tumultuous period of the Crusades, Abraham sincerely wanted to bridge the differences between Jews, Christians, and Muslims. He believed that his mystic speculations would achieve that goal.

His mysticism differed from earlier cabala. Abraham based his ideas on the doctrine of the ten *Sefirot* ("Divine Emanations") and enlarged on German cabalistic teachings such as combining letters, finding the numerical value of Hebrew words, and interpreting the letters of a word as an abbreviation of a sentence. He believed that the different combinations of Hebrew letters and words held within themselves the very forces of creation and that, through his cabala, practioners could receive prophetic powers and commune with the deity, human reason becoming guided by God's reason. He called this process the "Way of the Divine

Name." His writings had a great influence on later developments of cabala.

Abraham ben Samuel Abulafia died in Barcelona about 1292.

Todros ben Judah ha-Levi Abulafia

POET OF HISTORICAL IMPORTANCE

Todros ben Judah ha-Levi Abulafia was a successful financier and a prominent figure in Spanish royal courts, but his lasting fame came through his poetry. His writings represent the last flowering of the golden age of Spanish Hebrew poetry and provide modern scholars with valuable historical material about the time in which he lived.

Todros was born in Toledo, Spain, in 1247. He traveled for a time with Don Isaac ben Don Solomon Zadok, apparently through whose influence Todros entered court circles. He composed a series of poems in honor of notable Jews close to the Castile courts of Alfonso X (who reigned 1252–84) and Sancho IV (who reigned 1284–95).

Todros divided most of his time between poetry and finance. However, another major diversion was having many liaisons with non-Jewish women, who served as inspirations for much of his poetry.

In 1281 King Alfonso ordered the arrest, and confiscation of the property, of many prominent Jews of Castile, including Todros. After the prisoners were released, the Rabbi Todros ben Joseph ha-Levi Abulafia called on them to change their behavior that had led up to their imprisonment, especially consorting with Muslim and Christian women. The poet, however, refused to alter his conduct.

Nevertheless, by 1289 Todros had regained his status at court, now under the reign of Sancho IV. Some years later he headed a group of Jewish financiers who received important monopolies from the king.

Todros collected his poetry into a volume that he called *Gan ha-meshalim ve-ha-hidot* ("Garden of Apologues and Saws"), consisting of about a thousand poems of many types: elegies, love songs, epigrams, dedications, personal poems, and sacred hymns. The principal value in the poems is their historical material. Many are autobiographical, referring, for example, to his imprisonment. The poems also shed light on the social and political conditions of his era, and he mentions many men who were great in his day but outside his poems are unknown to history.

The last certain date mentioned in his poems is 1295. Todros ben Judah ha-Levi Abulafia died sometime after that year, perhaps about 1306.

SAMUEL BEN MEIR HA-LEVI ABULAFIA

ROYAL MINISTER AND PHILANTHROPIST

Samuel ben Meir ha-Levi Abulafia—as treasurer, diplomat, and personal adviser—was one of the major forces behind the throne of King Pedro the Cruel of Castile. With success came great wealth and influence, which Samuel used generously for the welfare of the Jewish community.

He was born in Toledo, Spain, in about 1320. As a young man he became steward of the estates of Don Juan Alfonso de Albuquerque, tutor to the king.

In 1350 Samuel began serving as royal treasurer for King Pedro. Within a few years he had reorganized the financial affairs of the kingdom and made Pedro the wealthiest sovereign in Spain.

When a court faction revolted in 1354, both the king and Samuel were imprisoned. By paying a large ransom, Samuel won their freedom.

After this episode, he became even closer to the king. Samuel helped Pedro in the latter's power struggle against the nobility by strengthening the financial state of the kingdom. The loyal treasurer-adviser removed unreliable tax farmers from their positions, replaced them with dependable people (often his own relatives or other Jews), and confiscated the property of rebel nobles.

He also served as a diplomat. In 1358 he was sent to Portugal to negotiate a political agreement between that kingdom and Pedro's.

During this period Samuel lived in princely fashion. In Toledo he occupied a large castle that in modern times became the El Greco Museum.

However, he did not lose contact with his Jewish community. Besides appointing many Jews to government positions, he provided the funds for building several synagogues in Castile.

In 1360 an opposing party accused Samuel of treason, and Pedro the Cruel ordered his old friend arrested. Samuel's property was confiscated and he was taken to Seville, where he was imprisoned and tortured to death.

Hayyim ben Moses Abulafia

LEADER OF THE TIBERIAS RESTORATION

Hayyim ben Moses (or Jacob) Abulafia served as rabbi in several cities. Late in life he achieved his greatest renown by leading the restoration of the ancient city of Tiberias, Palestine. He was also a prolific author of religious writings.

Hayyim was born in Palestine in about 1660. When he was a boy, his family moved from Hebron to Jerusalem, where he studied with Moses Galante and others. In 1699 Hayyim went on a mission to Salonika, in 1712 became rabbi in Smyrna, in 1718 moved to Safed to serve as rabbi there, and in 1721 was reappointed rabbi of Smyrna, where he remained for nearly twenty more years.

He had two sons and two daughters. His son Isaac would eventually succeed him in his rabbinic position, while Issachar would become head of the talmudic academy at Sofia.

Hayyim believed that the messianic era was near and that a

prerequisite to it was the restoration of Tiberias, which had been in ruins for many years. In 1740, at the invitation of the Arab ruler of Galilee, the sheikh Dahir al-'Amr, Hayyim moved to Tiberias and began rebuilding the city. In addition to constructing houses, outer and inner walls, and a synagogue, he laid out roads and marketplaces, cultivated fields, and planted vineyards. He sent his sons and sons-in-law to other regions to solicit aid for the restoration.

During 1742–43 Dahir engaged in war with Suleiman, pasha of Damascus. Hayyim supported the sheikh and encouraged the Jews to remain in Tiberias. Two campaigns ensued. The first ended when the seige of Tiberias was raised after eighty-five days. The second ended with the death of Suleiman. Hayyim declared the dates of those events holidays, which the Jews of Tiberias thereafter observed annually.

His published writings date from his second tenure in Smyrna. Among those works are *Mikra'ei kodesh* ("Holy Convocations," 1729), comments on the laws of Passover and on other topics; *Yosef lekah* ("Increasing Doctrine," 1729–32), homilies on the Pentateuch; and *Shevut Ya'akov* ("Captivity of Jacob," 1734), novellae on the Haggadah in *Ein Ya'akov*.

Hayyim ben Moses Abulafia died in Tiberias in 1744.

THE
ADLERS

T HE ADLERS WERE THE MOST FAMOUS acting family in the Yiddish theater. Many of them went on to great careers on the English-language stage as well.

The patriarch was Jacob Adler (1855–1926), who was not only the preeminent Yiddish actor of his time but also the principal force in changing the Yiddish theater repertory from light operettas to serious dramas and tragedies. Born in Odessa, the Ukraine, he established himself as an actor in Europe before settling in New York City, where he helped to develop the budding Yiddish theater.

Jacob came from a family known for its rabbis. One of his granduncles was Nathan Marcus (or Nissim Hillel) Adler (1803–1890), the chief rabbi of the united Hebrew congregations of the British Empire. Nathan himself was a son of a well-known German rabbi and a grandnephew of David Tevele Schiff, chief rabbi of London from 1765 to 1792. One of Nathan's sons, Hermann Adler (1839–1911), succeeded him as chief rabbi.

Jacob had three wives and eight children who survived to adulthood, all eleven of whom entered the theater. By far the most accomplished actress of his wives was the third—Sara Adler (née Levitzky, 1858–1953). As she assisted Jacob in his quest to reform the Yiddish theater, she became a pioneering realist on the stage and the acknowledged leading Yiddish actress of her era.

Jacob's children had a profound impact on both the Yiddish

and the English-language theaters. They often performed onstage in Yiddish plays with each other and with Jacob and Sara in various combinations. Five children, in particular, had memorable careers. Celia (1890–1979) came to be referred to as the First Lady of the Yiddish Theater. Frances (1891–1964), too, rose to the top ranks of Yiddish actresses. Jay (1896–1978) became a reliable character actor in innumerable English-language films, such as *The Juggler* (1953) and *Lust for Life* (1956). Stella (1902–1992) was an outstanding Yiddish and English-language stage actress and one of the most important acting teachers in American history. Luther (1903–1984), a major star in the Yiddish and English-language theaters, appeared as a character actor on many television programs and in motion pictures, including *Wake of the Red Witch* (1949) and *Voyage of the Damned* (1976).

The Broadway actress Francine Larrimore (real name, Fanya Levovsky, 1898–1975) was Jacob's niece, daughter of his sister, Soore (Adler) Levovsky. Frances married a member of the Schoengold Yiddish-theater family and had a daughter, Lulla Rosenfeld (née Schoengold, 1914–), who wrote the valuable book *Bright Star of Exile: Jacob Adler and the Yiddish Theatre* (1977), revised as *The Yiddish Theatre and Jacob P. Adler* (1988).

Jacob Adler

YIDDISH THEATER REFORMER

Jacob Adler was the most prominent figure in the establishment of the American Yiddish theater. Striving toward lofty artistic goals rather than quick commercial success, he reformed the Yiddish theater by shifting the emphasis from light fare to serious dramas and tragedies and by forging a deep emotional bond between actor and audience.

Jacob Pavlovitch Adler was born in Odessa, the Ukraine, on February 12, 1855. He was the son of the wheat merchant Feivel Abramovitch and Hessye (Halperin) Adler. His parents gave him the Hebrew name Yankev (Jacob) and called him by several nicknames, including Yankele.

He worked briefly in the Russian civil service, tried his hand at journalism, and finally found his true vocation on the Yiddish stage. After the 1881 assassination of Czar Alexander II by political terrorists, Alexander III initiated an era of repression, especially against the Jews. In August 1883 he issued an edict forbidding the Yiddish theater in Russia. Later that year Jacob immigrated to England. From 1883 to 1887 he and his small company were among the first Yiddish performers in London.

In early 1887 Jacob arrived in the United States. He tried unsuccessfully to establish a Yiddish theater in Chicago, stayed briefly in New York City, returned to London, and then performed for two years—to great acclaim—in Warsaw, Poland. In 1889, after a short stopover in London, he returned to New York City, determined to make a success of the young American Yiddish theater (which had started in 1882).

He joined Maurice Heine's company and, after appearing in a couple of poorly received plays, scored a series of major successes during 1889–90, especially in *Moishele Soldat* ("Soldier Moishele," also known as *The Russian Soldier*) and in *La juive* ("The Jew"). In the spring of 1890 he left Heine and teamed up with Boris Thomashefsky for performances with the latter's Yiddish troupe in Philadelphia and Chicago.

In 1891 Jacob married the actress Sara Heine (née Levitzky), who had recently divorced Maurice Heine. It was Jacob's third marriage, the first two also being to actresses. With his first wife, Sophia Oberlander (stage name, Sonya Michelson), he had his daughter Rivke (Hebrew for Rebecca, nicknamed Nunia) Vera, who died in childhood, and his son Abram (Abe). After Sophia's death, Jacob married Dinah Shtettin, with whom he had his daughter Celia (originally Tzirale) before divorcing in 1891. With a mistress in the mid-1880s, Jennya Kaiser, he had his son Charles (Charlie). With Sara he had five more children: Frances (originally Fanya, nicknamed Nunia), Jay, Julia, Stella, and Luther.

Jacob strongly disagreed with Thomashefsky's dependence on operettas to draw audiences. "The time had come," he later explained, "when our theater would touch on the deeper places of life, when plays of a more serious kind would find a place on our stage. And this task of deepening our theater, of so to speak 'tragicizing' it, fell, in great measure, on me."

He left Thomashefsky's troupe, established his own company, and, in the fall of 1891, began staging plays at the Union Theater in New York City. Jacob was the first Yiddish actor to dispense entirely with the traditional Yiddish operetta repertory and to rely solely on the classics and on modern European plays. In 1892 he formed the Independent Yiddish Artists Company, whose purpose was to present "serious portrayals of life." Simultaneously he commissioned a play from the best contemporary Yiddish playwright, Jacob Gordin.

The result was *The Yiddish* (or *Jewish*) *King Lear* (1892), a free adaptation of Shakespeare's *King Lear*. Jacob Adler himself starred as Dovid Moishele, a merchant blinded by his own wealth and power. He gives his fortune to his two scheming daughters and disowns his third daughter, who refuses to flatter him. After his wicked daughters drive him into poverty, he forces them to back down; but, disgusted with them and with his own foolishness, he chooses the street, where he begs for alms. This play and Jacob's powerful performance changed the Yiddish theater forever from a parochial form of amusement into an art form of universal human significance. The role remained one of his staples for the rest of his career.

Jacob also made a tremendous impression with his appearances in the title role of Gordin's *The Wild Man*. The character is a retarded man who sinks into a morass of sexual madness, murder, and suicide.

In 1901 Jacob appeared as a sympathetic Shylock in a Yiddish translation of Shakespeare's *The Merchant of Venice*. "The idea I tried to give," he explained, "was that Shylock from the first was governed by pride and not lust for revenge." His performance was so impressive that he was engaged to play in Broadway productions of the work in 1903 and 1905, speaking his part in Yiddish while the other players spoke in English.

In 1903 the Grand Theater was founded in New York City as the first playhouse ever built specifically for Yiddish productions. The following year Jacob took possession of the Grand.

In 1909 Jacob first appeared in the title role of Gordin's *Elisha ben Avuya*, which proved to be another lasting success. Set in the early Christian era, the play shows Elisha as a man of honor and integrity who is tricked out of his fortune, condemned by his own people, abandoned by his family, and driven to suicide.

Jacob starred in the silent film *Michael Strogoff* (1914). In it he played the title character, who foils a rebellion in czarist Russia.

Jacob was adored by his audiences. Long after English-speaking theater performances and audiences on Broadway and elsewhere became restrained, the palpable emotional connection between Yiddish performers and audiences endured. That mutual support was developed principally by Jacob Adler.

By cultivating higher tastes and by creating an emotional bond between players and audiences, Jacob became the most important figure of his time—and perhaps of any time—in the American Yiddish theater.

In 1920 a stroke forced him to retire. Jacob Adler died in New York City on March 31, 1926.

SARA ADLER

GREATEST YIDDISH ACTRESS OF HER TIME

Sara Adler was a pioneering realist in the American Yiddish theater. Through her unique ability to portray both strength and delicacy in hundreds of serious roles, she became the greatest Yiddish actress of her time.

She was born in Odessa, the Ukraine, in 1858. Her original name was Sara Levitzky. As a child she studied singing and yearned to perform on the mainstream Russian stage. However, she soon learned that to achieve a high position in the Russian theater, she would have to enter the Russian Orthodox church. Sara, rather than convert, joined a Yiddish acting troupe and married its manager, Maurice Heine.

After the assassination of Czar Alexander II in 1881, Alexander III initiated repressions against the Russian people, especially the Jews. In 1883 he banned the Yiddish theater in Russia. Therefore, in 1884 the Heines immigrated to the United States. Sara worked at the Oriental Theater in the Bowery section of New York City, becoming popular in operettas.

In 1890 she divorced Heine to marry the Yiddish tragedian Jacob Adler, with whom she had five children. She supported Jacob's efforts to reform the Yiddish theater by replacing light fare with serious dramas and by performing in a realistic style instead of with empty traditional mannerisms.

From the 1890s to the 1920s, Sara appeared in hundreds of plays, including masterpieces by Shakespeare, Ibsen, and Tolstoy. Her performances as Katusha Maslova in Jacob Gordin's version of Tolstoy's *Resurrection* established her as the preeminent actress in the Yiddish theater. Another memorable role for her during those years was in Gordin's *The Homeless*, a drama of immigrant life, in which she played a simple Russian-Jewish housewife who goes literally insane when her husband leaves her for another woman.

After Jacob's death in 1926, Sara performed only occasionally, but she appeared at least once a year till she was past the age of eighty. In 1939 a special evening was held in her honor at the New Yorker Theater, where she appeared once more as Katusha Maslova in the third act of *Resurrection*.

Sara Adler died in New York City on April 28, 1953, at the age of ninety-five.

STELLA ADLER

AMERICA'S PREEMINENT TEACHER OF ACTING

Stella Adler appeared in nearly two hundred stage productions in the United States and abroad. She virtually grew up as an actress on the Yiddish stage, and she attained great success in many English-language plays. But she is best remembered today as the finest teacher of acting in her time.

She was born in New York City on February 10, 1902 (some sources give 1901). Her parents soon thrust her into their theater life. "In my family," she later said, "immediately you could barely walk, you were put on the stage. All the children were." She made her own debut in 1906, in her father's production of *Broken Hearts*. For more than a decade after that, she played both girls' and boys' roles in a wide variety of classical and contemporary works for her parents' group and for other companies. In the early 1920s she broadened her range to include English-language productions.

In the mid-1920s Stella began to study acting at the new American Laboratory Theater school, founded and operated in New York City by former members of the famed Moscow Art Theater. The directors of the company introduced her to the revolutionary Stanislavsky acting technique and allowed her to act in many of the company's productions.

In the late 1920s she appeared for two seasons at the Living Place Theater with the renowned Yiddish actors Bertha Kalich and Jacob Ben-Ami. During 1930–31 she took a series of leading roles with the Yiddish Art Theater.

In 1931 Stella joined the new Group Theater, founded by Lee Strasberg, Cheryl Crawford, and Harold Clurman (who became the second of her three husbands). The Group Theater differed from the typical commercial theater company by consisting of an ensemble of players, directors, designers, and writers committed to staging productions that Clurman called "artistic wholes."

To help achieve that artistic unity, Strasberg trained all of his actors with a technique based on the Stanislavsky system that he, like Stella, had learned at the American Laboratory Theater. In rehearsals, Strasberg called for much improvisational work and for exercises in what he called "affective memory," the memory of an emotion that the actor had felt in the past.

The Group Theater had a no-star policy, so Stella sometimes played leading roles and other times small parts in the company's productions. Among her most memorable roles were those as the spiritually tortured Sarah Glassman in *Success Story* (1932), the Jewish matriarch Bessie Berger in *Awake and Sing!* (1935), and the indomitable Clara in *Paradise Lost* (1935). She also directed some Group Theater productions, notably *Golden Boy* in a Euopean tour of 1938–39.

After the Group Theater dissolved in 1941, Stella spent several years performing with other Broadway companies and directing commercial theatrical productions, such as the musical *Polonaise* (1945). Her last stage appearance came in London in 1961. She appeared in only a few films, including *Shadow of the Thin Man* (1941).

While her acting career was winding down, Stella became increasingly involved with teaching. She never fully approved of Strasberg's interpretation (called the Method) of Stanislavsky's system. "The emphasis was a sick one," she said of Strasberg's affective memory exercises. "You couldn't be on the stage thinking of your own personal life. It was just schizophrenic."

In 1934 she took a leave of absence from the Group Theater and studied for several months in Paris, France, with Stanislavsky himself, learning the master's revised system of acting. He taught her, she reported, that "the source of acting is imagination and that the key to its problems is truth, truth *in the circumstances of the play*." When she returned to the Group Theater, she urged the company to concentrate on the emotional experiences of the characters in the play instead of on the actors' personal memories. She openly challenged Strasberg's authority by giving acting lessons to some of the group's members.

In the early 1940s Stella began teaching at Erwin Piscator's Dramatic Workshop at the New School for Social Research in New York City. In 1949 she left that institution to establish the

Stella Adler Theater Studio, later called the Stella Adler Conservatory of Acting, also in New York City. There she created a two-year program of classes in acting, makeup, mime, movement, playwriting, rehearsal technique, Shakespeare, speech and voice production, stage direction, and other subjects. Her workshop topics included play analysis and characterization.

Stella based her acting classes on Stanislavsky's revised technique, which was "more externalized" than the Method version favored by Strasberg at his Actors Studio. The latter focused his students on memories of their own past personal experiences. Stella, however, encouraged her students to develop characters by studying the play's text, understanding the historical period of the story, and using their imaginations to create pasts that logically belonged to their characters. "I don't want you to be stuck with your own life," she told a class. "It's too little." Her many prize students included Marlon Brando, Eddie Albert, Warren Beatty, and Robert De Niro.

She had three marriages. The first was to Horace Eleascheff, with whom she had a daughter. Her second marriage was to the writer-director Harold Clurman, with whom she worked at the Group Theater. Her final marriage was to Mitchell Wilson, a physicist and novelist.

Stella summarized her highly successful teaching system in the book *The Technique of Acting* (1988). She died in Los Angeles, California, on December 21, 1992.

Luther Adler

DISTINGUISHED STAGE, FILM, AND TELEVISION ACTOR

Luther Adler learned the craft of acting in the Yiddish theater and went on to become one of the most distinguished English-language stage actors of his time. In his later years he was an important character actor in movies and a featured performer in live productions during television's early years.

He was born in New York City on May 4, 1903. The original form of his given name was Lutha. He studied acting under his father and from 1908 to 1921 appeared in plays with his father's Yiddish company.

In 1921 he entered the English-language theater, working in New York City in *The Hand of the Potter* (1921) and touring in *Sonya* (1922). After changing his first name to Luther, he made his Broadway debut by playing Leon Kantor, a young violinist with a self-sacrificing mother, in *Humoresque* (1923). Throughout the rest of the 1920s he worked steadily on the English-language stage, notably as Samuel Kaplan, a law student, in *Street Scene* (1929).

After spending 1930–31 on the Yiddish stage, Luther joined his sister Stella with the Group Theater, where he began with a minor role in *Night over Taos* (1932). Then, over the next several years, he gave some of the most memorable stage performances of the time. He played the ambitious, vicious Sam Ginsburg in *Success Story* (1932), the radical professor Julian Vardaman in *Alien Corn* (1933), the steadfast physician Dr. Gordon in *Men in White* (1933), and the crippled war veteran Moe Axelrod in *Awake and Sing!* (1935). Perhaps the most important role of his career was as Joe Bonaparte, who abandons a promising career as a violinist to earn money as a boxer, in *Golden Boy* (1937).

The Holocaust prompted Luther to participate in stage works that focused the general public's attention on the plight of Jews. In 1943 he appeared in Ben Hecht's pageant *We Will Never Die*, which recited great Jewish names in the arts and sciences, dramatized the contributions of American Jewish war heroes, and presented reports about the slaughters in Nazi Europe. In 1946 Luther directed Hecht's drama-pageant *A Flag Is Born*, a production that explained the cause of Zionism.

He devoted the late 1940s and early 1950s primarily to film work. Luther made his movie debut in *Lancer Spy* (1937), but it was his role as a beligerent Dutch tycoon in *Wake of the Red Witch* (1949) that finally established him as an important movie character actor.

His heavy features often led filmmakers to cast him as a villain. He played a crime boss, for example, in *D.O.A.* (1950), and in *The Desert Fox* (1951) he portrayed Adolf Hitler.

From the early 1950s on, he divided his time among stage, television, and movie projects. On the stage his roles included Shylock in *The Merchant of Venice* (1957), Willy Loman in *Death of a Salesman* (1960), Henry Drummond in *Inherit the Wind* (1961), and Tevye in *Fiddler on the Roof* (1965).

He contributed fine performances to a number of broadcasts during television's golden age of live productions. Among the plays that he appeared in were "Hedda Gabler" on *The U.S. Steel Hour* (1954) and "The Plot to Kill Stalin" on *Playhouse Ninety* (1958). He later guest-starred on many dramatic series, including *Twilight Zone* (1965) and *Hawaii Five-O* (1972). In 1971 he had a regular role in the series *The Psychiatrist*.

Luther appeared in the films *The Magic Face* (1951), *The Girl in the Red Velvet Swing* (1955), and *The Last Angry Man* (1959). In *Cast a Giant Shadow* (1966) he played Jacob Zion in a story about the Israeli War of Independence, fought during 1948–49. In *The Man in the Glass Booth* (1975) he was the judge in the trial of a Jew who claims that he is a Nazi war criminal and who becomes obsessed with the idea that he can absorb Nazi guilt and Israeli hatred. His later films included *Voyage of the Damned* (1976) and *Absence of Malice* (1981).

From the late 1930s to the late 1940s, Luther was married to the great Jewish actress Sylvia Sidney, with whom he had a son. In his last years he was married to Julia Hadley Roche.

Luther Adler died at his home in Kutztown, Pennsylvania, on December 8, 1984.

THE
BEGINS

T HE BEGINS ARE ONE OF THE MOST IMPORTANT political families in the history of Israel. The conservative Likud party, in particular, owes much to Menachem Begin (1913–92) and his son, Benjamin Begin (1943–).

Menachem first made his mark in the mid-1940s as a saboteur against the British, who rebuffed his demand for a politically independent Jewish state. When Israel was finally formed in 1948, he went into politics, helping to found a new party that eventually became the Likud. In 1977 he was elected the first Likud prime minister of Israel. His career was crowned in 1978, when he was awarded the Nobel Peace Prize for his efforts to negotiate peace with Egypt.

Benjamin entered politics in 1988 as a member of the Knesset (parliament). In 1993 he ran for the leadership of the Likud party, losing to Benjamin Netanyahu. When Netanyahu became prime minister in 1996, he brought Benjamin Begin, a former geologist, into the new government as the science minister.

MENACHEM BEGIN

NOBEL PEACE PRIZE WINNER

After working as an ardent Zionist during the 1930s and as commander of the militant Irgun Zvai Leumi (National Fighting Or-

Menachem Begin (left) with U.S.
President Jimmy Carter.

ganization) from 1943 to 1948, Menachem Begin entered Israeli politics, rising to serve as the nation's prime minister from 1977 to 1983. Known for his extreme hard-line views against the Arabs before he became prime minister, Begin surprised most observers by developing greater flexibility in his dealings with Arab neighbors after taking over the nation's leadership. For his efforts to achieve peace with Egypt, Begin was awarded the Nobel Peace Prize in 1978.

Menachem Wolfovitch Begin was born in Brest Litovsk, in a Polish region then ruled by Russia, on August 16, 1913. His parents were Wolf (in Hebrew, Ze'ev Dov) and Hassia (Kossovsky) Begin. Wolf was secretary of the Jewish communal organization in the city. "From my early youth," Menachem later recalled, "I had been taught by my father . . . that we Jews were to return to Eretz Israel."

At the age of ten Menachem joined Ha-Shomer ha-Tza'ir, a Zionist scouting organization that trained its members for kibbutz life. In 1929 he joined Betar (or B'rit Trumpeldor), a militant youth organization dedicated to establishing a Jewish state in Israel.

Meanwhile, he continued his education. In 1935 he graduated from the University of Warsaw with a master of jurisprudence degree.

From 1936 to 1938 he served as general secretary of the Betar branch in Czechoslovakia. Returning to Poland, he became the commander of the Polish Betar early in 1939.

Also in 1939 he married Aliza Arnold in Poland. They had a son and two daughters.

In May 1939 the British set up restrictions on Jewish immigration to Palestine. Menachem responded by leading protests outside the British embassy in Warsaw. As a result, he was arrested by Polish police and held for several months. After his release, he fled Warsaw just ahead of the invading German forces and went to Vilnius, Lithuania. (Both of his parents and his only brother were killed during the Nazi Holocaust.)

In July 1940 the Soviet Union annexed Lithuania. Because of his Betar activities, Menachem was seen as a threat to the Soviets, who arrested him and sentenced him to eight years as a slave laborer in Siberia. However, in 1941 the Soviets released Menachem and thousands of other Polish prisoners, many of whom formed a Polish army in exile to help the Soviets fight the Germans in World War II.

His unit was sent to Transjordan, from where, in May 1942, he entered Palestine. He soon took charge of the local Betar organization in Jerusalem.

Released from the Polish army, Menachem, in December 1943, became commander of the Irgun Zvai Leumi, a paramilitary force dedicated to immediate direct action to establish a Jewish state in Palestine. Under his leadership, the Irgun demanded a politically independent Jewish state in Palestine and an open-door policy for refugees from Hitler's Europe. When rebuffed, he initiated a campaign of sabotage against the British administration in Palestine. He developed a reputation as a ruthless terrorist. The British offered a $30,000 reward for his capture, and even David Ben-Gurion, later Israel's first prime minister, publicly condemned Menachem as a fascist.

However, in December 1947 the underground phase of Irgun ended when the United Nations decided to partition Palestine. Fighting broke out between the region's Jews and Arabs, and the Irgun was reorganized into a regular military unit. In May 1948, after the Jewish state declared its independence, Menachem announced that the Irgun would be disbanded so that its members could join the new Israeli army.

In July 1948 Menachem and his former Irgun associates formed a new political organization, the Herut ("Freedom") party. Its principal goal was to include in the modern Jewish state all the

Menachem Begin

land of the ancient kingdom of Israel.

Menachem was elected to the Knesset (parliament), where he led the opposition to the ruling Mapai (in 1968 renamed Labor) party till 1967. In 1965 Herut joined the Liberal party to form Gahal, of which Menachem became chairman.

From 1967 to 1970 he was a member of the National Unity government as a minister without portfolio. In 1973 Gahal and other right-wing parties formed the powerful new Likud ("Unity") bloc, which in 1977 replaced Labor as the country's dominant party.

On June 21, 1977, Menachem took office as Israel's sixth—and the nation's first non-Labor—prime minister. Though he was well known for his uncompromising stand on retaining the territory occupied by Israel during the 1967 Arab-Israeli War, he responded favorably when, in November 1977, President Anwar Sadat of Egypt made an unexpected peace initiative. The initial talks faltered, but President Jimmy Carter of the United States intervened and invited Menachem and Sadat to America to continue their negotiations at Camp David, the presidential retreat. After a thirteen-day conference, the two leaders, in a historic ceremony at the White House, publicly shook hands and signed preliminary peace agreements. The formal peace treaty, in which Israel agreed to return most of the Sinai region to Egypt in return for a full peace, was signed on March 26, 1979. For their efforts, Menachem and Sadat shared the 1978 Nobel Peace Prize.

However, tension in the Middle East remained high, and Menachem retained most of his hard-line views. During the early 1980s his opposition to the establishment of a Palestinian state continued. In 1981 he ordered the bombing of a nuclear reactor near Baghdad, Iraq.

The beginning of the end of his leadership came with Israel's ill-starred military incursion into Lebanon in 1982. Grieved by the casualties in that conflict and then by the death of his wife, Aliza, in November of that year, Menachem became noticeably listless. On September 15, 1983, he resigned the office of prime minister.

He spent the rest of his life in near seclusion, living with one of his daughters, Leah, in a Jerusalem apartment. Menachem Begin died in Tel Aviv on March 9, 1992.

Benjamin Begin

A POWERFUL FORCE IN THE LIKUD PARTY

Benjamin Begin became a Likud party member of the Israeli parliament, the Knesset, in 1988. By the early 1990s, the Likud prime minister of Israel, Yitzhak Shamir, was personally grooming him for the highest levels of government. In 1996 Benjamin was named the science minister in the cabinet of the new Likud prime minister, Benjamin Netanyahu.

Benjamin Ze'ev Begin was born in Jerusalem, Palestine, on March 1, 1943. His parents were Menachem Wolfovitch and Aliza (Arnold) Begin. Benjamin studied in Israel and the United States, joined his reserve unit during the 1973 Yom Kippur War, volunteered for two years of service in the regular army after the war, and then went to work as a geologist.

From 1977 to 1983, Menachem led Israel as its first Likud party prime minister. After Menachem's retirement, Likud officials began to see political potential in his son, whose ideas, appearance, and mannerisms closely mirrored those of his father. The officials persuaded Benjamin to run for a seat in the Knesset on the Likud ticket. He did so, and in 1988 he won an election that put him into the parliament.

He openly expressed his debt to his father. "The political equipment I come with," he admitted, "I learned at home." Like

Menachem, he wanted to keep Israel strong and to expand Jewish settlements in occupied territories.

In the late 1980s and early 1990s, Yitzhak Shamir, the Likud prime minister, adopted Benjamin as a protégé. When Menachem died in 1992, Benjamin inherited much of his father's political influence and became a leader of the Likud party.

The following year, Shamir having retired, Benjamin Begin ran against Benjamin Netanyahu for the official leadership of the Likud party. New party rules, under which the leader is elected by a direct vote of party members instead of by a small central committee, opened the door to an American-style campaign emphasizing television advertisements, at which Netanyahu excelled because of his good looks and his on-camera experience as a television commentator.

Benjamin Begin lost the election but retained a powerful voice in the party and in the nation. A hard-line conservative, he frequently spoke out in the mid-1990s against the ruling Labor party's peace strategies that he felt would weaken Israel's security.

When Netanyahu was elected prime minister of Israel in 1996, Benjamin Begin used his power in the Likud party to influence Netanyahu's decisions in forming a new cabinet. Benjamin Begin himself, because of his training as a geologist, became the new minister of science.

THE
BRONFMANS

THE CANADA-BASED BRONFMAN FAMILY has been a major force in the world business community for four consecutive generations. There are two main branches of the family, one controlling the fabulously successful Seagram alcoholic beverage firm and the other heading the huge conglomerate Edper Enterprises.

The founder of the dynasty was Ekiel (short for Yechiel) Bronfman, who immigrated to Canada from Bessarabia in 1889. He engaged in various ventures, eventually building up a profitable hotel business. His four sons—Abraham ("Abe," 1882–1968), Harry (1886–1963), Samuel (1889–1971), and Allan (1895–1980)—assisted Ekiel in his business operations.

The principal figure in that generation was Samuel, who went into the liquor business, acquired the old distilling firm of Joseph E. Seagram and Sons, and built it into one of the world's most successful companies. All three of his brothers helped in various executive capacities. Abe served as a vice president under Samuel and helped to form the United Jewish Relief Agency. Harry directed Seagram's production and construction and was a founder of the Canadian Jewish Congress. Allan, a barrister, became a vice president of the family firm and, like his brothers, engaged heavily in philanthropy.

The third generation of Bronfmans in the New World was blessed with an abundance of business talent. Gerald

Bronfman (1911–86), Harry's son, became president and director of various major Canadian businesses and supported many Jewish charities. Samuel's two sons, Edgar Miles Bronfman (1929–) and Charles Rosner Bronfman (1931–), became executives at Seagram. Edgar succeeded his father as head of the firm and wielded great influence as president of the World Jewish Congress. Charles held various executive positions at Seagram and founded the Charles R. Bronfman (CRB) Foundation. Edward M. Bronfman (1927–) and Peter Frederick Bronfman (1929–96), Allan's sons, established and controlled Edper Enterprises, the largest corporate empire in Canada.

The fourth generation of Bronfmans is well represented by Edgar Miles Bronfman's second of four sons, Edgar Miles Bronfman, Jr. (1955–). The younger Edgar succeeded his father as head of Seagram and led the family's 1995 takeover of MCA, the Hollywood entertainment conglomerate. Paul Arthur Bronfman (1957–), Edward's son, is president of Comweb Corporation, a Canadian film and television production company.

SAMUEL BRONFMAN

FOUNDER OF THE BLENDED WHISKEY EMPIRE

Samuel Bronfman virtually invented blended whiskey as a commercial product. With it, he turned a declining Canadian distillery, Joseph E. Seagram and Sons, into one of the world's most successful businesses.

He inherited his business acumen from his father, Ekiel (short for Yechiel) Bronfman, who had owned a gristmill and a tobacco plantation in Bessarabia before pogroms drove him out of the country. In 1889 Ekiel sailed for the New World with his wife— Minnie Bronfman (née Elman)—and their children. Samuel was born on February 27, 1889, either in Soroki, Bessarabia, or in mid-Atlantic during the trip (not, as he later claimed, in 1891 in Canada).

The family settled initially in Wapella, Saskatchewan, but soon moved to Brandon, Manitoba. Ekiel tried several businesses with modest success, including horse-trading. Some horse-trading was done in a bar, where young Samuel noticed people buying drinks and said to his father, "Instead of selling horses, we should be selling drinks." (*Bronfman*, incidentally, is Yiddish for "brandy man" or "distiller.")

During 1902 and 1903 Ekiel borrowed money from distillers and liquor store owners (who were glad to help start up a new customer for themselves) and purchased a hotel in Emerson, Manitoba, which included, of course, a well-stocked bar. Later Ekiel, with his sons, opened other hotels in various Canadian provinces. Samuel was the guiding spirit of the family's hotel business, whose chief source of revenue was the bar receipts.

He clearly saw a brighter future for the family in the liquor business itself. His first independent venture, in 1916, was to purchase a liquor store in Montreal, Quebec. But his principal activity, begun at about the same time, was to establish a mail-order firm that sold liquor throughout the Canadian provinces.

Just before Prohibition took effect in the United States in 1920, Samuel took advantage of some Americans' panicky last-minute sellouts of raw, overproof alcohol and bought several hundred thousand gallons at bargain prices. He thinned the alcohol with an equal amount of water, added about half as much again of real whiskey, plus some caramel for color and a dash of sulfuric acid (to speed the aging process). Thus he created a whole new category of alcoholic beverage—blended whiskey. Formulas changed over the ensuing years, and eventually blends became the most popular and largest-selling whiskey in North America. "Distilling is a science," Samuel said; "blending is an art."

In the early 1920s Samuel had to abandon his mail-order firm because the Canadian provincial governments took over the retail sale of liquor. He began selling his products to distributors who smuggled liquor into the United States to supply the huge American underground market that flourished during the Prohibition years. Besides manufacturing his blends, he imported European whiskeys. The company that he established in 1924 was called Distillers Corporation, Ltd., headquartered in Montreal.

In 1928 Samuel acquired a Waterloo, Ontario, distilling firm that was founded in 1857 and named Joseph E. Seagram and Sons in 1870. Samuel merged his old company with the new one to form Distillers Corporation-Seagrams, Ltd., which eventually consisted of many divisions and subsidiaries.

Also in 1928 he began maturing huge stockpiles of whiskey in Canadian warehouses in anticipation of the end of American Prohibition. His gamble paid off. In 1933 sales of liquor in the United States became legal, and Samuel went from a millionaire to a billionaire.

In 1930 he hired a Scotsman, Calman Levine, as his master blender. In 1934 Levine produced a formula called Seagram's Seven Crown (because it was the seventh formula out of about two dozen finalists, while *Crown* brought to mind elegance and high quality). Within two months it was the best-selling whiskey in the United States, and within ten years the best in the world. The company continued to grow rapidly, and by the late 1940s it was the number one distiller in the United States. By the early 1970s it was the world's largest distiller, owning dozens of distilleries and wineries in various countries and producing well over one hundred different brands of alcoholic beverages.

In his later years Samuel engaged in a wide range of activities outside his business. From 1939 to 1962 he headed the Canadian Jewish Congress, and in 1940 he created that body's Refugee Committee, which helped to save some seven thousand lives during World War II. He also served as a leader in many other organizations, such as the World Jewish Congress, the Canadian Mental Health Association, and the Canada-Israel Corporation. Samuel was a Mason and a member of B'nai B'rith. Among his many philanthropic gestures were his donation of the Biblical and Archeological Museum in Israel and his creation of the Saidye Bronfman Cultural Center in Montreal.

In 1951 Samuel bought an estate in Tarrytown, New York, but

he never became an American citizen. In 1957 he oversaw the construction of the famous Seagram world headquarters building in New York City.

Samuel's family played a major role in his life and business. In 1922 he married Saidye Rosner, whose father, like Samuel's, was a Canadian immigrant from Bessarabia. They had two sons and two daughters. The boys, Edgar and Charles, entered the family business. One daughter, Minda, married the French baron Alain de Gunzberg, with whom the Bronfmans bought into European real estate and insurance, purchased a fleet of tankers, and invested in a chain of resorts. Most of those European ventures were carried out in partnership with de Gunzberg's distant relatives in the famous Rothschild family. The other daughter, Phyllis, became an artist-architect, helped in the design of the Seagram building in New York City, and founded the Canadian Centre for Architecture.

Samuel was greatly concerned about the future of his business empire and his family. From the early days of his business ventures he brought in family members, including his brothers Harry and Allan and some nephews. However, before acquiring Joseph E. Seagram and Sons, he saw that company decline under a management divided among too many heirs, and he was determined not to allow the same problem destroy his own business and family. Therefore, he bought out various family members and made other maneuvers to assure his two sons of complete control of the empire. In the 1950s he gave control of the United States operations to Edgar, while Charles remained in Montreal to head the Canadian branch. Samuel retained overall leadership as head of the parent company, Distillers Corporation-Seagrams, Ltd. (later Seagram Company, Ltd.).

Samuel Bronfman died in Montreal on July 10, 1971.

EDGAR MILES BRONFMAN

HEAD OF THE SEAGRAM COMPANY

In the 1950s and 1960s, Edgar Miles Bronfman held various positions with his father's company, Distillers Corporation-Seagrams, Ltd. (later Seagram Company, Ltd.). During those years he launched programs of development that not only revitalized the firm's competitiveness in the alcoholic beverage industry but also expanded the company's interests into other fields. In 1971 he succeeded his father as head of the firm.

Edgar was born in Montreal, Quebec, on June 20, 1929. He was the older son of Samuel and Saidye (Rosner) Bronfman.

As a youth Edgar earned money by working as a golf caddy and a department store employee; when he was older, he worked in two New York City investment firms—the Empire Trust Company and Carl M. Loeb, Rhoades and Company. He later explained his industriousness: "If you went to father to ask for money, you had to explain why. If you earned it, you didn't have to explain."

In 1951 he graduated with a B.A. degree and honors in history from McGill University in Montreal. During college vacations, he worked for his father and learned the distilling business. "Nobody ever told me I had to get in," he has recalled, "but a kid gets the feeling early that joining the business is his natural destiny." After graduation he entered the family firm, and from 1953 to 1955 he was responsible for all Canadian plants.

In 1955 he went to New York City to become chairman of the administrative committee for Joseph E. Seagram and Sons, the American subsidiary of the parent company. In 1957, after Edgar threatened to leave the firm unless he was given more authority, Samuel gave him the presidency of the American branch, which Edgar held till 1971.

In the 1950s the firm's position in the industry was slipping because of changes in Americans' drinking habits —from blended whiskeys (a Seagram specialty) to Scotch, bourbon, and nonwhiskeys (gin, vodka, rum, brandy, and wine). Edgar undertook what *Time* magazine (March 5, 1965) called the "most ambitious marketing program ever undertaken by any distiller." He introduced a gin, a vodka, bottled cocktails, various rums, four liqueurs, and new varieties of Scotch; and he began importing wines.

Besides revolutionizing his firm's products, Edgar modernized the company's management by improving the methods of distribution, putting more money into advertising and promotion, and upgrading the market research. Edgar put new emphasis on international marketing, and by 1965 Seagram was selling its products in 119 countries. It became the first liquor company to exceed $1 billion in annual sales.

Edgar M. Bronfman, Sr.

Edgar, with his brother (Charles) and sisters (Minda and Phyllis) increased the family wealth through investments outside the liquor business. By 1966 they owned twelve shopping centers and held stock in such major firms as Allied Chemical and British-American Oil. By 1969 the Bronfmans were the largest private landowners in Canada.

Edgar had a special personal interest in the entertainment industry. He invested in the Broadway productions *The Apple Tree* (1966) and *1776* (1969). In 1967, through his efforts, the Bronfman family became the largest single stockholder in the Metro-Goldwyn-Mayer (MGM) film company. In May 1969 Edgar took over the chairmanship of MGM, but later that year he lost controlling interest in the company and resigned from the board. In early 1970 he became chairman of Sagittarius Productions, which managed a music corporation and produced films and stage shows.

After succeeding his father as head of Seagram in 1971, Edgar led the family firm to even greater heights of success and influence. In the 1980s he expanded the company's interests in oil. Eventually Seagram owned 24.2 percent of the oil and chemical giant E. I. du Pont de Nemours and Company, parent company of Conoco oil.

During 1993–94 Seagram bought 14.99 percent of the media and entertainment giant Time Warner, Inc. Edgar called entertainment "one of the great growth sectors for the 1990s and beyond."

In March 1995 Edgar led the family's strong opposition to Conoco's planned petroleum products activities in Iran. The following month Seagram sold most of its shares in E. I. du Pont de Nemours and Company and used the revenues to buy 80 percent of MCA, the well-known media and entertainment company.

Like his father, Edgar has been extremely active in a wide range of causes. He has served as president of the World Jewish Congress, chairman of the Anti-Defamation League of B'nai B'rith in New York City, head of the Samuel Bronfman Foundation, and a leader of many other organizations. Edgar has often participated in important events of international concern for Jews. For example, in 1987, as head of the World Jewish Congress, he met with Soviet Union officials and helped to convince them to permit large-scale Jewish emigration out of Russia.

Again like his father, Edgar has utilized family connections in various business ventures. Through his first marriage, to Ann Margaret Loeb in 1953, Edgar's family developed connections with her family's Loeb, Rhoades and Company, which aided the Bronfmans in several business transactions, such as the purchase of Texas Pacific Coal and Oil Company. After his divorce in 1973, he was married briefly to the titled Englishwoman Lady Carolyn Townshend. Later he married another Englishwoman, Eileen Webb, who converted to Judaism. His first marriage produced four sons and one daughter.

Edgar named as his successor his second son, Edgar Miles Bronfman, Jr., who became president in 1989 and chief executive officer in 1994. The elder Edgar retired from active management but remained with the firm as chairman of the board.

He began to devote himself largely to his role as president of the World Jewish Congress. In that capacity, he has represented the Jewish people in their claims against Swiss banks believed to be holding vast sums of money belonging to Holocaust victims. In May 1996, after years of pressure, especially by Edgar Bronfman, Swiss bankers agreed to facilitate efforts by Holocaust survivors and their relatives to recover funds from the banks.

Charles Rosner Bronfman

FOUNDER OF CHARLES R. BRONFMAN FOUNDATION

Charles Rosner Bronfman has held various executive positions with the family's Seagram Company. And, like other family members, he has been active in other fields of interest. He has had a particularly profound impact on the Jewish community through the work of his Charles R. Bronfman (CRB) Foundation.

Charles was born in Montreal, Quebec, on June 27, 1931. He was the younger son of Samuel and Saidye (Rosner) Bronfman. Samuel built the alcoholic beverage firm of Joseph E. Seagram and Sons into one of the world's great business successes. It eventually consisted of many subsidiaries under the parent company, Distillers Corporation-Seagrams, Ltd., later the Seagram Company, Ltd.

After studying at McGill University in Montreal (1948–51), Charles joined Seagram in 1951. In the mid-1950s his father named him to head the Canadian branch of the business. During the succeeding years, he held various executive positions with the family enterprise. In 1971, on Samuel's death, Charles's older brother, Edgar, became head of the company, while Charles took the position of executive vice president of the parent firm. Later he held the titles of chairman of the executive committee (since 1975) and cochairman of the board (since 1986).

From 1968 to 1980 he owned the Montreal Expos major league baseball team. In 1985 he was inducted into the Canadian Baseball Hall of Fame.

Charles married Andrea Morrison in 1982. They had one son and one daughter.

Charles has been associated with many Jewish charities. He is a past president of the Allied Jewish Community Services of Montreal. Other organizations that he has supported include the Canadian Jewish Congress and the Canadian Council of Christians and Jews.

His principal interest is his own Charles R. Bronfman (CRB) Foundation of Montreal. He and his wife founded the private organization in 1986. The foundation has over $100 million in assets and directs 66 percent of its annual available funds of $7 million toward Jewish causes. In 1987 he created the Israel Experience program, in which his foundation pays for trips by American and Canadian Jewish teenagers to Israel as a way of reaffirming Jewish identity and heritage. In 1993 several major Jewish institutions joined CRB as partners in the project, pledging to send fifty thousand Jewish teens a year to Israel by the year 2000, up from nine thousand in the mid-1990s.

EDWARD AND PETER BRONFMAN

FOUNDERS OF EDPER ENTERPRISES

The brothers Edward M. and Peter Frederick Bronfman founded Edper Enterprises, the largest corporate conglomerate in Canada. The firm has controlled many of the nation's most important companies.

Edward was born on November 1, 1927, and Peter on October 2, 1929, both in Montreal, Quebec. They were the sons of Allan and Lucy (Bilsky) Bronfman. Allan was the younger brother of Samuel Bronfman, who built the Seagram alcoholic beverage empire.

Edward and Peter graduated from American colleges. The elder brother received a B.Sc. degree (1950) at Babson College in Massachusetts, while the younger earned a B.A. degree (1952) from Yale University in Connecticut. Both brothers married (Peter, in fact, three times), and each had three children—Edward three sons, and Peter one son and two daughters.

Edward and Peter began their business careers at Seagram. But to ensure that his own sons would ultimately control the business, Samuel nudged his nephews out of the firm. He did, however, provide them with $25 million in stock, which they used as seed money to start Edper Enterprises in the 1960s. From the beginning, Peter headed the business, which was headquartered in Toronto, Canada.

Throughout the 1970s and 1980s, the brothers continued to add companies to their conglomerate, diversity being their hallmark. From 1971 to 1978 they owned the Montreal Canadiens professional hockey team. By the late 1980s they held major interests in such important Canadian companies as the forest products giant MacMillan Bloedel, the brewer John Labatt, the real-estate developer Bramalea, and the London Life Insurance Company. The central holding company was called Edper (*Ed*ward + *Peter*) Enterprises, from which was derived the name for the whole corporate empire—the Edper Group. The group consisted of over five hundred private companies and over forty public companies.

However, the recession of the late 1980s and early 1990s severely hurt Edper Enterprises, especially their natural resources and real-estate holdings. The group's single largest investment, the natural-resources conglomerate Noranda, dropped from $476 million in earnings in 1988 to only $62 million in 1992. Edper was also adversely affected by the collapse of the Reichmann family's real-estate company, Olympia and York Developments, in 1992. The Bronfmans and the Reichmanns, another successful Jewish Canadian family, had many business connections.

To solve the problem, Edper sold some companies and reorganized its structure. The Bronfmans sold their entire holdings in two of their most prestigious companies, MacMillan

Bloedel (49 percent of the company's stock) and John Labatt (37 percent), and reduced their Bramalea interest from 72 percent to 20 percent.

By December 1995 Edper was able to pull off a major business coup. The board of Olympia and York (USA), the American subsidiary of the bankrupt Olympia and York Developments of Toronto, approved a division-of-property deal giving 75 percent of the property of Olympia and York (USA) to a group headed by the Bronfmans of Toronto. With this deal, Edward and Peter Bronfman revealed once again the ingenuity and boldness that helped them to create one of the world's great business empires.

On December 1, 1996, Peter died in Toronto. He had held the title of senior chairman of the Edper Group, Ltd., while Edward was president of the Broncorp division of their business. Both brothers were active in community affairs. Edward served as national cochairperson of the Council for Christians and Jews and as a member of the board of governors at Hebrew University of Jerusalem. Peter was president of Montreal's Jewish General Hospital and engaged in many other philanthropies.

EDGAR MILES BRONFMAN, JR.

SUCCESSOR TO EDGAR MILES BRONFMAN

In June 1994 Edgar Miles Bronfman, Jr., succeeded his father as chief executive officer of the Seagram Company, the multibillion-dollar distilled spirits business. Less than a year later he made a dramatic move by agreeing to purchase 80 percent of MCA, the Hollywood entertainment conglomerate.

Edgar was born in 1955, the second son of Edgar Miles and Ann (Loeb) Bronfman. He grew up in Purchase, New York, and then in New York City.

Though he was proud of the accomplishments of his father, who greatly expanded the Seagram empire, and of his grandfather Samuel Bronfman, who founded it, Edgar as a young man did not want to enter the family business. His first interest was the entertainment industry. While still a high-school student, he worked as a production assistant and script reader for the film producer David Puttnam.

After graduating from high school, Edgar opted to skip college and go full-time into the entertainment business. He soon moved to Hollywood, California, where this phase of his career was highlighted by his work as producer of the film *The Border* (1982).

In 1979 he married Sherry Brewer, an African-American actress. The relationship caused a brief estrangement between Edgar and his father because the older man worried about the difficulties of an interracial marriage.

Soon, however, the father sought a reconciliation. Despite the fact that his firstborn son, Samuel, was already an executive at Seagram, the father wanted to be succeeded as head of the firm by Edgar, who possessed the kind of leadership qualities that the elder Bronfman thought the company needed. When Edgar received the offer to join Seagram for the purpose of eventually taking charge of the business, he accepted. He later explained that there were many reasons why he said yes, but the main reason was his "incredible pride in this company and in the family."

Edgar began working for Seagram in early 1982 as assistant to the office of the president in New York City. Within a few months he transferred to Seagram International, the company's European branch. During his two years in Europe, he proved himself an astute businessman. He led the acquisitions of Oddbins, which soon grew into one of the most successful liquor store chains in England, and of Matheus Müller, a sparkling-wine manufacturer that strengthened Seagram's business in West Germany.

In 1984 Edgar returned to the United States and became president of the manufacturing, marketing, and sales division of Joseph E. Seagram and Sons, the company's American subsidiary. At that time the consumption of alcoholic beverages in the United States was beginning to decline as people became more health conscious. Edgar reacted decisively. He cut costs by eliminating some jobs, distributors, and advertising agencies. And he increased profits by getting rid of some of the firm's inexpensive brands, including Calvert whiskey, which had low profit margins, and concentrating on the marketing of high-profit-margin products, such as Chivas Regal.

In 1986, impressed with his son's leadership, the elder Bronfman officially named Edgar as his eventual successor. In 1988, as the next step toward that goal, Edgar became executive vice president of the United States operations of the Seagram Company and of Joseph E. Seagram and Sons, and he was elected to Seagram's board of directors. The following year he was named president and chief operating officer of the Seagram Company, in charge of the daily operations of the entire firm, while his father, as chief executive officer, still retained ultimate control of the company.

To ensure the company's growth, Edgar set up a dual strategy: expand Seagram's liquor business and diversify the firm's interests. In the late 1980s he tapped further into world liquor sales by purchasing Martell cognac, with which Seagram could take advantage of the rapidly growing cognac market in Asia. In 1993 he obtained the right to distribute Absolut Vodka in the United States and in some foreign markets. As one step in diversifying the company, he acquired, in 1988, Tropicana Products, makers of fruit juices. But he, like his father before him, had in mind an even greater degree of diversity.

In 1981 the elder Bronfman had invested Seagram funds in E. I. du Pont de Nemours and Company, the giant oil and chemical concern. By the early 1990s, the dividends from Seagram's nearly 25 percent stake in du Pont accounted for a large portion of Seagram's income. Now Edgar, too, wanted to buy into a company with huge growth potential. He set his sights on an industry that he already knew well: communications and entertainment. In 1993 he began acquiring stock in the media giant Time Warner, Inc., and by May 1994 Seagram owned 14.99 percent of the company (Time Warner prevented anyone from owning more than 15 percent of its stock).

In June 1994 the elder Bronfman retired from active management (though he remained with the firm as chairman of the board). In accordance with his wishes, the directors elected Edgar to succeed his father as chief executive officer of the Seagram Company; he also retained his previous title of president.

In March 1995 Edgar and other family members led the opposition to Conoco's plan for petroleum production activities in Iran. The family had leverage because Seagram was a major shareholder in Conoco's parent company, E. I. du Pont de Nemours and Company.

The following month, at Edgar's insistence, Seagram agreed to acquire 80 percent of MCA, the Hollywood conglomerate whose holdings included Universal Pictures, recording and video companies, and publishing concerns. To raise cash for the purchase price, about $5.7 billion, he sold most of Seagram's interest in du Pont. It was a risky move, du Pont having played a major role in Seagram's growth for over a decade, but Edgar was convinced that American popular culture was the new growth industry.

Edgar's marriage to Sherry Brewer lasted till 1991, when they divorced. They had one son and two daughters. In 1994 he married Clarissa Alcock, daughter of a Venezuelan oil company executive.

Edgar Miles Bronfman, Jr., is a member of the board of trustees of various institutions, including the New York City Public Broadcasting Service affiliate WNET. He was appointed to a White House advisory group, the Export Council, by President Bill Clinton.

THE
DAYANS

THREE GENERATIONS OF DAYANS have played important roles in the settling and development of modern Israel. Shmuel Dayan (1891–1968), born in the Ukraine, immigrated to Palestine in 1908. There he helped to found the first kibbutz and the first moshav. Later he became a leading Israeli politician. His wife, Devora Dayan (née Zatulovsky), was a leader of the women's labor movement, a writer and editor in the labor press, and a representative to the United Nations Relief and Rehabilitation Administration.

They had two sons. The elder, Moshe Dayan (1915–81), led Israel to crucial military victories over the Arabs, served in the Knesset (Israeli parliament), and held high ministerial posts in the Israeli government. His younger brother, Zohar (1926–48), died in the Israeli War of Independence. A book of Zohar's poems and letters was published posthumously in 1950.

Moshe's three children have had memorable careers. Yael (or Yaël, 1939–) married Tat-Aluf Dov Sion (an officer in the Israeli Army), became a successful journalist and novelist, and was elected a member of the Labor party to the Knesset. She gained notoriety in 1992 when she met with a Palestine Liberation Organization (PLO) official, at that time an act prohibited by Israeli law. Ehud ("Udi," 1942–) served in a navy commando unit during the 1973 Yom Kippur War, later became estranged from his father, and wrote a book, *Life as a Side Show* (1982), critical of Moshe.

Assaf ("Assi," 1945–) served in the Yom Kippur War as a mortar-
man and became a well-known actor, appearing, for example, in
the films *The Day the Fish Came Out* (British-German, 1967) and
Operation Thunderbolt (Israeli, 1978).

SHMUEL DAYAN

ISRAELI PIONEER

Shmuel Dayan helped to found the first kibbutz and the first
moshav in Israel. Later he was an important pioneer in Israeli
politics as well, serving as one of the original members of the
Knesset (parliament).

Shmuel (also spelled Shemuel, anglicized as Samuel) was born
in Zhashkov (or Zaskow), the Ukraine, in 1890. His paternal
grandfather and great-grandfather had been highly respected rabbinic judges. But his father, Reb Avraham, held a variety of jobs
and remained poor his entire life, ending as an itinerant peddler.
It was Reb Avraham, however, who adopted the family name because of his forebearers' calling (*dayan* being Hebrew for "a judge
in a rabbinic court"). On his maternal side, Shmuel descended
from Rabbi Pinhas of Koritz, a great Hasidic leader of the eighteenth century.

As a youth Shmuel joined the Zionist movement and moved
to Palestine in 1908. In 1909 a small group of settlers established
Deganya Alef, the first kibbutz (collective farm), located just south
of the Sea of Galilee. In 1911 Shmuel moved to Deganya Alef
when the original handful of farmers was replaced by a larger
commune of workers, who gave the kibbutz permanence. In 1920
he was among the original settlers of Deganya Bet, a new kibbutz
created to provide land for immigrant farmers and formed from a
section of Deganya Alef. The following year found him in the
Jezreel valley, where he helped to create Nahalal, the first moshav
(village that combines features of cooperative and private farming).

Shmuel was also a political activist. He represented the moshav movement at Zionist congresses and in the political labor party known as Ha-Po'el ha-Za'ir ("The Young Worker"). In 1930 that organization merged with a Zionist socialist party to form a larger labor party, the Mapai (the name is formed from the initials of Mifleget Po'alei Eretz Israel ["Palestine Workers' Party"]), in which he became a leader. When the modern state of Israel was formed in 1948, he was elected on the Mapai ticket to the first session of the Knesset, where he held a seat till 1959.

Shmuel published books and articles about Deganya, Nahalal, and the moshav movement. His works include *Nahalal* (1936), *Moshav ovedim* ("Workers Settlements," 1945), *Pioneers in Israel* (1961), and *Man and the Soil* (1965).

In 1914 he married Devora Zatulovsky (1890–1956), a writer, editor, leader of the women's labor movement, and a representative to the United Nations Relief and Rehabilitation Administration. They had two sons, one of whom, Moshe, became a famous Israeli military commander and statesman.

Shmuel Dayan died in Jerusalem, Israel, on August 10, 1968.

Moshe Dayan

SYMBOL OF ISRAELI SECURITY

Moshe Dayan served Israel as a military commander and as a statesman. In his later years, he and his black eye patch—he had lost an eye in battle—came to symbolize modern Israel, where citizen-soldiers kept the nation secure by triumphing against great odds.

He was born in Deganya Alef, Palestine, in May 1915. His parents were Shmuel and Devora (Zatulovsky) Dayan. Shmuel was a founder of Deganya Alef, the first kibbutz; and in 1921 he was one of the original settlers of Nahalal, the first successful moshav, where Moshe was raised.

As a young man, Moshe was a guard in the village fields. Later he joined special night squads commanded by the British officer Orde Wingate, from whom Moshe learned guerrilla warfare. The squads were formed to defend Jewish and British facilities from Arab rebel bands during the revolt of 1936–39.

In 1939 the British government issued a document that favored Arab nationalism in the region. The British intended to limit Jewish immigration to Palestine, to restrict Jewish purchases of Arab land, and to block the establishment of a Jewish state.

The Haganah, a Jewish defense force to which Moshe had belonged since 1929, now had to go under-

Moshe Dayan

ground. Discovered, he was arrested and imprisoned by the British in 1939. Two years later he was released.

By then World War II had started, and the Jews and the British needed each other. From 1941 to 1944 Moshe served as a scout for British forces in Palestine and Syria. In a crucial campaign, he led Palestinian Jewish troops that joined with British and Free French units in the liberation of French-mandated Syria from the Vichy (pro-German) administration. During this military action, he lost his left eye; thereafter, he wore a black eye patch.

Later in the war, he helped to set up a radio-broadcasting network. It was designed to give British intelligence officers access to information in case Palestine should fall to the Germans.

After the war, Moshe returned to farming on a kibbutz. He also served as a lieutenant colonel in the Haganah reserve.

During Israel's War of Independence (1948–49), the Haganah disbanded so that its members, including Moshe, could blend into the regular army of the new state of Israel. He led a battalion on the Syrian front and rose to the top military command of the Jerusalem area. In 1949 he participated in the armistice negotiations between Israel and Jordan.

From 1953 to 1958 Moshe served as chief of staff of the Israeli armed forces. In 1956 he planned and led the invasion of the Sinai Peninsula. That successful operation firmly established his reputation as a military commander.

In 1958 he left the army to enter politics. The following year he was elected to the Knesset (parliament) as a member of the Mapai (Labor) party.

In December 1959 Prime Minister David Ben-Gurion appointed Moshe minister of agriculture, a post he held till November 1964. He then joined Ben-Gurion in forming Rafi, a socialist faction of the Labor party. In 1965 he was elected to the Knesset again, this time under the Rafi banner.

In 1967, during the tense days just before the Six-Day War, a national unity government was formed, and the prime minister, Levi Eshkol, appointed him minister of defense. Moshe thus took the highest civilian role in the ensuing war with the Arabs, cooperating with the chief of staff, Yitzhak Rabin, in directing all operations. After the conflict, Moshe administered the territories conquered and occupied by Israel.

During the early 1970s, his growing reputation gave him increasing influence in Israel's foreign affairs. However, when Egypt and Syria launched a surprise attack on Israel on October 6, 1973 (Yom Kippur), Moshe was severely criticized for the nation's lack of preparedness. When Rabin, of the Labor party, became prime minister in 1974, Moshe left his post as minister of defense.

In 1977 he returned to the cabinet as the foreign minister under Prime Minister Menachem Begin, of the conservative Likud party. The following year Moshe became one of the chief architects of Begin's peace initiative with Egypt. But in October 1979, angered by Begin's plan to assert Israeli sovereignty over the occupied West Bank, legally still a part of Jordan, Moshe resigned.

He had two marriages. In 1935 he married Ruth Schwartz, who

was active in the development of home industries during the early years of Israel and was founder and managing director of Maskit, a government-sponsored company that produced and marketed Israeli handicrafts. Moshe and Ruth separated in 1971 and divorced in 1972. In 1973 he married Rachel (or Rahel) Corem. His first marriage produced a daughter and two sons.

In 1981 Moshe formed a new political party, Telem, which advocated unilateral Israeli withdrawal from the areas occupied in the 1967 conflicts. But he did not live long enough to develop the movement.

Moshe Dayan died in Tel Aviv on October 16, 1981.

Yael Dayan

PROMINENT ISRAELI LIBERAL

Yael (or Yaël) Dayan is one of Israel's most controversial liberal politicians. She was born in Nahalal, Palestine, on February 12, 1939, the eldest of the three children of Moshe and Ruth (Schwartz) Dayan.

Yael traveled abroad for the United Jewish Appeal; spent two years in the army; wrote several novels; served as an army press liaison during the Six-Day War (1967); married, in 1967, an army colonel, Tat-Aluf Dov Sion, with whom she had two children; worked at an army hospital during the Yom Kippur War (1973); and wrote *My Father, His Daughter* (1985), about her relationship with her father, a military leader and statesman.

In 1992 Yael was elected as a Labor candidate to the Knesset. She soon made right-wing enemies by fighting for gay rights, women's rights, and the establishment of a Palestinian state. In 1992 she met with a Palestine Liberation Organization (PLO) official when such a meeting was against Israeli law. In 1993, after the ban was lifted, she became the first Knesset member to talk with PLO chairman Yasser Arafat. For her left-wing views, Yael Dayan has received hate mail and death threats.

THE
GOLDSMIDS

T HE GOLDSMIDS WERE ACTIVE IN ENGLISH and English Jewish life from the eighteenth to the twentieth century. The family, originally named Goldschmidt, developed in Germany, but a branch later moved to Amsterdam, the Netherlands, where they became prosperous merchants. In the mid-1700s Aaron Goldsmid (c. 1715–82) immigrated to London, England, and, with his son George Goldsmid (c. 1743–1812), established the mercantile firm of Aaron Goldsmid and Son, later known as Goldsmid and Eliason. Aaron became a treasurer in the Great Synagogue.

He had three other sons. Asher Goldsmid (c. 1750–1832) co-founded the firm of Mocatta and Goldsmid, bullion brokers to the Bank of England. Benjamin Goldsmid (c. 1753–1808) and Abraham Goldsmid (c. 1756–1810) became prominent financiers, were active in Jewish affairs, engaged in philanthropy, and did much to break down social prejudice against Jews in England.

The next generation of the family was led by Isaac Lyon Goldsmid (1778–1859), eldest son of Asher. Isaac became a wealthy financier, helped to establish the University of London, worked for the emancipation of the Jews, and was created a baronet, the first professing Jew to receive an English hereditary title.

From Isaac came several more notable Goldsmids. His eldest child, Anna Maria Goldsmid (1805–1889), was a writer, a translator, and an activist in communal affairs. His second child, Francis

Henry Goldsmid (1808–1878), was the first Jewish barrister in England, the first Jewish queen's counsel, a long-standing member of Parliament, a prolific writer, and an activist in both the Jewish and the non-Jewish communities. Francis's younger brother, Frederick David Goldsmid (c. 1812–66), also served in Parliament.

The next generation of Goldsmids had three outstanding members. One of Frederick's nine children, Julian Goldsmid (1838–96), followed him in Parliament and held many leadership roles in Jewish affairs. Frederick's youngest sibling, Emma Goldsmid (1819–1902), married Nathaniel Montefiore (1819–83), with whom she had Claude Joseph Goldsmid Montefiore (1858–1938), a biblical scholar and Jewish activist. The third person of note in this generation, Albert Edward Williamson Goldsmid (1846–1904) belonged to a line of Benjamin's descendants who renounced Judaism. Albert, Benjamin's great-grandson, made an avowed return to the faith, had a distinguished career in the military, and actively engaged in Jewish affairs, notably as a member of the Council of the Anglo-Jewish Association and as president of the Maccabeans.

ABRAHAM GOLDSMID

FINANCIER AND PHILANTHROPIST

Abraham Goldsmid made a major contribution to English life and government through his financial activities. His philanthropies aided not only the Jewish community but also the public at large.

He was born in Amsterdam, the Netherlands, in about 1756. His parents were Aaron and Catherine (de Vries) Goldsmid. Aaron, a merchant, moved with his family to England when Abraham was a child.

In 1877 Abraham and his older brother Benjamin formed a bill-broker business. They developed a reputation for integrity, and their business connections grew steadily. After 1792 they became wealthy through their dealings with the English government. They were the first members of the stock exchange to break the monopoly on public loans held by the banking clique.

Abraham married Ann Eliason of Amsterdam. They had six children.

Abraham and Benjamin served in all the offices of the Great Synagogue. They raised a large sum of money for the building and endowment of Neveh Zedek, the first large Ashkenazic charitable institution in England. Among their contributions to the general welfare was their establishment of the Royal Naval Asylum, which the government later turned into a hostel for sailors' children.

The Goldsmids' friendship with the sons of George III helped to break down social prejudice against Jews in England. Their association with Lord Nelson had the same effect.

In his later years Benjamin was subject to fits of depression, and he finally committed suicide in 1808. Abraham then continued to operate the business alone.

In 1810 he jointly contracted with the firm of Barin for a huge government loan. However, his rivals and enemies on the stock exchange succeeded in depreciating the value of the scrip of the new loan, thus diminishing his own fortune as well. When it became clear that he could not meet his liabilities, Abraham Goldsmid committed suicide on September 28, 1810, in Morden, near London.

ISAAC LYON GOLDSMID

FIRST JEWISH BARONET IN ENGLAND

Isaac Lyon Goldsmid was one of the most esteemed Jews in English history. He amassed a large fortune through his financial dealings, worked for general social and educational progress, and led the fight for Jewish emancipation. His achievements were publicly acknowledged when he was made a baronet, the first Jew to receive that honor in England.

Isaac was born in London on January 13, 1778. His parents were Asher and Rachel (Keyser) Goldsmid. Asher, an older brother of Abraham Goldsmid, was a cofounder of Mocatta and Goldsmid, bullion brokers to the Bank of England. As a young man Isaac entered his father's firm.

In 1804 he married his cousin Isabel, daughter of Abraham Goldsmid. They had two sons and five daughters.

Isaac had considerable success in financing railways. But his most extensive financial operations involved dealing in the precious metals of Portugal, Brazil, and Turkey. He ultimately accumulated great wealth through his career as a financier.

Isaac took a major role in founding the University of London (later University College) in 1825. In 1834 he helped to establish the University College (or North London) Hospital, serving as its treasurer from 1839 to 1857. He also worked for the reform of the penal system.

The greatest interest in his life was the cause of Jewish emancipation. After an 1829 parliamentary act provided civil rights for Roman Catholics in England, he began to seek the same rights for Jews. Through his efforts the Jewish Disabilities Bill was introduced in the House of Commons in 1830, where it passed in 1833. But for many years it failed to pass in the House of Lords. Finally, in 1859, largely thanks to Isaac's lobbying, the bill became law, granting civil and political rights to Jews.

In 1841, for his many contributions to English life, Isaac was made a baronet. He was the first professing Jew to be granted a hereditary title in England.

Isaac Lyon Goldsmid died in London on April 27, 1859.

Francis Henry Goldsmid

LAWYER, POLITICIAN, AND JEWISH ACTIVIST

As the first Jewish barrister in England and the first Jewish queen's counsel, Francis Henry Goldsmid broke important paths for the Jewish people. He also served in Parliament, produced many writings, and worked for Jewish civil and political emancipation.

He was born in London on May 1, 1808. His parents were Isaac Lyon and Isabel (Goldsmid) Goldsmid. Isaac became the first Jewish baronet in English history. Isabel was a first cousin of Isaac, daughter of his uncle Abraham Goldsmid.

Francis was privately educated as a classical scholar. He then carefully selected law as his profession for the specific purpose of opening a new career to his coreligionists. In January 1833 he was admitted to Lincoln's Inn, thus becoming England's first Jewish barrister. His legal career reached its apex in 1858, when he was named the first Jewish queen's counsel.

In 1839 Francis married his cousin Louisa Goldsmid, daughter of Moses (or Moshe) Goldsmid, his father's youngest brother. They had no children.

As a young man, he joined his father in the pursuit of Jewish emancipation. Francis wrote many influential pamphlets on the subject, including *Remarks on the Civil Disabilities of British Jews* (1830), *A Few Words Respecting the Enfranchisement of British Jews Addressed to the New Parliament* (1833), and *Reply to the Arguments Advanced against the Removal of the Remaining Disabilities of the Jews* (1848).

In 1859 his father died and Francis succeeded to the baronetcy. In the same year, the Jewish Disabilities Bill was passed, and in 1860 he took advantage of his new freedom by running for, and winning, a seat in Parliament, which he held for the rest of his life. He was the recognized spokesman for the Jewish community in Parliament.

Like his father, Francis actively supported the University College and the University College Hospital. He was treasurer of the hospital from 1857 to 1868.

In 1841 Francis established the Jews' Infant School, one of the earliest schools of its kind. He also helped to found the Reform Synagogue in 1841 and the Anglo-Jewish Association in 1871.

Francis Henry Goldsmid died in an accident at the Waterloo train station in London on May 2, 1878.

Julian Goldsmid

MEMBER OF PARLIAMENT AND JEWISH LEADER

Julian Goldsmid was a worthy successor to previous Goldsmids, who had contributed so richly to English life, both in general and especially in the Jewish community. He served for thirty years in Parliament and held many positions of leadership in Jewish communal affairs.

Julian was born in London in 1838. His parents were Frederick David and Caroline (Samuel) Goldsmid. Frederick, the younger brother of the famed lawyer Francis Henry Goldsmid, became a member of Parliament.

In 1866, the year his father died, Julian was elected to Parliament, where he held a seat for the rest of his life. At one time he served as deputy speaker of that distinguished body.

Julian married Virginia Philipson. They had eight daughters.

In 1878 his uncle Francis died and Julian succeeded him as the third and last Goldsmid baronet.

Like Francis, Julian was active in the Anglo-Jewish Association, holding the offices of vice president (1871–86) and president (1886–95). He also served as president of the Russo-Jewish Committee (1882–94), in which capacity he leveled many official protests against Russian persecutions of Jews. From 1883 till his death, he was president of the Jews' Infant School.

Julian Goldsmid died in Brighton, England, on January 7, 1896.

CLAUDE JOSEPH GOLDSMID MONTEFIORE

BIBLICAL SCHOLAR AND JEWISH ACTIVIST

Claude Joseph Goldsmid Montefiore played a major role in the twentieth-century movement to apply rabbinic material in a sympathetic, constructive way to the field of New Testament scholarship. He also promoted the cause of liberal reform within English Jewry and furthered both Jewish and non-Jewish educational ventures.

Claude was born in London on June 6, 1858. His parents were Nathaniel Mayer and Emma (Goldsmid) Montefiore. Claude was a grandson of Isaac Lyon Goldsmid, first baronet; a nephew of Francis Henry Goldsmid, second baronet; and a cousin of Julian Goldsmid, third baronet. In 1883 Claude officially added the name of Goldsmid to his original surname.

He studied privately and at Balliol College, Oxford, where he was influenced by the religious liberalism of Benjamin Jowett. After graduating in 1881, Claude continued his studies in Berlin. There he met a Romanian Jew, Solomon Schechter, who tutored him in rabbinic literature and with whom he returned to England.

Born to wealth, hence leisure, Claude used his time to serve the causes of scholarship, reform, and education. He earned a special niche for himself in the world of biblical scholarship by spreading among Christian readers a knowledge of the rabbinic writings and their relationship to the New Testament. His literary works in this field include *The Synoptic Gospels* (two volumes, 1909; second edition, 1927), *Some Elements of the Religious Teachings of Jesus* (1910), *Judaism and St.Paul* (1914), and *Rabbinic Literature and Gospel Teachings* (1930). In 1930 he was awarded the British Academy medal for biblical studies.

He also wrote extensively about Liberal Judaism (called Reform Judaism in the United States) and the need for changes in Jewish religious life in England. As joint editor (1888–1908) of the *Jewish Quarterly Review*, he produced a long list of articles on this subject. His books include *Liberal Judaism* (1903) and *Outlines of Liberal Judaism* (1912; second edition, 1923).

Claude helped to found, and was the principal force behind, the Jewish Religious Union for the Advancement of Liberal Judaism, as well as a Liberal Jewish synagogue. He often preached at the synagogue, which he served as president from 1910 till his death.

Claude made important contributions to Jewish and non-Jewish education in England. In 1892 he delivered the Hibbert lectures, published that year as *The Origin and Growth of Religion as Illustrated by the Religion of the Ancient Hebrews*. He helped to support the Cambridge lectureship in rabbinic studies, served as president of the Anglo-Jewish Association from 1896 to 1921, and held the same office at the University College of Southampton from 1915 to 1934.

Claude was married twice. In 1886 he wedded Thérèse Schorstein, with whom he had a son before she died in 1889. In 1902 he married Florence Fyfe Brereton Ward, with whom he had no children.

Claude Joseph Goldsmid Montefiore died in London on July 9, 1938.

THE
GUGGENHEIMS

THE GUGGENHEIMS CAME to the United States dirt poor in the mid-nineteenth century and through daring, innovative programs in both business and philanthropy became one of the wealthiest, most influential families in American history. They built their fortune primarily in mining and metallurgy, but Guggenheims have proven themselves leaders not only in industry but also in such diverse fields as aeronautics and rocketry, archaeology, art patronage, finance, literature, military service, and politics. No family in America has had a greater impact as benefactors of foundations.

From at least the early 1700s to the early 1800s, the Guggenheims were financial and intellectual leaders in the German-speaking ghetto village of Lengnau, Switzerland. But by the time Simon Meyer Guggenheim (1792–1869) came along, the family fortune had disappeared. In 1847 he immigrated to the United States and settled in Philadelphia, Pennsylvania, with his family.

It was Simon's only son, Meyer (1828–1905), who established the family business empire in America, at first in manufacturing and merchandising, later in mining and smelting. In 1877 he set up a holding company—M. Guggenheim's Sons—for his varied interests. In 1901 the family assumed leadership of the United States mining industry by gaining control of the American Smelting and Refining Company (ASARCO). In 1916 the holding company was renamed Guggenheim Brothers.

Meyer had eight sons and three daughters. One son died young. The others all rose to prominence. Isaac (1854–1922), the eldest, concentrated his efforts on the family's lace-importing business, taking only a minor role in mining and other interests. Daniel (1856–1930) headed the family enterprises after his father's death, established the Daniel and Florence Guggenheim Foundation, and was a pioneer in funding research in aeronautics and rocketry. Murry (1858–1939), the statistics expert, chaired the ASARCO finance committee, was a partner in the family's holding company, and established the Murry and Leonie Guggenheim Foundation to fund a free dental clinic for poor children in New York City. Solomon Robert (1861–1949) helped to run the family's enterprises, amassed one of the world's largest collections of abstract paintings, and commissioned Frank Lloyd Wright to build the revolutionary Solomon R. Guggenheim Museum of Art in New York City.

Benjamin (1865–1912) developed the family's mining interests in Colorado and elsewhere, retired in 1901, and died a hero when he gave his life jacket to a woman and assisted others into lifeboats as the S.S. *Titanic* sank on April 15, 1912. Simon (1867–1941) helped to run the family's mining and smelting enterprises, served a term as United States senator, and, in memory of his deceased son, established the John Simon Guggenheim Memorial Foundation for awarding Guggenheim Fellowships to scholars. Simon's twin brother, Robert (1867–76), died in a fall from a horse. William (1868–1941) developed the Guggenheim mining and smelting interests in Mexico in the 1890s, retired in 1901, and engaged in philanthropic, intellectual, and artistic pursuits.

Daniel had two sons and a daughter. M. Robert (1885–1959) worked for a time in the family's business and served as United States ambassador to Portugal (1953–54), but his principal claim to fame was as one of the most spectacular wastrels in American history. However, his younger brother, Harry Frank (1891–1971), was a Renaissance man of incredible energy and accomplishment: he led the family from 1930 to 1971; furthered his father's businesses and philanthropies, especially aeronautics and rocketry;

established his own Harry Frank Guggenheim Foundation; and distinguished himself as a man of both thought and action in a variety of fields, including aviation and publishing. Daniel's daughter, Gladys Eleanor (1895–1980), married Roger W. Straus, whose family owned Macy's department store; exercised influence at ASARCO through her husband, who rose to the presidency of the company; and served as president of the Daniel and Florence Guggenheim Foundation. Their son Roger W. Straus, Jr., became America's leading literary publisher through his company of Farrar, Straus and Giroux.

Murry's only son, Edmond Alfred (1888–1972), helped to develop the world's richest copper mine (in Chile), worked briefly as a partner in Guggenheim Brothers, served as president of the Murry and Leonie Guggenheim Foundation, and devoted much of his life to golf, yachting, and other sports. Benjamin had three daughters, one of whom, Peggy (originally Marguerite, 1898–1979), was an important art patron who established the famous Peggy Guggenheim Collection of modern art.

Because later generations produced many more daughters than sons, the name Guggenheim has passed down to only a small number of people. However, the Guggenheim energy and talent are still alive, as in Peter O. Lawson-Johnston (1927–) and Iris Cornelia Love (1933–), both Episcopalians but members of the Guggenheim bloodline. The former is the son of Barbara (Guggenheim) Lawson-Johnston, the daughter of Solomon Robert Guggenheim. When Harry Frank Guggenheim died in 1971, he made Peter, his second cousin, his principal heir, so that Peter immediately gained control of many businesses within the former Guggenheim empire, as well as two foundations (the Solomon R. Guggenheim and the Harry Frank Guggenheim foundations), through which Peter exerts great cultural influence. Iris Cornelia Love is the daughter of Audrey (Josephthal) Love, the daughter of Edyth (Guggenheim) Josephtahl, the daughter of Isaac Guggenheim. Iris is widely regarded as the foremost woman archaeologist in the United States and perhaps in the world.

Meyer Guggenheim

FOUNDER OF THE GUGGENHEIM EMPIRE
AND FAMILY DYNASTY

With an astonishing degree of business genius and an unusual courage in taking risks, Meyer Guggenheim founded a business empire by developing worldwide mining interests that dominated the industry for decades. Perhaps an even greater achievement was his molding of his sons into men strong enough to carry on his business enterprises and cultured enough to turn their wealth into life-enhancing projects.

Meyer was born in Lengnau, Switzerland, on February 1, 1828. His parents were Simon Meyer and Schäfeli (Levinger) Guggenheim. Simon was a tailor, while Meyer worked as a peddler throughout Switzerland and Germany. In 1847, eleven years after the death of Schäfeli, Simon sought a better life by leaving Lengnau for the United States. With him on the journey were his son, Meyer; his five daughters; his financée, Rachel Weil Meyer; and Rachel's children by her first marriage.

They arrived in America in 1848 and settled in Philadelphia, Pennsylvania. Simon soon married Rachel, and he and Meyer went to work as peddlers of lace, spices, shoestrings, stove polish, and other items. The younger Guggenheim noticed that stove polish was a good seller but that his profit margin was extremely small. Showing initiative, he began to manufacture and sell his own polish at a much larger profit. He also made a success of selling coffee essence.

By 1852 his products were doing well enough for him to marry Barbara Meyer, his stepsister. They had eight sons (one of whom died in childhood) and three daughters.

Meyer was never satisfied with any single success. He always sought to improve the family's position through new ventures. "Roasted pigeons," he often said, "do not fly into one's mouth." One had to work to get those roasted pigeons. He opened a grocery store, speculated in clothing and food during the Civil War, became a wholesale merchant of spices, manufactured lye, and invested in a railway. In 1872 he and a partner set up the firm of Guggenheim and Pulaski, importers of fine Swiss laces and embroideries.

In 1877, after his partner retired from the business, Meyer reorganized the company as M. Guggenheim's Sons (incorporated in 1882). He took into the business his four oldest sons, who had already been educated and apprenticed for their roles in the embroidery firm.

In 1881, despite the fact that his lace and embroidery business was doing extremely well, Meyer gambled in an entirely new field by buying the controlling interest in two lead and silver mines near Leadville, Colorado. The gamble paid off beyond his wildest expectations. In August of that year the mines began to yield the bonanza that would lay the groundwork for the Guggenheims' later worldwide empire of copper, silver, and gold.

Meyer soon realized that he could dramatically increase his profits by doing the same thing he had done with stove polish: cutting out the middleman—in this case, the smelter who refined the ore. In 1888 he formed, with a minority partner (later bought out by the Guggenheims), the Philadelphia Smelting and Refining Company and built a new smelter at Pueblo, Colorado. This was the first step toward the Guggenheims' control of the smelting industry in America.

Meyer signed over his controlling share of the smelting company to the lace and embroidery firm of M. Guggenheim's Sons. The three younger sons, who were brought into the company as equal partners with their four older brothers, soon went into the field to learn the mining and smelting business. Gradually Meyer phased out the lace and embroidery business, and the four older sons shifted their efforts to the new family enterprise.

In 1888 and 1889 Meyer moved the family from Philadelphia to New York City. He added more smelters, mines, and metallic ores to the business, which became so powerful that in 1901 the Guggenheims gained control of the American Smelting and Refining Company (ASARCO), a trust composed of the country's largest metal-processing plants. In effect, the family now ran the United States mining industry.

In his last years, Meyer had the satisfaction of knowing that he could leave his business in the capable hands of his sons, whom he had personally trained in business tactics and in the importance of family unity. He was also a role model for them as a philanthropist, giving much to Jewish charities.

Meyer Guggenheim died in Palm Beach, Florida, on March 15, 1905.

DANIEL GUGGENHEIM

SUCCESSOR TO MEYER GUGGENHEIM

Daniel Guggenheim headed the ever-expanding Guggenheim business empire after the death of his father, Meyer; established the influential Daniel and Florence Guggenheim Foundation; and provided pioneer funding in aeronautics.

He was born in Philadelphia, Pennsylvania, on July 9, 1856. When he was a teenager, he was sent to Switzerland by his father to learn the elder Guggenheim's business of manufacturing and importing Swiss embroideries. After eleven years (1873–84) in Switzerland, Daniel returned to the United States while the family was shifting its emphasis to mining and smelting, to which he soon adapted.

In the same year of his return, 1884, Daniel married Florence Schloss. They had two sons and one daughter.

The second of Meyer's seven living sons, Daniel quickly proved himself to be the ablest. He was largely responsible for the basic Guggenheim strategy of controlling and integrating the supply of metallic ores and the process of smelting and refining. It was he, too, who negotiated the Guggenheim takeover in 1901 of the American Smelting and Refining Company (ASARCO), a trust consisting of America's largest metal-processing plants; Daniel headed ASARCO till 1919 and exercised a dominant influence

Daniel Guggenheim

on it in the 1920s. He expanded the family's interests by building smelters and refineries and by initiating and directing explorations for new sources of ore supply, such as mines producing tin in Bolivia, gold and copper in Alaska, diamonds in Africa, and copper and nitrate in Chile. He also oversaw the restructuring of the family's business from M. Guggenheim's Sons to Guggenheim Brothers in 1916.

Daniel continued his father's tradition of philanthropy. "Money, to me," he once wrote to his son Harry, "for the luxury that it will give me has very little value. But money is power, and the power is the thing to use, not to abuse." Using money wisely, "you can accomplish a great deal in the world for yourself and the world. For yourself, because of the satisfaction you will obtain from accomplishing for the world." In addition to making anonymous donations, he formed the Daniel and Florence Guggenheim Foundation, which dispensed millions to a variety of charities in the United States and abroad, including hospitals and medical institutes in Chile, the Congo, and Israel.

His son Harry interested him in aviation. In 1925 Daniel donated the money to establish the Daniel Guggenheim School of Aeronautics at New York University, America's first school of aeronautics. The following year he created the Daniel Guggenheim Fund for the Promotion of Aeronautics, which helped to change the emphasis of aviation from stunt flying to the development of "its commercial, industrial, and scientific aspects." He lived long enough to see the aeronautics fund do its work so well that early in 1930 it was liquidated, having accomplished its goals.

Meanwhile, in 1929 he formed the Daniel Guggenheim Fund for the Measurement and Investigation of High Altitudes, with money advanced from the Daniel and Florence Guggenheim Foundation. This was a visionary project, prompted by his friend Charles Lindbergh, set up specifically to aid the pioneering research in rocketry by Robert H. Goddard. At that time rocketry was generally an object of jokes, but Daniel's family got the last laugh when, forty years later, Goddard's work led to the rockets that sent men to the moon.

In his last years, Daniel gradually turned over the management of his affairs to Harry. Daniel's wife, Florence (1863–1944), took a leading role in Guggenheim charities. She also served as treasurer of the Women's National Republican Club for many years.

Daniel Guggenheim died at his country home near Port Washington, Long Island, on September 28, 1930.

Solomon Robert Guggenheim

FOUNDER OF THE GUGGENHEIM MUSEUM

Solomon Robert Guggenheim, the fourth son of Meyer Guggenheim, assisted in the development of the family's mining and smelting enterprises. But his greatest achievements were as an art collector, as the founder of the Solomon R. Guggenheim Foundation for the promotion of art, and as the man who commissioned the revolutionary Guggenheim Museum.

He was born in Philadelphia, Pennsylvania, on February 2, 1861. At the age of fourteen he was sent by his father to study at the Concordia Institute in Zurich, Switzerland. Later he joined his three older brothers as a partner in M. Guggenheim's Sons, a company founded by Meyer for the importing of Swiss laces and embroideries. Sol, as he was called, remained for some years in Europe to learn, and help run, the business. In the 1880s Meyer struck it rich in the mining business, into which he brought his sons. Sol handled the sale of the embroidery factories.

Returning to America, he began to familiarize himself with the mining industry. In the early 1890s he helped to develop the family's mining concerns in Mexico. He settled in New York City, the family's headquarters, in 1895 and helped to run various divisions of the Guggenheim empire till he retired from full-time business activities in 1919.

In 1895 he married Irene Rothschild, no relation to the famous European Rothschilds. Sol and Irene had three daughters.

Irene interested Sol in collecting paintings, mostly by old masters. But in 1927 he met the baroness Hilla Rebay von Ehrenwiesen, a painter who introduced him to modern art. He soon began to build a huge collection of works by such moderns as Wassily Kandinsky, Paul Klee, Fernand Léger, and Laszlo Moholy-Nagy. In 1937 he established the Solomon R. Guggenheim Foundation "for the promotion and encouragement of art and education in art." In 1939 the foundation rented temporary housing on East Fifty-fourth Street in New York City for the Solomon R. Guggenheim Collection.

In 1943 Sol commissioned the great architect Frank Lloyd Wright to design and build a permanent museum for the collection (and later additions) on Fifth Avenue in New York City. Sol did not live to see the building, which was completed in 1959, ten years after his death. The Solomon R. Guggenheim Museum is one of the most famous and controversial structures in America. A radical departure from traditional museum design, the building spirals upward and outward in coils of massive white concrete, while the interior exhibition space consists of a six-story spiral ramp encircling an open area lighted by a glass dome. During 1990–92 the museum underwent restoration and expansion.

Besides his philanthropies in art, Sol gave generously to other causes, especially to hospitals. He was a staunch conservative Republican and an active golfer, hunter, and yachtsman till his old age.

Solomon Robert Guggenheim died at his Sands Point, Long Island, home on November 3, 1949.

Simon Guggenheim

FOUNDER OF THE GUGGENHEIM FELLOWSHIPS

Simon Guggenheim, Meyer Guggenheim's sixth son, played a major role in the building of the Guggenheim mining empire and served one term as a United States senator. But his most lasting contribution to the world was the creation of the foundation that grants the important Guggenheim Fellowships.

Simon was born in Philadelphia, Pennsylvania, on December 30, 1867. He had a twin brother, Robert, who died as a child in an accident. Simon studied at a business school in Philadelphia and then spent some time in Spain learning Spanish, which came in handy when the family's business spread to Spanish-speaking countries in the New World.

In 1888 he went to Colorado to help run the family's mining business there. When the Guggenheims took control of the American Smelting and Refining Company (ASARCO) in 1901, Simon became a member of the board of directors.

Meanwhile, in 1898, he married Olga Hirsch, daughter of a wealthy realtor and diamond merchant. They had two sons.

Also in the 1890s he became active in Colorado politics. As one of the younger brothers in the family, he felt he needed to do something on his own to win the respect of his older siblings. In 1904 he opened a political office in Denver, and in 1907, after running an openly corrupt campaign of buying votes, he was elected by the Colorado legislature to the United States Senate as a Republican. During his term in office (1907–1913) he promoted federal projects for his state and developed a reputation as the most conservative member of the Senate.

After leaving the Senate, Simon returned to executive positions in the family's business. In 1919 he succeeded his brother Daniel as president of ASARCO, a position he held till his death.

In later life he took an increasing interest in philanthropy, prompted especially by the death of his seventeen-year-old elder son, John Simon, following a mastoid operation in 1922, and by the mental deterioration of his younger son, George Denver (who committed suicide in 1939). In 1925 Simon and his wife established the John Simon Guggenheim Memorial Foundation. John had shown promise as a scholar, so Simon set up the foundation to provide grants of money to research scholars and creative artists under the freest possible conditions, without any pressure to obtain specific results. Over the years, Guggenheim Fellowships have enabled thousands of scholars and artists to study, research, travel, and create at a pace and to a degree not otherwise possible. Today hundreds of fellowships are granted annually to citizens of the United States, Canada, other countries of the Western Hemisphere, and the Philippines.

Simon was a benefactor of other causes as well. He gave money to the Colorado School of Mines and the University of Colorado. Though not strongly attached to Judaism (he and his wife attended an Episcopalian church), he nevertheless contributed to Jewish causes, such as Hebrew Union College in Cincinnati, Ohio.

Simon Guggenheim died in New York City on November 2, 1941.

Harry Frank Guggenheim

Renaissance Man

The most versatile member of the Guggenheim family was Harry Frank Guggenheim, son of Daniel and grandson of Meyer. Harry led the family after his father's death; developed his father's businesses and philanthropies, especially aeronautics and rocketry; established a new foundation in his own name; and distinguished himself as an aviator, aviation pioneer, naval officer, United States ambassador, civic leader, author, publisher, racehorse owner, and museum president. In an era of increasing specialization, he was a rare throwback to the Renaissance man of wide-ranging achievements.

Harry was born in West End, New Jersey, on August 23, 1890.

He studied science for a year at Yale University, learned about mining and metallurgy in Mexico at one of his family's properties, and earned B.A. (1913) and M.A. (1918) degrees in engineering at Pembroke College, Cambridge University, England.

Inheriting his father's and grandfather's energy, determination, daring, and golden touch, Harry became the acknowledged leader of the Guggenheims after his father's death in 1930. He kept that role till his own death over forty years later.

His business instincts added some $40 million to the family fortune. He began his work for the family in 1913 when he became a director of several copper compa-

The Harry Frank Guggenheim Foundation

Harry Frank Guggenheim

nies affliated with the Guggenheims' interests. In 1916 he joined Guggenheim Brothers as a partner and promoted the family's mining enterprises in South America. He served as executive director of the Guggenheims' Chile Copper Company, owner of the world's largest copper deposit. When the majority of the partners decided to sell Chile Copper in 1923, Harry resigned from the partnership in protest.

In 1949 he rejoined Guggenheim Brothers and in his later years was the firm's senior member. He also served as chairman of the board at the Guggenheims' Anglo-Lautaro Nitrate Corporation of Chile, producer of more than half of the world's natural nitrate and iodine.

Besides assisting in the development of his father's business ventures (such as the Chile Copper Company), Harry aided his father's philanthropies. From 1926 to 1930 Harry served as presi-

Florence Guggenheim

dent of the Daniel Guggenheim Fund for the Promotion of Aeronautics, through which he set up projects to win public support for safe, commercially feasible passenger travel by air. One early project was to finance a nationwide tour of the Richard E. Byrd North Pole plane in 1926.

In his later years Harry directed the Daniel and Florence Guggenheim Foundation, which distributed grants for a wide range of causes, including aviation. Using funds from his father's foundation, Harry established aeronautics schools and centers at a number of universities, including Cornell, Princeton, and Columbia. The best known of the schools came to be the partially Guggenheim-funded Jet Propulsion Laboratory (JPL) at the California Institute of Technology (Caltech) in Pasadena. By mid-century virtually all of America's senior aerospace engineers were graduates of Guggenheim-sponsored schools.

In 1929 Daniel began funding the pioneering research in rocketry by Robert H. Goddard. After Daniel's death, Harry renewed Goddard's grants over and over again, often in the face of strong opposition by his own advisers. But Daniel's vision and Harry's persistence eventually paid off. Before Goddard died in 1945 he developed the essential features of the Saturn V rocket system that propelled Apollo XI and the first men to the moon in 1969. In fact, about two hundred patents to Saturn's rockets once belonged to Goddard and the Daniel and Florence Guggenheim Foundation. In 1951 Goddard's widow and the foundation filed a lawsuit against the United States government for infringement of

Goddard's work. In 1961 the government awarded Mrs. Goddard and the foundation $1 million.

In the mid-1960s Harry set up the Harry Frank Guggenheim Foundation. Again he showed the Guggenheim trait of boldly breaking new ground: unlike any other foundation, it was dedicated to developing a program to improve "man's relation to man." Among the projects that the foundation later funded were studies in "dominance interaction in early peer group formations among children"; studies of the "political and economic behavior of females in Israeli kibbutzim"; and research on prehistoric man in Africa, including the work of Dr. L. S. B. Leakey. The foundation also

The Harry Frank Guggenheim Foundation

Harry Frank Guggenheim

gave money to the United Jewish Appeal, the Holocaust Survivors Memorial Foundation, the Medical University of North Carolina, and other causes. Harry once stated his philosophy of philanthropy: "Inherited wealth should be used for the progress of man. . . . People who make a business of pleasure are seldom happy." This philosophy was virtually the same as his father's.

Harry's interest in aviation began during World War I, in which he served as a lieutenant in the United States Naval Aviation Forces in Europe. He rose to the rank of lieutenant commander before leaving the service in December 1918.

Later he served as a member of a committee of experts that studied the limitation of air armaments for the disarmament commission of the League of Nations (1927), represented United States commercial aviation at the Third Pan-American Conference (1927), was selected by President Calvin Coolidge as a delegate to the International Conference on Civil Aeronautics (1928), and was appointed by President Herbert Hoover to the National Advisory Committee for Aeronautics, on which he served for nearly a decade (1929–38).

During World War II he returned to active military duty and became commanding officer at Mercer Field in Trenton, New Jersey, which tested and commissioned combat planes for the navy. In 1943 he was promoted to commander and was awarded the commmendation ribbon. Later he served on the aircraft carrier U.S.S. *Nehenta Bay* in the Pacific and won another commendation ribbon. In 1945 he made the rank of captain.

His role as a public servant was highlighted in 1929 when President Hoover appointed him United States ambassador to Cuba, where he served till 1933. Harry's earlier work for the Guggenheim Brothers in Chile and Mexico had given him an opportunity to learn Spanish and to gain an understanding of problems in Latin American countries. However, his term in Cuba was marred by the brutal dictatorship of Gerardo Machado and the violent reaction of rebels. Harry knew that the dictatorship was evil, but because of his innate conservatism and his experience as a business executive in Latin America, he could not support the Cuban rebels who threatened law and order. His resulting acquiescence in Machado's tyranny established an American nonintervention policy in Cuba that resulted less than thirty years later in the communist revolution led by Fidel Castro.

In later years he continued his public service in other capacities. From 1936 to 1942 he was president of the citizens' committee on the control of crime in New York City. In 1946 he was appointed chairman of the board of the New York City Airport Authority; Harry soon divested himself of the position when, at his recommendation, the board's work was turned over to the Port of New York Authority and thus freed from municipal politics.

He also had an intellectual side. His book *The Seven Skies* (1930) consists of a collection of essays on the history and development of flying. *The United States and Cuba: A Study in International Relations* (1934) recommends changes in the commercial association between the two countries.

In 1939 Harry founded *Newsday*, a Long Island, New York, newspaper, primarily so that his third wife, Alicia Patterson, could run it. He kept 51 percent of the stock and managed the paper's financial affairs, while she had 49 percent and controlled the paper's operations. *Newsday* experienced tremendous growth during the 1940s to 1960s as New Yorkers rushed into the suburbs, and it became America's largest suburban daily. In 1954 the paper won a Pulitzer Prize for its meritorious public service. After Alicia died in 1963, Harry took over complete control. In 1970 he sold *Newsday* to the Times Mirror Company.

Another interest in his late years was raising and racing horses. His horse Dark Star won the Kentucky Derby in 1953.

After the death of his uncle Sol in 1949, Harry took over the administration of the Solomon R. Guggenheim Foundation for the promotion of art. And after the 1959 completion of the Solomon R. Guggenheim Museum (which he himself renamed from Museum of Non-Objective Art), he served as president of that institution. One of his greatest pleasures as president was receiving the Justin K. Thannhauser Collection, including thirty-four Picassos.

Harry married three times. By his first marriage, in 1910 to Helen Rosenberg, daughter of a New York City businessman, he had two daughters. By his second marriage, in 1923 to Caroline Morton, a member of the family that founded Morton Salt, he had another daughter. Those marriages were stormy and unhappy, but the third, in 1939 to Alicia Patterson, was enduring. Daughter of the founder of the *New York Daily News* and great-granddaughter of the founder of the *Chicago Tribune*, Alicia was well suited to be the wife of the founder of *Newsday*. Their marriage lasted till her death in 1963.

Harry Frank Guggenheim died at his home near Sands Point, Long Island, on January 22, 1971.

Peggy Guggenheim

FOUNDER OF THE PEGGY GUGGENHEIM COLLECTION

Peggy Guggenheim was one of the most important art patrons and art collectors of the twentieth century. Among the artists whom she personally patronized was Jackson Pollock. Her large collection of modern art is housed at her former home in Venice, Italy.

Peggy (originally Marguerite) was born in New York City on August 26, 1898. She was the second of three daughters of Benjamin and Florette (Seligman) Guggenheim. Her maternal grandfather, James Seligman, had made a fortune in banking, and her father had prospered in his family's enterprises till he went into business for himself, two years before he drowned during the sinking of the S.S. *Titanic* in 1912. From both sides of her family, Peggy inherited the wealth that she would apply to art. However, because her father had left the Guggenheims' partnership early, she never had the amount of money that was available to most of the other branches of the family.

Early in life she acquired a love of art from her father. After studying under private tutors till she was fifteen, she attended a private school for Jewish girls in New York City, the Jacobi School, from which she graduated in 1915. She then studied Italian and other subjects, came into her fortune in 1919, and went to Europe for a visit that lasted twenty-one years.

In Paris she married the writer-painter Laurence Vail in 1922 (divorced 1930). They had a son and a daughter.

Influenced by Vail, Peggy began to live a bohemian lifestyle in the 1920s. During those years she also read books on Italian art and studied great paintings throughout Europe.

She knew little about modern art, but with encouragement and advice from friends, such as the artist Marcel Duchamp, she opened a modern art gallery, the Guggenheim Jeune, in London in 1938. Her shows included works by many avant-garde artists, including Jean Cocteau and Wassily Kandinsky. From each show, she bought at least one work to encourage the artists. Thus began her remarkable collection of modern art.

In 1939 she made plans to replace the art gallery with a museum of modern art, but the outbreak of World War II ended the project. Despite the war, she went to France and continued to buy works of art till the invading Germans forced her to return to the United States in the summer of 1941.

Later in 1941 she married the painter Max Ernst (divorced 1946). In 1942 she opened another avant-garde art gallery, the Art of This Century in New York City. There she showed her permanent collection and gave special exhibitions, including one-man shows by Jackson Pollock, Robert Motherwell, Mark Rothko, and other modern painters. More than any other art patron, she helped spawn what came to be known as the New York school of abstract expressionists.

Peggy believed that Jackson Pollock was the most promising of the painters she discovered. From 1943 to 1947 she dedicated herself to furthering his career, partly by signing a contract with him that guaranteed him a monthly salary.

Shortly after World War II ended, she returned to Europe and settled in Venice, Italy. In 1949 she bought and moved into the eighteenth-century Palazzo Venier dei Leoni on the Grand Canal in Venice. For the rest of her life, she displayed her art collection to the public at her Venice palazzo and, periodically, in other European cities. Her collection was unique in Europe because of its historic survey of modern art and especially its representation of American abstract expressionism. The Italians called her L'Ultima Dogaressa ("The Last Duchess"). Peggy sponsored a number of Italian painters, including Tancredi Parmeggiani. But in her late years she added little to her collection, finding that contemporary art had become a "business venture" producing "painting that isn't painting anymore."

In 1969 she exhibited nearly her entire collection at the Solomon R. Guggenheim Museum in New York City, named after her uncle Sol and maintained by the Solomon R. Guggenheim Foundation, which he had established. Later she willed her home and art to the foundation, which, since her death, has both operated the Guggenheim Museum in New York City and directed the Peggy Guggenheim Collection at the palazzo in Venice. Among the art displayed at her former home are early cubist works by Pablo Picasso and Georges Braque, modern sculpture by Henry Moore, a mobile by Alexander Calder, surrealist works by Max Ernst and Salvador Dali, and American paintings by Jackson Pollock and Mark Rothko.

Peggy prided herself on living an unconventional life. She recorded that life openly in her memoirs: *Out of This Century* (1946) and *Confessions of an Art Addict* (1960). In the 1970s she combined those two books and updated them in a volume published posthumously in 1980.

Peggy Guggenheim died in Camposampiero, near Venice, on December 23, 1979. She was buried in her beloved Venice, only a few hundred kilometers from the Switzerland birthplace of her grandparents Meyer and Barbara. The Guggenheims had come full circle.

THE
HASMONEANS
(OR MACCABEES)

THE HASMONEANS WERE A FAMILY OF PRIESTS, military
leaders, and princes who ruled the Jews in the first
and second centuries B.C.E. (Many dates in the history
of the Hasmoneans are disputed among scholars. The dates given
below may differ slightly from those found in some other sources.)

Mattathias (died c. 166 B.C.E.), the aged head of a priestly family, began the Jewish revolt against the religious oppression of
the Syrians in 167 or 166 B.C.E. One of his ancestors was surnamed Hasmon (also recorded as Hashmon/Hasmoneus), from
which came the later family name of Hasmonean. Mattathias had
five sons: John (or Johanan, died 160 B.C.E.), called Gaddi, the
eldest; Simon (or Simeon, died 134 B.C.E.), called Thassi, the
second eldest; Judah (died 160 B.C.E.), called Maccabee, the
middle son; Eleazar (died 162 B.C.E.), called Avaram, the second
youngest; and Jonathan (died 142 B.C.E.), called Apphus, the
youngest.

The third son, Judah Maccabee (in Latin, Judas Maccabaeus),
succeeded his father as leader (c. 166–160 B.C.E.) of the rebellion.
The name Maccabee was a title of honor—probably meaning
"Hammer," "Hammerer," or "Extinguisher"—given to him be-
cause of his effectiveness as military leader in the war against the
Syrians.

89

Later the name Maccabee was extended to include Judah's father and his four brothers. Jonathan succeeded Judah as military leader (160–142 B.C.E.) of the Jews, and in 152 he became high priest in Jerusalem, thus beginning the high priestly Hasmonean line. Simon (ruled 142–134 B.C.E.) succeeded Jonathan, won independence for Judaea, and was rewarded by being made high priest and ruler of the Jewish nation. The offices were hereditary, so Simon became the first of the Hasmonean dynasty.

Simon's descendants were also known as Maccabees. He was followed by his youngest son, John (or Johanan) Hyrcanus I (c. 175–104 B.C.E., ruled 134–104); Hyrcanus I's son Judah Aristobulus I (c. 140–103 B.C.E., ruled 104–103), the first Hasmonean to adopt the title of king of the Jews; Aristobulus I's brother Alexander Yannai (or Jannai/Jannaeus, died 76 B.C.E., ruled 103–76); Alexander Yannai's widow, Salome Alexandra (died 67 B.C.E., ruled 76–67); her son John (or Johanan) Hyrcanus II (died 30 B.C.E., ruled 67 and 63–40); Hyrcanus II's brother, Judah Aristobulus II (died 49/48 B.C.E., ruled 67–63); and Aristobulus II's son Mattathias Antigonus (died 37 B.C.E., ruled 40–37), the last Hasmonean king.

Later generations of Hasmoneans continued, however, to play important roles in Jewish history, especially three named Aristobulus. One, who lived from 52 to 35 B.C.E., was a prince of Judaea and the last Hasmonean high priest. The grandson of both Hyrcanus II and Aristobulus II (the youth's mother was the daughter of Hyrcanus II, while his father was a son of Aristobulus II), young Aristobulus was killed by Herod the Great, his brother-in-law, who feared the boy's ambition to supplant Herod as king. Another Aristobulus, a prince of Judaea who died in 6 B.C.E., was a son of Herod the Great, a nephew of the preceding Aristobulus, and the father of Herod Agrippa I (also known as Julius Agrippa I, 10 B.C.E.–44 C.E.), who became king of Judaea. Herod had this Aristobulus, too—his own son—executed. The grandson of the preceding Aristobulus was the Aristobulus who was king of Chalcis (52–75 C.E.) and of Armenia Minor (55–75). He was married to the Salome who brought about the death of John the Baptist.

The Books of the Maccabees are four Greek books written by Jews. All of the books appear in some manuscripts of the Septuagint (a pre-Christian Greek version of the Jewish Scriptures, adopted by Greek-speaking Christians). Jews and Protestants regard none of the books as canonical, but the first two books are accepted as Scripture in the Septuagint and by Roman Catholic and Eastern Orthodox churches. I Maccabees is a contemporary history of the events in Judaea from the time of Mattathias to the death of Simon Maccabee. II Maccabees focuses on the Jews' revolt against the Syrians and concludes with Judah Maccabee's victory over the Syrian general Nicanor in 161 B.C.E. It also introduces the Jewish holiday of Hanukkah, commemorating the purification of the Temple of Jerusalem after its defilement by the Syrians. III Maccabees is misnamed, having nothing to do with the Hasmonean family or the revolt in Judaea. IV Maccabees is a philosophical discourse on the martyrdom of Jews persecuted by the Syrians.

The Hasmonean period had a great impact on the formation of the Jewish identity. By overcoming huge obstacles and powerful enemies to regain freedom in their own time, the family created a prototype of Jewish faith, will, and courage for all time.

MATTATHIAS

FIRST LEADER OF THE REVOLT AGAINST THE SELEUCIDS

Mattathias, a priest and landowner of Modein (or Modi'in), near Jerusalem, began and led the early stages of the war of national resistance against the Seleucid Empire of Syria, which, in the second century B.C.E., attempted to destroy the Jewish religion and to hellenize the Jewish people. In the process, Mattathias raised his family, the Hasmoneans, to a position of power and leadership that it would hold in Jewish military, religious, and political life for many generations to come.

In the second century B.C.E. Judaea lay between the great powers of Egypt and Syria. The Ptolemies ruled in Egypt and the Seleucids in Syria. As a province of Egypt in the third century B.C.E., Judaea had enjoyed religious freedom. But in 200 B.C.E. the Seleucid emperor Antiochus III the Great took Palestine away from the Ptolemies. In 175 Antiochus IV Epiphanes began his attempts to rid the world of the Jewish religion and to hellenize Judaea. In 172 he made Menelaus the Judaean high priest, an act that infuriated most Jews because he was a Hellenist and because he did not belong to the descendants of Zadok, who had held the office of high priest since the time of King Solomon. In 168 the Jews of Jerusalem began an uprising, which Antiochus IV used as a pretext to invade the city, massacre the rebellious Jews, take over (with the cooperation of Menelaus) the Temple, and build Acra, a fortress used as a Seleucid military base. The following year he dedicated the desecrated Temple to the Olympian god Zeus.

During that same period, 168–167 B.C.E., the Seleucid emperor issued a series of anti-Jewish decrees in which he forbade the observance of the Sabbath, the reading of the Law of Moses, and the practice of circumcision. Jews were ordered to renounce their religion, sacrifice to the Greek deities, and eat, on demand, the flesh of animals prohibited by Jewish law, such as the pig. He backed up these decrees with military force, including torture and execution.

Mattathias, who saw the imminent end of Judaism, turned his home in the village of Modein into a center of resistance. With him were his five sons: John, Simon, Judah, Eleazar, and Jonathan.

Mattathias initiated the resistance movement in 167 or 166 B.C.E. by killing a Seleucid officer who was trying to enforce the emperor's decrees. The family and their followers then fled to the Judaean hills, where they embarked on a guerrilla war of national resistance against the invading Syrians and simultaneously a civil war against Jews who acquiesced in the paganization or collaborated with the Syrians.

Many pious Jews opposed Mattathias because they believed that God forbade them to rebel against the king. One group of rebels, the Hasideans, at first refused to fight on the Sabbath and soon were massacred. As a result of that disaster, Mattathias declared that defensive warfare on the Sabbath was permissible, a ruling that caused even more pious Jews to defect from his side.

The elderly Mattathias died in the Gophna hills about 166 B.C.E. and was laid to rest in the family tomb just outside Modein. At his death, he was the leader of only a small guerrilla band. However, he ensured the ultimate success of his rebellion by naming as his successor his third son, Judah.

JUDAH MACCABEE

PRESERVER OF THE JEWISH RELIGION

In the brief time, about six years, allotted to him as a leader in Judaea, Judah Maccabee achieved a greatness matched by few others in the history of the Jewish people. He led a series of stunning military victories over the far mightier Seleucid armies, repealed the Syrian king's anti-Jewish decrees that threatened to extinguish the Jewish people's spiritual life, restored and purified the Temple of Jerusalem after its defilement by the Syrians, and, in his rededication of the Temple, originated the holiday of Hanukkah.

When Judah's father, Mattathias, began his rebellion against the religious oppression of Antiochus IV Epiphanes, king of the Syrian Seleucid Empire, Judah and his four brothers joined him. Judah was in charge of training the soldiers in guerrilla tactics. About 166 B.C.E., the dying Mattathias named Judah his successor, even though Judah had two older brothers. Mattathias must have seen Judah's outstanding leadership qualities.

In fact, the resistance movement desperately needed a new leader. Mattathias had alienated many Jews whom he regarded as collaborators and many pious Jews who were opposed, in principle, to warfare against the king.

The charismatic Judah, however, had remarkable success in uniting his people, including pious Jews, to fight against the imperial troops. Believing himself a divinely appointed leader and a successor to Moses and Joshua, he would pause before battle to assemble his men, to "watch and pray," and to read the Torah together. Then they would blow their trumpets, as in the days of Joshua, and attack the enemy. He was a brilliant general, especially in organizing his troops into effective units and motivating them in a great cause. During 165–164 B.C.E., he led a series of great battlefield successes against Seleucid forces, notably at Beth Horon, Emmaus, and Beth Zur.

In 164 B.C.E. Judah recaptured Jerusalem, which had been taken over by the Syrians three years earlier. In December of that year, he had priests cleanse the Holy Place, erect a new altar, and reconsecrate the sanctuary. The Hebrew word for this act, *hanukkah* ("dedication"), is still the name of the annual festival that commemorates the event.

For his accomplishments, Judah was given the honorific name of Judah Maccabee (in Latin, Judas Maccabaeus). *Maccabee* probably means "Hammer(er)" (because he "hammered" the enemy) or possibly "Extinguisher" (because he "extinguished" Hellenism from Judaea).

In 163 B.C.E., Antiochus IV died. He was succeeded by the very young Antiochus V Eupator, with Lysias in control as regent. The following year, in the name of the sovereign, Lysias annulled the anti-Jewish decrees, thus conceding religious freedom to the Jews. Menelaus was removed as high priest and executed.

However, later that year, 162 B.C.E., Antiochus V and Lysias were themselves executed, and Demetrius I Soter became emperor. Demetrius I appointed, or approved the earlier appointment of, Eliakim (or Jakim, hellenized as Alcimus) as high priest in Judaea. Eliakim was accepted by some Jews but not by the Hasmoneans, who opposed him because he was a Seleucid choice installed by the power of foreign troops. Judah continued the war, not only to gain absolute religious freedom but also to win political independence for Judaea.

In 162 B.C.E. his brother Eleazar was killed in a bizarre way. During a battle at Beth Zechariah, Eleazar put his sword into the underbelly of an elephant, which he may have thought carried the Syrian king or commanding general. The beast died and fell on Eleazar, crushing him to death.

In 161 B.C.E., Judah concluded a treaty of friendship with the powers in Rome, from whom he hoped to receive help in his war with the Syrians. This treaty, however, marked the first step toward the eventual takeover of Judaea by Rome.

Meanwhile, Judah continued to score military successes. In 161 B.C.E. he won a spectacular victory over a royal force led by the general Nicanor at Adasa, north of Jerusalem.

A year later Judah Maccabee was killed during a battle with a Seleucid army at Elasa. His three remaining brothers recovered his body and buried it in the family tomb near Modein.

JONATHAN MACCABEE

FIRST HASMONEAN HIGH PRIEST

Jonathan Maccabee, though the youngest of the Hasmonean brothers, succeeded his sibling Judah Maccabee as the military leader in the Jewish war of independence against the Seleucid Empire. Later he became the first Hasmonean high priest.

He was also known as Jonathan Apphus. Because of the prominence of Judah Maccabee, the honorific title Maccabee came to be applied as well to the rest of his family, including Jonathan.

After Judah's death in 160 B.C.E., Jonathan led a band of guerrillas who refused to recognize the authority of Eliakim (or Alcimus), the high priest appointed by the Syrian emperor. Jonathan and his followers successfully withstood the efforts of Demetrius I Soter (reigned 162–150 B.C.E.) to suppress them, but in 160 B.C.E. Jonathan's eldest brother, John (or Johanan), was killed by Arab raiders.

Jonathan was a brilliant diplomat. Though he refused to compromise with the superior Seleucid forces, he concentrated on political maneuvering rather than military confrontations. He took advantage of internal power struggles in Syria to win concessions for himself and the Jewish people. In 152 B.C.E. Alexander Balas, who was a contender for the Syrian crown and who wanted Jonathan's support, appointed Jonathan the first Hasmonean high priest, thus making him, in effect, both the secular and the religious leader of Judaea. (This appointment abrogated the prerogative of the priestly line of Zadok, which had lasted since the time of King Solomon, about eight hundred years earlier. Such breaking of tradition alienated strict upholders of the Law, who formed a strong anti-Hasmonean party.)

In 150 B.C.E. Alexander Balas killed Demetrius I in battle and became the new Syrian emperor. He then extended Jonathan's power by officially appointing him military commander and political governor of Judaea.

In 145 B.C.E. a son of Demetrius I defeated Alexander Balas, who was killed. Demetrius II Nicator, the new Syrian emperor, confirmed Jonathan as high priest and gave Judaea greater autonomy.

During 144–143 B.C.E., Tryphon (formerly the general Diodotus) set up Antiochus VI Dionysos, the infant son of the late Alexander Balas, as a rival to Demetrius II for the Syrian throne. Tryphon, as regent, followed Demetrius II in confirming Jonathan as the political and religious leader of Judaea.

During this period, Jonathan defeated the forces of Demetrius II at Hazor and at Hamath. He also renewed his brother Judah's pact with Rome. Unlike Judah, however, Jonathan tried to avoid military conflict with the Syrians, preferring instead to use guile and political leverage to obtain his goals.

Nevertheless, the Seleucid chief minister, Tryphon, saw Jonathan as a threat, lured him into a trap at the Gates of Acre in Ptolemais, and had him killed at Bascama, just north of the Sea of Galilee, in 142 B.C.E. Jonathan was buried in Bascama, but his brother Simon recovered the body and had it interred in the family tomb near Modein.

Simon succeeded Jonathan as leader of the revolt.

Simon Maccabee

FIRST OF THE HASMONEAN DYNASTY

Simon (or Simeon) Maccabee, in 142 B.C.E., succeeded his brother Jonathan as leader of the revolt against the Seleucid Empire. Later Simon became the first of his family to receive the official endorsement of the Jewish people as their high priest and military-political leader. The title being hereditary, Simon thus became the first member of the great Hasmonean dynasty.

Simon was the last survivor of Mattathias' five sons, but he earned his position of primacy not by default but through the strong personal character and leadership he had shown while serving quietly and loyally under his father and his brothers. When the dying Mattathias named Judah his successor, he also described Simon as one who was "wise in counsel" and who "shall be a father to you." Like his father and his brothers, Simon, or Simon Thassi, was granted his brother Judah's honorific title of Maccabee.

After taking over the leadership, Simon successfully resisted Tryphon, the Seleucid chief minister who, in 142 B.C.E., dethroned the child emperor, Antiochus VI Dionysos, and declared himself king. Simon wisely made a treaty with Demetrius II Nicator, the Seleucid ruler who opposed the rebel Tryphon for the Syrian throne. In exchange for Simon's support, Demetrius II, in 142, granted Judaea exemption from taxes—in effect, full independence.

Judaea owed much to Simon. In 141 he took possession of the Acra, the Seleucid fortress and garrison near the Temple of Jerusalem, and he conquered the port city of Jaffa and the strategic town of Gezer. All of Jerusalem was now under Maccabean control, and Judaea was once again an independent state.

In gratitude, a great assembly of Jews in Jerusalem in 140 made Simon and his descendants hereditary high priests, military commanders, and chief executives of the nation. He was the first Hasmonean to be so honored by his own people, Jonathan having been appointed high priest and ruler by the Seleucids. The assembly's actions gave legitimacy to the Hasmonean status as the family of the high priesthood, displacing the family of Zadok, which had held the high priesthood since the time of the First Temple.

However, the assembly specifically denied the Hasmoneans the title of king. At that time, a king's powers usually included presiding over a nation's legislative and legal systems. Simon and his heirs were not granted lawmaking or judical authority. He was to be an ethnarch, with the right of leadership in military and political matters.

Simon brought peace and security to Judaea, especially in Jerusalem. He supplied the people with plenty of food, equipped them well for defense, protected the poor, rid the country of lawbreakers, furnished the Temple with new splendor, and prevented major military conflicts from erupting.

In spite of all these accomplishments, Simon died violently, not through battle with external forces but through treachery within his own family. In 134 B.C.E. Simon and two of his three sons (Mattathias and Judah) were assassinated by his son-in-law, Ptolemy, the governor of Jericho, who hoped for a reward from the current Syrian king, Antiochus VII Sidetes.

Nevertheless, Simon's surviving son, John (or Johanan), succeeded to the throne because of the support he received from the army and the people. John came to be known as Hyrcanus I.

JOHN HYRCANUS I

RULER WHO EXTENDED JEWISH CONTROL

John (or Johanan) Hyrcanus I, youngest son of Simon Maccabee, ruled Judaea as ethnarch and high priest from the death of his father in 134 B.C.E. till his own death in 104. He consolidated and extended the areas of Jewish control. Under his leadership, Judaea became more powerful than it had been since the time of King Solomon.

John Hyrcanus I was born in about 175 B.C.E. In 137 he and his brother Judah commanded the force that repelled the invasion of

Judaea led by Cendebeus, the general of the Syrian king Antiochus VII Sidetes. In 134 Hyrcanus I's brother-in-law, Ptolemy, the governor of Jericho, murdered Hyrcanus I's father and two older brothers, Mattathias and Judah. Hyrcanus I then succeeded to the high priesthood and the highest authority in Judaea.

During the early part of his rule, he deferred to the powerful Antiochus VII (reigned 139–129 B.C.E.). Unwilling to risk the loss of all the recent improvements in the condition of the Jewish people, John avoided a military confrontation with the Syrian king by agreeing to resume the practice of paying tribute. Even though the king confirmed Judaea's autonomy, politically the Jews were again, in effect, a subject people.

However, after the king was killed in battle with the Parthians in 129, the Syrian Empire collapsed in civil war. Hyrcanus I took advantage of his enemy's weakness at this time and restored Judaea's independence. He successfully thwarted Syrian incursions by alliance with Rome and conquered the neighboring territories of Samaria and Idumaea (or Edom). Hyrcanus I forced the Idumaeans (or Edomites) to convert to Judaism, the first known example of conversion imposed by the Jews in their history. (It was at this time that Antipas, the governor of Idumaea, converted to Judaism; thus, in later years, his grandson Herod the Great and great-grandson Herod Agrippa I were Jews by religion.)

To mark the nation's renewed independence, Hyrcanus I became (apparently) the first Hasmonean to mint his own coins. Each coin was inscribed, in Hebrew, "John the High Priest and the Commonwealth of the Jews." The second term (in Hebrew, *Hever ha-Jedudim*) was the name of an assembly that was viewed as embodying the will of the people. Hyrcanus I, as ethnarch, was head of the assembly.

During his rule, the well-defined split occurred between the religious parties of the Pharisees and the Sadducees. The former were a scholarly sect with popular backing. The latter were an aristocratic sect that included the priesthood.

Hyrcanus I marked a turning point in the history of the Hasmoneans. Unlike his grandfather Mattathias, a religious and patriotic zealot who interpreted Scripture liberally according to real-life situations (as when he allowed fighting on the Sabbath), Hyrcanus I was worldly and urbane. He became in spirit a Sadducee, an upper-class conservative who accepted only the Written Law as authoritative.

His was the last reign under which Judaea was a powerful, united state. Hyrcanus I died in 104 B.C.E. and was succeeded, through treachery, by his eldest son, Judah Aristobulus I.

JUDAH ARISTOBULUS I

FIRST HASMONEAN KING OF THE JEWS

Judah Aristobulus I, eldest son of John Hyrcanus I, succeeded his father as ethnarch and high priest shortly after the latter's death in 104 B.C.E. He soon took the title of king (reigned 104–103), becoming the first of his house to adopt that title and the first king of the Jews since the Babylonian captivity (sixth century B.C.E.).

Judah Aristobulus I was born in 140 B.C.E. When his father died in 104, the throne, according to the wishes of Hyrcanus I himself, was passed to his wife, while the high priesthood went to the eldest of his five sons, Aristobulus I. However, soon after his father's death, Aristobulus I seized the throne and cast his mother (some sources say stepmother) into prison, where she starved to death. He also imprisoned or killed all of his brothers.

Contrary to the decision of the great Jerusalem assembly held during Simon's reign and to the will of the people, Aristobulus I called himself king, a title that none of his Hasmonean predecessors had presumed to take. He favored the Greeks in Judaea (thus opening the door to Hellenization), supported the Sadducees, and conquered Galilee, where he converted the Ituraeans to Judaism.

In 103 B.C.E., after a reign of only one year, Aristobulus I died of illness. He was succeeded by his brother Alexander Yannai.

Alexander Yannai

HASMONEAN COMMITTED TO AGGRESSIVE WARFARE

Alexander Yannai (or Jannai/Jannaeus) succeeded his brother Judah Aristobulus I in 103 B.C.E. His reign was marked by his penchant for waging war both inside and outside the Jewish nation.

From his brother, Alexander Yannai inherited the titles of high priest and king. He relinquished the title of king for a time, but then he reassumed it.

His years of rule were marred by his aggressive warfare. Presumably he wanted to fulfill biblical prophecies of an invincible king. Indeed, under his rule, the nation enlarged to about the size of King David's kingdom. However, eventually he encountered many defeats, which pious Jews interpreted as evidence that he was not the king foretold.

Alexander Yannai further aggravated many Jews through his efforts to hellenize Judaea. Pharisees strongly opposed him on this account. A Jewish revolt against him broke out, and from 89 to 84 B.C.E. he waged civil war against his own subjects.

He managed to stay in power till his death in 76 B.C.E. Alexander Yannai was succeeded by his widow, Salome Alexandra.

Salome Alexandra

RULER OF THE HASMONEAN GOLDEN AGE

Queen Salome (or Salina/Shlomzion) Alexandra was the widow of, and successor to, King Alexander Yannai. Her short, tranquil reign (76–67 B.C.E.) was perhaps the golden age of the Hasmonean dynasty.

She was born in 139 B.C.E. Her first marriage was to Judah Aristobulus I. When he died, she married his brother Alexander Yannai.

By her second marriage she had two sons: John Hyrcanus II and Judah Aristobulus II. Alexander Yannai realized that the hot-headedness of his sons made them unsuitable for the throne. In contrast, his wife's mellow wisdom and strong will made her his logical successor.

When she became queen in 76 B.C.E., Salome could not, of course, take the role of high priest. That position was taken by her elder son, Hyrcanus II, while Aristobulus II had command of the army. However, throughout her rule, she dominated both of her sons.

As queen, she was relieved of the pressures her male predecessors had felt to fulfill prophecies of an invincible king. Consequently, she abandoned warfare as an instrument of policy. She also won the support of the Pharisees, who had strongly opposed her late husband.

After Queen Salome Alexandra died in 67 B.C.E., the peace that she had brought died with her. Her two sons soon started a civil war.

JOHN HYRCANUS II, JUDAH ARISTOBULUS II, AND MATTATHIAS ANTIGONUS

LAST OF THE HASMONEAN DYNASTIC RULERS

The brothers John (or Johanan) Hyrcanus II and Judah Aristobulus II, by fighting between themselves for power after the death of their mother, Salome Alexandra, created a civil conflict that weakened the kingdom and enabled the Romans to conquer Judaea in 63 B.C.E. The country was stripped of the conquests made by earlier Hasmoneans, and the brothers ended the dynasty of their great family. Only a brief flicker of independence (40–37 B.C.E.) remained under Mattathias Antigonus, a son of Aristobulus II.

When Alexander Yannai died in 76 B.C.E., his wife, Queen Salome, became the ruler of Judaea. Under her authority, her elder son, Hyrcanus II, served as high priest, while her younger son, Aristobulus II, commanded the army.

On Salome's death in 67 B.C.E., Hyrcanus II assumed the rulership of Judaea. But he reigned for only three months before his brother, supported by the army, drove him from power and took the king's crown for himself.

Hyrcanus II sought the advice of Antipater, satrap of Idumaea, who saw the weak-willed Hasmonean as a vehicle for his own ambition and encouraged him to wage war on Aristobulus II. With military aid from the nearby Arab kingdom of Nabataea, Hyrcanus II engaged in a brutal struggle with his brother for the throne of Judaea.

Finally, in 63 B.C.E., the Roman general Pompey intervened. Like others, he felt that he could control Judaea through Hyrcanus II. Pompey took Jerusalem by force, abolished the Judaean monarchy, named Hyrcanus II high priest and ethnarch, sent Aristobulus II to Rome, and confiscated most of the lands conquered by the Hasmoneans. Judaea, no longer an independent state, became a Roman province.

During the rest of his life, Hyrcanus II was manipulated by both Romans and Jews. He was deprived of his office for a time by the Roman military commander Aulus Gabinius but was restored by the greater Roman power of Julius Caesar. Even in office, Hyrcanus II was merely a figurehead; the real power lay in the hands of the wily Antipater and his sons—Jews with strong Roman connections.

Antipater came from an Idumaean family (his father was Antipas, governor of Idumaea) that had converted to Judaism under Hasmonean rule. He was appointed minister of the affairs of state in Judaea by Julius Caesar, and he virtually ran the country in that position. In 42 B.C.E. Phasael and Herod, Antipater's sons, were appointed rulers of Judaea by Mark Antony, thus rendering Hyrcanus II powerless.

During those years, Aristobulus II escaped from Rome, returned to Judaea, and renewed his war with Hyrcanus II. Aristobulus II was supported by many Jews who still hoped that the prophesied

invincible king would be a Hasmonean. However, he was repeat-
edly defeated by the Romans, who recaptured him and returned
him to Rome. Eventually Julius Caesar released him and sent him
back to Judaea to oversee Caesar's interests there in opposition to
Pompey. Aristobulus II was poisoned to death by Pompey's
adherents in 49 or 48 B.C.E.

Hyrcanus II's fate was no better. In 40 B.C.E. the invading
Parthians, at the instigation of his ambitious nephew Mattathias
Antigonus (a son of Aristobulus II), cut off Hyrcanus II's ears to
disqualify him from serving as high priest. After serving the next
several years in forced exile in Babylon, Hyrcanus II was allowed
to return to Jerusalem. In 30 B.C.E. Herod, by then the Roman
king of Judaea and still fearful of popular support for
the Hasmoneans, had Hyrcanus II executed.

The last Hasmonean ruler was Mattathias Antigonus. In 40
B.C.E., besides having Hyrcanus II disfigured, Antigonus got rid
of Antipater's two powerful sons, causing the suicide of Phasael
and forcing Herod to flee to Rome. As a Hasmonean, Antigonus
won the broad support of the Jewish people and ruled as king for
three years. However, Herod, appointed by Rome as the king of
Judaea, returned with a mercenary army of Romans and, in 37
B.C.E., defeated and executed Antigonus.

Ironically, it was through Herod (known as Herod the Great,
reigned 37–4 B.C.E.), the man who instigated the deaths of the
last two Hasmonean rulers, that the Hasmonean bloodline remained for some generations at or near the Judaean throne. Herod
married Mariamne, granddaughter of both Hyrcanus II and
Aristobulus II and niece of Antigonus. Herod Agrippa I (10 B.C.E.–
44 C.E.), king of Judaea from 41 to 44 C.E., was the grandson of
Herod and Mariamne and thus the great-great-grandson
of Hyrcanus II and Aristobulus II and the great-grandnephew
of Antigonus.

THE
HERZOGS

FEW FAMILIES HAVE HAD AS PROFOUND AN INFLUENCE on both the political and the spiritual sides of Israeli life as the Herzogs.

Isaac Halevi Herzog (1888–1959) immigrated to Palestine in 1936 to succeed Abraham Isaac Kook as the second chief Ashkenazic rabbi. As chief rabbi during the Holocaust period and during the birth of the state of Israel, he guided the spiritual lives of Jews in both the depths of despair and the heights of joy.

His son Chaim Herzog (1918–97) had a varied career in military intelligence, law, business, journalism, and politics. He was best known as Israel's most powerful and popular president (1983–93).

An ordained rabbi, Yaakov Herzog (1921–72), Chaim's brother, combined his father's spiritual strength and his brother's political wisdom. Yaakov served the Israeli government in many capacities, notably as an adviser to prime ministers and as ambassador to the United States and to Canada.

ISAAC HALEVI HERZOG

CHIEF ASHKENAZIC RABBI OF ISRAEL

Isaac Halevi Herzog was a famed rabbinic scholar, philosopher, and author who helped Jews reconcile modern living with the demands of the Talmud. In 1936 he was named the chief rabbi of the Ashkenazim in Palestine, and in 1948 he became the first to hold that important position in modern Israel.

Isaac was born in Lomza, Poland, in November 1888. His parents were Joel and Liba (Cirowitz) Herzog. Isaac was first educated by his father, a talmudist who held rabbinic positions in Paris, France, and Leeds, England. At the University of London, Isaac earned the degrees of B.A. (1909), M.A. (1911), and D.Lit. (1914).

Ordained in 1910, he accepted his first appointment as rabbi in 1915, becoming head of the Jewish community of Belfast, Ireland (later Northern Ireland). He then served as chief rabbi of Dublin, Ireland (1919–25), and chief rabbi of the Irish Free State (1925–36).

In 1936 he was elected to succeed Abraham Isaac Kook as chief rabbi of the Ashkenazic community in Palestine. As chief rabbi during the Nazi campaign to exterminate the Jews, Isaac engaged in diplomatic negotiations, personal appeals, and public prayers for the relief of his people. During and after the Holocaust, he traveled extensively in Europe and the United States to arrange the transfer of Jews, especially children, to Palestine.

A Zionist, Isaac used his influence as chief rabbi to obtain the support of world leaders for the creation of the state of Israel. In 1948 his lifelong dream was realized when modern Israel was born. A leading spokesman for the Orthodox position, he spent the rest of his life trying to restore Israel as a religious state. "True democracy," he said, "does not mean a spiritless, godless state. Although the state will not interfere with the freedom of the individual, it must bear the specific impress of a God-conscious people."

Isaac believed that Israel should be governed by religious law. He pointed to Israel's laws of marriage, divorce, and rabbinic courts as examples of the kind of legislation that he wanted the Knesset (parliament) to pass in all areas of life.

Isaac himself worked on establishing practical solutions to many halakic problems that had long been of purely academic interest, such as Sabbath observance and dietary laws within the framework of a modern state and society. He was especially interested in securing recognition for halakic standards in marital and personal relations.

Much of his scholarship and philosophy can be found in his writings. In 1920 he wrote *Divrei Itzhak* ("The Words of Issac"), which deals with the laws of sacred objects and purification. *Ohel Torah* ("The Tabernacle of Torah"), published in 1948, received the Rav Kook prize for rabbinic literature from the city of Tel Aviv. His major work, *Main Institutions of Jewish Law*, was a planned five-volume analysis of the evolution of the Jewish legal system; only two volumes, written in English and then translated into Hebrew, were published (1936–39). Three volumes of his responsa, containing valuable rabbinic guidance on contemporary issues, were published posthumously.

He was married in 1917 to Sarah Hillman, daughter of a rabbi who was the assessor to the chief rabbi of the British Empire. They had three sons.

Isaac Halevi Herzog died in Jerusalem on July 25, 1959.

Chaim Herzog

SIXTH PRESIDENT OF ISRAEL

Soldier, military intelligence expert, lawyer, businessman, author, broadcast journalist, and statesman, Chaim Herzog made a major impact on the state of Israel. From 1983 to 1993 he served as perhaps the most powerful and popular president in the nation's history.

Chaim was born in Belfast, Ireland (later Northern Ireland), on September 17, 1918. His parents were Isaac Halevi Herzog, then chief rabbi of Ireland, and Sarah (Hillman) Herzog. Both parents came from families of eminent rabbinic scholars. Chaim grew up speaking English, Hebrew, Yiddish, and Gaelic.

In 1936 the family moved to Palestine, where Isaac had been appointed chief rabbi. Chaim studied in Jerusalem, Ireland,

and England. He obtained his bachelor of laws degree at the University of London and was called to the bar at Lincoln's Inn in 1942.

During World War II he served as an officer with the British army. He saw combat duty as a tank commander in the elite Guards Armored Division and was wounded in action. Later he directed British intelligence operations in northern Germany, where he helped to identify a captive Nazi soldier as Heinrich Himmler.

In 1947 Chaim married Aura Ambache, whose sister, Susan, married the Israeli statesman Abba Eban. Chaim and Aura had three sons and one daughter.

After being discharged from the British army, he joined the Haganah, the Jewish underground in Palestine. During the 1948 War of Independence he served with the Israeli army as chief of staff of the brigade that opened up the supply road to Jerusalem.

After the war, Chaim directed military intelligence for the Israeli Defense Forces (1948–50); served as defense attaché in Washington, D.C. (1950–53), and Ottawa, Canada (1953–54); returned to Israel as a field commander (1954–59); and again functioned as chief of military intelligence (1959–62).

From 1962 to 1972 he was employed as managing director of G.U.S. Industries, one of Israel's top industrial investment firms. During those years he began to establish his reputation as Israel's best-known military and political commentator through his radio and television broadcasts and his newspaper articles. After the Six-Day War of 1967 he was appointed the first military governor of the occupied West Bank. In 1972 he left G.U.S. Industries to form the Tel Aviv law firm of Herzog, Fox and Neeman.

In 1975 Chaim took a three-year leave of absence from his law practice to accept an appointment as Israel's chief delegate to the United Nations (UN). In November of that year the UN's General Assembly adopted an Arab-sponsored resolution defining Zionism as "a form of racism and racial discrimination." On the floor of the General Assembly, Chaim defiantly tore up a copy of the resolution, just as his father had once torn up a British edict aimed at limiting Jewish immigration to Palestine. During his three years at the UN, Chaim gave many memorable addresses in support of Israeli causes.

After completing his term at the UN, he returned home to resume his law practice. In 1981 he became a Labor party member of the Knesset (parliament).

Two years later Chaim was elected to a five-year term as Israel's president. In his hands the largely ceremonial position soon became much more important than it had been before. Because of his acknowledged stature, both principal political parties, Labor and Likud, looked to him to mediate their disputes. Special-interest groups, such as farmers and nurses, appealed to him for help that they could not get from ordinary politicians. On the international scene, he became the first Israeli president to make an official visit to the United States.

However, Chaim also sparked much controversy. As president he had exclusive power to pardon citizens convicted of crimes; in 1985–86 he was criticized for pardoning the Shin Bet (Israeli security service) director, who allegedly had ordered the execution of two Palestinian bus hijackers, and seven Shin Bet operatives, who had not yet been charged with any crime.

But most Israelis saw Chaim's efforts in a positive light. He was especially popular for his outspoken defense of Israel in its dealings with Arab countries and the Palestine Liberation Organization (PLO).

In 1988 he was elected to a second five-year term as president. It was marked by the same characteristics that had distinguished his first five years.

In March 1993 he was succeeded by Ezer Weizman. Chaim continued, however, to be active on the public affairs scene. In April 1993, for example, he attended the dedication of the new Holocaust Memorial Museum in Washington, D.C.

His books chronicle and analyze the most important events and issues in Israel's history. They include *Israel's Finest Hour* (1967), on the Six-Day War of 1967; *The War of Atonement* (1975), on the Yom Kippur War of 1973; *Who Stands Accused?* (1978), on countries that sheltered terrorists holding hostages and specifically on the rescue of Jewish hostages at Entebbe, Uganda, in 1976; *The Arab-Israeli Wars* (1982), on Israel's military adventures; and *Heroes of Israel* (1989), on courageous individuals who helped create and protect Israel.

Chaim Herzog died in Tel Aviv on April 17, 1997.

YAAKOV HERZOG

ISRAELI DIPLOMAT

Yaakov Herzog served Israel for many years in a variety of governmental posts at home and abroad. In the late 1950s and early 1960s, he represented Israel in the United States and then in Canada.

Yaakov (or Ya'acov, anglicized as Jacob) David Herzog was born in Dublin, Ireland, in December 1921. His parents were Isaac Halevi and Sarah (Hillman) Herzog. Both parents came from families of eminent rabbinic scholars. At the time of Yaakov's birth, Isaac was chief rabbi of Dublin; later he became chief rabbi of the Irish Free State and then chief rabbi of the Ashkenazic community in Palestine, where Yaakov went to live with his father and the rest of the family.

During World War II Yaakov began his diplomatic career by accompanying or representing his father on missions to Christian religious and political leaders in attempts to save the Jews of Europe. After the war Yaakov continued to make such trips to rescue surviving European Jews.

In the new state of Israel, he was appointed director of the department of Christian matters within the Ministry for Religious Affairs. He distinguished himself through his delicate negotiations with Christians regarding the handling of holy places in Jerusalem and elsewhere.

Later he joined the Foreign Ministry and soon became director of its United States department. During the 1956 Sinai military campaign he assisted Prime Minister David Ben-Gurion, serving as the latter's political liaison.

Because of his great skill in communicating with people at high levels of government, Yaakov was appointed Israeli minister to the United States in 1957. He held that post till 1960 and then served as ambassador to Canada (1960–63). While he was in Canada, he earned a doctorate in international law at the University of Ottawa.

In 1965 Yaakov, who had been an ordained rabbi since his youth, was elected chief rabbi of the British Commonwealth. However, illness prevented him from taking the position when it was available.

In 1966 he joined Prime Minister Levi Eshkol's staff as an adviser in political affairs. Four months later he also took on the role of director general of the prime minister's office, thus becoming the premier's foreign adviser, speech writer, and document drafter. When Eshkol was succeeded by Golda Meir in 1969, Yaakov retained both positions—political adviser and director general—but with somewhat less influence.

The principle that guided Yaakov through his entire career was that there existed an important link between the Israeli state and the Diaspora. "The concept of the community of the Jewish people," he said, "is inherent in its faith."

Yaakov married Pnina Shahor, daughter of Rabbi Zalman Shahor, scion of a well-known rabbinic dynasty. With Pnina, Yaakov had one son and two daughters.

In December 1971 he suffered a fall in his home, incurring a brain injury. Yaakov David Herzog died in Jerusalem on March 8, 1972.

THE
HILLELS

ONE OF THE MOST IMPORTANT and influential
Jewish families in the ancient world was that established
by Hillel (fl. c. 70 B.C.E.–c. 10 C.E.), the greatest sage of
the Second Temple period and the founder of the talmudic school
known as the House of Hillel. His family claimed Davidic descent.

Hillel rose to the position of *nasi* ("prince," or president) of the
Sanhedrin, the Jewish supreme court. The Roman term for his
status was *patriarch*, the official leader of the Palestinian Jews. The
patriarchs for the next several hundred years belonged to the Hillel
family.

Gamaliel I (fl. early first century C.E.), Hillel's grandson, was
the first to be given the title of *rabban* ("our master"). Simeon ben
Gamaliel I (fl. middle of first century C.E.), Gamaliel I's son, was a
leader in the rebellion against Rome. Gamaliel II (fl. late first
to early second century C.E.), Simeon ben Gamaliel I's son, led the
Jewish restoration after the fall of Jerusalem to the Romans in 70
C.E. Simeon ben Gamaliel II (fl. second century C.E.), Gamaliel
II's son, reestablished the authority of the *nasi* after it had been
destroyed by the Romans in revenge for the revolt led by Simon
Bar Kochba.

Judah ha-Nasi (c. 135–e. 220 C.E.), Simeon ben Gamaliel
II's son, compiled the Mishnah and had two distinguished sons:
Gamaliel III (fl. first half of third century C.E.), who succeeded

Judah ha-Nasi as head of the Sanhedrin, and Simeon ben Judah ha-Nasi (fl. first half of third century C.E.), who was appointed *hakham* (head of the yeshiva and third in authority at the Sanhedrin). Gamaliel III also had two important sons: Judah Nesiah (or Judah II; *nesiah* is Aramaic for "prince," equivalent to Hebrew *nasi*; fl. middle of third century C.E.), who served as *nasi*, and Hillel (fl. middle of third century C.E.), a scholar.

Gamaliel IV (fl. late third century C.E.) succeeded his father, Judah Nesiah, as *nasi*. The office was then passed, from father to son, from Gamaliel IV to Judah Nesiah II (or Judah III, fl. late third to early fourth century C.E.); Hillel II (fl. middle of fourth century C.E.), under whose authority the Jewish calendar came to be fixed by rules rather than by proclamation; and Gamaliel V (fl. second half of fourth century C.E.).

The last *nasi* was Gamaliel VI (died 426 C.E.). In 415 a Roman order removed Gamaliel VI from the post of *nasi* as a penalty for having built a synagogue without authorization and for having defended the Jews against the Christians. With Gamaliel VI the centuries-long patriarchate held by the Hillel family came to an end.

HILLEL

FOUNDER OF A LINE OF PATRIARCHS

Hillel, or Hillel ha-Zaken ("Hillel the Elder," an epithet used to distinguish him from later Hillels), was the first distinct personality in, and the foremost master of, talmudic Judaism, the branch of Jewish thought and tradition that created the Talmud, a body of commentaries on the Oral Law. He was so highly regarded in his own time that he was promoted to the status of patriarch, an office that remained hereditary in his family for several centuries.

Hillel was born in Babylonia about 70 B.C.E. He studied the Torah there and under the Pharisees in Jerusalem, where he arrived when he was about the age of forty. A reliable biography of his life is difficult to relate because of the many legends associated with his name, but much about him can be known through his wide-ranging achievements.

In Jerusalem he was at first treated with disdain because of his Babylonia origin (one of his epithets was "the Babylonian"). Nevertheless, with his great learning, he rose to a position of prominence among the Pharisees, the spiritual leaders of the Jewish people during most of the Second Temple era. Eventually he was appointed *nasi* ("prince," or president) of the Sanhedrin, the Jewish supreme court. The Roman term for his status was *patriarch*, the official leader of the Palestinian Jews. As such, he served as spiritual leader of the people during the stressful reign of terror under King Herod the Great. Hillel adopted a basically quietist policy, though he did criticize the lavish, ostentatious lifestyles of the rich and powerful families in the Jerusalem of his time.

As head of the Sanhedrin, Hillel presided over the Jewish people's supreme religious and legal authority. He shared power with a vice president, first with a man named Menahem, who resigned, and then with Shammai, who opposed Hillel's liberal views on Bible interpretation.

Hillel was committed to the idea that traditional law based on the Bible was flexible and open to adjustment to fit changing situations in human life. His Seven Rules became the basis of rabbinic hermeneutics, the study of the methodological principles of Bible interpretations. He founded the Bet Hillel ("House of Hillel"), a talmudic school that liberated texts and law from slavishly literal interpretation of Holy Scripture. Without Hillel a severe rigidity might have developed in the inherited traditions.

He instituted many legal reforms motivated by social concern. One of the most notable pertained to the repayment of debts. He replaced the rule of Deuteronomy (which canceled debts in the sabbatical year of release) with a provision that the accounting for debts be put under the jurisdiction of a court. His intention was to help both the borrower and the lender. Because of his un-

derstanding of the needs of his age and because of his persuasive-
ness and personal reputation as a great sage, Hillel's view of biblical
interpretation became established as the legal norm.

Hillel was also an important teacher of the Torah.
Many teachers in his day, including Shammai, discriminated in
the choice of pupils, favoring those with wealth and good breeding.
Hillel, however, rejected that practice. He taught Torah to laborers on their way to work and gladly received questioners at his
own home. The Torah, he said, should be studied unselfishly for
its own sake, not for ulterior motives. Learning alone could re-
fine the student's character and raise him to the level of a genu-
inely pious man. He taught using a question-and-answer format,
much in the manner of the Greek philosopher Socrates (some of
Hillel's Seven Rules also show a Hellenistic influence). He believed that the teacher should teach through personal example,
and the concept of "serving scholars" has been part of rabbinic
pedagogy ever since.

Above all, it was as a *hasid* ("a man of pious action") that Hillel
made his mark in Jewish history. He performed every action "for
the sake of heaven," motivated by the desire to do God's will.
The very model of the ideal Jewish sage, he was apparently a man
of extraordinary virtues.

Traditional storytellers' accounts picture him as a rock of patience; even when repeated attempts were made to insult him, he
retained his equanimity and civility. He advocated peaceful conduct, loved all people, studied diligently, taught altruistically, and
cheerfully trusted in God.

The texture of his saintliness can be felt in his sayings and ethical maxims. Many of them form the basis of modern Judaism and
Christianity. For example, "The more property, the more anxi-
ety; the more schooling, the more wisdom; the more counsel, the
more understanding; the more righteousness, the more peace."
And: "Do not withdraw from the community. Do not be sure of
yourself till the day you die. Do not judge your fellowman till
you have stood in his place. And do not say, 'When I have time, I
will study'; you may never find time." Perhaps his best-known

maxim is the following: "What is hateful to you, do not do to your fellowmen. This is the whole Torah; all the rest is its explanation." In the *Pirke avot* ("Ethics of the Fathers") in the Mishnah (the authoritative collection of Oral Law), Hillel is quoted more than any other talmudic sage.

Hillel played an extremely important role in the history of Judaism. His hermeneutical rules expanded and revolutionized Jewish tradition. His emphasis on ethical conduct, tolerance, and humility greatly influenced the shape of both Judaism and Christianity. His liberal teachings were used as justifications for modern movements of Jewish dissent. And his cultivation of a sense of Jewish community based on learning rather than on the power of the state led to the formation of "classical Judaism."

Hillel died about 10 C.E. The patriarchs down to about the fifth century, when the patriarchate came to an end, were his descendants.

GAMALIEL I

THE FIRST RABBAN

Gamaliel I, grandson of Hillel, was a *tanna* ("teacher"), one of a select group of Jewish masters who lived during the first two centuries C.E. and whose interpretations of biblical law and Hebrew oral tradition are recorded in the Mishnah and other works. He showed tolerance for the emerging Judeo-Christian sect and is mentioned twice in the New Testament. His stature was so great that he became the first to earn the honorific title of rabban.

Gamaliel I flourished early in the first century C.E. Tradition states that he succeeded his father, Simon, and his grandfather Hillel (to whose school of thought he belonged) as president of the Sanhedrin. He was a contemporary of King Agrippa I, who consulted him on halakic problems. As the supreme halakic authority, he issued proclamations to the Jewish communities in

Palestine and in the Diaspora concerning many problems, such as tithes.

One of the Sanhedrin's most important powers was the regulation of the Jewish calendar. Gamaliel I issued rules to assure the examination of witnesses who had seen the new moon and who thus could enable the court to proclaim the beginning of another month.

In ritual law he was strict. But his theory of civil law was that laws should be broadly interpreted and applied to promote the welfare of society. He established a number of lenient ordinances, especially regarding women and non-Jews. His regulations limited the husband's rights in divorce and made it easier for a woman to collect her marriage portion from her husband's estate. He relaxed the biblical rules of evidence to prove the death of the husband and to free the wife from the constrained status of an *agunah* (a woman whose husband has deserted her or has disappeared and who may not remarry till she gives proof of his death or obtains a bill of divorce).

Gamaliel I insisted that Gentiles be given equal charitable treatment with Jews. He ruled that their needy should be given material support, their sick should be visited, their dead should be eulogized and buried, their mourners should be comforted, and they should not be discriminated against when gathering their dues.

Gamaliel I enjoyed the highest reputation as a teacher of the Law. He stressed the duties of study and scrupulous observance of religious ordinances.

In Acts 5:34–39 of the New Testament, he successfully intervened on behalf of the apostles of Jesus to save them from destruction during a meeting at the Sanhedrin. "Ye men of Israel," he said, "take heed to yourselves what ye intend to do as touching these men." He reminded them of previous sects that had come and gone with no lasting effect. "And now I say unto you, Refrain from these men, and let them alone: for if this counsel or this work be of men, it will come to naught: But if it be of God, ye cannot overthrow it; lest haply ye be found even to fight against God." In Acts 22:3, Saint Paul tried to influence the Jews by stating that he himself was a Jew brought up "at the feet of Gamaliel, and taught according to the perfect manner of the law of the fathers."

The usual term applied to a talmudic sage was *rabbi* ("my master"). Gamaliel I, however, won a great distinction by being the first to be honored with the title of *rabban* ("our master"), which denoted a level higher than rabbi. The title was passed on to his descendants who followed him as presidents of the Sanhedrin, beginning with Simeon ben Gamaliel I, his son. Like his grandfather Hillel, Gamaliel I was given the title of *ha-Zaken* ("the Elder") as a term of respect and as a means of distinguishing him from later Gamaliels.

"When Rabban Gamaliel the Elder died," says the Talmud, "regard for the Torah ceased, and purity and piety died."

SIMEON BEN GAMALIEL I

LEADER IN REBELLION AGAINST ROME

Simeon ben Gamaliel I suceeded his father, Gamaliel I, as head of the Sanhedrin. He was active in the middle decades of the first century C.E. and played a key role in the rebellion against Rome (66–73), during which the Temple was destroyed.

Little is known about the details of his life. Like his father, he issued proclamations to the Jewish communities both inside and outside Palestine. He informed the people of the Sanhedrin's decision to intercalate a month in leap years and instructed them regarding their tithing duties. When rejoicing during the water-drawing festival at the Temple, he juggled with eight lighted torches.

Simeon ben Gamaliel I was greatly respected, even by his opponents. The Jewish historian Flavius Josephus, whom Simeon bitterly opposed, praised him: "A man highly gifted with intelligence and judgment; he could by sheer genius retrieve an unfortunate situation in affairs of state." Simeon's character is reflected in his own words in the Avot (1:17): "I have lived all my life among the wise, and I have found nothing of better service than silence; not learning but doing is the chief thing; and he who is profuse of words causes sin."

When the Jews rebelled against Roman rule in 66 c.e., Simeon ben Gamaliel I, as head of the Pharisaic party, joined with the Sadducean high priest Anan to lead the rebellion. He also spoke out courageously against the extremist Jews when they established their dictatorship over Jerusalem and the Temple.

Simeon ben Gamaliel I died during the rebellion, probably at the hands of the Romans. He is thus traditionally included among the Ten Martyrs (ten Jewish sages who traditionally, though not all historically, were tortured and martyred by the Romans in the second century c.e.).

Gamaliel II

LEADER OF JEWISH RESTORATION

Gamaliel II, also known as Gamaliel of Jabneh, a son of Simeon ben Gamaliel I, presided over the Jewish national-religious restoration after the fall of Jerusalem to the Romans in 70 c.e. His great achievement was to unify the important Jewish laws and rituals during a time of external oppression by Rome and intense conflicts within the Jewish community itself.

He was born about the middle of the first century c.e. After the Romans conquered Jerusalem and destroyed the Temple in 70 c.e., many Jews took refuge in the city of Jabneh, where Johanan ben Zakkai set up a school of Judaism whose members inherited the authority of the Sanhedrin of Jerusalem. However, Johanan had many enemies in the Jewish community because he had not fully supported the revolt against Rome. In about 80 c.e. he was pressured into relinquishing the leadership of the Jabneh sect to Gamaliel II, who enjoyed broad support because his father, Simeon ben Gamaliel I, had been a leader in the rebellion.

Gamaliel II played a crucial role in restoring the Jewish faith, which had been seriously weakened by the loss of the Jerusalem Temple and of Jewish political autonomy. He firmly established the authority of the Sanhedrin and the academy at Jabneh by making it the base for many of the most outstanding Jewish scholars of the time. More importantly, he unified the sages, who often disagreed with each other, in their production of a body of theological, legal, ritual, and ethical teachings that later became the basis of the Mishnah, the collection of Jewish traditions forming the main part of the Talmud. His own opinions are quoted in this code about seventy times.

Gamaliel II designed regulations that helped maintain the religious customs and unity of the Jewish people without the benefit of the Temple. He ruled that Hillel's liberal interpretations of Jewish law, not Shammai's stricter views, were authoritative, thus ending a serious division between Jewish spiritual leaders. He gave special attention to the regulation of prayer ritual, notably by standardizing the principal prayer, the Amidah. He ruled that a seder was to be held on the eve of Passover, without sacrifice. He shifted the emphasis at Passover to the national and historical by means of the Haggadah (the ritual for the seder), which raised national freedom to a paramount value. He changed the character of the Day of Atonement by introducing the idea of repentance to atone for one's sins as a substitute for sacrifice, which had ceased with the destruction of the Temple.

Gamaliel II sought to unify the Jewish people in their dispersion by establishing a single body of Halakah (Jewish law), whose rulings were binding on everyone. He further unified Jews by asserting his authority to standardize the Jewish calendar and to fix the dates of festivals.

Gamaliel II also unified the Jewish world by reinforcing ties with the Diaspora. He renewed the practice of sending emissaries to foreign Jewish groups, he established communal institutions for Jewish education and financial assistance in the Diaspora, and his agents abroad collected contributions for the Jewish centers in Palestine.

Besides his duties as president of the Sanhedrin, he was the political leader of the nation. He made frequent journeys to Rome as the head of delegations to the Roman government, often meeting with Emperor Domitian.

Rome recognized Gamaliel II as patriarch (leader of the Jewish people). His reforms raised the power and prestige of the patriarchate.

However, in his personal dealings he was sometimes overbearing and dictatorial. He excommunicated his own brother-in-law. In a debate with Joshua ben Hananyah, he unnecessarily humiliated the elderly scholar. Because of his harsh methods he was deposed, replaced by Eleazar ben Azariah. But later Gamaliel II was reinstated and the two shared office. Thereafter, a tension remained between him and the Sanhedrin as to their respective authority.

Gamaliel II died before 132 c.e. He was buried, at his own request, in simple garments and with no display, thus establishing the tradition that all funerals should be alike so that the poor are not embarrassed.

SIMEON BEN GAMALIEL II

CONSOLIDATOR AND TEACHER

Son of Gamaliel II and father of Judah ha-Nasi, Simeon ben Gamaliel II (fl. second century c.e.) stood between two giants in Jewish history. But his own achievements, too, were outstanding. He consolidated the status of the office of *nasi* and produced a rich body of halakic teachings.

When Simeon ben Gamaliel II was very young, the Romans destroyed the house of the *nasi* in revenge for the Jewish revolt led by Simon Bar Kochba. After the persecution subsided and his life was safe, Simeon ben Gamaliel II was appointed *nasi* of the new Sanhedrin assembled at Usha.

However, the years during which the Sanhedrin had functioned without a *nasi* made Simeon's position difficult. He had to regain the people's belief in the necessity of the office.

During the absence of a *nasi*, leadership was in the hands of the *ab bet din* ("father of the supreme court"), who was a kind of vice president, supported by the *hakham* (head teacher at the academy). The *av bet din* was Nathan the Babylonian; the *hakham* was Meir.

Simeon made a deliberate effort to cooperate with the members of the Sanhedrin. He behaved modestly and humbly, and he even accepted Sanhedrin members' rulings in practical halakah.

However, like his father, Simeon ben Gamaliel II believed in strengthening the power and authority of the office of the *nasi*. "When the *nasi* enters," Simeon decreed, "all the people shall rise"; but "when the *av bet din* enters, one row rises on one side and one row on the other," and "when the *hakham* enters, everyone rises (as he passes) and (then) sits down." This decree aroused the ire of Nathan and Meir, who for a time planned to remove Simeon from office, but eventually they accepted his decision. In another act to strengthen his office, Simeon restored the dependence of Babylon on Palestine, especially in regard to the intercalation of months.

By cooperating with the members of the Sanhedrin, by being moderate yet capable in his leadership, and by standing firm on the authority of his office, Simeon consolidated the status of the *nasi* and reestablished it as the highest institution in the nation.

His halakic teachings extended to all fields of the law and revealed a special interest in practical solutions to daily problems. He favored changes according to circumstance and local custom. Primarily concerned with the common good, he opposed the issue of ordinances too difficult for the majority to bear. In religious matters he generally took the more lenient point of view. On the subject of marriage he was known for his efforts to protect the interest of the wife. He also sought to improve the condition of the slave, holding that it was a religious duty to help slaves obtain their freedom.

Simeon ben Gamaliel II left behind some well-known haggadic

sayings, such as "The world rests on three things: justice, truth, and peace" and "One need not erect monuments to the righteous, for their works preserve their memory."

Judah ha-Nasi

COMPILER OF THE MISHNAH

Judah ha-Nasi played a role of tremendous importance in the history of Judaism. The spiritual and political leader of Jews during a key period in the ancient world, he was one of the last of the *tannaim* ("teachers" or "masters of the Oral Law") and performed the crucial service of compiling the Mishnah, a collection of Jewish traditions and the basic part of the Talmud. In his lifetime he was held in such high regard that he was named *ha-Nasi* ("the Prince"). In the centuries since his death, rabbinic tradition has held that no one after Moses has combined knowledge and authority more thoroughly than Judah ha-Nasi.

His father was Simeon ben Gamaliel II, who was the son of Gamaliel II. Simeon ben Gamaliel II flourished in the second century of the common era, served as head of the Sanhedrin, and established the patriarchate in Usha. His opinions are often quoted in the tannaitic texts, and his death and last will and testament are described at length in the Talmud and Midrash. He was buried at Bet She'arim, thus establishing that city as a necropolis for Jews of both Palestine and the Diaspora.

The great Judah ha-Nasi, Simeon ben Gamaliel II's son, was born about 135 to 138 C.E. He was taught not only by his father but also by several other masters of the time, including Simeon ben Yohai, the reputed author of the *Zohar*. About 165 to 170, Judah succeeded his father as patriarch of the Palestine Jewish community and consequently as head of the Sanhedrin. He lived most of his life in Galilee, first in Bet She'arim and later in Sepphoris.

Judah ha-Nasi wielded great power as the spiritual and political leader of the Jews. He reserved for himself the right to appoint judges and teachers and to regulate the laws of the sabbatical year.

His almost unlimited authority sprang not only from his status as the most revered rabbi of his time but also from his great wealth. He inherited large tracts of land, increased them, and farmed them intensively, producing wine and vegetables. He also raised cattle, manufactured wool and linen, and exported and imported these products in his own ships. He used his wealth to support scholars and aid the needy.

Judah ha-Nasi is best known as the compiler of the Mishnah, a systematic collection of accumulated Oral Law that became the basis of Jewish thought, second in importance only to the Scriptures. Because the Written Law, the Pentateuch (the Five Books of Moses), could not cover all possible situations in daily life, a body of Oral Law had developed over the centuries. To preserve that tradition, to reduce its vast chaos down to a manageable size, and to help the people know which statements were to be regarded as normative, Judah ha-Nasi, in cooperation with the leading teachers of his time, selected and organized the Oral Laws into the work known as the Mishnah ("Instruction").

He arranged it into six orders (divisions) according to subject matter: agriculture, festivals, marriage, civil law, the temple service, and ritual purity. He made profound contributions to the Oral Law by determining which rabbinic opinions were authoritative, carefully preserving minority opinions in case laws should be changed in the future and a precedent for these changes be required, and omitted laws that were obsolete or lacking in authority. The Mishnah became the subject for commentaries by later sages. The commentaries came to be known as the Gemara ("Completion"). The Mishnah and the Gemara together make up the Jerusalem (or Palestinian) and Babylonian Talmuds.

Judah ha-Nasi's opinions are quoted many times, not only in his own Mishnah but also in the rest of the halakic literature. Some of his prayers have found places in the daily liturgy, such as the prayer for protection against arrogance, against bad company, and against a hard law case or litigant. His haggadic sayings are well known, such as "Be as punctilious in observing a light as a weighty commandment, for you do not know their relative reward"; "Do not be deceived by the outward appearance of age or youth; a new pitcher might be full of good old wine, while an old one might be empty altogether"; "A man should revere his father and mother as he reveres God, for all three are partners in him."

Because of his great stature within the Jewish community, Judah was called by several honorific names, notably *ha-Nasi* ("the Prince" or "the Patriarch"). Others included *rabbenu* ("our teacher") and *rabbenu hakadosh* ("our holy teacher"). In the halakic literature, he is quoted in the name of *Rabbi* ("the Master").

Judah ha-Nasi died about 217 to 220 c.e. Like his father, he was buried in the necropolis of Bet She'arim.

Judah had named his son Gamaliel III to succeed him as *nasi*, while his son Simeon ben Judah ha-Nasi was to become *hakham* (head of the academy and third in rank at the Sanhedrin). Both sons put finishing touches to their father's Mishnah.

THE
IBN EZRAS

T HE IBN EZRAS WERE ONE OF THE MOST PROMINENT families during the golden age of Spanish Jewry (900–1200). Moses ben Jacob ibn Ezra (c. 1060–c. 1139) wrote sacred and secular poetry unsurpassed in its mastery of poetic style and structure in the Hebrew language. His three brothers—Isaac, Joseph, and Zerahiah (all fl. late eleventh and early twelfth centuries)—were eminent scholars.

Medieval authorities believe that Moses and his brothers were related (though the exact relationship is uncertain) to Abraham ben Meir ibn Ezra (c. 1092–c. 1167), a poet, grammarian, philosopher, astronomer, and biblical commentator. Abraham's son Isaac ibn Ezra (fl. twelfth century) was also a distinguished Hebrew poet.

MOSES BEN JACOB IBN EZRA

SACRED AND SECULAR HEBREW POET

One of the most highly regarded Hebrew poets in history, Moses ben Jacob ibn Ezra broke new ground in his development of secular verse and created a uniquely introspective kind of penitential prayer. He also wrote treatises on poetry and philosophy.

Moses was born into a wealthy, cultured family in Granada, Spain, in about 1060. His three brothers became scholars.

Moses and one of his nieces fell in love, but her father, Moses' brother, refused permission for them to marry, giving the girl instead to another of Moses' brothers. Deeply affected by this episode, Moses became estranged from his siblings, left Granada, and spent much of the rest of his life as a wanderer.

His failed love affair influenced his entire life's work. To express the emotions set loose by his loss, he became one of the earliest Hebrew poets of secular verse, in which he celebrated love, wine, and the beauty of nature, while also bemoaning faithlessness and, eventually, the onset of old age. When his former love died in childbirth, he wrote a profound elegy.

In later years he produced mostly introspective, melancholic penitential prayers (*selihot*), for which he earned the epithet *ha-Sallah* ("Writer of Penitential Poems"). Many of them came to be included in the Sephardic liturgy for New Year and the Day of Atonement.

Moses also wrote two important prose treatises in Arabic, in which language he was known as Abu Harun Musa. One, on the art of poetry, was originally titled *Conversations and Recollections*, later translated into Hebrew as *Shirat Yisrael* ("Song of Israel"). It is a valuable literary history of his era, dealing with Arabic, Castilian, and Jewish poetry. The other treatise, translated into Hebrew as *Arugat ha-bosem* ("The Bed of Spices"), summarizes thoughts gathered from other philosophers on such topics as the attributes of God and the nature of man.

Moses ben Jacob ibn Ezra died about 1139.

ABRAHAM BEN MEIR IBN EZRA

HEBREW POET, SCHOLAR, AND BIBLICAL COMMENTATOR

Abraham ben Meir ibn Ezra earned a reputation as a poet and scholar in several different fields. Today he is best remembered for his pathbreaking biblical commentaries.

Abraham was born in Tudela, Zaragoza, Spain, in 1092 or 1093.

Little is known about his activities as a young man in Muslim Spain. He may have had five sons, four of whom probably died as infants or children. Only one, Isaac, is known by name.

In 1140 Abraham moved to Rome, and in 1145 he began life-long wanderings throughout Europe. The reason for his root-lessness is not clear, though one conjecture is that his son's abandonment of Spain and apparent conversion to Islam made Abraham himself feel lost. Another factor in his wanderlust was probably his poverty, which led him to feel unattached to any area or group. His later writings are marked by a bitter sense of exile, making touching references to his native land and calling himself, in Hebrew, *ha-Sefaradi* ("the Spaniard").

Abraham wrote both sacred and secular poetry. His religious poems reflect his deep faith. The secular poems, written in Hebrew, are often mystical, with frequent flashes of irony and humor. In his later years, he sometimes alluded to his poverty and misfortune in his verse, as in these lines: "Were I to deal in candles, / The sun would never set; / Were selling shrouds my business, / No one would ever die!"

Abraham displayed a wide-ranging scholarly aptitude. By translating into Hebrew the Arab-language books of Spanish-Jewish grammarians and philosophers, he opened a vast new spectrum of knowledge to European Jews unfamiliar with Arabic. He also wrote original Hebrew grammatical and philosophical treatises. His *Sefer yesod mora ve-sod ha-Torah* ("Treatise on the Foundation of Awe and the Secret of the Torah") analyzes Torah precepts and their significance.

Abraham had deep knowledge of mathematics and astronomy. He introduced a decimal system of numeration into Hebrew science, and he made calculations of the planets.

However, his greatest work was his biblical commentaries, which include expositions on the Book of Job, the Book of Daniel, the Psalms, and the Pentateuch. He is widely regarded as the first Jewish Bible critic and, in his philological approach, a forerunner of modern biblical criticism. For example, he hinted that the passage in Deuteronomy 34 recounting the death of Moses was written by Joshua. Similarly, the last twenty-six chapters of Isaiah may have been written by a "second Isaiah," who lived and taught during the Babylonian exile.

Abraham's philosophical commentaries reveal him as a Neoplatonic pantheist. In this departure from traditional biblical interpretation he was a precursor of the seventeenth-century Jewish philosopher Spinoza.

Abraham's versatile knowledge and creativity made him one of the most remarkable Jews in the medieval world and gave him an esteemed reputation that grew in later generations. He is believed to be the model for Robert Browning's famous poem "Rabbi Ben Ezra."

Abraham ben Meir ibn Ezra died in 1164 or 1167, probably in Calahorra, Spain, or in Rome.

Isaac ibn Ezra

HEBREW POET

Isaac ibn Ezra (fl. twelfth century) left an outstanding legacy as a Hebrew poet. He is also well known in history as secretary to Abu al-Barakat.

Isaac was probably born in Spain. His father was the great Hebrew poet-scholar Abraham ben Meir ibn Ezra.

As a young man Isaac left Spain. He spent most of his life in the Near East.

In Baghdad he became a court poet as well as a pupil of, and an assistant to, the philosopher-physician Abu al-Barakat. In 1143 Abu dictated an Arabic commentary on Ecclesiastes to Isaac, who, in the introduction to the work, wrote a long poem in praise of his master.

When, in his old age, Abu converted to Islam, so, apparently, did Isaac. In one of his poems, he reveals that he did convert but that he remained a Jew at heart.

Many of Isaac's secular poems have survived. His works are fully worthy of belonging to that long line of distinguished Hebrew poetry produced by the ibn Ezras.

THE
KOOKS

THE KOOK (OR KUK) FAMILY was a distinguished rabbinic line that developed in eastern Europe. During the twentieth century the family's most outstanding members moved to the Holy Land, where they made a profound impact on the region's religious and political life.

Abraham Isaac Kook (1865–1935) immigrated to Palestine in 1904. He was an active Zionist and the first Ashkenazic chief rabbi of modern Palestine.

Saul Hone ben Solomon Zalman Kook (1879–1955), a younger brother of Abraham, also immigrated to Palestine in 1904. There Saul engaged in business, supported cultural and educational organizations, and wrote scholarly articles on the Bible and on Hebrew folklore, literature, and linguistics.

Zvi Yehuda Kook (1891–1982), Abraham's only son, became head of the Merkaz ha-Rav yeshiva (founded by his father) in Jerusalem, where his stress on Zionism and the spiritual aspect of Israel made his seminary unique. He was also the spiritual leader of the Gush Emunim ("Bloc of the Faithful") movement, which pressed for Jewish settlement of areas captured during the 1967 Six-Day War.

ABRAHAM ISAAC KOOK

FIRST ASHKENAZIC CHIEF RABBI OF MODERN PALESTINE

Zionist, philosopher, and educator, Abraham Isaac Kook did much to shape the direction of modern Jewish Palestine. He became the first Ashkenazic chief rabbi of Palestine under the League of Nations mandate to Great Britain to administer the region.

Abraham Isaac ha-Kohen Kook (or Avraham Yitzhak HaCohen Kook; the surname is sometimes recorded as Kuk) was born in Greiva (or Griva/Grieve), Latvia, in 1865. His father was a Hasidic (mystical) rabbi, while his mother descended from a line of Mitnagged (Orthodox, non-Hasidic) rabbis. Abraham studied under his father and at the yeshiva in Volozhin, and he came under the influence of the Musar (personal piety) movement, which acknowledged no dichotomy between the sacred and the secular.

While a student at Volozhin, he married the daughter of Rabbi Eliyahu David Rabinovitz-Tomin. They had one son.

After serving as rabbi in small eastern European towns (1888—1904), he immigrated to Palestine in 1904 to become chief rabbi of Jaffa. There he supported the pioneer Jewish settlements and encouraged the settlers to return to a religious lifestyle.

During a 1914 trip to attend a planned conference, Abraham was stranded in Europe by the outbreak of World War I. He was briefly interned as an alien in Germany, but he escaped to England via Switzerland. In London he served as rabbi of a synagogue and solicited popular support for the British government's Balfour Declaration (1917), on the basis of which the League of Nations gave Great Britain a mandate to establish and administer a Jewish homeland in Palestine.

After the war he returned to Palestine, and in 1919 he was appointed chief rabbi of the Ashkenazic community of Jerusalem. In 1921 he was elected chief rabbi for all of Palestine, a position he held for the rest of his life.

Also in 1921 he founded in Jerusalem the Merkaz ("Center"), the beginning of what would become a yeshiva that reflected his interest in Zionism and in the universality of studies. The yeshiva became known as Merkaz ha-Rav (or Merkaz Harav, "Center of the Rabbi") in honor of its founder.

Abraham's greatest quality was his ability to bring together different points of view within the Jewish world. He played a major role in paving the way for the independent state of Israel by breaking down barriers between groups so that Jews could unite in their most important quest—building their homeland. Abraham himself embodied that unification of disparate elements: a deeply religious mystic, he also took a strong interest in human affairs; a devout student of the Torah, he also advocated the study of secular sciences; and a religious Zionist, he also embraced the secular elements of the movement.

Abraham was a prolific writer. His works reflect his varied interests, with special emphasis on his philosophical and mystical insights. He developed what he called a philosophy of repentance, in which humankind's separation from God is not an objective fact but a consequence of human "forgetfulness" of a higher existence. Repentance, and therefore restoration of unity with the divine, can be achieved through the Torah. In his *Orot ha-teshuvah* (published in English as *Rabbi Kook's Philosophy of Repentance*), he explored these ideas. In his collection of essays called *Orot ha-kodesh* ("Lights of Holiness"), he expounded his mystic view that the Jewish national revival is part of the divine plan for strengthening faith against modern heresy. He also wrote novellae, responsa, and a commentary on the Talmud.

Abraham Isaac Kook died in Jerusalem on September 1, 1935.

Zvi Yehuda Kook

EDUCATOR AND SPIRITUAL LEADER

Zvi Yehuda Kook greatly influenced the spiritual life of Israel through his directorship of the Merkaz ha-Rav yeshiva in Jerusalem. His effect on the nation's political life was nearly as great because of his role as the spiritual father of the Gush Emunim ("Bloc of the Faithful") movement to settle the regions captured by Israel during the 1967 Six-Day War.

Zvi Yehuda (or Tzevi/Zevi/Avi Judah) ben Abraham Isaac ha-Kohen Kook was born in Zimel, near Kaunas (or Kovno), Lithuania, in 1891. His father, Abraham Isaac Kook, was at that time rabbi in Zimel.

In 1904 Zvi moved with his parents to Palestine and later studied at the Etz Chaim yeshiva in Jerusalem. When his father established the Merkaz (later Merkaz ha-Rav or Merkaz Harav) yeshiva in that city in 1921, Zvi soon joined him in administering the seminary. After his father's death in 1935, Zvi succeeded him as head of the institution. Continuing his father's Zionist philosophy and inclusive method of education, Zvi strongly influenced generations of students from all elements of the Jewish people. Like his father, he exuded a positive attitude toward Zionism, helping to lay the groundwork for the birth of Israel in 1948. Also like his father, he emphasized the need for couching the new nation in a spirit of religious renewal.

In his later years Zvi became the spiritual leader of Israeli ultranationalists. His outspoken belief in the right of Israel to its biblical geography inspired the Gush Emunim organization, which pressed for the Jewish settlement of the West Bank of the Jordan River and resisted efforts to return the Sinai peninsula to Egypt. He personally led his Gush Emunim followers to Horon and Jericho. He was also the spiritual leader of the National Religious party, which called for a return to the roots of Judaism.

Zvi's political convictions sprang from his religious convictions. "We are not a nation of conquerors," he explained. "We are returning to the land of our fathers. No one, no prime minister, has the authority to renounce any part of the country." Arabs, he said, have civil rights as individuals but not as a nation. "The country belonged to us for generations past in accordance with history, the Bible, and the Prophets."

Like his father, Zvi produced many writings. He wrote a number of articles dealing with halakic attitudes toward contemporary events, and he edited and published much of his father's literary output.

Zvi Yehuda Kook died in Jerusalem on March 9, 1982. He was childless, his wife having died early in their marriage.

THE
LEHMANS

THE FIRST GENERATION OF LEHMANS in the United States founded the influential Lehman Brothers investment banking firm. For over one hundred years the company played a major role in financing the recovery of depressed regions (such as the post-Civil War South) and the development of new industries (including television). In later generations the family produced not only a steady stream of outstanding Lehman Brothers partners but also great achievers in such fields as law, politics, and philanthropy.

In 1844 Henry Lehman (1821–55), a Bavarian immigrant in Montgomery, Alabama, opened a mercantile business. Soon he was joined by Emanuel (1827–1907) and Mayer (1830–97) Lehman, his brothers. They established Lehman Brothers, at first a general store, later a commodities trader, and finally a New York City investment banking firm.

The next generation, the first born in the United States, was incredibly talented. Emanuel's son Philip (1861–1947) and Mayer's son Arthur (1873–1936) became partners in the firm and, in the early years of the twentieth century, led the shift in emphasis from commodities trading to investment banking. Arthur's wife, Adele Lehman (née Lewisohn), added a rich dimension to the family through her activities as a philanthropist and art collector.

Mayer's sons Irving (1876–1945) and Herbert (1878–1963) entered other fields. Irving became the chief judge of the New York

Court of Appeals. Herbert joined Lehman Brothers but gained his greatest renown in politics, winning elections to the New York governorship and the United States Senate.

The following generation was led by Allan Lehman (1885–1952) and Robert Lehman (1891–1969). The former was a son of Mayer's son Sigmund, himself a partner in the family firm. Allan served as a general partner at Lehman Brothers from 1908 to 1952 and supported many charitable organizations. Robert, the principal partner at Lehman Brothers for over forty years, changed the nature of the firm's partnership and pioneered the founding of new and neglected industries.

Orin Lehman (1922–), Allan's son, worked as an economist for Lehman Brothers (1947–52) and then moved on to a variety of executive positions elsewhere, such as chairman of Colgreene Broadcasting Company (1968–75). He is noted for his public service in many roles with city, state, and federal organizations, notably as the longtime head of the New York State Office of Parks, Recreation, and Historic Preservation.

HENRY, EMANUEL, AND MAYER LEHMAN

FOUNDERS OF LEHMAN BROTHERS

Lehman Brothers, originally a dry-goods retail store and later a commodities trader, became one of the most important American investment banking houses of the twentieth century. It was founded by the German immigrant brothers Henry, Emanuel, and Mayer Lehman.

All three brothers were born in Bavaria: Henry in 1821, Emanuel in 1827, and Mayer in 1830. Their parents were Abraham, a cattle merchant, and Harriet (Rosenheim) Lehman.

The first to leave the family's hometown of Rimpar, near Würzburg, and immigrate to the United States was Henry, who settled in Montgomery, Alabama, and opened a mercantile business, known as H. Lehman, in 1844. In 1847 Emanuel immigrated and joined his brother's business, which became H. Lehman and Bro. Soon Mayer arrived, and in 1850 the three brothers began operating a general store together, with Mayer finally becoming a full partner in 1853. As late as 1854 the firm was still doing business as H. Lehman and Bro., but soon the company adopted the name of Lehman Brothers. Following Henry's death in 1855, Emanuel and Mayer headed the business.

Much of the firm's trade was with cotton planters to whom it extended credit for supplies till the cotton crop was sold. Often the company took cotton in payment for its goods. In this way Lehman

Mayer Lehman

Brothers became engaged in cotton trading, shipping its supply of the commodity to northern states and to Europe.

In 1856 Emanuel opened an office in New York City, but the Civil War interrupted its operations. During the war, the brothers supported the Confederacy. Mayer, in fact, was entrusted with caring for the Alabama prisoners in northern states.

In 1865, after the war ended, the brothers moved their headquarters to New York City. They expanded their range of commodity trading to sugar, coffee, petroleum, and other products.

The brothers' success early led them into the investment banking field. At the close of the Civil War they lent Alabama $100,000 and served for several years as fiscal agents for the state.

During the rest of the 1800s the firm continued to engage in both commodities trading and investment banking. The Lehmans' commodity activities still centered on the cotton industry. They acquired two large cotton factories, one near Montgomery and one in New Orleans. As investment bankers, they promoted the development of many southern ventures, including railroads, iron and steel furnaces, coal mines, and real estate. Later they helped to form two banks: the Mercantile National Bank (which merged with the Irving Trust Company) and the Mutual Alliance Trust Company (which became the Manufacturers Trust Company).

Emanuel married Pauline Sondheim of New York City. They had two sons and two daughters. Mayer married Babette Newgass, like the Lehmans an immigrant from Bavaria. They had five sons (one of whom died in infancy) and two daughters. Emanuel's daughter Harriet married Mayer's son Sigmund, a partner in Lehman Brothers.

Mayer Lehman died in New York City in 1897. Emanuel Lehman died there in 1907.

ARTHUR LEHMAN

LEHMAN BROTHERS PARTNER, 1901–1936

Arthur Lehman, in his thirty-five years as a partner in Lehman Brothers, helped to transform the firm from a medium-sized commodity business into a major investment banking house. He was also a noted philanthropist and art collector.

Arthur was born in New York City on June 1, 1873. He was the third of five sons, and the second of the four who survived to adulthood, of Mayer and Babette (Newgass) Lehman, both natives of Bavaria. Mayer, with his two older brothers, had formed in 1850 the company that would become Lehman Brothers, at first a dry-goods store and later a firm trading in cotton and other commodities.

After attending Dr. Julius Sachs's private school in New York City, Arthur studied at Harvard (A.B., 1894). He then gained practical business experience with Lehman, Stern and Company, a New Orleans cotton firm that his family controlled.

In 1898 he joined Lehman Brothers and three years later became a partner in the firm. Arthur played a large role in redirecting Lehman Brothers from commodities trading to investment banking. The company pioneered the financing of what were then new industries, such as automobile, aviation, and motion-picture companies; mail-order houses, including Sears, Roebuck (1906); and department store chains, such as F. W. Woolworth (1912).

Arthur helped to organize the Marine Midland Trust Company and the Southern States Land and Timber Corporation, which in the early 1900s purchased and reclaimed large tracts of land in the Upper Everglades and thereby helped to open lower Florida. In 1929 he became president of the newly formed Lehman Corporation, an investment trust.

Arthur was one of the founders of the Federation of Jewish Philanthropies, which he served not only as a substantial benefactor but also as an early president and as treasurer of the Joint Distribution Committee. He donated a new administration building, Lehman Hall, to Harvard, and he held trusteeships with the New School for Social Research and the Museum of the City of New York. An avid art collector, he specialized in Italian and English fifteenth- and sixteenth-century tapestries, paintings, and illuminated books.

He was married in 1901 to Adele Lewisohn, daughter of the financier Adolph Lewisohn. They had three daughters.

Arthur Lehman was a senior partner at Lehman Brothers when he died suddenly at his home in New York City on May 16, 1936.

Adele Lewisohn Lehman

PHILANTHROPIST AND ART COLLECTOR

Adele Lewisohn Lehman, wife of the investment banker Arthur Lehman, combined the qualities of a nineteenth-century woman who dutifully fulfilled her social obligations and a twentieth-century woman who actively pursued social progress. She became one of the most prominent philanthropists and art collectors of her time.

Adele Lewisohn was born in New York City on May 17, 1882. She was the daughter of Adolph, a financier and philanthropist, and Emma (Cahn) Lewisohn.

In 1901 she married Arthur Lehman of Lehman Brothers. They had three daughters.

Adele grew up at a time when women of her high economic and social class were expected to engage in philanthropy. She accepted her duty and followed her husband into the Federation for Jewish Philanthropies, which he had helped to found. For many years she served as honorary vice president of the women's division and raised funds for the organization.

She was also a member of the board of directors of the New York Service for Orthopedically Handicapped. The service ran a summer camp, sponsored a workshop where crippled girls were taught manual skills, and maintained a free school where it was shown that children with cerebral palsy were educable.

Adele was an avid collector of all forms of art, including paintings, tapestries, and sculptures. She and Arthur acquired many pieces that were later donated to museums, including the Metropolitan Museum of Art in New York City.

After her husband died in 1936, she expanded her interests. As a young woman, she had supported the woman suffrage movement. Now she regained her impulse to have an impact on contemporary political and sociological issues. She became active in the League of Women Voters, serving as vice president in 1945. In 1954 she established the Arthur Lehman Counselling Service to provide psychiatric help for people suffering from personal, marital, or family problems.

In her later years she spent much of her time painting. Many of her works are floral pieces and landscapes.

Adele Lewisohn Lehman died in Purchase, New York, on August 11, 1965.

Irving Lehman

CHIEF JUDGE OF THE NEW YORK COURT OF APPEALS

Unlike his siblings, Irving Lehman never joined the family investment-banking firm, Lehman Brothers. Instead, he became a lawyer and a distinguished jurist, his career capped with his years as chief judge of the New York Court of Appeals, the state's highest court. He was also one of America's most prominent leaders of the Jewish community.

Irving was born in New York City on January 28, 1876. He was the fourth of five sons, and the third of the four who survived to adulthood, of Mayer and Babette (Newgass) Lehman, both natives of Bavaria. Mayer, with his two older brothers, had formed in 1850 the company that would become Lehman Brothers, originally a dry-goods store before turning to commodities trading and then investment banking. All three of Irving's brothers went into the firm.

He, however, had a different agenda. After attending Dr. Julius Sachs's private school in New York City, he studied at Columbia University, where he earned the degrees of A.B. (1896), A.M. (1897), and LL.B. (1898). He served as a law clerk in the office of Marshall, Moran, Williams and McVickar, and in 1901 he became a member of the firm. Later he was a partner in Worcester, Williams and Lehman.

In 1901 he married Sissie Straus, daughter of Nathan Straus, the co-owner of Macy's department store and a noted philanthropist. Irving and Sissie had no children.

In 1908 he was elected to the Supreme Court of the State of New York on the Democratic ticket. He was assisted in the election by his father-in-law, a major contributor to the Democratic party and a close friend of the powerful Democrat Alfred E. Smith. When his fourteen-year term expired in 1922, Irving won reelection with the backing of both parties. The following year, again with bipartisan support, he was elected to a fourteen-year term on the state Court of Appeals. In 1937 he was reelected, and from 1940 till his death he served as chief judge of the court.

Irving's juridical philosophy was that the law had to accomodate itself to societal changes. He had, for example, a liberal view of the state's power to regulate the economy. By broadly interpreting the state's police power (that is, the power to protect the welfare of the whole community), he held that the legislature could fix the prices of certain commodities and authorize the setting of minimum wages. His point of view in this matter was in opposition to most legal precedents.

On civil liberties issues, too, he was ahead of his time. He protected religious liberty at every opportunity, banned racial discrimination in a postal employees' association, and condemned the use of third-degree tactics by police.

Irving was one of the principal shapers of the Jewish Welfare Board. He served as its president from 1921 to 1940 and oversaw its post-World War I transition from a wartime service agency for American Jews in the armed forces to a national coordinator for Jewish community-center work. He was also president of the Ninety-second Street YMHA and of Temple Emanu-El, both in New York City, and a member of the executive committees or boards for the American Jewish Committee, the Jewish Theological Seminary, and the Union of American Hebrew Congregations.

Irving Lehman died at his home in Port Chester, New York, on September 22, 1945.

HERBERT HENRY LEHMAN

GOVERNOR AND SENATOR

Herbert Henry Lehman joined his family's firm of Lehman Brothers, investment bankers, but his principal life work was in public service. As New York governor and United States senator, he had a leading role in the liberal political movement of his era. He also devoted himself to philanthropy and community affairs.

Herbert was born in New York City on March 28, 1878. He was the fifth of five sons, and the youngest of the four who survived to adulthood, of Mayer and Babette (Newgass) Lehman, both natives of Bavaria.

Herbert attended Dr. Julius Sachs's college preparatory school in New York City and then Williams College (B.A., 1899). After graduation from college he worked for the J. Spencer Turner Company, cotton manufacturers, where he rose to become vice president and treasurer.

In 1908 he left that job to join Lehman Brothers. Mayer and his two older brothers had founded an early form of the company in 1850.

Herbert Lehman

It was originally a dry-goods store and later a commodities trader. But in the early years of the twentieth century, the firm was changed, largely by Herbert's older brother Arthur, into an important investment banking house.

In 1910 Herbert married Edith Louise Altschul, whose father was also an investment banker. They had two sons (one of whom was killed in World War II) and one daughter.

When America entered World War I, Herbert volunteered as a civilian textile-procurement specialist in the Navy Department, where he met Franklin D. Roosevelt, at that time the assistant secretary of the navy. Later in the war Herbert became a captain in the army, where he served as a textile procurer, a contract adjuster, and a member of the War Claims Board. In June 1919 he resigned from the army with the rank of colonel.

After the war ended he became involved in liberal Democratic politics, especially through his support of the popular New York politician Alfred E. Smith. When Smith won the Democratic nomination for the presidency in 1928, Herbert was rewarded with a top post in the Democratic National Committee.

Later that year he was elected lieutenant governor of New York, while his friend Franklin D. Roosevelt won the governorship. Herbert, unlike most lieutenant governors, actively participated in running the state goverment. Roosevelt called him "my good right arm." In 1930 they were both reelected.

In 1932 Roosevelt won the presidency of the United States and Herbert was elected governor of New York. He served four terms as governor, winning two-year terms in 1932, 1934, and 1936, and the state's first four-year term in 1938.

As governor, he supported Roosevelt's liberal New Deal national policies and presided over a state admini- stration known as the "Little New Deal." Herbert instituted reforms in labor legislation, in the regulation of public utilities, and in goverment appointments, which became biparti- san under his leadership. He also managed, despite the Great Depression, to turn a 1933 deficit of $90 million into a surplus of $6 million by 1938.

In 1940 his brother Irving was elected chief judge of the New York Court of Appeals. Thus, from 1940 to 1942 New York, for the only time in its history, had brothers heading both the execu- tive and the judicial branches of its government.

Herbert grew more and more concerned with inter- national affairs, including the fate of European Jews. A few days before the end of his fourth term in December 1942, he resigned as governor to become director of the newly created Office of Foreign Relief and Rehabilitation Operations in the State Department, and in November 1943 he was elected the first director of the United Nations Relief and Rehabilitation Administration. After many accomplish- ments in refugee relief during World War II and imme- diately afterward, he resigned in March 1946.

Later in 1946 he ran unsuccessfully for the United States Senate. But three years later he won a special election to fill a vacated seat in the Senate for one year, and in 1950 he was reelected to a full six-year term. During his time in the Senate (November 1949 to January 1957) he championed civil rights, minority rights, and liberalized immigration policies; and he was one of the first to speak out against Senator Joseph R. McCarthy and McCarthyism. Herbert was referred to as "the conscience of the Senate."

After retiring from the Senate in early 1957, he remained active. In 1959 he helped to launch a campaign to end bossism in New York City politics.

His philanthropic work began early in his life. By the turn of the century Herbert had already begun a lifelong association with the Henry Street Settlement, where he was a trustee. Early in World War I he helped to found the Joint Distribution Committee for collecting and distributing funds for the relief of Jews in Europe and Palestine. He also served as a director of the National Council of the Boy Scouts of America and the National Conference of Christians and Jews.

In late 1963 he was scheduled to receive the Presidential Medal of Freedom, the nation's highest civilian honor. "Citizen and Statesman," the citation read, "he has used wisdom and compassion as the tools of government and has made politics the highest form of public service." However, the award had to be given posthumously because he died in New York City on December 5, 1963.

ROBERT LEHMAN

LEHMAN BROTHERS LONGTIME PRINCIPAL PARTNER

Robert ("Bobbie") Lehman was the principal partner at Lehman Brothers, investment bankers, for over forty years. As such, he initiated many profound changes in the nature of the firm's partnership and its investment strategies, pioneering the funding of industries previously shunned by Wall Street investors. He also acquired an important art collection and contributed to art education.

Robert was born in New York City on September 29, 1891. He was a grandson of Emanuel Lehman, one of the founders of Lehman Brothers, and the son of Philip and Carrie (Lauer) Lehman. Philip ran Lehman Brothers during the crucial early 1900s, when the company was changing from commodities trading to investment banking.

Robert attended the Hotchkiss School and Yale University (B.A., 1913). After caring for his father's art collection for several years, he enlisted in the army and served as a captain of artillery in France during World War I.

In 1919 he joined Lehman Brothers. In 1921 he became a partner, and by 1925 he was the bank's principal partner.

Robert soon made far-reaching innovations in the business. One important change was his calling for the recruitment of the firm's first nonfamily partners. This step energized the company's internal competition.

He also turned the bank increasingly away from product producers, in whom Wall Street traditionally invested, and toward other industries, especially retail business, soon a Lehman specialty. Federated Department Stores, F. W. Woolworth, Gimbels, Macy's—these and other retail merchandisers received financial services from Lehman Brothers.

Robert broke more new ground by investing in the entertainment industry. He created America's largest vaudeville circuit by consolidating the Keith-Albee and Orpheum theaters; funded motion-picture studios, including Twentieth Century-Fox; and, in the late 1930s, sponsored the first public underwriting of a television company, Allan B. DuMont Laboratories.

Robert led Lehman Brothers into early investments in the airline industry. In 1929 he helped to fund the Pan American Airways expansion in South America and was named to its board of directors. In that same year Lehman Brothers helped to create the Aviation Corporation, which later became American Airlines. Robert also helped to finance other airlines, including Continental.

In his personal life, he was interested in racehorses and art. From the 1940s through the 1960s he raised and raced dozens of horses.

His art collection was one of the finest private collections in the United States. Some of his thousand or so paintings were exhibited at the Louvre in Paris in 1957. He also collected Gothic tapestries, Renaissance furniture, and other art works. In 1963 he endowed a chair of art history at Yale University, and in 1967 he gave $1 million to the Institute of Fine Arts at New York University. Also in 1967 he became chairman of the board of trustees at the Metropolitan Museum of Art, which received by donation his art collection in 1969.

Robert had three marriages. In 1923 he married Ruth Rumsey, but they divorced in 1931 with no children. In 1932 he married Ruth Owen Meeker, with whom he had a son. His final marriage, in 1952, was to Lee Anz Lynn; they had no children.

Robert Lehman died in Sands Point, Long Island, on August 9, 1969.

THE
MAIMONS

THE MAIMONS WERE THE FOREMOST FAMILY of scholars in medieval Jewry.

Maimon ben Joseph (c. 1110–c. 1165), a highly respected scholar, guided and comforted the Jews who were forced to convert to Islam. He wrote an important epistle on this topic as well as a book on the laws of prayer, a commentary on the Torah, and other works.

His son Moses ben Maimon became famous under the name of Moses Maimonides (1135–1204), widely regarded as the greatest postbiblical figure in Judaism. His contributions in philosophy and talmudic scholarship have for centuries influenced Jews and non-Jews alike.

Moses Maimonides' only son, Abraham ben Moses Maimon (1186–1237), succeeded his father as head of the Egyptian Jews. Abraham made his own mark as a scholar, writing a comprehensive halakic code and other works.

MAIMON BEN JOSEPH

SCHOLAR AND SPIRITUAL GUIDE

Maimon ben Joseph was one of the most outstanding Jewish scholars of his time. In his life and writings he guided and comforted Jews who had been forced to convert to Islam, and his principles greatly influenced the philosophy of his son Moses Maimonides.

Maimon was born in Spain in about 1110. He studied in Lucena under Joseph ben Migash and then became a distinguished rabbi in Córdoba.

Though a part of Islamic Spain, Córdoba had long allowed its Jewish citizens religious freedom. But in 1148 a fanatic Islamic sect, the Almohads, captured the city and began forcing Jews to submit to Islam or to leave. For the next eleven years Maimon and his family—including a daughter and two sons (Moses and David)—lived in Córdoba by publicly disguising their beliefs and privately practicing their Judaism.

About 1159 Maimon and his family moved to Fez, Morocco. While he was in Morocco, he forbade the people to follow the popular false prophet Moses Dari.

In 1165 the family briefly visited Palestine before moving to Egypt, finally settling in Fostat, near Cairo. There they were free to practice their faith openly.

Maimon wrote many scholarly works. One of the most widely known and influential was an open letter of consolation to Jews forced to convert to Islam. He had two goals in the letter: to comfort the forced converts and to preserve Judaism. His basic premise, later adopted by his son Moses, was that Islam, being free from a personification of the Deity, was not an idolatrous religion; therefore, he opposed martyrdom to avoid conversion. Thus Jews could in good conscience accept Islam publicly while retaining Judaism in their hearts.

In his letter Maimon emphasized the importance of belief in the divinity of the mission of Moses, whose virtues lie at the core of the work. Maimon compared such belief with belief in God. This idea was later utilized in Moses Maimonides' Thirteen Principles.

Maimon wrote important Talmud commentaries, later often quoted by his son Moses. Other works by the father include responsa, a commentary on the Torah, and a book on the laws of prayer and the festivals.

Maimon ben Joseph died shortly after arriving in Egypt, probably in 1165 or 1166.

MOSES MAIMONIDES

FOREMOST INTELLECTUAL OF MEDIEVAL JUDAISM

Philosopher, theologian, talmudic scholar, physician—Moses Maimonides, known as Rambam (an acronym for Rabbi Moses ben Maimon), utilized all of these roles to raise himself above all others in intellectual achievement among Jews in the Middle Ages. He was arguably the most gifted and influential Jew since biblical times.

Originally named Moses ben Maimon, he was born in Córdoba, Spain, on March 30, 1135. His father was the learned scholar Maimon ben Joseph. Moses studied under his father and other masters, and he early developed a surprising depth in his understanding of Judaism and other subjects.

In 1159 he moved with his father and other family members to Fez, Morocco. There Moses continued his studies in rabbinics and Greek philosophy and added medicine to them. In 1165 the family moved to Palestine and then to Egypt, settling in Fostat, near Cairo.

Soon after arriving in Egypt, his father died. Then, in 1169, a shipwreck took the life of his younger brother, David, a prosperous jewelry merchant who had supported Moses' scholarly work. Faced with the need to earn a living, Moses took advantage of his earlier medical studies and became a practicing physician. In 1177 he was appointed head of the Jewish community of Fostat (his leadership was recognized throughout Egypt and much of the rest of the Mediterranean region), and in 1185 he became court physician to the Egyptian sultan Saladin. Moses held both positions for the rest of his life.

He was married twice. His first wife died young. In Egypt he took a second wife, the sister of a man named ibn Almali, one of the royal secretaries. Ibn Almali himself married Moses' only sister. One son, Abraham, came of Moses' second marriage.

In his earliest writings Moses was influenced by Aristotelian philosophy and astronomy. At the age of sixteen he wrote a treatise on technical terms used in logic. Another early piece was an essay on the Jewish calendar. He composed both of these works in Arabic.

His mature writings are headed by three great works. In his *Commentary on the Mishnah*, also written in Arabic, he clarified words and

Maimonides

phrases, often calling on his knowledge of science, archaeology, and theology. The work includes several introductory essays that explore general philosophical issues in the Mishnah. One of the essays summarizes Judaism in the famous Thirteen Articles of Faith.

His *Mishneh Torah* ("The Torah Reviewed" or "The Second Torah"), written in Hebrew, is a monumental synthesis and codification of all Jewish law and doctrine. The most comprehensive work of its genre, it covers the full range of classical rabbinic law, including laws that were outdated even in Moses Maimonides' own day, such as laws of the Temple and laws concerning the government of a Jewish monarchy in biblical times. Central to the importance of this code are its many ethical, religious, and philosophical discussions.

Moses' third major work is *The Guide for the Perplexed*, written in Arabic and later translated into Hebrew and other languages. In it he called for a form of Judaism based on rational philosophy, blending ideas from science, philosophy, and religion. He wrote it as a response to the confusion felt by many contemporary Jews who were torn between the doctrines of Aristotelian philosophy and a literal reading of rabbinic Judaism.

Besides producing those three towering literary achievements, Moses wrote a number of significant works of lesser scope. *The Book of the Commandments*, written in Arabic as a digest of laws for unsophisticated readers, enumerates the 613 biblical commandments and classifies them into the fourteen categories around which Moses structured his *Mishneh Torah*. *Hilkhot ha-Yerushalmi* ("Laws of Jerusalem"), written in Hebrew, is a digest of the laws in the Palestinian Talmud. His other works include essays and letters in which he comforted Jews who had been forcibly converted to Islam, addressed the nature of the Messiah, and explored astrology. He also wrote a number of works on medicine, including a popular miscellany of health rules.

Moses' advanced views, notably his rationalistic approach to religious doctrines, created a controversy that began in his lifetime and lasted for centuries. But eventually he was universally acknowledged as a pillar of traditional faith and the greatest of all Jewish philosophers. His writings greatly influenced later intellectuals, both Jews and non-Jews, including medieval scholastic writers Benedict de Spinoza, Gottfried Leibniz, and Moses Mendelssohn.

Moses Maimonides died in Egypt on December 13, 1204. He was buried in Tiberias in the Holy Land, where his grave is still a shrine for pilgrims.

ABRAHAM BEN MOSES MAIMON

DEFENDER OF MOSES MAIMONIDES

Abraham ben Moses Maimon (also called Abraham Maimuni or Abulmeni) earned a significant reputation as an independent Jewish scholar. But he is best remembered today for his intellectual defenses of his father, Moses Maimonides.

Abraham was born in Fostat, Egypt, in 1186. He had the difficult task of following in the footsteps of his illustrious father, the greatest Jewish scholar of the medieval period. Abraham succeeded his father as the head of the Egyptian Jews and as a physician at the Egyptian court.

Not content to rest solely on the family laurels, he cultivated a great depth of learning in his own right. Nevertheless, the memory of his father dominated his life, and he spent much of his career combating attacks on the ideas of Moses Maimonides. For example, when Daniel ben Saadia Hababli objected to Maimonides' talmudic writings, Abraham responded with coolly learned explanations. However, when his father's religious sentiments were questioned by anti-Maimonideans, the son reacted with heated indignation.

Abraham produced a large body of writings, notably a comprehensive halakic code that was later edited and published in English as *The High Ways to Perfection* (two volumes, 1927 and 1938). He also wrote responsa, a public letter addressed to the opponents of his father's philosophical system, and an unfinished commentary on the Pentateuch.

Abraham ben Moses Maimon died in Fostat in 1237.

THE
MENDELSSOHNS

FOR THREE GENERATIONS in the late eighteenth and early nineteenth centuries, the Mendelssohns were the leading symbol of Jewish assimilation into German culture.

Moses Mendelssohn (1729–86), a renowned philosopher, greatly contributed to the emancipation and assimilation of European Jews through his leadership of the Haskalah (Jewish Enlightenment).

His son Abraham Mendelssohn (1776–1835), a banker, married Lea Salomon (daughter of wealthy Berlin Jews) in 1804. In 1813 he personally paid to equip a volunteer armed force to fight against French invaders. After the victory over the French, he became a town councillor in Berlin and rose to great social prominence. His home developed into the most important salon in Berlin. It was the site of many theatrical performances, literary readings, and concerts. Guests included famous people of music, science, theater, philosophy, and other fields.

Abraham and Lea had four children: Fanny (1805–1847), Felix (1809–1847), Rebecka (1811–58), and Paul (1813–74). In 1816 Abraham, somewhat of a religious skeptic because of his early exposure to his father's rationalist philosophy, had his children baptized into the Lutheran church for the purely practical purpose of attaining civil equality for them. In 1822, when Abraham and Lea also converted, the family took the dual surname

Mendelssohn Bartholdy (without a hyphen, which was adopted later by Paul's descendants). The name Bartholdy was borrowed from Lea's brother, originally named Jakob Salomon, who had changed his surname to Bartholdy after purchasing a Berlin garden formerly owned by someone of that name.

Fanny, who married the painter Wilhelm Hensel, became an excellent pianist and composer. She published songs, piano works, and choral pieces. Rebecka studied singing and married the mathematics professor Peter Dirichlet. Paul was a cellist and financier. The pride of the generation was Felix, who became one of the most important figures in the history of Western music. Abraham described himself as "a mere dash" between Moses and Felix. "Once I was the son of my father," he lamented; "now I am the father of my son."

Moses Mendelssohn

GREATEST JEWISH PHILOSOPHER OF THE EIGHTEENTH CENTURY

Moses Mendelssohn was the principal initiator of the Haskalah, a movement among eighteenth-century European Jews to acquaint the Jewish masses with European languages and secular education and culture. The Haskalah was the Jewish form of the Enlightenment.

Moses was born in Dessau, Anhalt (a former state in central Germany), on September 26, 1729. Son of a poor Jewish scribe named Menachem Mendel Dessau (or Mendel of Dessau), Moses was originally known as Moses Dessau. He later took the surname Mendelssohn, a Germanized form of the Hebrew *ben Mendel* ("son of Mendel"). His new name reflected his belief in the acculturation to German life that he sought for other Jews.

In 1743 he followed his Talmud teacher, Rabbi David Fränkel, to Berlin, Prussia. There Moses lived for years in terrible poverty while he engaged in secular studies against the wishes of many local Jewish elders, who forbade the learning of German and tried

Moses Mendelssohn

to restrict access to Christian sources of information. But Moses had an obsessive hunger for knowledge. By the age of twenty he had studied not only Hebrew and the Talmud but also German, French, English, Latin, Greek, mathematics, literature, and philosophy.

In 1750 Moses accepted a job as tutor of the children of Issak Bernhard, a silk manufacturer. Later Moses entered Bernhard's business, first as a bookkeeper and then as a partner.

In 1762 Moses married a young Jewish woman named Fromet Gugenheim. They had three sons and three daughters who reached maturity.

Though physically disadvantaged by being extremely small, frankly unattractive, and hunchbacked, Moses cultivated an intellect, integrity, and charm through which he became one of the few Jews to overcome the social and legal restrictions of his time. He was widely admired and honored in the gentile world, where he was known by such epithets as "the Jewish Socrates" and "the German Plato."

In his early writings Moses concentrated on general philosophical issues. He was a popular philosopher in the sense that his concerns were empirical and nonsystematic, and his style was easy to read. His first work, *Philosophical Speeches* (1755), praises the German philosopher Leibniz. His *Letters on Feelings* (1755) stresses the spiritual significance of human feelings.

In 1763 he wrote his "Essay on Evidence in Metaphysical Science," comparing the demonstrability of metaphysical propositions with that of mathematical propositions. The essay won a prize from the Prussian Academy of Arts and prompted King Frederick the Great to grant Moses the status of "protected Jew," exempting him from the legal disabilities to which Jews were usually subjected.

In *Phaedo; or, On the Immortality of the Soul* (1767), Moses defends the idea of immortality against the prevalent mechanistic philosophy. The soul, Moses says, is simple and indestructible. The book is presented in the form of a dialogue in imitation of Plato's *Phaedo*.

In 1769 the Swiss theologian Johann Caspar Lavater challenged Moses to become a Christian unless Moses could refute the arguments for Christianity. Moses deplored religious controversy; but, after a great internal struggle—leading, in fact, to a nervous breakdown in 1771—he answered the challenge and in the process reaffirmed his religious heritage. In essence, Moses replied that the deism of the En
lightenment, which he himself had helped to develop into a universal religion of reason, was identical with Judaism.

The Lavater episode marked a turning point in Moses Mendelssohn's career. He now began his true life's work: the emancipation and assimilation of European Jews.

Moses had always been deeply involved with the Jewish community. He had composed prayers, hymns, and sermons for use in Berlin synagogues. And Jewish groups and individuals had often sought his advice.

But now, in the 1770s, Moses began to make a conscious effort to build a permanent bridge between the Christian and Jewish communities. For example, in 1778 he wrote a précis of Jewish laws and customs for use in Prussian courts.

From 1780 to 1783 he prepared a version of the Pentateuch translated into German but printed (in 1783) in Hebrew characters, a symbolic fusion of the German and Jewish cultures. The translation and accompanying commentary had a revolutionary impact on German Jewry who, through it, learned the German language and received a rational explanation of the Torah.

Moses supported a modernization of Jewish education,

including European-style secular studies. In 1781 he initiated a Jewish Free School in Berlin. Other cities soon adopted a similar plan.

The great culminating work of his life was *Jerusalem; or, On Religious Power and Judaism* (1783). In this book Moses asserts that there is no essential conflict between the truths of religion and those of reason. One proof of this assertion is the fact that all monotheistic religions tend to be merely different interpretations of one eternal truth. Therefore, societies should practice religious and political toleration, separation of church and state, and freedom of thought and conscience for Jews and non-Jews alike.

Moses almost single-handedly guided German Jews out of the ghetto and into the movements for emancipation and assimilation. Through his advocacy of religious toleration and through the prestige of his intellectual accomplishments, he did much to further the emancipation of Jews from the social, cultural, political, and economic restrictions placed on Jews in Germany. Through the example of his own life, he showed that it was possible to combine the tenets of Judaism with the rationality of the Enlightenment, a blend that he formulated and expressed as the hallmark of the Haskalah movement, which had as its main goal the assimilation of Jews into the mainstream of modern European culture. He fought against the extremism of both anti-Semites and conservative Jews for the cultural and political union of Christians and Jews. "What a world of bliss we would live in," he said, "if all men adopted the true principles which the best of the Christians and the best of the Jews hold in common."

Moses Mendelssohn, the greatest Jewish philosopher of the eighteenth century, died in Berlin on January 4, 1786.

Felix Mendelssohn

CONCERT INNOVATOR AND UNIQUE COMPOSER

Felix Mendelssohn, grandson of the philosopher Moses Mendelssohn, holds a dual place in music history: he laid the groundwork for modern symphonic organizations and concerts, and he composed a rich body of music in a personal blend of romantic and classical elements.

Jakob Ludwig Felix Mendelssohn was born in Hamburg, Germany, on February 3, 1809. He was the second of the four children, and the older of the two sons, of Abraham and Lea (Salomon) Mendelssohn. Abraham, a wealthy banker, was a son of Moses Mendelssohn, the famed philosopher. When Felix was two years old, his family moved to Berlin, a hotbed of anti-Semitism. Despite the boy's baptism into the Lutheran church in 1816, the sensitive Felix suffered much from anti-Semitism, including at least one stoning. In 1822 the family changed its surname to Mendelssohn Bartholdy to deemphasize its Jewish origins.

As an adult, Felix, proud of his heritage but thoroughly assimilated into German culture, adopted an ambivalent attitude toward his religious-racial identity. He considered himself a Protestant, largely because of his deep commitment to the Lutheran musical tradition of Johann Sebastian Bach. Yet he was known to refer to himself frankly as a Jew. When Felix began to earn an international reputation, his father urged him to drop the name Mendelssohn ("If Mendelssohn is your name, you are ipso facto a Jew") and become simply Felix Bartholdy. But Felix refused. He knew that because of his famous grandfather, Moses, people preferred to call the young musician Mendelssohn, under which name he scored his early successes. He therefore saw to it that the world knew him as Felix Mendelssohn, though many of his works were published under the name Felix Mendelssohn Bartholdy.

Felix was educated privately at his Berlin home, at first by his parents (his father teaching arithmetic and French, his mother teaching German, literature, and the fine arts, including piano) and later by a succession of teachers in many fields. His music studies included piano, violin, viola, cello, voice, theory, and composition.

Felix's earliest extant compositions date from 1820, when he was eleven years old. The young composer's artistic growth was helped immensely by the wealth of his father, who hired large ensembles of musicians to perform his son's works, including symphonies and comic operas, under Felix's own direction in the family home.

The rich cultural atmosphere in the home nurtured Felix's natural gifts into an early blossoming. Stimulated by some lines from Goethe's *Faust*, young Mendelssohn, in 1825, wrote his *String Octet*. The following year he composed what is still his most popular work: the overture to Shakespeare's play *A Midsummer Night's Dream*. No one in the history of Western music, not even Mozart, has written such gloriously inspired and polished music at the tender ages of sixteen and seventeen.

In March 1829 Felix conducted a revival of Bach's *St. Matthew Passion* at the Berlin Singing Academy. It was the first performance of the work since the composer's death in 1750 and the event that ushered in the modern realization of Bach's true stature.

From 1829 to 1835 Felix, because his parents felt that traveling was essential for a complete education, made a series of visits to leading European music capitals. Many of his compositions were directly affected by his travels. For example, his 1829 visit to Edinburgh generated the first ideas for his *Third* (or *Scottish*) *Symphony* (1842). In the same year, a stormy steamship crossing to the Hebrides (islands off the west coast of Scotland) and a visit to the famous cave there inspired his concert overture *The Hebrides* (1830), also known as *Fingal's Cave*. An 1830 visit to Italy occasioned the beginning of his *Fourth* (or *Italian*) *Symphony* (1833).

From 1833 to 1835 he served as the music director of the provincial German town of Düsseldorf. He directed Catholic church music, organized concerts, conducted operas, and arranged several Handel oratorios for performance, an activity that inspired his own Handel-like oratorio *St. Paul* (1836). During 1829–35 he also composed many of his early poetic little piano pieces called *Songs without Words*.

In 1835 Felix was asked to take over the Gewandhaus Concerts in Leipzig. He jumped at the opportunity to rise from the sleepy village of Düsseldorf to a major city—especially because Leipzig had been the home of his idol, Bach. The years that Felix spent in Leipzig (1835–47) as conductor, music organizer, and performer were the most significant period of his life.

He revolutionized orchestral playing. Previously orchestras had been directed by one of the performers, usually the first violinist. Felix was among the first independent, baton-wielding conductors in the modern sense, and he trained the Gewandhaus Orchestra into one of the most precise ensembles of the era.

His work as a music organizer in Leipzig was also revolutionary. Before he arrived, the most frequently played composers had been minor, now-forgotten figures. But he cultivated his audiences' musical appreciation by programming the finest music available, both old and new. He made Mozart and Beethoven the backbone of his repertory, followed by Bach, Handel, Haydn, and Weber. One of the most important music events of the era was the world premiere of Schubert's *Ninth* (or *Great*) *Symphony*, conducted by Felix in 1839, eleven years after the composer's death. He also encouraged, with performances, such living composers as Frédéric Chopin, Franz Liszt, and Robert Schumann. Felix developed a close friendship with Schumann and his wife, the pianist Clara Schumann (née Wieck), whom Schumann married in 1840.

Not only important composers but also eminent performers were attracted to the Gewandhaus Concerts under Felix. He invited such soloists as the pianists Franz Liszt and Anton Rubinstein, the violinist Joseph Joachim, and the singer Jenny Lind. Felix himself performed as a pianist and organist.

Moreover, he did away with the customary variety programs and began to organize concerts in the modern fashion: an overture, a large-scale work, a concerto or another large-scale work, and a shorter piece. He refused to go along with the tradition of separating the movements of a symphony by inserting lighter forms of music.

His innovations at the Leipzig Gewandhaus—training the orchestra into a precision unit, playing important old works as well as significant new ones, recruiting outstanding performers, and organizing well-structured programs—laid the groundwork for modern symphonic organizations and concerts.

During his Leipzig years, Felix went though great changes in his personal life. In November 1835 he was shattered by the death of his father. In March 1837 he married Cécile Jeanrenaud, daughter of a deceased Calvinist pastor. They had five children, none of whom was musically gifted.

Cécile was a cultured woman, but she was unmusical. It was his sister Fanny, a pianist and composer, to whom Felix always turned for musical discussion and advice.

While retaining his connection with the Gewandhaus Concerts, Felix performed other major musical functions. In 1841 the king of Prussia asked him to take charge of an expanded program of musical activities in Berlin. One of his duties there was to compose incidental music for plays, including Shakespeare's *A Midsummer Night's Dream* (1842). In some of the pieces for that work, he used themes from the overture that he had written sixteen years earlier. The music is particularly remarkable for having so thoroughly captured an English spirit. In fact, Felix was an Anglophile, and in his numerous visits to England, that nation fully returned his affection.

Discouraged by a lack of cooperation from his superiors in Berlin, Felix finally withdrew from his post there in 1844. Meanwhile, however, in 1843 he had become the first director of the newly established Leipzig Conservatory, where he again proved successful at organization. He formed a faculty that included some of the finest musicians of the time, such as Ferdinand David (violin) and Robert Schumann (piano and composition).

In May 1847 Felix's sister Fanny suddenly died. He composed

his last great work, the deeply moving F-minor *Sixth String Quartet* (1847), as a memorial for Fanny.

Already having shown signs of increasing weakness before his sister's death, Felix could not recover from the emotional and physical drain that he suffered when he lost her. After a series of strokes, he died in Leipzig on November 4, 1847, at the age of only thirty-eight. He was buried in Berlin, next to Fanny.

Felix Mendelssohn's music combines romantic and classical elements. Living during a period of growing romanticism, he often adopted the romantics' use of literature and other extramusical stimuli to inspire compositions. He was strongly influenced in that direction by the philosopher Hegel (whom Felix met at his parents' home), who held that even instrumental music should not only have its own abstract structure but also express something, however indeterminate. Yet, influenced by his father's conservatism, the classical sense of form and aristocracy in the works of the author Goethe (whom young Felix met several times), as well as his own personal inclinations, Felix wrote music that, despite the romantic extramusical references, displays the techniques, forms, clarity, elegance, and grace of eighteenth-century classical and preclassical music.

By his mid-teens, he had already absorbed the romantic and classical elements of his creative nature and developed his own personal characteristics as well, such as small-scale rhythmic figures, melodies that incorporate a variety of motives, and flexibility in the use of traditional forms. The *String Octet* exemplifies all of these characteristics, as do the incidental music to *A Midsummer Night's Dream*, the *Italian* and *Scottish* symphonies, and many of his other compositions.

As the founder of modern symphonic organization and concerts and as the composer of a unique blend of romantic and classical elements, Felix Mendelssohn earned a place of special distinction in the history of Western music and proved to be a worthy final member of three generations of outstanding Mendelssohns.

THE
NETANYAHUS

T HE NETANYAHUS HOLD A PROMINENT PLACE in the history of modern Israel. In both theory and practice, they have aided Israel's creation and continued strength.

In the early 1920s, Benzion Netanyahu (1910–) moved from his native Poland to Palestine, where he became one of the intellectual fathers of the revisionist movement, a militant Zionist wing that eventually evolved into Israel's Likud political party. Later, in the United States, he had a long, distinguished career as a professor of, and writer on, Jewish studies.

His sons—Jonathan (1946–76), Benjamin (1949–), and Iddo (1952–)—took more activist roles in Israel's affairs. The first served as field commander of the famous July 1976 Israeli raid that rescued over one hundred hostages held by terrorists at an airport in Entebbe, Uganda. Jonathan ("Yoni"), the only Israeli commando killed during the mission, became a national hero. Benjamin was elected prime minister of Israel on the Likud ticket in May 1996, becoming the youngest to hold that office, the first to be voted for directly by the Israeli people, and the most distinctly hard-line prime minister in many years in his views toward the Arabs. Iddo, like both of his older brothers, served in the Sayeret Matcal ("Border Reconnaissance"), an elite antiterrorist army unit.

Benzion Netanyahu

HISTORIAN

Early in his career, Benzion Netanyahu made his mark as a Zionist writer and editor. Later he became one of the world's most respected professors and writers of Jewish history.

He was born in Poland on March 25, 1910. His parents were Nathan and Sarah (Lurie) Mileikowsky. Nathan, a rabbi who gave Zionist lectures, immigrated with his family in 1920 to Palestine, became an educator, and changed the family name to the Hebrew *Netanyahu* ("God gave").

Benzion adopted his father's Zionist views, becoming an early activist in the militant revisionist movement. The revisionists believed that revenge attacks against the enemies of Zionism were justified and that the borders of the modern Jewish state should include the land that is now Jordan. After graduating from Hebrew Teachers Seminary in Jerusalem (teacher's diploma, 1929) and Hebrew University of Jerusalem (M.A., 1933), Benzion co-edited the Hebrew monthly *Betar* (1933–34), edited the revisionist daily *Hayarden* ("The Jordan," 1934–35), and edited the Zionist Political Library in Jerusalem and Tel Aviv (1935–40).

From 1940 to 1948 he lived in the United States as the executive director of the New Zionist Organization of America in New York City. In 1944 he married Cela Segal, daughter of a Lithuanian-American businessman who had earlier lived in Palestine. They had three sons. In 1947 Benzion earned a Ph.D. degree at Dropsie College (later the Annenberg Research Institute) in Philadelphia, Pennsylvania.

In 1948 he returned to the Holy Land, now the new state of Israel. There, in Jerusalem, he became the editor in chief of the *Encyclopedia Hebraica*, a position he held till 1962.

In 1957 Benzion came back to the United States as a visiting professor of Hebrew language and literature at Dropsie College. From 1959 to 1962 he was again in Israel, finishing his tenure with the *Encyclopedia Hebraica*. In 1962 he resumed his position at

Dropsie College, where from 1966 to 1968 he served as professor of medieval Jewish history and Hebrew literature. He then taught Hebraic studies at the University of Denver, Colorado (1968–71).

In 1971 he began his long association with Cornell University in Ithaca, New York. He served as professor of Judaic studies (1971–78), chairman of the department of Semitic languages and literatures (1971–75), and professor emeritus (since 1978).

Benzion, as editor and writer, has produced a huge volume of literature in Jewish studies. He edited and contributed to Theodore Herzl's *Letters, 1896–1904* (in Hebrew, 1937; second edition, 1949); edited Israel Zangwill's *Road to Independence: Collected Works on the Jewish Question* (in Hebrew, 1938); edited *Zionews* (of the New Zionist Organization of America, 1942–44); edited and contributed to Max Nordau's *Collected Works* (in Hebrew, four volumes, 1954–62); coedited the *Jewish Quarterly Review* (1959–60); served as general editor of the first volume of *The World History of the Jewish People* (1964); and issued many similar works.

His original book-length scholarly studies have had great impact in their fields. They include *Don Isaac Abravanel: Statesman and Philosopher* (1953; third edition, 1972) and *The Marranos of Spain* (1966; second edition, 1973).

Perhaps his greatest acheivement was his success in raising his sons. All three—Jonathan, Benjamin, and Iddo—served in the elite Sayeret Matcal ("Border Reconnaissance") army unit. Jonathan became a national hero when he was killed leading the famous raid that rescued over one hundred Jews held by terrorists at Entebbe, Uganda, in 1976. In 1996 Benjamin was elected prime minister of Israel for the Likud party, which had evolved from the revisionist movement.

In 1995 Benzion published his monumental *The Origins of the Inquisition in Fifteenth-Century Spain*. He dedicated the work "with unrelieved grief to the memory of my beloved son Jonathan."

JONATHAN NETANYAHU

LEADER OF THE RAID ON ENTEBBE

Jonathan Netanyahu was one of Israel's most promising young military commanders. He led the famous July 1976 operation that rescued over one hundred hostages in Entebbe, Uganda, where he was killed.

Jonathan, or Yonatan ("Yoni"), was born in the Harlem section of New York City on March 13, 1946. He was the oldest of the three sons of Benzion and Cela (Segal) Netanyahu. Benzion, a zealous Zionist, had lived much of his life in Palestine, and when the Israeli War of Independence broke out in 1948, he returned with his family to Israel.

They settled in 1949 in Talpiot and moved in 1953 to Katamon, both suburbs of Jerusalem. Jonathan began school in Jerusalem, studied for a time in the United States while his father taught at Dropsie College (1957–59), spent more time in Jerusalem (1959–62), and returned to the United States (1962), where he finished high school.

In 1964 Jonathan joined the Israeli army and volunteered for the paratroops. He rose to first lieutenant and became a platoon leader. During the Six-Day War in 1967, he fought in the Sinai and on the Golan Heights, where he was wounded in his left elbow and lost the full use of that arm.

Shortly after the war, he was married in Israel. He and his wife, Tutti, had two children, neither of whom survived. Jonathan and Tutti separated in 1972.

During a brief interlude away from the military, he studied history and philosophy at Harvard University (1967–68). Returning to Israel (1968), he studied mathematics and philosophy at Hebrew University.

In 1969 he rejoined the paratroops and was assigned to a reconnaissance unit, having been recruited by his younger brother Benjamin, already a member. Jonathan became a captain in 1970, distinguished himself as a company leader in campaigns along

Israel's borders, rose to second in command of a battalion, and in May 1973 was promoted to major.

That summer he studied at Harvard University, but in the autumn he returned to Israel to fight in the 1973 Yom Kippur War. He led a paratroop unit on the Golan Heights and in Syria.

In December 1973 he began to attend the Sinai Armored School to learn how to command an armored tank battalion. In March 1974 he became a company commander with a tank battalion on the Golan Heights, and just two months later he was given command of an entire battalion. Jonathan greatly improved the fighting condition of the unit and led it in battle against the Syrians till the July cease-fire. At the end of his tour with the tank corps, he gave his battalion an address that has been printed in military manuals. He spoke of the responsibilities of command, stressed the importance of attention to detail, and exhorted the soldiers to strive for perfection.

In 1975 he left the tank corps for a paratroop command. In that same year, he received the Distinguished Conduct Medal for his role during the 1973 Yom Kippur War.

In late June 1976 four terrorists (two Palestinians and two West Germans) hijacked an Air France airplane, originating in Tel Aviv and destined for Paris, after its takeoff from Athens, Greece, and forced it to land at Entebbe, Uganda. The terrorists released the non-Jewish passengers but detained over one hundred hostages, mostly Israeli citizens, at the airport. The price demanded for the freedom of the Jews was the release of dozens of terrorists in several countries. The government of Israel immediately planned a rescue operation, made extremely difficult by the great distance involved (over two thousand miles) and the hostility of the Ugandan president, Idi Amin, who supplied the terrorists with a guard of sixty Ugandan soldiers.

Jonathan, by now a lieutenant colonel, was selected as the field commander of the operation. He himself sketched the plan for the complex, dangerous mission. Because of the great distance, the limited time, and the vulnerability of the hostages, a full-scale army could not be sent. The rescue had to be made by a small force acting with lightning speed and with no margin for error. Once the plan was made, Jonathan ruthlessly drilled his soldiers over and over again, constantly striving for perfection.

On July 3, at 3:30 P.M. local time, four airplanes took off from Israel. Seven hours later they arrived at Entebbe. Jonathan and his force jumped off their airplane, ran to the terminal housing the hostages, and killed the terrorists. While Jonathan stood by the entrance to the terminal, a Ugandan sniper in the control tower shot him. Mortally wounded, Jonathan was placed aboard one of the airplanes. Less than an hour after the rescue force arrived, the airplane carrying the freed hostages (three of whom had been killed in the operation) left for the flight back to Israel.

By thoroughly drilling his soldiers to perfection, he ensured the success of one of the greatest rescue missions in history. Jonathan Netanyahu died on the airplane after the mission was completed. The official date was listed as July 4, 1976.

A collection of his letters was posthumously edited by his brother Benjamin and published as *Self-Portrait of a Hero: The Letters of Jonathan Netanyahu, (1963–76)* (1980), with notes by Benjamin and a Foreword and an Afterword by both Benjamin and Iddo, Jonathan's other brother. "Death . . . doesn't frighten me . . . ," Jonathan wrote in a letter when he was only seventeen. "I do not fear it, because I attribute little value to a life without purpose. And if I should have to sacrifice my life to attain its goal, I'll do so willingly."

Benjamin Netanyahu

ISRAEL'S GET-TOUGH PRIME MINISTER

When he was elected prime minister of Israel in May 1996, Benjamin Netanyahu became the youngest ever to win that office and the first to be elected directly by popular vote. Most significantly, he represented a fundamental change in the nation's direction because of his strong opposition to the land-for-peace diplomacy that his recent predecessors had used in dealing with the Arabs.

Benjamin, or Binyamin ("Bibi"), was born in Tel Aviv on October 21, 1949, and he spent his early years living in Jerusalem suburbs. He was the middle of the three sons of Benzion and Cela (Segal) Netanyahu. His father had been a zealous Zionist in the militant revisionist movement, which evolved into the Likud political party. Benzion, who became a noted professor of, and writer on, Jewish studies, often told Benjamin and his brothers about the struggle to create the Jewish state and about the revisionists' belief that revenge attacks against Arabs were justified and that the borders of Israel should include Jordan.

At the age of fourteen Benjamin moved with his family to the United States, where his father had accepted a teaching position at Dropsie College in Philadelphia, Pennsylvania. In the spring of 1967 Benjamin finished high school and returned to Israel to witness the June Six-Day War, in which Israel tripled its size by capturing lands formerly controlled by Arabs.

Later that year he joined the Israeli army and was accepted into a secret unit called Sayeret Matcal ("Border Reconnaissance"), an elite force specializing in antiterrorist raids behind enemy lines. In one of his earliest missions, in 1968, he and his team blew up thirteen unoccupied airplanes at Beirut International Airport in Lebanon in retaliation for the hijacking of an El Al airplane by Lebanon-based Palestinian terrorists. In 1972 he and other Sayeret soldiers stormed an airplane that had been hijacked by terrorists and forced to park at an airport outside Tel Aviv. He received an arm wound in the operation, which successfully rescued one hundred people. Benjamin became a captain and recruited his brothers, Jonathan and Iddo, into the unit. For a short time, all three brothers served together, achieving legendary status in the country.

When his tour of service ended in 1972, Benjamin returned to the United States and enrolled at the Massachusetts Institute of Technology (MIT). A year later he fought with Israel in the Yom Kippur War, serving in the Sinai and on the Golan Heights. Resuming his studies, he earned a B.A. degree in architecture and an

M.B.A. degree in business management (1976). From 1976 to 1978 he worked as a management consultant for the Boston Consulting Group.

In 1978 he moved back to Israel, where he founded the Jonathan Institute, a memorial to his brother Jonathan, who had been killed while leading the famous rescue of one hundred Israelis held hostage by terrorists at Entebbe, Uganda, in 1976. Benjamin organized the institute, located in Jerusalem, to study the origins of, and the best ways to combat, terrorism. He also honored his brother's memory by collecting and editing Jonathan's letters, publishing them as *Self-Portrait of a Hero: The Letters of Jonathan Netanyahu, (1963–1976)* (1980).

Benjamin Netanyahu

Yeshiva University Public Relations Department

After serving for two years as executive director of the Jonathan Institute, Benjamin worked from 1980 to 1982 as a marketing manager for Rim Industries, a Jerusalem furniture company. During those years he became increasingly involved in Israeli politics, aligning himself with the Likud party, to whose birth his father had contributed. Benjamin may have been influenced in his new interest when he edited his brother's letters, in some of which Jonathan revealed that he was considering leaving his army career to enter politics. Benjamin now began to fulfill his dead brother's ambition.

In 1982, through his acquaintance with Moshe Arens, a Likud leader recently named ambassador to the United States, Benjamin became deputy chief of mission at the Israeli Embassy in Washington, D.C. He served effectively for two years.

From 1984 to 1988 he held the important post of Israel's permanent representative to the United Nations in New York City. Because of Benjamin's thorough knowledge of English and his willingness to speak bluntly, American journalists often sought him out for comments on Middle Eastern issues.

In 1988 he resigned his United Nations post and entered electoral politics, winning a seat in the Knesset, Israel's parliament. He was also appointed deputy minister of foreign affairs. In January 1991 he gained international renown when he served as his country's chief spokesperson during the Persian Gulf War. During American television interviews he reflected his nation's strength and patience in allowing the United States to resolve the conflict while Israel endured Scud missile attacks from Iraq under the direction of President Saddam Hussein. Benjamin was also in charge of his government's contacts with the foreign press during the Madrid peace conference in October 1991 between Israel and its Arab neighbors. He showed a remarkable ability to "spin" information to his government's advantage.

Shortly after the Madrid conference, Prime Minister Yitzhak Shamir of the Likud party asked Benjamin to take the post of deputy minister in the prime minister's office. Benjamin accepted the job and held it till June 1992, when Shamir was replaced as prime minister by the Labor party's Yitzhak Rabin.

Shamir soon announced his retirement from public life, and an election was scheduled to select his replacement as head of the Likud party. A new system would allow the party's members to vote directly for their leader, who had previously been chosen by a small central committee. The new campaign emphasized American-style television interviews and political advertisements, in which Benjamin, because of his good looks and on-camera experience, had an advantage over his opponents. In March 1993 he won the election and became, at forty-three, the youngest person ever to lead a major Israeli political party.

For the next three years, from his seat in the Knesset, Benjamin served as the nation's official spokesperson for the opposition to the Labor-led government. He disagreed with Prime Minister Rabin's decision to recognize the Palestine Liberation Organization (PLO) and with the 1993 peace agreement in which Israel conceded territory in the Gaza Strip and the West Bank to Palestinian self-rule. Benjamin argued that the Palestinians should have control over their civilian affairs but that Israel's security depended on its military presence in those areas.

During this time he was heavily engaged in literary activity. He had earlier prepared *International Terrorism: Challenge and Response* (1981) and *Terrorism: How the West Can Win* (1986), which he edited from speeches given by various authorities at, respectively, 1979 and 1984 terrorism conferences he had hosted through the Jonathan Institute. His own writings include the books *A Place Among Nations: Israel and the World* (1993) and *Fighting Terrorism: How Democracies Can Defeat Domestic and International Terrorists* (1995).

Throughout 1994 and 1995, as more and more West Bank towns came under PLO control, Israeli right-wing extremists grew increasingly hostile toward Rabin. On November 4, 1995, he was assassinated as he left a peace rally in Tel Aviv by a non-Likud right-wing fanatic. Many Israelis, including Rabin's widow, Leah, publicly blamed Benjamin for not controlling the climate of hate that preceded the murder. He vigorously defended himself against the criticism, which he labeled "a classic case of guilt by association."

After Rabin's death, the foreign minister, Shimon Peres, took over the office of prime minister till an election could be held for a new national leader. Benjamin, the Likud candidate for the office, engaged in a heated campaign against Peres, the Labor candidate. Though Benjamin's popularity had slipped because of the criticism he received after the Rabin assassination, a rash of suicide bombings by Islamic fundamentalists in Israel in February and March raised his ratings because his principal theme was that Labor softness toward the PLO would increase the danger for Israel. Though by the time of the election he had conceded that the Israeli-Palestinian peace process should continue, he still felt that the Labor government had gone too far too fast; he promised to slow down the process so that the safety of Israelis would not be left in the hands of the PLO.

In late May 1996 Benjamin won the election by less than 1 percent of the popular vote. However, among Jewish citizens—as distinct from the Palestinian Israelis who voted—he led Peres by 55.5 percent to 44.5 percent. His strongest support came from Orthodox Jews, who feared that the Labor government was secularizing the country. This was the first election in which Israelis voted directly for their prime minister (instead of for members of parliament only); as in his 1993 run for the Likud leadership, he showed a remarkable flair for broad appeal through his polished public-relations image. Benjamin became the youngest Israeli prime minister; in fact, at forty-six, he was the first under the age of sixty.

One important aid in his victory was his third wife, Sara, a child psychologist. Israeli tradition did not allow her to take a major role in the campaign, but her intelligence and photogenic qualities provided excellent support for her husband. Three years earlier, during his campaign for the Likud leadership, Benjamin, to avoid being blackmailed, went on Israeli television and admitted to having had an extramarital affair. Sara stood by him. At the time of his election to the prime ministry, they had two sons. He also had a daughter from his first marriage, which, like his second, ended in divorce.

After his election Benjamin kept his campaign promise of a new get-tough policy toward Arabs in general and the PLO in particular. He sought peace—but only peace with assured security for Israel and its citizens. At a September 4, 1996, meeting with PLO leader Yasser Arafat, "I transmitted to the Palestinians," Benjamin reported, "that the era of one-sided giving is over, that the Palestinians will now have to give and not only receive."

In late September 1996 he gave permission for Israelis to open a previously sealed exit door for a tourist tunnel in Jerusalem. The door is located in the Muslim Quarter, and Palestinian protesters, upset at what they regarded as Israel's flaunting of its control over the city, immediately rioted. Prime Minister Benjamin Netanyahu, refusing to accept violence as a tool of diplomacy, vowed to keep the tunnel exit open.

THE
OCHSES

T HE OCHS FAMILY made important contributions
to American publishing. Their chief claim to fame
was their development of the *New York Times* into one
of the world's greatest newspapers.

Julius Ochs (1826–88) was born in Germany and immigrated
to the United States, where he became a merchant and a civic
leader. His eldest of three sons, Adolph Simon Ochs (1858–1935),
became a publishing tycoon, controlling various periodicals, notably the *Chattanooga Times* and the *New York Times*. Adolph's
younger brothers, George Washington Ochs Oakes (1861–1931)
and Milton Barlow Ochs (1864–1955), worked for Adolph's publishing empire in various editorial and executive capacities.
George, for example, edited *Current History*, and Milton served
as president of the Chattanooga Times Printing Company.

Adolph's only child, Iphigene Bertha Ochs (1892–1990), married Arthur Hays Sulzberger, through whom the *New York Times*
passed into the hands of the Sulzberger family. Adolph's nephew
Julius Ochs Adler (1892–1955) was the son of Adolph's sister Ada
and her husband, Harry Clay Adler, who was chairman of the board
of directors and general manager of the *Chattanooga Times*. Julius
worked at the *New York Times* as treasurer and vice president (1919–
35) and as general manager (1935–55). George Washington Oakes
(1909–1965), son of George Washington Ochs Oakes, became a
successful journalist and author.

JULIUS OCHS

PROMOTER OF PUBLIC WELFARE

Dissatisfied with his lot in Germany, Julius Ochs immigrated to the United States and engaged in various business enterprises. He showed his gratitude to his new homeland by serving as a leader in local military affairs during the Civil War and by participating in a wide range of activities for the public welfare.

Julius was born in Fürth, Bavaria (later part of Germany), on June 29, 1826. His parents were Lazarus and Nannie (Wetzler) Ochs. Lazarus spoke several languages fluently and was an authority on rabbinic law.

Julius, too, had linguistic gifts, and at an early age he could converse in German, English, French, and Italian. However, his apparent destiny of a professional career evaporated when, at his father's death, one of his brothers apprenticed him to a bookbinder. Julius disliked the work and escaped it in 1815 by immigrating to the United States and settling in Louisville, Kentucky, where some of his family members (a brother and two sisters), who had arrived earlier, were living.

Because of his knowledge of languages, he got a job teaching at the Female Academy in Mount Sterling, Kentucky. Soon, however, the school went bankrupt. During the next dozen years he was associated with business ventures in many cities, spending much of his time in the South, where his contact with slavery made him a firm abolitionist.

In 1855 he married Bertha Levy, a refugee from Rhenish Bavaria after the revolution of 1848. They had three daughters and three sons. The sons all became prominent in the journalistic world: Adolph Simon, George Washington, and Milton Barlow.

During the Civil War Julius lived in Cincinnati, Ohio. Despite his long previous residence in the South and his wife's Southern sympathies, he decided to help the Union side. In 1861 he organized a military company known as Julius Ochs Company, which became a part of Lieutenant Colonel A. E. Jones's Independent

Battalion of Ohio Volunteers and did guard duty in the state. Julius served both as captain and as adjutant to Jones. Later Julius moved to Knoxville, Tennessee, where he was an officer in a Union regiment that protected the city.

After the war he continued to live in Knoxville for thirteen years. In 1878 he went to Chattanooga to become treasurer of the *Chattanooga Times*, which his son Adolph had recently acquired.

Julius was noted for his integrity, kindness, tolerance, and devotion to the faith of his fathers. He poured all these virtues into many public activities. From 1868 to 1872 he was a justice of the peace and a member of the Knox County, Tennessee, court. In 1872 he was a delegate to the national convention of Liberal Republicans and supported Horace Greeley for the presidency. He was one of the commissioners who built the first bridge across the Tennessee River at Knoxville. For the small Jewish community in Knoxville, he acted as rabbi.

At Chattanooga he organized the first humane society there and helped to establish Erlanger Hospital. Julius also helped to build up a thriving Jewish congregation in the city, again acting as rabbi. He composed the light opera *The Megilah; or, The Story of Esther* for performance by Sabbath-school children. A synagogue erected in 1927 was named the Julius and Bertha Ochs Memorial Temple.

Julius Ochs died in Chattanooga on October 26, 1888.

Adolph Simon Ochs

THE MAN WHO SAVED THE *NEW YORK TIMES*

Adolph Simon Ochs was an American publisher who took over the failing *New York Times* and built it into one of the world's outstanding newspapers. He fought off the competition from the powerful yellow (sensational) journalism of his era and succeeded through a policy of comprehensiveness, accuracy, and balance—a policy reflected in his famous slogan, "All the News That's Fit to Print."

American Jewish Archives, Cincinnati Campus, Hebrew Union College-Jewish Institute of Religion

For Ida

Adolph Simon Ochs

Adolph was born in Cincinnati, Ohio, on March 12, 1858. His parents were Julius and Bertha (Levy) Ochs. Julius was a well-known social activist. The family moved to Knoxville, Tennessee, where Adolph, at the age of eleven, went to work as an office boy for a local newspaper, the *Knoxville Chronicle*. He had very little formal schooling, but his cultured parents gave him a good informal education. As Adolph later said, "The printing office was my high school and university."

In his teens he tried various jobs in several cities but always returned to Knoxville and the newspaper industry, learning the entire range of its news, business, and mechanical branches.

In 1877, at the age of nineteen, Adolph helped to establish a new publication, the *Chattanooga Dispatch*, and became its editor in chief. However, the newspaper soon failed.

In 1878 he borrowed $250 and bought a controlling interest in the *Chattanooga Times*. It, too, was on the verge of failure, but as its publisher (1878–1935) he developed it into one of the leading newspapers in the South. He was successful because, he said, he produced a paper that was "clean, dignified, and trustworthy."

Adolph also founded a business paper, the *Tradesman*, and helped to establish the Southern Associated Press, of which he was chairman from 1891 to 1894. From 1900 till his death he was a director of the nationwide Associated Press.

In 1883 he married Effie Miriam Wise, daughter of Rabbi Isaac M. Wise, the great leader of Reform Judaism. Adolph and Effie's only child, Iphigene Bertha Ochs, married Arthur Hays Sulzberger, who obtained control of the *New York Times* after Adolph's death.

In 1896 the *New York Times* was facing bankruptcy. Adolph thought he could save it. But the bulk of his Chattanooga profits were tied up in a real-estate deal. So when he invested $75,000 to become the publisher of the *New York Times*, most of the money, as in Chattanooga eighteen years earlier, was borrowed. The venture was quite a gamble. If he succeeded in making the paper pay for three consecutive years, he was to become its majority stockholder. But his prospects were poor: he had a dying property, a discouraged staff, little working capital, and competition from papers backed by large fortunes.

Adolph took complete control on August 18, 1896, and immediately began to implement the same principles he had practiced in Chattanooga. He insisted on printing documented news free from personal and partisan bias at a time when such bias was common in other newspapers. Despite his need for all the advertising money he could get, he refused advertisements that he deemed dishonest or improper.

At that time New York City journalism was dominated by the "yellows," papers that emphasized sensationalism by focusing on crime and salacity and by reporting such stories with typographical excesses. To distance himself from such papers, Adolph adopted the slogan "All the News That's Fit to Print," first used in the *New York Times* on October 25, 1896, and still carried daily on the front page of the paper. The eventual success of the *New York Times* had the effect of raising the standards of both news and advertising throughout the industry.

However, that success did not come overnight. For a while he even had difficulties meeting the payroll. By late 1898 the paper was near collapse. Some of its executives wanted to emphasize its "quality" appeal by raising its price from three cents a copy to five cents. Adolph then had his greatest inspiration and took his biggest gamble by deciding instead to reduce the price to one cent. The "yellows" had built up huge circulations by charging one cent, and that price became a symbol of sensation-seeking papers. There was a good chance that if Adolph charged one cent for the *New York Times*, people would think that it, too, was turning yellow, so that it would lose its previous readers and simultaneously fail to garner new readers who actually wanted to read the "yellows." Adolph, however, believed that many people bought the "yellows" only because the papers were cheap and that they would buy the *New York Times* instead if they could get it at the same price. He was right. Within a year circulation had tripled. By 1900 he was able to purchase the controlling interest in the paper.

Under his leadership the *New York Times* expanded its coverage of foreign affairs, added financial news, offered book reviews, led in the development of rotogravure printing of pictures, began in 1913 to publish *The New York Times Index* (the only complete United States newspaper index), and continued to increase its circulation. His paper gave outstanding coverage to such events as the sinking of the *Titanic* (1912), World War I (1914–18), and Charles Lindbergh's transatlantic flight (1927).

Adolph retained ownership of the *Chattanooga Times*, which was directed by his brother Milton and his brother-in-law Harry Clay Adler, and later by his nephew Adolph Shelby Ochs. In 1901 Adolph purchased the *Philadelphia Times* and in 1902 the *Philadelphia Public Ledger*. He merged the two papers, put his brother George in charge of it, and then sold it after a little more than a decade of ownership. His pledge of $500,000 made possible the publication of the *Dictionary of American Biography*.

Adolph Simon Ochs died during a visit to Chattanooga on April 8, 1935.

George Washington Ochs Oakes

EDITOR OF *CURRENT HISTORY*

George Washington Ochs Oakes, like his father, Julius Ochs, was greatly interested in public affairs, and he served four years as mayor of Chattanooga, Tennessee. But his principal life's work was as an editor of various periodicals, notably *Current History*.

George Washington Ochs was born in Cincinnati, Ohio, on October 27, 1861. He was the second of the three sons of Julius and Bertha (Levy) Ochs. In 1865 the family moved to Knoxville, Tennessee, where George attended public and private schools and earned money by delivering newspapers. He studied for three years (1876–79) at East Tennessee University (later the University of Tennessee) but left after his junior year to join his family in Chattanooga. (In 1880, when his class graduated, he was awarded the B.A. degree because of the outstanding record he had achieved during his three years of attendance.)

His elder brother, Adolph Simon Ochs, had purchased the *Chattanooga Times*, where George now began his journalistic career, starting as a reporter. Two years later he was made city editor, a year later news editor, and in 1884 managing editor. In the late 1880s he assumed the leadership of the *Tradesman*, an industrial periodical controlled by the *Chattanooga Times*. In 1896, when Adolph moved to New York City to take control of the *New York Times*, George returned to the *Chattanooga Times* to run it for his brother.

During his years in Chattanooga he was actively engaged in public affairs. In 1891 he was appointed police commissioner. The following year he was a delegate to the National Democratic Convention, where he delivered a speech in support of Grover Cleveland. From 1893 to 1897 George served two terms as mayor of Chattanooga. He administered his office with such efficiency that the city debt was nearly eliminated even though a low tax rate was maintained—all this while he was setting up new school buildings, a park system, and a city hospital. After he left the mayor's office he served as president of the board of education. He also helped to establish the first public library in the city and became its president.

In 1900 his brother Adolph placed him in charge of the publication of a daily edition of the *New York Times* at the Paris Exposition. In 1901, after he returned to the United States, he became general manager of the *Philadelphia Times*, which Adolph had recently purchased. The following year Adolph acquired the *Philadelphia Public Ledger*, merged it with the *Philadelphia Times*, and placed the combined publications into George's hands.

In 1907 George married Bertie Gans of Philadelphia. They had two sons.

After more than a decade of running the Philadelphia paper for his brother, George suddenly found himself under the authority of Cyrus H. K. Curtis, to whom Adolph had sold the paper. George, in conflict with the new owner's policies and methods, resigned at the end of 1914.

In early 1915 Adolph invited George to New York City to become an officer and a director of the New York Times Company. In March 1915 George took over the editorship of the *New York Times Current History* (later simply *Current History*). An auxiliary of the *New York Times*, the periodical aimed to provide an impartial record of economic, political, and military developments arising from World War I. Through his editing of *Current History*, George did more than almost anyone else to develop public opinion on the underlying issues at stake in the struggle.

World War I deeply affected George. He was greatly embittered against the Germans by their conduct during the war. Far too old for active war service, he nevertheless enlisted as a private in the New York militia. Not wanting to pass down to his descendants a name of German origin, he sought, and was granted, permission by a Philadelphia court to change his name to George Washington Ochs Oakes (sometimes recorded as Ochs-Oakes).

After the war ended, *Current History* continued to report on important events around the world. It reflected George's own wide-ranging intellectual interests as well as his strongest personal characteristic—tolerance. Though he was conservative in politics, orthodox in economic beliefs, and strict in morals, he welcomed differing points of view among contributors to *Current History*.

George Washington Ochs Oakes had nearly finished the requirements for the degree of Ph.D. at Columbia University when he died in New York City on October 26, 1931, one day short of his seventieth birthday.

THE
PRITZKERS

T HE PRITZKERS, beginning with the law firm of Pritzker and
Pritzker in 1901, have developed a wide range of ventures,
especially hotels and manufacturing, to build one of the
most massive fortunes in the United States. The Pritzker trade-
marks have always been the teamwork of family members and the
vastness of their philanthropies.

They got their start in America in 1881, when nine-year-old
Nicholas Pritzker (1872–1957) left Kiev, Russia, with his family
for a new life. In 1901 he founded the Chicago law firm of Pritzker
and Pritzker, which became the basis of the family business.

The two driving forces in broadening the family's business interests were Nicholas's sons Abram Nicholas Pritzker (1896–1986)
and Jack Nicholas Pritzker (1904–1979). They invested in real
estate and other ventures and were so successful that beginning
in 1936 the family law firm handled only one client—the growing Pritzker financial empire.

The family business continued to expand under the direction
of Abram's three sons: Jay Arthur Pritzker (1922–), the financial
genius who acquired troubled companies; Robert Alan Pritzker
(1926–), the production genius who turned those companies into
moneymakers that eventually made up the Marmon Group; and
Donald Nicholas Pritzker (1932–72), who created the fabulous
Hyatt chain of hotels. Jack's son, Nicholas J. Pritzker (1945–),
also played a major role in the development of the Hyatt hotels.

The fourth generation of American Pritzkers is well represented by Thomas Jay Pritzker (1950–), son of Jay and Marian (Friend) Pritzker. Thomas, a lawyer, became a partner in Pritzker and Pritzker in 1976 and president of the Hyatt Corporation in 1980. Donald's daughter, Penny Sue (1959–), runs Hyatt's Classic Residences (luxury accomodations for the elderly) and the family's Coast-to-Coast Savings and Loan.

ABRAM NICHOLAS PRITZKER

FOUNDER OF THE PRITZKER EMPIRE

Abram Nicholas Pritzker founded a business group whose holdings at the time of his death were estimated at $1.5 billion. He controlled over two hundred businesses in a wide range of industries, including real estate and manufacturing. The group's best-known property was the Hyatt chain of hotels. He also became a prominent philanthropist.

Abram was born in Chicago, Illinois, on January 6, 1896. His parents were Nicholas J. and Annie (Cohen) Pritzker. Nicholas had immigrated to Chicago from Russia as a nine-year-old in 1881. In 1901 he founded the law firm of Pritzker and Pritzker, which became the foundation for the family business. His three sons—Harry, Abram, and Jack—all joined the firm.

Abram earned a bachelor of philosophy degree at the University of Chicago (1916), served in the navy during World War I, and graduated from Harvard Law School (1920). Returning to Chicago, he joined his father's law firm. However, he found business more interesting than law and, with his brother Jack, began to invest in real estate and other ventures. By 1936 he and Jack had become so successful in business that they left their father's law practice. At about that time the law firm stopped taking outside clients, reserving its efforts for the growing Pritzker business interests.

During the 1930s Abram created a business strategy that became a key factor in the Pritzker family's success for the next fifty years.

He transferred most of his assets to a series of trusts that he set up to avoid paying taxes. Eventually he reportedly had more than a thousand such trusts, which family members drew on for their various business operations. The Pritzkers, then, owned all of their interests collectively but were free to function individually.

In 1942 Abram negotiated the deal that gave the Pritzkers their first taste of true wealth. He purchased the troubled Cory Corporation, a Chicago maker of coffee percolators and small appliances, for $25,000 in cash and $75,000 in notes. For the next twenty-five years, with his partner, James W. Alsdorf, managing the business, the company was a consistent moneymaker, turning out annual profits of $3 million to $4 million in the 1960s. In the late 1960s Abram sold Cory Corporation for $27.5 million.

By then he was being assisted by members of the family besides Jack. Abram had married Fanny L. Doppelt, with whom he had three sons: Jay, Robert, and Donald. As his sons expanded the family business into ever-greater diversity, he increasingly took the role of general overseer, leaving the acquisitions and daily operations to the younger Pritzkers. By Abram's last years the family reportedly owned 266 companies and subsidiaries, including the Hyatt chain of hotels and the Marmon Group of manufacturers.

The sons abided by his principal philosophy of business. "We don't believe in public business," he explained. "Any public corporation that seeks vast expansion has a conflict with shareholders who follow the daily market and are not thinking of future gains and tax benefits." Thus, he kept the business strictly within the family.

Though a religious skeptic, Abram supported Jewish communal affairs. He was active with the Jewish Federation, the Combined Jewish Appeal, the Young Men's Jewish Council, and various Jewish charities in Chicago. A non-Zionist, he nevertheless gave huge contributions to Israel. He also directed the Pritzker Foundation, which averaged about $4.5 million a year in distributions. In 1968 he gave the University of Chicago, his alma mater, $16 million to establish the Pritzker School of Medicine. Abram endowed the prestigious Pritzker Architecture Prize, awarded annually for outstanding lifetime creative achievements in architecture. Other favorite recipients of his donations included the Michael Reese Hospital in Chicago, which had given his penniless father an over-coat in 1881, and the Wicker Park Elementary School, which Abram himself had attended.

In 1970 he first wife, Fanny, died. As an elderly man, he took a second wife, Lorraine.

In 1975 Abram, a chief petty officer in the navy during World War I, was given a cruise on an aircraft carrier. While aboard, he agreed to accompany the pilot of a fighter plane when it was cata-pulted into flight from the deck. At the age of seventy-nine, he was probably the oldest person ever to take such a ride.

Abram Nicholas Pritzker died in Chicago on February 8, 1986, at the age of ninety.

JACK NICHOLAS PRITZKER

THE PRITZKER REAL-ESTATE EXPERT

With his brother Abram, Jack Nicholas Pritzker was one of the two driving forces in broadening the scope of the Pritzker family from the original law firm into a huge business conglomerate. His special expertise was in real estate.

Jack was born in Chicago, Illinois, on January 6, 1904. His parents were Nicholas J. and Annie (Cohen) Pritzker.

After earning a bachelor's degree at the University of Michigan (1926) and a law degree at Northwestern University (1927), he joined his father's Chicago law firm, Pritzker and Pritzker. There he worked with his brothers Harry and Abram.

Jack, like Abram, was more interested in business than law. They joined forces in various ventures, notably in real estate. As the Great Depression forced Chicago property values down, Jack and Abram invested in real estate at rock-bottom prices and then waited for them to go up again. The strategy worked. With profits from real estate and other projects, the brothers were able to leave their father's law firm in 1936 to concentrate on business.

During World War II Jack rose to the rank of lieutenant commander in the navy reserve. In 1944 he married Rhoda Goldberg, with whom he had a son.

As Abram and other family members increasingly turned toward financial and manufacturing interests, Jack remained the one most closely involved with real estate. He made property purchases for the family's chain of hotels: Hyatt Corporation in the United States and Hyatt International Corporation abroad. His role was similar in the development of the Pritzker's hugely successful Marmon Group of manufacturing companies.

In his late years he served as a director of Hyatt International. He was also an honorary director of the Jewish Children's Bureau of Chicago.

Jack Nicholas Pritzker died in Chicago on October 30, 1979.

Jay Arthur Pritzker

FINANCIAL GENIUS OF THE FAMILY

Jay Arthur Pritzker succeeded his father, Abram Nicholas Pritzker, as head of the family business empire. The family controls hundreds of companies, including the Hyatt hotels. Jay's main contribution has been his financial wizardry, especially his ability to sense value in troubled companies and to negotiate for their purchase by the Pritzkers.

He was born in Chicago, Illinois, on August 26, 1922, the eldest of the three sons of Abram and Fanny (Doppelt) Pritzker. When Jay was a youngster, his father discussed business deals with him and his brothers. A brilliant student, Jay finished high school when he was just fourteen, graduated from Northwestern University at eighteen, served in the navy during World War II, and earned his law degree at Northwestern in 1947.

Also in 1947 he married Marian Friend. They had three sons and two daughters.

In 1948 Jay became a partner in the family law firm of Pritzker and Pritzker. In the early 1950s he and his younger brother Robert began to play increasingly large roles in the family's business ventures. They specialized in buying financially troubled manufacturing companies and rejuvenating them into profitable enterprises. Jay sought out small concerns that were doing poorly but, he felt, had good potential. He negotiated for them, bought them, and then handed them over to Robert, whose skill in operations brought the companies back to life.

Eventually the brothers united these companies into the Marmon Group, which comprised dozens of firms. Purchased at bargain rates, the companies nearly always became profitable for the Pritzkers. Jay avoided high technology businesses, concentrating instead on manufacturers of such basic goods as gloves, industrial casters, refined copper, brake drums, and railroad tank cars.

Jay also acquired a vast range of other properties for the family. He bought the first Hyatt hotel (1957) and then assigned his youngest brother, Donald, the task of developing it into a hotel chain; helped to build the Centex industrial park in suburban Chicago (early 1960s); purchased *McCall's* magazine (1973); acquired Braniff International Airlines (1983); and invested in numerous other ventures. In some cases, such as *McCall's* and Braniff, Jay sold the properties after a brief ownership, but generally the family took on projects for the long haul. By the mid-1980s the Pritzkers owned well over two hundred companies and subsidiaries.

In the early 1980s Jay succeeded his father, who died in 1986, as head of the family business empire. He has long served as chairman of the Hyatt Corporation, Hyatt International, and the Marmon Group, Inc.

In the 1990s Jay was involved in two well-publicized lawsuits. In 1993 Paul S. Dopp, a New Jersey businessman, won a jury trial on the issue of whether Jay had used "deceit or duress" to breach a

1984 contract for them to buy two hotels together. In 1993 and 1994 Jay Pritzker and Donald J. Trump slapped each other with lawsuits in a legal feud over the management of the Grand Hyatt Hotel in New York City, jointly owned by Trump and the Pritzkers and managed by the Pritzker family's Hyatt Corporation. Trump complained that the Pritzkers used questionable accounting, while Jay countered that Trump was at fault for failing to remain solvent, pledging his stake in the hotel as collateral for bank loans, and refusing to pay his share of repairs at the hotel. In 1995 Jay and Trump settled their dispute out of court. Details were not announced, but reportedly the compromise called for renovations at the hotel and for Trump to be given a role in management.

ROBERT ALAN PRITZKER

PRODUCTION GENIUS OF THE FAMILY

Robert Alan Pritzker is the principal force behind the great success of the Marmon Group, the largest business interest of the Pritzker family. The Marmon Group is a collection of dozens of manufacturing companies that were doing poorly till Robert's production genius turned them into profitable firms.

He was born in Chicago, Illinois, on June 30, 1926, the middle of the three sons of Abram and Fanny (Doppelt) Pritzker. After finishing high school he earned a B.S. degree in industrial engineering at the Illinois Institute of Technology (1946), studied business administration at the University of Illinois, and acquired six years of practical production experience outside the family business.

In 1953 his older brother, Jay, purchased the Colson Company, a small, struggling manufacturer of bicycles, rocket parts, and industrial casters. Jay asked Robert to take over Colson. Robert dropped the bicycle and rocket-parts divisions, made a success of the caster business, and acquired a number of related small companies and integrated them with Colson.

Soon Jay and Robert repeated the Colson success story with other troubled manufacturing concerns. Jay, the lawyer and financial man, bought the companies, and Robert, the engineer and operations man, turned them around. "The deals I make," Jay said, "create a lot of problems for Bob. But he is a master at finding a way to make sick companies work."

Robert invested huge sums of money to make sure that his plants had the best possible equipment. With about sixty companies to run, with such wide-ranging products as gloves, refined copper, and railroad tank cars, he developed a decentralized management style, allowing his general managers great freedom. In turn, they produced huge profits for the Marmon Group, the Pritzkers' name for the unifed companies.

Robert has been married twice. By his first marriage, to Audrey Gilbert, he had a son and two daughters. His second marriage, to Irene Dryburgh, produced a son and a daughter.

Robert became the president and chief executive officer of the Pritzker's Marmon Corporation. He has also served as a member of the board of directors of the Pritzker's Hyatt Corporation, as chairman of the Pritzker Foundation (and thus the guardian of the many Pritzker philanthropies), and as an executive for many other enterprises in the Pritzker business empire.

DONALD NICHOLAS PRITZKER

PRESIDENT OF HYATT CORPORATION

The most prestigious property in the Pritzker business empire is the Hyatt chain of hotels. The family member who, more than anyone else, built the chain was Donald Nicholas Pritzker.

He was born in Chicago, Illinois, on October 31, 1932, the youngest of the three sons of Abram Nicholas and Fanny (Doppelt) Pritzker. Abram led the Pritzker family into the financial stratosphere through his diversified investments.

After earning a bachelor's degree at Harvard University (1954), serving to the rank of lieutenant (j.g.) in the navy reserve (1954–56), and taking a law degree from the University of Chicago (1959), Donald joined his two older brothers, Jay and Robert, who were in the midst of acquiring a vast array of business interests. Jay had purchased the Hyatt House hotel in Los Angeles in 1957 and now asked Donald to build a chain of Hyatts.

Donald soon built a second hotel, in Burlingame, near San Francisco, California, and by 1961 he had raised the number to six hotels. In 1967 he gave the project a new direction and a major boost when he induced Jay to purchase the Atlanta Regency hotel, renamed the Hyatt Regency. The Regency was one of the first of the modern luxury downtown hotels and the first to be built with a vast atrium in its center, where a large shaft of air and light shot upward for several stories in the middle of the lobby. In the future, more and more of the Hyatt hotels were erected in downtown areas and were constructed around the atrium concept.

By 1972 Donald had built the hotel chain into one of America's fastest-growing, most respected operations. He served the domestic division, Hyatt Corporation, as executive vice president (1960–63) and as president (1963–72). The foreign division, Hyatt International Corporation, had hotels in Hong Kong, Manila, and elsewhere; Donald headed it as president for the last four years of his life (1968–72).

Outside his business duties, Donald was active in Jewish communal affairs. A resident of Atherton, near San Francisco, he served as a director of Mount Zion Hospital and of the Jewish Welfare Federation, both in San Francisco.

He married Susan Sandel in 1958. They had two sons and one daughter.

While in Honolulu, Hawaii, to attend the opening of a hotel not in the Hyatt chain, Donald Nicholas Pritzker died of a heart attack on May 6, 1972, at the age of only thirty-nine.

RASHI
AND FAMILY

RASHI (1040–1105) WAS A RENOWNED medieval French commentator on the Bible and the Talmud. His familiar name is an acronym from the Hebrew initials of his title and original name: Rabbi Shlomo Yitzhaqi (or Solomon, son of Isaac).

He had three daughters, all of whom married prominent Jewish scholars. Jochebed married Meir ben Samuel (c. 1060–c. 1135), a student of Rashi and one of the founders of the school of tosaphists (writers of critical and explanatory glosses on the Talmud) in northern France. Miriam married Judah ben Nathan (fl. late eleventh and early twelfth centuries), another of Rashi's pupils who became an early writer of tosaphoth. Rashi's third daughter, probably named Rachel, married a scholar named Eliezer (fl. late eleventh and early twelfth centuries).

Rashi's grandchildren were among the greatest scholars of their generation. Jochebed and Meir ben Samuel had four sons. The first became known as Ribam, an acronyn for Rabbi Isaac ben Meir (fl. mid-twelfth century), another early tosaphist. His brother Samuel ben Meir, or Rashbam (c. 1080–c. 1174), earned an outstanding reputation as a talmudist and Bible commentator. Solomon ben Meir (fl. twelfth century), known as "the father of the grammarians," interpreted texts especially through his scholarly understanding of language. The fourth brother, Jacob ben Meir (1100–1171), was a highly influential talmudic authority and one of the most important tosaphists. His honorific name was Rabbenu ("Our Master") Tam ("Respected Scholar").

Rashi's daughter Miriam and her husband, Judah ben Nathan, also had a well-known son. He was Yom Tov (fl. twelfth century), a learned rabbi.

The next generation, Rashi's great-grandchildren, was led by Isaac ben Samuel of Dampierre (c. 1115–c. 1185), usually referred to as Ri (or RI, for Rabbi Isaac), as in Ri the Elder. His mother was the daughter of Jochebed and Meir ben Samuel. With Rabbenu Tam, his uncle and teacher, Isaac ben Samuel holds a central position among the tosaphists.

This remarkable family had at least one more memorable figure. Elhanan ben Isaac of Dampierre (died 1184), a son of Isaac ben Samuel of Dampierre, was a notable tosaphist who was martyred under unknown circumstances.

RASHI

GREATEST BIBLICAL AND TALMUDIC COMMENTATOR

Rashi was a French rabbinic scholar whose commentaries on the Bible and the Talmud form the basis for the traditional study of those two pillars of the Jewish religion. He also wrote penitential hymns and responsa.

He was born in Troyes, Champagne, France, in 1040. His original name was Shlomo (or Shelomo) Yitzhaqi (or Yitzhaki)—that is, Solomon ben Isaac (Solomon, son of Isaac). The honorific name of Rashi is an acronyn from the Hebrew initials of his full title and name: Rabbi Shlomo Yitzhaqi.

His father, Isaac, was a scholar whom the son often quoted. Rashi's mother was the sister of the liturgical writer Simeon ben Isaac.

At an early age Rashi went to study in Worms and then in Mainz, the Rhenish centers of Jewish learning. He was taught the traditions associated with the great Rabbi Gershom ben Judah. About 1065 Rashi returned to Troyes, where he established his own academy, served as rabbinic judge of the community, and earned his livelihood as a vintner.

In his Bible commentary Rashi combined the two basic methods of interpretation: the literal (or *peshat*) and the nonliteral (or *derash*). He sought the plain meaning by drawing on his knowledge of grammar and syntax and by carefully considering the text and the context. But his commentaries are also rich in the use of folklore and symbolism to explain the deeper meanings of passages. His clear, concise Hebrew language, his familiarity with everyday occupations, and his blend of literal and nonliteral interpretations account for the enormous popularity

Rashi

of his work. In fact, the first Hebrew book to be printed, in 1475, was Rashi's Bible commentary.

His writing exerted great influence not only in the Jewish world but also in the gentile. It was studied and emulated in the fourteenth century by the Franciscan scholar Nicholas of Lyra, whose work in turn was a source for Martin Luther during the Reformation in the sixteenth century.

In his commentary on the Talmud, Rashi maintained a greater consistency of technique than he did in his work on the Bible. The Talmud required a more purely literal clarification of its meaning for at least three reasons: (1) the existence of variant copies of the text raised the question of the authenticity of the different versions, (2) the Aramaic language of the Talmud was difficult for many readers to understand, and (3) the talmudic arguments themselves were often obscure.

Rashi prepared what he believed to be the true text. In his commentary he drew heavily on the collective achievements of earlier Franco-German scholars, but he gave his writing a uniquely oral tone that reflects the work's classroom origin at his Troyes academy. His commentary explains the text in its entirety. In fact, text and commentary are interwoven so as to form a unified whole. His interpretations were subsequently incorporated into all printed editions of the Talmud.

Rashi's work on the Talmud was continued by a school of commentators called tosaphists, who composed tosaphoth ("additions"), which are further glosses on the Talmud or on Rashi's own explanations. The school was founded by Rashi's sons-in-law and was lifted to its apex by his grandsons.

Rashi's biblical and talmudic commentaries are a valuable source of information for students of Old French. In those works he provided thousands of Old French equivalents for obscure or technical Hebrew words.

Rashi also composed penitential hymns (*selihot*) and about 350 responsa. The hymns focus on the harshness of exile and the comforting belief in redemption. The responsa answer questions about Jewish law and reveal his gentle character and liberal approach to matters of ritual.

Rashi had three daughters. All three married Jewish scholars, two of whom—Meir ben Samuel and Judah ben Nathan—earned great renown by founding the school of tosaphists.

Rashi died in Troyes on July 13, 1105.

RASHBAM

BIBLE COMMENTATOR AND TALMUDIST

Rashbam was a highly esteemed biblical commentator known for his strictly literal interpretations of the text. He also helped to start the school of tosaphists and became one of its most important members.

He was born in Ramerupt, near Troyes, in northern France,

about 1080–85. His original name was Samuel ben Meir. The honorific name of Rashbam reflects the close connection between his reputation and that of his maternal grandfather, the great Rashi. Rashbam's mother, Jochebed, was a daughter of Rashi, and his father was Meir ben Samuel, a pupil of Rashi and one of the first tosaphists.

Rashbam studied under his father and under Rashi himself. Rashi is said to have accepted some of his grandson's opinions and changed his own biblical and talmudic commentary accordingly.

Rashbam earned his livelihood by raising sheep and growing grapes. His life was marked by simplicity and devotion to scholarly pursuits, though he did participate in open disputes with Christians.

He apparently wrote commentary on all the books of the Bible, but only his work on the Pentateuch has survived in nearly its entirety. His biblical commentaries are devoted to what he often referred to as "the profound literal meaning of the text." He strongly condemned earlier commentaries, including those of his grandfather, that did not adhere to the literal meaning. Nevertheless, he respected, and was greatly influenced by, Rashi. In fact, some of Rashbam's explanations are identical to his grandfather's.

Rashbam carefully sought out accurate texts of the Bible as the basis for his work. His style is clear and concise, focused strictly on the topic and language of the passage under discussion.

He was the first Bible commentator to incorporate into his commentaries attacks on Christian theology. He often repeated the phrase "according to the literal meaning of the text and in answer to sectarians" (that is, Christians).

Besides his work in biblical commentary, Rashbam earned a reputation as an early and important tosaphist. However, only a small number of his halakic writings are extant. The most significant are his supplements to the unfinished portions of Rashi's talmudic commentary, notably in *Bava Batra*. Rashbam's commentaries, verbose but lucid, are included in standard editions of the Talmud.

He died in Ramerupt about 1174.

RABBENU TAM

GREATEST SCHOLAR OF HIS ERA

Rabbenu Tam was a talmudic authority whose decisions on Jewish law had far-reaching consequences in medieval Europe. He also wrote a wide range of highly regarded religious works, including tosaphoth and poetry.

Rabbenu Tam was born in Ramerupt, near Troyes, in northern France, in 1100. His original name was Jacob ben Meir. For his great intellectual and religious achievements, he was given the honorific name of Rabbenu ("Our Master") Tam ("Respected Scholar"). He was one of the four sons of Meir ben Samuel, who was a pupil of Rashi and one of the first tosaphists, and Jochebed, a daughter of Rashi.

Rabbenu Tam studied under his father and under his older brother Samuel ben Meir (Rashbam). In Ramerupt, Rabbenu Tam earned a livelihood as a wine merchant and financier, had four sons, and headed a rabbinic academy that attracted the finest scholars of the generation. Recognized as the greatest scholar of the age, he received halakic questions from all parts of the world.

In 1147 a band of crusaders attacked him because he was a veritable symbol of Jewry. They wounded his head five times as revenge for the five wounds that Jews allegedly inflicted on Jesus. After he was saved by a passing knight, he fled to the nearby town of Troyes.

There he became a leading participant in synods that were called to develop rules governing relations between Jews and Christians. Rabbenu Tam took the forefront in settling terms from the Jewish side. He called for three principal rules: (1) disputes between Jews would be resolved by Jewish authorities, (2) the law against polygamy would be reinforced, and (3) no Jew could lightly challenge the legality of a Jewish deed of divorce.

Rabbenu Tam's major work on Jewish law is the *Sefer ha-yashar* ("Book of the Righteous"). It contains legal decisions, responsa, and tosaphoth. He tended to give lenient decisions within the halakic framework.

Religious poetry played a special role in his output. He wrote many such poems and approved their introduction into the liturgy. Eventually some of his poems were incorporated into the Hebrew prayer book.

Rabbenu Tam died in Troyes on June 9, 1171.

ISAAC BEN SAMUEL OF DAMPIERRE

LEADING TOSAPHIST

With his uncle Rabbenu Tam, Isaac ben Samuel of Dampierre is the central figure in the history of tosaphoth as a system of study and as a literary genre. He also wrote responsa of great historical and cultural value.

Isaac was probably born in Ramerupt, near Troyes, in northern France, about 1115. He came to be referred to by the initial letters of his title and first name: Ri (or RI, for Rabbi Isaac), as in Ri the Elder or Ri of Dampierre. His father was Samuel of Dampierre, who was the son of Simhah ben Samuel of Vitry. Isaac's mother was the daughter of Jochebed, herself the daughter of the great Rashi. By both parents, then, Isaac was related to distinguished Jewish families of scholars and community leaders.

He studied under his uncle Rabbenu Tam, whom he served as an assistant. After the master left Ramerupt, Isaac went to live in Dampierre. For the rest of his life he followed his uncle's teachings and rulings.

Isaac and his uncle Rabbenu Tam raised tosaphoth activity to its peak achievements. On nearly every page of the printed tosaphoth, Isaac is mentioned. Unfortunately, little of his tosaphoth writing has survived in its original form, but his teachings are interwoven in the published tosaphoth handed down by his pupils, such as Samson ben Abraham of Sens.

Isaac's responsa are also important. They cast light on the lives of contemporary Jews and reflect a humility and gentle approach unique in responsa of the time.

He had many well-known pupils whom he strongly influenced. Among them were Abraham ben Nathan ha-Yarhi and one of Isaac's own two sons, Elhanan ben Isaac of Dampierre, also a tosaphist.

Isaac ben Samuel of Dampierre died about 1185.

THE
REICHMANNS

T HROUGH HUGE REAL-ESTATE PROJECTS, such as the World Financial Center in New York City, the Reichmanns of Toronto, Canada, became fabulously wealthy—"the Rothschilds of the New World." At the peak of their success they were believed to be the fourth richest family in the world, with assets estimated at $12.8 billion. However, bankruptcy in 1992 and the death of the Reichmanns' most promising heir in 1994 left the family devastated. Since then, they have made a remarkable comeback.

The family patriarch was Samuel Reichmann (1898–1975), who in 1921 married Renée Gestetner (1899–1990). Both were Hungarians whose families belonged to the Oberlander ultra-Orthodox wing of Judaism. In Hungary, Samuel and Renée had a daughter (Eva) and two sons: Edward (1925–) and Louis (1927–). Fearing a Russian invasion, Samuel and his family moved to Vienna, Austria, in 1928. There three more sons were born: Albert (1929–), Paul (1930–), and Ralph (1933–). To escape the Nazis, the family fled to France in 1938 and then to Spain and Morocco in 1940.

In Morocco, Samuel prospered as a currency trader who also dabbled in construction. Renée became famous during World War II for sending food parcels to inmates of Nazi concentration camps, for smuggling forged Spanish passports to Jews in Hungary, and for turning the family's home into a haven for refugees.

In the 1950s, as Islamic fervor and political instability swept through Morocco, the Reichmanns moved to Canada. There they opened a ceramic-tile business and then branched out into real estate through their York Developments company, later called Olympia and York Developments.

Edward and Louis left the family enterprises to pursue other interests. But Albert, Paul, and Ralph—led by Paul—built Olympia and York into one of the world's richest, most powerful real-estate developers. After Samuel died in 1975 the matriarch, Renée, remained active in the family business as honorary chairman of the board and assistant secretary till her death. In 1974 they built in Toronto the world's tallest building outside the United States. Later they bought New York City skyscrapers and became the city's largest private owner of commercial property.

But in 1992 their most ambitious project, the seventy-one-acre Canary Wharf commercial development in London's East End dockyards, failed, sending Olympia and York into bankruptcy. The family lost control of the company.

Then, in 1994, David Reichmann (1960–94), son of Ralph Reichmann, suddenly died. David had pulled out of the Canary Wharf deal before it collapsed and had set up a communications company in Israel. Many insiders believed that David was the heir apparent, in terms of intelligence and charm, to the current leader of the clan, his uncle Paul.

Despite these setbacks, the family has rebounded. In October 1995 Paul, with a small group of investors, bought back Canary Wharf from the banks that had taken it over. He thus showed the business acumen and tenacity that had always characterized the Reichmann family.

Paul Reichmann

ARCHITECT OF THE REICHMANNS' SUCCESS

The principal figure in the spectacular rise of the Reichmanns into one of the world's wealthiest families was Paul Reichmann. Through his leadership of the family's Olympia and York Developments company, he pioneered virtually every commercial real-estate trend over a three-decade period.

Paul was born in Vienna, Austria, in 1930, the fifth of the six children and the fourth of the five sons of Samuel and Renée (Gestetner) Reichmann. The family escaped the Nazis by fleeing to France in 1938 and to Spain and then Morocco in 1940. During the 1940s, while his brothers joined their father's currency-trading business, Paul pursued religious studies. He spent five years at talmudic colleges in England.

However, when family members began moving to Canada to start new business ventures in the mid-1950s, Paul joined them. Edward set up Olympia Trading Company in Montreal, later bought Montreal Tile, and then formed Olympia Floor and Wall Tile, a building-supplies company that Ralph soon took over. Paul joined Ralph, and in 1957 they moved the tile business to Toronto. The brothers wanted to build a warehouse, but the bids by contractors were so high that Paul decided to contract the building himself. He saved the family over $50,000 and found the building industry so attractive that he handed over his part of the tile business to Ralph and went into real-estate development full-time.

In 1958 Paul set up York Developments, named after the surrounding county, to handle the family's real-estate business. He started buying industrial properties and putting them up for sale or lease. When Samuel finally moved to Canada in 1959, the money he brought with him enabled the new family enterprises to expand even further. In the 1960s the Reichmann construction business became Toronto's biggest developer, earning a reputation for providing good quality at a fair price. The family combined its two business names into Olympia and York Developments, incorporated in 1969.

In 1973 the Reichmanns began work on First Canadian Place, a white marble office tower of seventy-two stories in downtown Toronto. The world's tallest building outside the United States, it gave the family international publicity. By using innovative construction techniques—notably trucking materials into the basement and then lifting them to the level where they were needed—Paul completed the building in only sixteen months and saved millions of dollars. In 1975 tenants began moving in.

When Samuel died in 1975, Paul and Albert emerged as the family's decision makers, with Paul as the chief strategist. Ralph continued to head the building-materials company; Edward and Louis, the oldest brothers, had already left Canada to engage in other businesses.

In 1977 the Reichmanns began their first operations in the United States when they bought eight prime Manhattan office towers. At the time, New York City had just narrowly missed bankruptcy and office vacancies were rapidly rising, so other major developers were staying away from the city. As a result, the Reichmanns got rock-bottom prices for the skyscrapers; when property values and rents began to climb in the late 1970s, Olympia and York reaped huge profits.

Over the next few years, the family used the money-saving construction techniques they had experimented with at First Canadian Place to build office towers in Boston, Miami, Los Angeles, and elsewhere in the United States. In 1980 they won a contract to build the world's largest financial center in New York City, eventually called the World Financial Center, which officially opened in October 1985.

Beginning in the late 1970s, the Reichmanns tried to diversify their investments. The new projects generally did not do as well as the real-estate ventures did. In 1981, for example, Olympia and York bought Abitibi-Price, a Canadian forest products giant. The company gradually declined, and by 1990 it was losing money. In the late 1980s Paul gave hundreds of millions of dollars as investments and loans to his friend Robert Campeau, an entrepreneur who was trying to take over a couple of United States department store chains. The deals went sour, and Paul withdrew.

At about that time, Paul began concentrating once again on real estate. For example, he led Olympia and York into financing the construction of an office tower in Moscow in the then Soviet Union.

In 1987 Paul took over the redevelopment of Canary Wharf, a seventy-one-acre section in London's East End dockyards. It became Europe's biggest real-estate development, including England's largest single office building, One Canada Square. Paul gambled that London would soon become the financial center of the new Europe. However, by the early 1990s London was in the midst of an office glut, the real-estate market severely declined, and the Reichmanns could not find enough tenants to support the expensive new complex. Added to that problem were the falling prices for energy and newsprint, the other key industries in Olympia and York's portfolio. In May 1992 the company filed for bankruptcy. In the restructuring that followed, the family lost control of Olympia and York.

By February 1993 Paul had rebounded and announced that he was forming a new Toronto-based partnership, Reichmann International. Joining forces with the American investor George Soros, Paul began to engage once again in gigantic real-estate deals, as in some Mexico projects beginning in late 1993.

In October 1995 Paul led a small group of investors (including the Tisch family and a Saudi prince) in buying back Canary Wharf from the banks that had taken over its administration. The price was about $1 billion. Paul, who had 5 percent of the project, announced that the group intended to continue developing Canary Wharf.

Despite Paul Reichmann's great wealth, he, his wife, and their five children live unpretentiously. He shuns publicity yet is widely praised and admired. His interests outside business still center on his scholarly religious beginnings. He speaks eight languages, collects Hebrew holy texts as a hobby, remains devoted to his Orthodox Jewish faith, and reportedly donates 10 percent of his income to Jewish charities. In Olympia and York's heyday, the company was famous for shutting down its offices and construction sites on the Sabbath and holy days and still bringing in projects on schedule.

ALBERT AND RALPH REICHMANN

PARTNERS IN OLYMPIA AND YORK DEVELOPMENTS

Albert and Ralph Reichmann were partners with their brother Paul in the firm of Olympia and York Developments, one of the world's most successful real-estate developers. Though Paul was the chief strategist, both Albert and Ralph made individual contributions to the family enterprises.

Albert was born in 1929 and Ralph in 1933, both in Vienna, Austria. They were the third and fifth, respectively, of the five sons of Samuel and Renée (Gestetner) Reichmann.

The family fled the Nazis in 1938 to France and in 1940 to Spain and then Morocco. In the 1940s and early 1950s, Albert and Ralph learned the intricacies of commerce under their father in his successful currency-trading business. But to escape the increasing Islamic fervor and political instability in Morocco, the family began looking for a new place to settle.

In 1954 their father, Samuel, sent his oldest son, Edward, to Canada to explore the business possibilities there. Edward set up Olympia Trading Company in Montreal, later bought Montreal Tile, and then formed Olympia Floor and Wall Tile, a Montreal-based building-supplies company. Over the next few years, three of his brothers arrived in Canada: Louis (the second son), Ralph, and Paul (the fourth son). Ralph came in 1956 and took over the tile company. The following year Paul joined him and moved the tile business to Toronto. Paul soon left the tile company to go into real-estate development, establishing what came to be known as

Olympia and York, the construction arm of the family enterprises. In 1959 the rest of the family—Samuel, Renée, and Albert—moved to Canada and joined the others in Toronto.

When the family patriarch, Samuel, died in 1975, Albert and Paul became the decision makers at Olympia and York, while Ralph, also a partner in that company, continued to head the family's original business, Olympia Tile. Louis and Edward, the two oldest brothers, left Canada to pursue other interests.

Albert went on to serve as chairman of Olympia and York. He was also a director of the firm's major subsidiaries, such as Abitibi-Price and Gulf Canada. Ralph held the title of general manager at Olympia and York. Like Albert, he also served as a director of company subsidiaries.

When Olympia and York's ambitious Canary Wharf commercial development in London failed in the early 1990s, the firm was driven into bankruptcy in 1992. The Reichmann brothers lost control of the firm, which was taken over by the banks.

However, in 1993 Albert and Ralph joined with Paul in a new partnership, Reichmann International. With it the brothers once again became involved in major real-estate developments. Late that year, for example, they invested in large-scale projects in Mexico.

DAVID REICHMANN

THE FALLEN HEIR

David Reichmann was widely regarded as the most promising heir to the Reichmann business empire. Only he, it was said, could rival the gifts of the family's leader, his uncle Paul Reichmann. Breaking new ground in the Reichmann family saga, David set out to forge a major high-technology business in Israel. But he had barely begun when he suddenly died at the age of only thirty-four.

David was born in Toronto, Canada, on January 2, 1960. He was the first of the five children of Ralph Reichmann, one of the three Reichmanns, with his brothers Paul and Albert, who controlled Olympia and York Developments, the greatly successful international real-estate firm headquartered in Toronto.

Like other Reichmanns, David was ultra-Orthodox, and he spent years studying in yeshivas in New Jersey, England, and Israel. At twenty-one, while still a student, he married Rachele Friedman, a young ultra-Orthodox woman from a wealthy family in Switzerland. They had five children.

In his early twenties David left the yeshiva and embarked on an intensive six-month private business-tutoring program taught by professors from Toronto's York University and paid for by his parents. He then served as a project manager for Olympia and York in Toronto and at the World Financial Center (built by the Reichmanns) in Manhattan, and he also worked for his father at Olympia Tile in Toronto.

But David was ambitious and anxious to build an empire of his own. He sold most of his stock in the family's Canadian companies, giving him a grubstake of about $200 million, and moved with his wife and children to Israel in 1991. The Israeli government-run telephone monopoly was on the verge of deregulating, and licenses for many services would soon be available. David dreamed of setting up an Israel-based telecommunications conglomerate that would dominate telephone services in the Middle East.

Settling in Tel Aviv, he founded Darcom, which stood for "David and Rachele's company." Astutely, he became a financial backer of Rabbi Eliezer Schach, who held great influence with the head of the Communications Ministry. Because of that connection, David was granted several of the new telecommunications licenses in 1992. However, these were limited licenses, for such services as videoconferencing and "callbacks," private long-distance lines a customer could phone to get a lower-cost Israeli dial tone. In 1993 he acquired a small company to run these services for him. By the end of the year, corporate customers were coming aboard at the rate of nearly $3 million in monthly sales.

Meanwhile, David pursued his real goal: the license to become Israel's second major long-distance carrier. To get that license, David felt he needed a partner. He made a deal with IDB Communications, a Los Angeles, California, outfit that could supply the necessary phone lines and equipment. Prospects looked good till November 1993, when a business newspaper exposé criticized the manner in which David obtained his licenses and warned that the Darcom-IDB alliance could become a monoply, driving up long-distance rates. Then, in early 1994, IDB phone lines began to malfunction.

David, under stress, spent six weeks in December 1993 and January 1994 in a Toronto sanatorium. However, by March he had worked out the company's problems well enough to obtain the right to use his new videoconferencing service to handle a speech by American Vice President Al Gore to a conference of hundreds of Israeli business leaders as well as Israeli Prime Minister Yitzhak Rabin.

But disaster lay just ahead. On May 31, 1994, IDB collapsed. Its auditors resigned, believing the company to be unprofitable, and its stock plummeted. David worried about getting a replacement partner to ensure that Darcom would continue to have lines and technology, both to remain in the running for the still ungranted long-distance license and even to stay in business at all.

What very few people knew at this time was that David's health was being undermined not only by business stress but also by a history of drug abuse. Unnaturally intense pressure, partly family-imposed and partly self-imposed, to live up to the Reichmann name had led to his addiction to drugs, especially cocaine.

David Reichmann died in Tel Aviv on August 2, 1994.

THE
ROTHSCHILDS

T HE ROTHSCHILD FAMILY is the most famous of all European banking dynasties. Founded in the late eighteenth century, the house accumulated legendary wealth and exerted unrivaled commercial influence in continental Europe and in England during the nineteenth century. In the twentieth century it continued to play a major role in world finance and industry.

The family's name derived from the red shield—in German, *rot* ("red") *schild* ("shield")—that identified the Frankfurt am Main, Germany, house where family ancestors once lived. For generations the Rothschilds were modest merchants in Frankfurt, though several members became distinguished rabbis.

The first to attain lasting prominence, and the founder of the dynasty, was Mayer Amschel Rothschild (1744–1812), who became financial adviser to the landgrave of Hesse-Kassel and built up a fortune during the French revolutionary and Napoleonic wars (1790s and early 1800s).

His principal asset was his five sons, who established family banking branches in Europe's major financial centers. Amschel Mayer (1773–1855) supervised the original business in Frankfurt. Salomon Mayer (1774–1855) opened an office in Vienna, Austria. Nathan Mayer (1777–1836) established himself in London, England. Carl (originally Kalmann) Mayer (1788–1855) set up a branch in Naples, Italy. And James (originally Jacob) Mayer (1792–1868) settled in Paris, France.

In all these cities, the family established banking houses that were separate but interdependent. Intermarriages among the various branches of Rothschilds further strengthened the family bonds.

In 1822 all five of Mayer's sons were made barons of the Austrian Empire. Thereafter, many family members in German-speaking countries styled themselves as von Rothschild, and in France and England as de Rothschild.

During the hundred years between the fall of Napoléon and the beginning of World War I, the Rothschilds were the world's leading private bankers. They also became leaders of the Jewish communities in the countries where they established themselves. In later generations the family produced not only financiers but also important politicians, scientists, art collectors, and philanthropists.

The Italian branch closed in 1861 and the Frankfurt in 1901. In 1938 the Nazis seized the Viennese house. But the London and Paris houses continued to be major factors in global finance throughout the twentieth century.

Nathan Mayer had seven children, of whom three had notable careers. Lionel Nathan (1808–1879), a banker and philanthropist who enhanced the importance of the family firm in London, forced the political emancipation of Jews in England through his struggle to take the seat in Parliament to which he was elected. Anthony (1810–76) was the first Rothschild baronet in England and a zealous Jewish communal activist. Mayer Amschel (1818–74) became known as a sportsman and art collector.

Carl Mayer's sons Mayer Carl (1820–86) and Wilhelm Carl (1828–1901) returned from Naples to Frankfurt, where they took over the direction of the parent firm. James Mayer produced three sons who had memorable careers: Mayer Alphonse (1827–1905), a worthy successor to his father as head of the Paris branch and a noted philanthropist; Gustave Salomon (1829–1911), another prominent member of the Paris firm; and Edmond James (1845–1934), one of the most important patrons of the Jewish revival in Palestine.

In the next generation of Rothschilds—the fourth, including the first Mayer Amschel, of the dynasty—Ferdinand James (1839–98), grandson of Salomon Mayer and great-grandson of the founder of the financial house, served in the English Parliament and acquired a notable collection of books and art works. Lionel Nathan's eldest son, Nathaniel Mayer (1840–1915), sat in the English House of Commons for twenty years (1865–85); was created Baron Rothschild, the first Jewish peer in England (1885); and then served in the House of Lords (1885–1915). He and his brothers, the art connoisseur Alfred Charles (1842–1918) and the sportsman-philanthropist Leopold (1845–1917), were among the close associates of King Edward VII. James Armand (1878–1953), a son of Edmond James, was an English politician, Zionist, and philanthropist.

The fifth generation distinguished itself as well. Lionel Walter (1868–1937), a son of Nathaniel Mayer, earned a reputation as a zoologist, served for many years in the English Parliament, and succeeded his father as the second Baron Rothschild. Nathaniel Mayer's other son, Nathaniel Charles (1877–1923), was a partner in N. M. Rothschild and Sons, the family's London-based merchant banking firm. Guy Edouard Alphonse Paul (1909–), a grandson of Mayer Alphonse, headed, for much of the twentieth century, the family's Paris branch, by then the principal center of Rothschild business interests. James Gustave Jules Alain (1910–82) and Elie Robert (1917–), grandsons of Gustave Salomon, also showed exceptional ability in their handling of Rothschild operations in France.

In the sixth generation, Miriam Louisa (1908–), Nathaniel Charles's eldest daughter, became a prominent scientist in many fields but won special renown as the world's leading expert on fleas. Nathaniel Mayer Victor (1910–90), Nathaniel Charles's only son, made contributions to zoology, headed England's famous Whitehall "think tank" in the early 1970s, served as an executive with Royal Dutch Shell, and succeeded Lionel Walter, his uncle, as the third Baron Rothschild.

Edmund Leopold (1916–), a grandson of Leopold, took over

the directorship of the family's London-based merchant banking firm in 1975. Philippe (1902–1988), a great-great-grandson of Nathan Mayer, headed the famed winemaking firm of Mouton-Rothschild.

Mayer Amschel Rothschild

FOUNDER OF THE ROTHSCHILD BANKING DYNASTY

Though he came from a family of humble shopkeepers, Mayer Amschel Rothschild set his sights high in the business world and established a business method that produced the great House of Rothschild banking dynasty. Perhaps his greatest achievement was to raise five sons of outstanding capability to carry on and expand the family's business interests.

Mayer was born in Frankfurt am Main, Germany, on February 23, 1744. His father, Amschel Moses Rothschild, had a small business as a merchant and banker in Frankfurt.

Mayer originally studied for the rabbinate at Fürth but eventually followed his father into the world of business, beginning by serving an apprenticeship of three years with the banking firm of Oppenheim in Hannover. In the 1760s Mayer, after his father's death, set up his own Frankfurt business, which combined the characteristics of a small bank and moneychanger's office with those of a mercantile firm. He dealt especially in luxury items, gold coins, and commercial papers.

His reputation for honest dealing brought him to the attention of the wealthy William IX, landgrave of Hesse-Kassel. In 1801 the landgrave appointed Mayer his financial agent. With his patron's support, Mayer soon took the first step in establishing the family's long career as loan contractors to European governments. In 1803 he lent twenty million francs to the government of Denmark. During this period Mayer set the pattern that his descendants would follow for generations: doing business with the highest political leaders and fathering as

Mayer Amschel Rothschild

many sons as possible to help run the family's affairs.

He married Gutele Schnapper, daughter of a Frankfurt shopkeeper, in 1770. They had five sons and five daughters. The five sons became great aids to him in his business: Amschel Mayer, Salomon Mayer, Nathan Mayer, Carl (originally Kalmann) Mayer, and James (originally Jacob) Mayer.

Mayer and his sons took advantage of the French revolutionary and Napoleonic wars (1792–1815) by trading with the warring countries in such basic items as wheat, cotton, and arms, and by making loans to the leaders of those nations. The family also set up the first great international financial clearinghouse, expediting the payment of England's subsidies to its allies—Austria, Prussia, and Russia—against France.

Mayer's great gift was his beguiling, dignified personal style in completing business transactions with the highest government powers. His sons, on the other hand, contributed craft and energy. Amschel helped and succeeded his father at the home office in Frankfurt, while Nathan set up an office in London in 1804, James settled in Paris in 1811, and Salomon and Carl established branches in Vienna and Naples, respectively, in the 1820s.

Mayer Amschel Rothschild lived long enough to see much of this expansion. He died in Frankfurt on September 19, 1812.

Nathan Mayer Rothschild

FOUNDER OF THE ROTHSCHILD BRANCH IN ENGLAND

One of the most important of all the Rothschilds was Nathan Mayer Rothschild, who established the family's greatly successful financial house in England.

Nathan was born in Frankfurt am Main, Germany, on September 16, 1777. He was the third son of Mayer Amschel and Gutele (Schnapper) Rothschild.

In the late 1790s Mayer sent Nathan to Manchester, England, as the family's representative in the cotton trade. In 1804 Nathan became a British citizen and opened a Rothschild business office in London.

He soon became an agent of the English government, taking a leading role in the payment of the nation's subsidies to its continental allies—Austria, Prussia, and Russia—in the war against France. The Rothschild family's many contacts on the Continent proved extremely useful to England during the Napoleonic Wars. For example, one of Nathan's agents, a man named Roworth, was the first to deliver to England the news of Napoléon's defeat at Waterloo in 1815. For his contributions during the Napoleonic Wars, Nathan, as well as his four brothers, was given the title of baron of the Austrian Empire (1822). Nathan himself never assumed the title.

After the coming of peace in 1815, the Rothschild's London house made even more rapid progress under Nathan's guidance. He arranged many large financial operations, including loans to the governments of England, France, Prussia, Russia, and Austria. During the commercial panic in London in 1825, the Duke of Wellington sought and followed Nathan's advice on the best way to meet the crisis. In 1835 Nathan raised millions of pounds to finance the emancipation of slaves in the British West Indies.

He married Hannah Cohen, daughter of a London merchant, in 1806. Her sister married Moses Montefiore. Nathan and Hannah had four sons and three daughters.

In 1836 he returned to Frankfurt to attend the wedding of his eldest son, Lionel Nathan. Nathan Mayer Rothschild died there on July 28, 1836.

JAMES MAYER ROTHSCHILD

FOUNDER OF THE ROTHSCHILD BRANCH IN FRANCE

James Mayer Rothschild founded the French branch of the Rothschild financial empire. He also became the leader of Jewish communal affairs in France.

James (originally Jacob) was born in Frankfurt am Main, Germany, on May 15, 1792. He was the youngest of the five sons of Mayer Amschel and Gutele (Schnapper) Rothschild.

In 1811, in the midst of the Napoleonic Wars, James settled in Paris, establishing there an office vital to the ongoing history of the Rothschild family business. He showed extraordinary skill in maintaining his position in Paris for over half a century despite many political upheavals in France. James played a crucial role in the financing of French railroad construction.

The Jewish community in France accepted James as its undisputed leader. He often used his influence with the French government to lobby for the fair treament of persecuted Jews in other countries.

In 1824 he married his niece Betty Rothschild, daughter of his older brother Salomon. They had four sons and one daughter.

James Mayer Rothschild died in Paris on November 15, 1868.

LIONEL NATHAN ROTHSCHILD

PIONEER JEWISH POLITICIAN

Lionel Nathan Rothschild succeeded his father, Nathan Mayer, as head of the Rothschilds' London financial house. But his greatest achievement came in politics, where his struggle to assume the Parliament seat to which he was elected brought about the political emancipation of Jews in England.

Lionel was born in London, England, on November 22, 1808, the eldest of the four sons of Nathan Mayer and Hannah (Cohen) Rothschild. After being educated in Göttingen, Germany, Lionel entered his father's business and, on Nathan's death in 1936, took over the management of the Rothschild operations in England.

Under Lionel's leadership, the London house expanded its influence in England and on the Continent. It issued eighteen large government loans, the most spectacular in 1875, when Lionel lent the English government enough money to buy control of the Suez Canal.

He was strongly anglicized in his private life. His homes became the sites for innumerable social occasions among the English elite, and his close friends included many English statesmen, notably Benjamin Disraeli. Lionel developed a fondness for the English sport of hunting with staghounds. He also owned racehorses, one of which, Sir Bevys, won the Derby in 1879.

Lionel used his influence to improve the condition of Jews in England and elsewhere. He applied his voice and his money to assist Jews in Russia, Poland, Romania, and Palestine. In London he supported Jewish institutions and served as president of the Great Synagogue.

His greatest contribution was his battle to win political freedom for Jews in England. In 1847 he was elected to the House of Commons, but when he refused to accept the words "on the true faith of a Christian" in the parliamentary oath of office, he was not allowed to take his seat. After being reelected by a large majority, he went to Parliament and demanded to be sworn in on the Old Testament—but again he was denied. He won further elections in 1852, 1854, and 1857 (twice). Each time he was denied permission to become an official member of Parliament.

The problem, however, lay not in the House of Commons but in the House of Lords. The House of Commons, between 1830 and 1857, passed nine bills allowing Jews to take the oath in a form they could accept. Each bill was rejected by the House of Lords. Early in 1858 a tenth bill was passed by the House of Commons. This time the House of Lords accepted most of the bill but deleted the specific clause affecting the Jews. A few months later, both houses passed a bill allowing each house of Parliament to determine the form of its own oath of office.

Finally, on July 26, 1858, eleven years after his first election, he became the first Jew to take a seat in the English Parliament. He served in the House of Commons from 1858 to 1868 and again from 1869 to 1874.

Like many other Rothschilds, he married a relative. In 1836 he wedded his first cousin Charlotte Rothschild, daughter of his uncle Carl Mayer Rothschild. They had three sons and two daughters. Charlotte was active in Jewish and other charities and published a series of writings called *Addresses to Young Children* (1858, 1859, and 1861).

Lionel Nathan Rothschild died in London on June 3, 1879.

NATHANIEL MAYER ROTHSCHILD

FIRST JEWISH PEER IN ENGLAND

Nathaniel Mayer Rothschild followed the family tradition by being a noted banker and philanthropist. Like his father, Lionel Nathan, he served many years in the English Parliament. He is now best remembered for being created Baron Rothschild, thus becoming the first Jewish peer in the history of England.

Nathaniel was born in London, England, on November 8, 1840. He was the eldest of the three sons of Lionel Nathan and Charlotte (Rothschild) Rothschild. Nathaniel was educated by private tutors and then at Cambridge University (taking no degree) and in Germany.

He became a member of the family's London firm, N. M. Rothschild and Sons, founded by his grandfather Nathan Mayer Rothschild. In 1879, on the death of his father, he took over the leadership of the company. He often used his firm to assist the English government. In 1882, for example, when Egypt was on the verge of financial collapse, he upheld the interests of England by financially assisting Egypt.

As a philanthropist, too, he won the admiration of the English people. At his firm, one department was devoted exclusively to the administration of the large sums set aside for donations to individuals, institutions, and public subscriptions. He was personally active in the operations of several hospitals and served as chairman of the British Red Cross Society during the early part of World War I.

Involved with nearly every important Jewish organization in England, he became the acknowledged lay head of the Anglo-Jewish community. Through his influence, anti-Semitic powers seeking loans were denied access to official London. He further assisted the Jewish world through huge donations for the relief of persecuted Jews abroad. In his later years, he was widely regarded as the preeminent Jew in the world.

From 1865 to 1885, he served in the House of Commons. During those years, he succeeded his uncle Anthony as second baronet (1876) and his father as Austrian baron (1879). In 1885 he was elevated to the English peerage as a baron. For the rest of his life he sat as the first Jew in the House of Lords. He was a close associate of King Edward VII, with whom he had attended Cambridge University.

Nathaniel married Emma Louisa Rothschild, daughter of his father's cousin Mayer Carl Rothschild of Frankfurt am Main, Germany, in 1867. They had two sons and one daughter.

Nathaniel Mayer Rothschild died in London on March 31, 1915.

LIONEL WALTER ROTHSCHILD

EMINENT ZOOLOGIST

Lionel Walter Rothschild succeeded his father, Nathaniel Mayer, as head of the banking firm of N. M. Rothschild and Sons and as second baron. But Lionel won his greatest international fame for his many contributions to human knowledge of birds, insects, and mammals and for his creation of a large zoological museum.

Lionel was born in London, England, on February 8, 1868. He was the eldest son of Nathaniel Mayer and Emma Louisa (Rothschild) Rothschild.

Because of delicate health as a child, Lionel studied for many years privately at home. Later he attended Bonn (Germany) and Cambridge (England) universities.

Following family tradition, he joined the Rothschild bank in London, studying finance under his father. He also followed his father by serving in Parliament (1899–1910). On his father's death in 1915, Lionel inherited the titles of third baronet and second baron.

In 1917, because of his Zionist sympathies and his prominent position in the Anglo-Jewish community, he received from Arthur James Balfour, the British foreign secretary, a letter declaring the English government's willingness to establish in Palestine a national home for the Jewish people. This letter came to be known as the famous Balfour Declaration.

The dominant interest in Lionel's life was zoology. In early childhood he began collecting insects. At Cambridge University he met the famed zoologist Alfred Newton, who helped Lionel blossom from an amateur collector into a serious naturalist.

On his father's estate at Tring, Buckinghamshire, Lionel set up buildings for storing collections of birds, insects, mammals, and animal-related books. In 1892 he opened his displays as a public museum. In 1894 he began to publish a periodical for the museum, *Novitates zoologicae*, which contained material gathered from zoological expeditions that Lionel sent out to regions where the animal life was little known. He himself attended such expeditions in Europe and North Africa. In 1908 he largely retired from his London work to devote himself to his zoological efforts. His museum held the largest collection of natural history specimens ever assembled by one man.

Lionel Nathan Rothschild died, unmarried, at Tring on August 27, 1937. He willed his museum and all its contents to the British Museum in London.

GUY EDOUARD ALPHONSE PAUL ROTHSCHILD

LEADER OF FRENCH HOUSE OF ROTHSCHILD

As senior member of the French branch of the Rothschild family, Guy Edouard Alphonse Paul Rothschild headed an influential bank as well as a huge holding company with mining, industrial, and financial interests. More than anyone else, he brought the Rothschild empire into the modern world.

Guy was born in Paris, France, on May 21, 1909. His parents were Edouard Alphonse James and Germaine Alice (Halphen) Rothschild. Edouard was the only son of Mayer Alphonse Rothschild, the eldest son of James Mayer Rothschild, founder of the French branch of the House of Rothschild.

After receiving his *licence* (equivalent to a master's degree) in law from the University of Paris, Guy entered the family banking business. His career was interrupted by World War II, during which he served in a mechanized cavalry unit, was briefly a German prisoner of war, tried to keep the family business afloat under both the Germans and the puppet Vichy government, moved to the United States in 1941 to reassemble part of the Rothschild assets, went to England in 1943, and fought with the Free French Army in the liberation of France in 1944. For his war service, he received the Croix de Guerre.

World War II wiped out the Austrian and German Rothschilds, leaving the French house, though greatly weakened, the most important branch on the Continent. Guy set about the task of restoring the French Rothschilds' economic empire. In 1949, on the death of his father, he became Baron Rothschild and inherited the presidencies of the Rothschild Frères (a bank) and the Compagnie du Nord (a large investment firm and holding company), though he had, in effect, been in control of the family business since 1940.

With these two financial bases and with the help of his cousins Alain (in full, James Gustave Jules Alain) and Elie Robert Rothschild—both, like Guy, great-grandsons of James Mayer Rothschild—he modernized and strengthened the firms under his control. In 1951, for example, he made Rothschild Frères the first bank in Paris to use an automatic data-processing system. He applied advanced management techniques, sought new kinds of investments overseas, and, in 1967, reorganized Rothschild Frères, since 1817 a private investment bank, into Banque Rothschild, an incorporated commercial bank with branches in several French and Italian cities. The new bank gave the Rothschilds tax advantages because they became principal shareholders rather than personal owners, and it offered better opportunities for expansion and development, its assets doubling within five years.

One of Guy's most successful ventures was the Société minière métallurgique de Peñarroya, of which he was president and director-general from 1964 to 1971. Founded by the Rothschilds in 1881, Peñarroya was an international mining company, the world's largest producer of lead and one of the largest producers of zinc and other metals. But because of outmoded management and mining techniques, the company was running at a deficit till Guy took personal command. He closed unprofitable mines, bought new equipment, diversified the products, and integrated the firm's operations.

Guy also headed other mining operations as well as firms involved in hotels, publishing, real estate, oil refining, construction, vineyards and wineries, and other ventures. He founded the investment companies Five Arrows Securities Company, Ltd., of

Toronto (1956) and New Court Securities Corporation of New York City (1967).

Guy married Alix Schey de Koromla of Hungary in 1937. By that marriage, which was dissolved in 1956, he had one son and adopted a daughter. In 1957 he married Marie-Hélène de Zuylen de Nyevelt van de Haar, the daughter of a Dutch baron. They had one son.

Guy was widely acknowledged the titular head of the French Jewish community, but because his second wife, Marie-Hélène, was a Roman Catholic, a controversy arose and he resigned his position. From 1950 to 1982 he served as president of the French counterpart of the United Jewish Appeal.

In his later years, he enjoyed breeding and racing horses. Baron Guy Edouard Alphonse Paul Rothschild published his autobiography as *Contre bonne fortune* ("The Whims of Fortune," 1985).

THE
SACHARS

THE SACHARS HAVE BEEN remarkably diverse in their fields of achievement. All members of the family, however, are unified by their dual qualities of energy and intellectuality.

The American Sachars inherited those traits from their Old World ancestors. Samuel Sachar (1869–1949) was born in Lithuania and came to the United States in the 1880s. Beginning with nothing but a will to work, he became a successful realtor in Saint Louis, Missouri. He married another immigrant, his cousin Sarah Abramowitz, a Jerusalem native and daughter of Saint Louis's chief Orthodox rabbi, Dov Ber Abramowitz, whose family had many authors and scholars. Samuel and Sarah produced three sons and three daughters.

The eldest son was Abram Leon Sachar (1899–1993). He wrote *A History of the Jews*, served for many years as the national director of the B'nai B'rith Hillel Foundations, and was the founding president of Brandeis University, the first Jewish-sponsored non-sectarian institution of higher learning in the United States.

All three of Abram's sons have had notable careers. Howard Morley Sachar (1928–) is a history educator and author. Edward Joel Sachar (1933–84) was a successful psychiatrist. David Bernard Sachar (1940–) has had a profound impact in the medical field of gastroenterology.

ABRAM LEON SACHAR

FOUNDING PRESIDENT OF BRANDEIS UNIVERSITY

Abram Leon Sachar capped his long, distinguished career by serving as the founding president of Brandeis University, the first Jewish-sponsored nonsectarian institution of higher learning in the United States. Earlier he had won renown as a writer of Jewish history, as a lecturer and news analyst, and as the national director of the B'nai B'rith Hillel Foundations.

Abram was born in New York City on February 15, 1899. He was the eldest of the six children of his immigrant parents, Samuel and Sarah (Abramowitz) Sachar. When Abram was seven, his family moved to Saint Louis, Missouri, where he attended Washington University, earning B.A. and M.A. degrees in history, both in 1920. In 1923 he received a doctorate in history from Cambridge University in England.

Returning to the United States, he soon joined the history faculty of the University of Illinois, where he remained for twenty-four years. In 1927 he succeeded Rabbi Benjamin Frankel as director of the original Hillel Foundation, which was founded at the University of Illinois. Later more chapters were established at about two hundred other universities. Sponsored by B'nai B'rith, the Hillel Foundations were, in Abram's words, "youth centers for Jewish students on American campuses." From 1933 to 1948 he served as national director of the organization, and from 1948 to 1955 he chaired the National Hillel Foundation Commission.

As early as 1929 he had to give up teaching because of time pressures from his Hillel work and his historical research. His first important book was *Factors in Modern Jewish History* (1927), while *A History of the Jews* (1929; fifth edition, 1965) became a major success. *Sufferance Is the Badge: The Jew in the Contemporary World* (1939) added to his reputation.

During these early years, he also lectured at most of the larger North American cities. In 1944 he became a news analyst on a

Howard Morley Sachar

Abram Leon Sachar (seated, right) with his wife, Thelma (seated, left), and their three sons: David, Howard, and Edward (standing, left to right).

Chicago radio station, and the following year he did similar work in New York City.

In 1948 he was invited to become the first president of Brandeis University, named in memory of United States Supreme Court Justice Louis D. Brandeis. When it opened under Abram's direction in 1948, Brandeis, located in Waltham, Massachusetts, had only 107 students and 13 faculty members. By the time of Abram's death it had 3,700 students and a full-time faculty of 360. During his years as president (1948–68), Abram raised $250 million for the school and oversaw its growth from a few structures to ninety buildings. He was the driving force behind the development of Brandeis into a major research institution. From 1968 to 1982 he held the post of chancellor of the university, serving as an ambassador for the institution.

In these later years, he also continued many of his earlier interests. Beginning in 1969 he presented a weekly National Educational Television program called *Course of Our Times*, an extension of his Brandeis lecture course on twentieth-century history. His later books include *The Course of Our Times* (1972) and *The Redemption of the Unwanted: From the Liberation of the Death Camps to the Founding of Israel* (1983).

He was married in 1926 to Thelma Horwitz, a student at Washington University. They had three sons.

Abram Leon Sachar died at his home in Newton, Massachusetts, on July 24, 1993, at the age of ninety-four.

HOWARD MORLEY SACHAR

HISTORIAN AND EDUCATOR

Howard Morley Sachar, eldest of Abram Leon Sachar's three sons, followed in his father's footsteps as a historian and educator. He has written many highly valued historical studies of modern Jewish history, Israel, the Zionist movement, the Middle East, and Jews in the United States. In the mid-1960s he began a long career as professor of history at George Washington University in Washington, D.C.

Howard was born in Saint Louis, Missouri, on February 10, 1928. His parents were Abram Leon and Thelma (Horwitz) Sachar. Abram wrote many important books on Jewish studies, notably *A History of the Jews* (1929; fifth edition, 1965), and became the founding president of Brandeis University.

Howard earned a B.A. degree at Swarthmore College (1947) and an M.A. degree at Harvard University (1950), where he also received a Ph.D. (1953). In his distinguished academic career he worked as an instructor of history at the University of Massachusetts—Amherst (1953–54); the director of the Hillel Foundations at the University of California, Los Angeles (1954–57) and Stanford University (1959–61); the director of the Jacob Hiatt Institute (of Brandeis University), Jerusalem, Israel (1961–64); and associate professor (1964–66) and full professor (1966–) of

Howard Morley Sachar

Howard Morley Sachar

history at George Washington University, Washington, D.C.

He married Eliana Steimatzky in 1964. They had two daughters and one son.

Howard has contributed articles to many important scholarly periodicals as well as to numerous popular media, including the *New York Times*, the *Washington Post*, the *New Republic*, and *Commentary*. Among his books are *The Course of Modern Jewish History* (1958); *Aliyah: The Peoples of Israel* (1964); *From the Ends of the Earth: The Peoples of Israel* (1964); *The Emergence of the Middle East, 1914–1924* (1969); *Europe Leaves the Middle East, 1936–1954* (1972); *A History of Israel* (1976); *Egypt and Israel* (1981); *Diaspora* (1985); *A History of Israel from the Aftermath of the Yom Kippur War* (1987); *A History of the Jews in America* (1992); and *Farewell España: The World of the Sephardim Remembered* (1994). Howard Morley Sachar, unlike many other academic writers, has been praised for his ability to produce works that are not only encyclopedic in knowledge but also readable in style.

Edward Joel Sachar

PSYCHIATRIST AND HORMONE EXPERT

Edward Joel Sachar was one of the most renowned psychiatrists of his time. He gained recognition as an authority on the roles of chemicals in mental illness.

Edward was born in Saint Louis, Missouri, on June 23, 1933.

He was the middle of the three sons of Abram Leon and Thelma (Horwitz) Sachar. Abram was a historian and the founding president of Brandeis University.

After receiving a B.A. degree from Harvard University (1952) and a medical degree from the University of Pennsylvania (1956), Edward interned at Beth Israel Hospital in Boston (1956–57), served his residency at the Massachusetts Mental Health Center (1957–59), performed a tour of duty in the Medical Corps of the United States Army (1959–61), and, in the 1960s, trained in psychoanalysis at the Boston Psychoanalytic Society and Institute. He worked as an associate in psychiatry at the Harvard Medical School (1964–66) and joined the Albert Einstein College of Medicine in the Bronx, New York, where he was an associate professor (1966–72) and a full professor (1972–76) of psychiatry, as well as the chairman of the department (1975–76). During those years he continued to study, graduating from the New York Psychoanalytic Institute in 1972. He also directed the psychiatry services at the Bronx Municipal Hospital Center.

In the final stage of his career, he served as professor of psychiatry and chairman of the psychiatry department of the College of Physicians and Surgeons at Columbia University in New York City (1976–81) till a stroke forced him to retire. He was also director of the New York State Psychiatric Institute and chief of psychiatry services at Presbyterian Hospital.

Edward specialized in depression and performed psychoendocrine research, the study of the relationship between psychological processes and hormones. He contributed numerous articles to professional journals and wrote the books *Topics in Psychoendocrinology* (1975) and *Hormones, Behavior, and Psychopathology* (1976).

Highly regarded by his colleagues, he served as secretary-treasurer of the American Psychosomatic Society and president of the Psychiatric Research Society. In 1975 he was awarded the Anna-Monika Foundation prize for his work in depression, and in 1981 his research won a gold medal from the Society of Biological Psychiatry.

Edward Joel Sachar died in New York City on March 25, 1984. He was survived by his wife, Hindy.

DAVID BERNARD SACHAR

GASTROENTEROLOGIST

David Bernard Sachar is one of the preeminent gastroenterologists of his time. He has taught, practiced, written, and performed research in the field since the 1960s.

David was born in Urbana, Illinois, on March 2, 1940. He was the youngest of the three sons of Abram Leon and Thelma (Horwitz) Sachar. Abram was a renowned historian and the first president of Brandeis University.

After earning a B.A. degree (1959) and a medical degree (1963) at Harvard University, David served his internship at Beth Israel Hospital in Boston (1963–65) and then worked as assistant chief of clinical research for the Pakistan-SEATO (Southeast Asia Treaty Organization) Cholera Research Laboratory in Dhaka, Bangladesh (1965–67). Returning to Beth Israel Hospital, he served his general residency (1967–68) before moving to Mount Sinai Hospital in New York City for his residency in gastroenterology (1968–70).

In 1970 he began to work as an instructor at the Mount Sinai School of Medicine in New York City, later rising to professor; in 1992 he became the first Burrill B. Crohn professor of medicine there. During those years he also practiced in the gastroenterology division at Mount Sinai Hospital, becoming director of the division in 1983 and vice chairman of the department of medicine in 1992.

David has written well over a hundred articles and chapters on natural history and on the treatment of inflammatory bowel disease. As an editor he has produced, to date, seven books and monographs. Among his achievements are his codevelopment of oral rehydration therapy for diarrhea and his creation of resources and standards for clinical teaching in gastroenterology.

David has been widely active and highly honored in his field. He cochaired a work group on inflammatory bowel disease for the National Institutes of Health (1973–75), was a member of the expert advisory panel on gastroenterology and nutrition at the United States Pharmacopeial Convention (1980–85), chaired the research development committee of the National Foundation for Ileitis and Colitis (1984–89), and served as the first American to be elected chairman of the International Organization for the study of Inflammatory Bowel Disease (1989–92). In 1991 he received the Distinguished Service award from the Crohn's and Colitis Foundation of America.

David Bernard Sachar married Joanna Maud Belford Silver in 1961. They had two sons.

THE
SASSOONS

T HE SASSOONS, known as "the Rothschilds of the East," attained fabulous wealth and influence in the Orient, especially during the British development of India and China in the nineteenth century. After establishing themselves in England they spanned the two worlds—Eastern and Western—more thoroughly than any other family. Merchants, industrialists, statesmen, scholars, philanthropists— the Sassoons were a family of incredibly diverse talent.

They were probably among the earliest Jews to move from ancient Palestine to Babylonia. Later, perhaps after a prolonged stay in Spain, they settled in Baghdad, where they lived for many centuries as wealthy merchant-bankers under successive Ottoman rulers. However, as the power of Baghdad declined, minorities could no longer depend on the goodwill of the Muslim governor of the city. By the end of the eighteenth century, the clan was threatened with extinction.

The first documented member of the family was Sason (or Sassoon) ben Saleh (1750–1830), whose full name was Sason ben Saleh ben David ben Jacob ben Saleh ben David. A merchant by trade, he was also the chief treasurer for the Baghdad governor and the lay leader of the Jewish community, his dual role noted in his titles of *sheikh* (Arabic "chief") and *nasi* (Hebrew "prince").

Sason ben Saleh had seven sons, one of whom, David Sassoon

(1792–1864) rose to distinction and founded the principal family line. David fled Baghdad because of persecution and settled in Bombay, India, where he set up a great commercial house, David Sassoon and Sons (later David Sassoon and Company), with agencies throughout the Orient.

He had eight sons. Albert (originally Abdullah David, 1818–96), became head of the family company after his father's death and was the first of many Sassoons to be made a knight (1872) and a baronet (1890). Elias David (1820–80) left the family business and set up a rival firm, E. D. Sassoon and Company. Sassoon David (1832–67), the first of the clan to settle in England and to wear Western clothes, advanced the family business interests in England, and became active in Jewish communal life there. Reuben David (1835–1905) also settled in England to work in the family business, but he became best known for his close friendship with the Prince of Wales, later King Edward VII.

Arthur (originally Abraham, 1840–1912) rose to a senior directorship of the family firm in England, was socially connected with King Edward VII, and became the best known of the brothers to the general public because of the lavish entertainments that he hosted. Aaron (1841–1907), who participated in neither business nor society, led a rather obscure life in England and, at his death, left his fortune to the poor. Solomon (1841–94), Aaron's twin, remained in the Orient, heading the family business interests in Shanghai, Hong Kong, and India. Frederick (originally Farraj Hayim, 1853–1917), the youngest son, moved to England, where he became chairman of the family firm in 1912, five years before his death.

Later generations of Sassoons also left their marks. Albert's son Edward Albert (1856–1912) headed the Sephardic Jewish community in England and served for many years in Parliament. He linked the family with the House of Rothschild by marrying Aline Caroline de Rothschild. Their son, Philip Albert Gustave David (1888–1939), was an important British statesman.

Elias's eldest son, Jacob Elias (1844–1916), expanded E. D. Sassoon and Company in India and became a well-known philanthropist. Elias's second son, Edward Elias (1853–1924), became prominent in business and society, while the latter's son Victor (1881–1961), in his turn, headed E. D. Sassoon and Company and was a leader of British Indian Jewry. Yet another of Elias's sons, Meyer Elias (1855–1924), had a son, Reginald Ellice (1893–1933), who was a hero in World War I, winning the Military Cross, and was later successful with the family business in India and China; he also rode racehorses and died after a fall from one of them.

Sassoon David's daughter, Rachel (or Richa, 1858–1927), married Frederick Beer and edited his *Sunday Observer* in England. Later she bought the *Sunday Times* and edited both newspapers simultaneously. Rachel was responsible for changing the *Sunday Times* from an independent liberal publication into a nonpartisan objective press.

Solomon married his grandniece Flora (originally Farha) Abraham (1859–1936), daughter of one of his brother Albert's daughters. After Solomon's death, Flora managed the family firm in Bombay for about seven years. She was also a highly respected Hebrew scholar. Solomon and Flora's son, David Solomon (1880–1942), was a noted bibliophile and Hebraist who wrote the posthumously published book *A History of the Jews in Baghdad* (1949). David's son, Solomon David (1915–85), became a rabbi, continued his father's work as a bibliophile, moved to Jerusalem, and produced scholarly writings, including *The Spiritual Heritage of the Sephardim* (1957).

Some branches of the family left the Jewish faith. The first to marry outside Judaism was Sassoon David's son Alfred (1861–95), who wedded a Christian and had three sons. One of them was the famous English writer Siegfried Lorraine Sassoon (1886–1967), who was raised as an Anglican and later converted to Roman Catholicism.

DAVID SASSOON

FOUNDER OF THE MODERN SASSOON DYNASTY

David Sassoon saved his prominent family from possible extinction by fleeing a mad ruler in Baghdad. Starting his life over again as a humble peddler at the age of thirty-seven, he soon founded David Sassoon and Sons and built it into one of the greatest business empires ever seen in the Orient.

He was born in Baghdad in 1792. His parents were Sason (or Sassoon) ben Saleh, born in the same city in 1750, and Amam Gabbai, daughter of a merchant. Sason descended from a long line of wealthy merchants who were the lay leaders of the Baghdad Jewish community and held the title of *nasi* ("prince"). Along with that status came an appointment from the Muslim governor of the city as chief banker (or treasurer), responsible for collecting taxes from the Jewish people. Sason, too, attained these positions, becoming *nasi* is 1778. He was also granted the honorary Arabic title of *sheikh* ("chief").

David entered the family business and married Hannah Joseph, daughter of a merchant. They had two sons and two daughters. She died in 1826, and two years later he married Farha Hyeem, whose father was also a merchant. They had six sons and four daughters.

When Sason retired in 1817, a non-Sassoon was named to replace him. But the successor was imprisoned during the reign of terror under Daud Pasha, the governor of Baghdad. David therefore became the unofficial leader of the city's Jews. In 1828 David himself was imprisoned by Daud Pasha and held for ransom. In 1829, after Sason paid the required amount, David, correctly assuming that Daud Pasha would soon arrest him again for more ransom, fled to Bushire, Persia. The rest of his family joined him in Bushire, where Sason died in 1830.

David, virtually penniless, began to work as a peddler. In early 1832 he moved to Bombay, India, where he opened his merchant business, David Sassoon and Sons (later David Sassoon and

Company). The business expanded rapidly, and within twenty-five years it was one of the most powerful in the Orient.

David was the sole owner till 1852, when his eldest son, Abdullah (later Albert) joined him in partnership. Eventually each of the other sons was also admitted to partnership after he had proved himself capable. David allowed his sons to acquire small independent fortunes, but he nipped avarice in the bud.

The company exported English textiles to the Orient, from which it imported native products to be sold to British traders. The firm dealt with a vast range of products, including silks, gums, spices, metals, and opium (at that time still a respectable commodity).

At first the company employed only Jews. It paid good wages and pioneered welfare schemes for workers and their families. When David sent his employees to new branches, he built synagogues and schools for them. In fact, most of the Jewish communities that came into existence in India and the Far East were located around the agencies of David Sassoon and Company.

David became a patriotic supporter of the British Empire, though he never learned to speak English. When he was naturalized as a British citizen in 1853, he signed the oath in Hebrew.

David's benefactions were enormous. The great patriarch of Eastern Jewry, he answered pleas from Jews throughout the Orient, and in his last years no Jewish beggar could be found in his home city of Bombay. He was the recognized judge of all disputes between Bombay Jews. In that city, he built many communal institutions, including, for the Jewish community, the Magen David synagogue, and, for the city as a whole, the Sassoon Industrial and Reformatory Institution for juvenile delinquents, the first of its kind in the Orient and the model for many others. In Poona, India, where he had a summer residence, he endowed the nonsectarian Sassoon General Hospital, built the Ohel David synagogue, and established the Sassoon Infirmary and Leper Asylum.

David Sassoon died in Poona in November 1864.

ALBERT SASSOON

SUCCESSOR TO DAVID SASSOON

On the death of David Sassoon, founder of the Sassoon business empire, Albert, David's eldest son, took control of the family firm in Bombay, India. Albert inherited his father's commercial ability and his philanthropic spirit.

Originally named Abdullah David, Albert was born in Baghdad on July 25, 1818 (some sources give 1817). He was the first son of David and Hannah (Joseph) Sassoon. Albert was educated in India, and in his early years he helped to establish his father's trade with China.

When his father died in 1864, Albert succeeded him as head of the family business. Under his leadership the company branched out from trade to manufacturing, insurance, and banking.

Albert contributed greatly to the development of Bombay, donating huge sums of money to various causes. His principal benefaction to the city was his construction (1872–75) of the first wet dock on the western coast of India. The project employed thousands of local workers and initiated Bombay's emergence as a major port city.

In 1872 he was made a knight, and the following year he visited England, receiving the freedom of the city of London for his "munificent and philanthropic exertions in the cause of charity and education, especially in our Indian empire." Soon afterward he settled permanently in England, where the family's business interests were increasingly centered. He acquired a mansion in London and another residence in Brighton. In both locations he associated with members of high British society, including the Prince of Wales, later King Edward VII. In 1890 he was created first baronet of Kensington Gore.

Albert also identified himself with the Jewish community. He donated liberally to Jewish charities and served as a vice president of the Anglo-Jewish Association.

In 1838 Albert married Hannah Moses, daughter of a Baghdad

merchant who had settled in Bombay. They had two sons and three daughters.

Albert Abdullah David Sassoon died in Brighton on October 24, 1896.

ELIAS DAVID SASSOON

FOUNDER OF E. D. SASSOON AND COMPANY

Elias David Sassoon, disliking his subordinate role in his family's business, set up his own independent firm, E. D. Sassoon and Company. The new company prospered even more than the original one.

Elias was born in Baghdad in 1820. He was the second son of David and Hannah (Joseph) Sassoon.

As a young man Elias was sent to China to develop and supervise the Sassoon business there. His work was successful, and he became an important force in the company.

But after his father died in 1864, he developed a rivalry with his older brother, Albert (originally Abdullah). In 1867 Elias left David Sassoon and Company and founded his own business, E. D. Sassoon and Company. Establishing himself in the Orient, Europe, Africa, and America, he directly competed against, and eventually outstripped, the family firm. Like his father, Elias employed large numbers of Jews and provided them with schools and synagogues, even in the most isolated locations.

He married Leah Gubbay, daughter of another Jewish family engaged in developing the Orient. They had five sons.

Elias David Sassoon died while visiting tea plantations in Colombo, Ceylon, in 1880.

SASSOON DAVID SASSOON

FIRST SASSOON TO SETTLE IN ENGLAND

Sassoon David Sassoon established the first David Sassoon and Company office in England and became the first member of his family to settle there. He was also more active than his brothers in the Jewish communal life of England.

Sassoon was born in Bombay, India, in 1832. He was the first son born to David and Farha (Hyeem) Sassoon but was the third son of David, who had two sons from an earlier marriage.

In his boyhood Sassoon was sent to Baghdad for a traditional Jewish education. While still in his teens he issued at Bombay the earliest numbers of the first Jewish periodical to be published in India. He then served his business apprenticeship in Shanghai.

In 1858 his father sent him to England, where Sassoon set up an office for the family business. He greatly advanced the David Sassoon and Company interests in England and fit in so well with English ways that he became the first of his family to wear Western clothes.

Raised by a strictly Orthodox father, Sassoon, though far from home, took a strong interest in London Jewish life. He served as warden of his synagogue, was a member of the council of the Jews' College, and functioned as examiner in Hebrew at the Jews' Free School. He also acquired a fine collection of Jewish art and literature.

Sassoon married Flora (or Farha) Reuben, daughter of Solomon Reuben of Baghdad. They had three sons and one daughter.

Near the end of his life he bought the historic estate of Ashley Park, near Walton on Thames. His widow built the public hall in Walton in 1879.

Sassoon David Sassoon died in London in July 1867.

SOLOMON SASSOON

HEAD OF THE SASSOON EMPIRE, 1877–94

Next to his eldest brother, Albert, Solomon Sassoon was the most capable businessman of the eight Sassoon brothers. He led the family firm, David Sassoon and Company, from 1877 till his death.

Solomon was born in Bombay, India, in 1841. His twin brother, Aaron, and he were the fourth and fifth sons of David and Farha (Hyeem) Sassoon but the sixth and seventh sons of David, who had two sons from an earlier marriage.

As a young man Solomon was sent to Shanghai and Hong Kong to develop the family's business interests. Returning to India, he took control of the firm's Bombay headquarters in 1877, Albert having moved to England. In addition to guiding David Sassoon and Company, he served as a director of the Bank of Bombay, a leader in the Chamber of Commerce, and a trustee of the Bombay Port.

Like his father, Solomon remained intensely devoted to the Jewish milieu. He was active in the Anglo-Jewish Association, held services at the private synagogue located in his mansion, and was a noted Hebraist and student of the Talmud.

Solomon married his grandniece Flora (originally Farha) Abraham, daughter of a daughter of his eldest brother, Albert. They had one son and two daughters.

Solomon Sassoon died in Bombay in 1894.

JACOB ELIAS SASSOON

SUCCESSOR TO ELIAS DAVID SASSOON

After the death of his father, Elias David, Jacob Elias Sassoon became head of E. D. Sassoon and Company, which he led into pathbreaking business endeavors. He was also a noted philanthropist.

Jacob was born in Bombay, India, in 1844. He was the eldest son of Elias David and Leah (Gubbay) Sassoon. Jacob assisted Elias when the latter left David Sassoon and Company in 1867 to found the rival firm of E. D. Sassoon and Company.

When Elias died in 1880, Jacob, one of the most brilliant businessmen in the Sassoon family, took control of the company. He greatly extended the business and established branches in England, where he lived in the 1880s.

Returning to Bombay, he led the development of the cotton textile industry in western India, setting up numerous mills and building the region's first dye works. The Jacob Sassoon Mill, India's largest, employed at one time fifteen thousand workers.

In 1909 he founded the Eastern Bank, Ltd., an exchange bank for Indian business. It was headquartered in London. In the same year, his achievements were recognized by British authorities, who made him a baronet.

Like other Sassoons, Jacob contributed large sums to many causes. He followed in his grandfather's footsteps by being a benefactor of Bombay. With his brothers, he built the Keneseth Eliyahu synagogue there. His other philanthropies included establishing the Jacob Sassoon European General Hospital, opening a free school for Jewish boys and girls, founding the Central College of Science, and leaving many endowments for the Bombay Jews whose families (like the Sassoons) had originated in Baghdad.

He married Rachel Simon Isaacs. They had no children.

Jacob Elias Sassoon died in Baghdad on October 23, 1916.

EDWARD ALBERT SASSOON

FIRST SASSOON POLITICIAN

Edward Albert Sassoon was the first member of the Sassoon family to choose politics as a profession. He also linked the family to the House of Rothschild through marriage.

Edward was born in Bombay, India, on June 20, 1856. He was

the younger of the two sons of Albert and Hannah (Moses) Sassoon.

In 1887 Edward married Aline Caroline de Rothschild, daughter of Baron Gustave de Rothschild of Paris, in a ceremony performed by the chief rabbi of France. Edward and Aline had a son and a daughter.

They established themselves in a London mansion and entertained such celebrities as Winston Churchill, John Singer Sargent, and H. G. Wells. Edward became head of the Sephardic Jewish community in England.

He joined the family firm, and when his father died in 1896 he succeeded to the chairmanship of the company as well as to Albert's baronetcy. However, he soon entered politics. He was elected to Parliament in 1899 and held the seat for the rest of his life. His main interest was in improving telegraphic communications between India and England, introducing a bill to make wireless equipment mandatory on vessels at sea.

In January 1911 he was thrown from a motor car, and thereafter he suffered poor health. Edward Albert Sassoon died in London on May 24, 1912.

FLORA (ABRAHAM) SASSOON

BUSINESS MANAGER AND HEBREW SCHOLAR

When her husband, Solomon, died, Flora Sassoon took over the management of David Sassoon and Company in Bombay, India. She also earned a reputation for her talmudic knowledge.

Flora Sassoon (originally Farha Abraham) was born in Bombay in 1859. She was the daughter of Ezekiel and Aziza (Sassoon) Abraham. Her mother was a daughter of Albert Sassoon, the eldest son of the founder of David Sassoon and Company.

When Flora wedded Albert's brother Solomon, she married her own granduncle. They had one son and two daughters.

In 1894 Solomon died and Flora took his place as manager of

the family's Bombay headquarters. She showed a good business head, keeping the firm on solid ground till 1901, when David Sassoon and Company was incorporated and she was eased out of her position by other members of the family.

Flora then moved to London, England, where she entertained scholars and public figures in a grand style. Judaism filled her life, even in her dealings with English high society. At her table kiddush was said, and Jew and non-Jew alike wore the yarmulke.

Flora was a master of Hebrew (as well as several other languages) and a student of the Talmud and talmudic literature. She was often consulted on questions of Jewish law. In 1924, at Jews' College in London, she delivered a learned discourse on the Talmud, and in 1930 she published an essay in the *Jewish Forum* on the great medieval biblical and talmudic commentator Rashi.

Flora, strictly Orthodox, was an active member of the Sephardic Jewish community in London. She helped found the London Jewish Hospital.

Flora Sassoon died in London on January 14, 1936.

VICTOR SASSOON

BANKER, PUBLIC FIGURE, AND RACEHORSE QWNER

Victor Sassoon attained distinction in three different fields of activity. He excelled in commerce, played a prominent role in public life, and became a famous owner of racehorses in England and India.

Ellice Victor Sassoon was born in Naples, Italy, on December 30, 1881. His parents were Edward Elias and Leontine (Levy) Sassoon. Edward's grandfather David Sassoon had founded the Sassoon business dynasty in India, while Edward's father, Elias David Sassoon, had established a new family enterprise, E. D. Sassoon and Company, also of India, a merchandising and banking firm later headed by Edward's brother Jacob and then by Edward himself.

Victor was educated in England, studying at Harrow and at Trinity College of Cambridge University. He developed an early interest in aviation, competing, for example, in a French airshow in 1912. In World War I he served in the British air force and retired with the rank of captain. He pioneered civil aviation in his family's home country of India.

By the end of World War I Victor, an exceptionally astute businessman, had already taken over active control of the vast interests of E. D. Sassoon and Company and its many branches in various countries. Victor was a pioneer in promoting the health and welfare of laborers. He set up programs to assist his own millworkers and encouraged other mill owners to do the same.

In 1930 he became chairman of the newly created E. D. Sassoon Banking Company, registered in Hong Kong and organized to finance the family's large-scale investments in Hong Kong, London, and elsewhere outside the company's home territory of India. In his later years, this concern became his primary business focus. After moving to Shanghai to oversee his Eastern banking interests, Victor encountered many difficulties by successive Japanese and Communist Chinese authorities, who appropriated much of his property. Frustrated by this development, he moved his personal headquarters to Nassau, the Bahamas.

During those years of business activity, Victor also participated in public affairs. He was a member of the Indian Legislative Assembly in 1922–23 and 1926–29. In 1929 he served on a royal commission studying the working conditions of laborers in India, the health and standard of living of workers, and the relations between employers and employees. Another public topic of concern to him was the question of government policy toward stabilizing the exchange value of the Indian rupee. To deal with this issue, Victor founded, and served as president of, the Indian Currency League.

As head of British Indian Jewry, he worked tirelessly to help Jewish refugees fleeing from Nazism in the 1930s and 1940s. Besides contributing funds for the immediate relief of the refugees, he hired as many of them as possible for his offices in India and China.

Victor had a long-standing interest in horse racing and breeding. He bought his first racehorse in 1924 and went on to become one of England's major owners, winning the Derby four times. In India, too, he earned a prominent place in thoroughbred history.

His original first name, Ellice, was a variant of Elias, often found in the Sassoon family. In 1924 his middle name, Victor, became his official given name when he used it in conjunction with his acceptance of the British baronetcy he inherited from his late father, who in turn had inherited it from his older brother, Jacob Elias Sassoon, the first baronet in the line.

Victor married late in life. In 1959 he wedded Evelyn Barnes of Dallas, Texas.

(Ellice) Victor Sassoon died in Nassau on August 12, 1961.

Philip Albert Gustave David Sassoon

BRITISH STATESMAN AND ART CONNOISSEUR

Philip Albert Gustave David Sassoon held a seat in the British Parliament for twenty-seven years. During those years he also held the important government posts of undersecretary of state for air (1924–29 and 1931–37) and, because of his knowledge of art, first commissioner of works (1937–39).

Philip was born in Paris, France, on December 4, 1888. He was the only son of Edward Albert and Aline Caroline (de Rothschild) Sassoon.

Philip was educated in England at Eton and at Christ Church of Oxford University. At the age of nineteen he chose British citizenship.

In 1912 his father, who had been a member of the British Parliament since 1899, died. Philip succeeded his father as third baronet of Kensington Gore. He also ran for and won his father's seat in Parliament that year. For some years thereafter he was the youngest member of the House of Commons. He remained in

Philip Sassoon

Parliament till his own death twenty-seven years later.

Early in World War I he held a commission in the Royal East Kent Yeomanry. Later he served as private secretary to Field Marshall Douglas Haig, commander in chief of the British armies. Philip initiated and implemented the plan of sending artists, such as John Singer Sargent, to the front to record their impressions of the fighting.

In 1924 Philip was appointed undersecretary of state for air, a post he held till 1929 and then again from 1931 to 1937. In that capacity he did much to promote the importance of aviation, especially the Royal Air Force. His only book, *The Third Route* (1929), is the story of his flying tour of British overseas air stations.

In 1937 he was appointed the first commissioner (minister) of works, responsible for parks, royal palaces, and ancient monuments. He was well suited to this post, being a connoisseur of all kinds of decorative objects, including paintings, china, old silver, and furniture. For many years he held annual art exhibitions at his London house in aid of charity. He was a trustee of the National Gallery, the Tate Gallery, and the Wallace Collection.

Philip never married. He was known as "the richest bachelor in England" and entertained a wide circle of friends, including T. E. Lawrence (of Arabia) and King Edward VIII, in London and at his country residence, Port Lympne, near Hythe.

Philip Albert Gustave David Sassoon died in London on June 3, 1939.

THE
SCHIFFS

THE SCHIFFS HAVE THE LONGEST continuous known record
of any Jewish family. They emerged in fourteenth-
century Germany, where, in Middle High German, *Schiff*
meant "vial," probably adopted by the family from the sign of
an apothecary or physician. Centered primarily in Frankfurt
am Main, the Schiffs for centuries produced many
prominent members. In the eighteenth century they shared a
Frankfurt house with the Rothschild family, with whom they
would long vie for the greatest prestige in the Jewish community.
However, the Rothschilds for generations were known principally as businessmen, while the Schiffs excelled not only in
business but also in such fields as scholarship and the rabbinate.

Meir ben Jacob ha-Kohen Schiff (1605–1641) was born
in Frankfurt; became rabbi in Fulda, Hesse; delivered sermons and
lectures famous for their wit and warmth; wrote profound talmudic
works; earned the title of MaHaRaM (or MaHaraM), an acronym
for Morenu Ha-Rav Meir Schiff; and died in Frankfurt. David
Tevele Schiff (died 1792) was born in Frankfurt and in 1765 became chief rabbi of the Great Synagogue in London, England,
where he spent the rest of his life.

In 1865 Jacob Henry Schiff (1847–1920), also a native of Frankfurt, immigrated to the United States, where he headed the important New York City investment banking firm of Kuhn, Loeb
and Company and became a noted philanthropist. Ludwig Moses

Schiff (1855–1930), Jacob's brother, was a leading banker and Jewish community leader in Frankfurt.

Otto Moritz Schiff (1876–1952), a nephew of both Jacob and Ludwig, was born in London, England. He devoted much of his life to Jewish communal work and became a leader in British relief of persecuted Jews in eastern Europe during the Nazi era. In America the same generation was well represented by Mortimer Leo Schiff (1877–1931), Jacob's only son. Mortimer succeeded his father as head of Kuhn, Loeb and Company and served with distinction as a philanthropist and as a leader in a wide variety of Jewish and non-Jewish organizations, including the Jewish Board of Guardians and the Boy Scouts of America.

Dorothy Schiff (1903–1989), Mortimer's daughter, crusaded for social progress through her role as publisher and editor in chief of the *New York Post*. John Mortimer Schiff (1904–1987), Mortimer's son, became a partner in Kuhn, Loeb and Company, succeeded Lillian D. Wald as president of the famous Henry Street Settlement in New York City, was active in the American Red Cross and the Boy Scouts of America, helped lead the Jewish Welfare Board, and engaged in philanthropy.

JACOB HENRY SCHIFF

HEAD OF KUHN, LOEB AND COMPANY

As head of the investment banking firm of Kuhn, Loeb and Company, Jacob Henry Schiff played a major role in financing the development of American railroads at the beginning of the twentieth century. He was also active in both Jewish and non-Jewish philanthropies.

Jacob was born in Frankfurt am Main, Germany, on July 10, 1847. His parents were Moses and Clara (Niederhofheim) Schiff. Moses, a stockbroker, belonged to an old family (traceable to the fourteenth century) of distinguished scholars, rabbis, and businessmen. One of Jacob's brothers, Herman, became a successful banker in London, England.

After being educated in secular and Jewish subjects at local schools, Jacob was apprenticed at the age of fourteen to a business firm. Four years later, in 1865, he immigrated to the United States and began to work in the brokerage business in New York City. In 1867 he joined the firm of Budge, Schiff and Company, and in 1870 he became a naturalized American citizen.

However, in 1872 his firm was dissolved. Moving back to Germany, he worked briefly in Hamburg and then, on the death of his father, returned to Frankfurt.

In 1874 Abraham Kuhn, senior partner at Kuhn, Loeb and Company of New York City, invited him to enter that firm. Jacob accepted

Jacob Henry Schiff

American Jewish Archives. Cincinnati Campus, Hebrew Union College-Jewish Institute of Religion.

the job in early 1875 and took with him many important business connections in Europe. He was thus able to place large quantities of American securities on the European market.

In May 1875 he married Therese Loeb, daughter of Solomon Loeb, head of Kuhn, Loeb. They had a daughter, Frieda, who married Felix M. Warburg, and a son, Mortimer. Both Felix and Mortimer entered Kuhn, Loeb and Company.

In 1885, on the death of Solomon Loeb, Jacob took charge of the firm. He concerned himself with financing many of the most important railroads in the East, especially the Pennsylvania Railroad and the Louisville and Nashville line.

In 1897 he gained much prestige in banking circles when he financially backed Edward H. Harriman's takeover of the bankrupt Union Pacific Railroad. A few years later the Union Pacific engaged in a sensational struggle with the Great Northern company for control of the Northern Pacific, in which Jacob backed

Jacob Henry Schiff

Harriman against James J. Hill and his banker, J. P. Morgan. The contest, ultimately inconclusive, brought about a panic on the stock market in 1901.

Jacob also aided various other ventures, including the American Smelting and Refining Company, the Westinghouse Electric Company, the Western Union Telegraph Company, and the Equitable Life Assurance Society. During the Russo-Japanese War of 1904–1905, he played a central role in the sale of Japanese bonds in the United States.

Jacob spent considerable time, effort, and money in philanthropy, both general and Jewish. He served as president of the Montefiore Hospital, contributed to the Henry Street Settlement and district nursing, was a member of the International Relief Board of the American Red Cross, and provided substantial aid for educational purposes, including the establishment of the Semitic Museum at Harvard University and of the departments of Semitic literature at the New York Public Library and the Library of Congress. Jacob helped to promote Tuskegee Institute and other historically black schools in the South.

He was a founder of the American Jewish Committee, organized in 1906 to help Jews in other countries. During World War I he supported the American Jewish Joint Distribution Committee, which relieved suffering in Europe, and the Jewish Welfare Board, which aided Jewish soldiers and sailors. He created a fund to publish the Schiff Library of Jewish Classics and donated heavily to the Jewish Theological Seminary of New York City and to the Hebrew Union College in Cincinnati, Ohio.

Jacob Henry Schiff died in New York City on September 25, 1920. He was succeeded as head of Kuhn, Loeb and Company by his son, Mortimer.

MORTIMER LEO SCHIFF

BANKER AND COMMUNITY LEADER

Mortimer Leo Schiff succeeded his father as head of the prestigious banking firm of Kuhn, Loeb and Company in New York City, but much of his time and energy went into public causes. He helped to found the Boy Scouts of America, and he supported a wide range of philanthropic interests.

Mortimer was born in New York City on June 5, 1877. His parents were Jacob Henry and Therese (Loeb) Schiff.

After graduating from Amherst College in 1896, he studied railroading in the United States and then banking in Europe. In 1900 he joined his father's firm, Kuhn, Loeb and Company. When Jacob died in 1920, Mortimer took charge of the company. He also became a director of many other enterprises, such as the Chemical Bank and Trust Company, Western Union Telegraph Company, and the American Railway Express Company. Mortimer served as vice president of the New York State Chamber of Commerce.

One of the founders of the Boy Scouts of America, he financially helped to promote the movement abroad as well. In 1931, shortly before his death, he was elected president of the organization's national council. His interest in promoting the welfare of children led him to assist the Jewish Board of Guardians in New York City, which he served for many years as president.

Mortimer was a major contributor to the Federation for the Support of Jewish Philanthropic Societies in New York City. Among the scores of other recipients of his generosity were the Jewish Theological Society of America, the Young Men's Christian Association, and the Henry Street Settlement.

He married Adele Neustadt in 1901. Their children had notable careers. Dorothy Schiff became the publisher of the *New York Post*, while John Mortimer Schiff followed in his father's footsteps as a partner at Kuhn, Loeb and Company, a supporter of the Boy Scouts, and a philanthropist.

Mortimer Leo Schiff died in Oyster Bay, Long Island, on June 4, 1931.

DOROTHY SCHIFF

PUBLISHER OF THE *NEW YORK POST*

Though she inherited a substantial family fortune, Dorthy Schiff was not satisfied with the traditional role of passive philanthropist. She rolled up her sleeves and worked as the publisher and editor in chief of the *New York Post* newspaper, which she used as a vehicle to crusade for social progress.

Dorothy was born in New York City on March 11, 1903, the daughter of Mortimer Leo and Adele A. (Neustadt) Schiff. Her grandfather Jacob Henry Schiff and later her father headed the investment banking firm of Kuhn, Loeb and Company.

Dorothy attended the Brearley School in Manhattan and then entered Bryn Mawr College, but she left after her freshman year because of poor grades. In 1921 she made her social debut.

Two years later she married Richard B. W. Hall, a broker. They divorced in 1932. Later that year she married George Backer.

In the early 1930s she began to take part in social welfare activities, including four years' work with the poor as a member of the Social Service Committee of Bellevue Hospital. However, "it seemed to me," she later complained of that experience, "that what we were doing was simply putting a little salve on the sore, not curing the disease."

Dorothy admired President Franklin D. Roosevelt's New Deal social welfare program. She felt that government aid was "far less demoralizing than private charities." During the 1930s she became a leader of the Democratic party in New York State, a director of the Women's Trade Union League of New York, the secretary-treasurer of the New York Joint Committee for the Ratification of the Child Labor Amendment, and a member of the New York City Board of Child Welfare.

Meanwhile, she invested some of her sizable inheritance in communications media, including radio stations. In June 1939 she became the majority stockholder of the *New York Post*. Alexander Hamilton had started the publication in 1801 as a pamphlet-newspaper. During the nineteenth century the paper supported liberal causes, such as Jacksonian democracy, labor organizations, and the abolition of slavery. Early in the twentieth century the Post went through a conservative period, but in the 1930s it regained its progressive tendencies and favored the New Deal. Dorothy continued the newspaper's liberal policy.

At first she held the positions of director, vice president, and treasurer, while her husband, George Backer, was publisher and president. However, in 1942 ill health forced Backer to resign, and Dorothy succeeded him in both of his roles, becoming New York City's first woman publisher. In 1943 she assumed the titles of owner and publisher.

In the same year, she divorced Backer and married Theodore Olin Thackrey, who had risen from assistant city editor of the *Post* to executive editor in 1939. She promoted him to editor and publisher in 1943.

In 1948 Dorothy and Thackrey had a public disagreement over the presidential election. Both opposed the Democratic candidate, Harry Truman, but she favored the Republican, Thomas E. Dewey, while Thackrey preferred the Progressive party candidate, Henry Wallace. In 1949, disturbed by Thackrey's alleged left-wing policies, she took over full control of the *Post*, and he left the newspaper. They subsequently divorced. Later that year she replaced Thackrey as editor with James A. Wechsler.

At that time the *Post*, with nearly fifty columnists, became known as the "column-happiest American daily." Through the years its columnists included such well-known writers and celebrities as

Drew Pearson, Sylvia Porter, Jackie Robinson, Eleanor Roosevelt, and Eric Sevareid. From 1951 to 1958 Dorothy herself wrote a column, "Publisher's Notebook" (later "Dear Reader").

During the 1950s the *Post* won two important lawsuits. In 1952 it published a series attacking the methods of the gossip columnist Walter Winchell. He countered by implying that the *Post* had communist leadings. The *Post* brought a lawsuit, and Winchell retracted. In 1957 the newspaper won a victory for freedom of the press when the New York State Court of Appeals ruled in favor of the *Post*'s demand for a transcript of a judge's charge to the jury in a manslaughter case of a policeman accused of killing a boy.

In 1961 Wechsler shifted his attention to the editorial page, and Dorothy herself began to manage the news department. The following year she became editor in chief, a newly created title. She kept her publication afloat during the 1962–63 New York City newspaper strike, from which the *Post* emerged as the city's only surviving afternoon daily. In the newspaper's reorganized form she had the titles of editor in chief, publisher, president, and treasurer.

The *Post* held the distinction of being the oldest newspaper in the United States with a direct line of daily publication. It was also New York City's only openly liberal, cause-conscious newspaper. Dorothy described her editorial policy as advocating "honest unionism, social reform, and humane government programs" and championing "the causes of civil rights and civil liberties."

In her later years with the *Post*, she upgraded the newspaper by moving it to new quarters and installing modern automated equipment. She also allowed herself a spacious eleventh-floor oval office.

During the mid-1970s the *Post* experienced heavy losses. As a result, Dorothy sold the newspaper in 1976 to the Australian entrepreneur Rupert Murdoch.

In her retirement years, she turned increasingly toward domestic interests. Needlepoint was one of her favorite activities.

Dorothy's first marriage produced a son and a daughter, her

second a daughter, and her third no children. In 1953 she married for a fourth time, her new husband being Rudolf G. Sonneborn, a petroleum executive. They separated in 1965 and later divorced.

Dorothy Schiff died in New York City on August 30, 1989.

THE
SELIGMANS

THE SELIGMANS PLAYED A KEY ROLE in the progress of Jews in the United States. Among Jewish immigrant families in America they were the first to achieve great prominence, the first to make the transition from merchants to bankers, and the first to attain a high level of social distinction, setting the tone for much of German-Jewish society in the United States, especially in New York City. After the family made a business alliance with the huge financial houses of Rothschild and Morgan in 1874, the Seligmans became known as "the American Rothschilds."

David Seligman (1790–1845) was a weaver in the village of Baiersdorf, Bavaria. When he married, his wife, Fanny Steinhardt, brought with her as a dowry a large stock of dry goods, with which the family opened a shop.

In 1837 the eldest of their eight sons, Joseph (1819–80), immigrated to the United States. He became a successful merchant and gradually sent for the rest of the family to join him in his business. In 1865 he formed J. and W. Seligman and Company, an investment banking firm. The *J.* was for Joseph and the *W.* stood for William (1822–1910), David's second-oldest son. Notable among the six other brothers were Jesse (1827–94), Leopold (1831–1911), and Isaac (1834–1927). After achieving success in the United States, several of the brothers returned to Europe to set up branches of the family firm; William, for example, went to

Paris and Leopold and Isaac to London. Joseph, the eldest, set an example for the rest of the family in his philanthropies and civic leadership.

The next generation of Seligmans followed the example of the first as business and community leaders. Four of Joseph's five sons entered the family firm, led by Isaac Newton (1855–1917). The other son, Edwin Robert Anderson (1861–1939), became an influential economist. Joseph's brother Jesse also contributed sons to the business, including Henry (1857–1 933) and Albert Joseph (1859–1935), the latter of whom founded his own A. J. Seligman and Company in 1919.

In London, too, the torch was passed to competent successors. Herbert Spencer (1872–1951), son of Leopold, became a highly decorated British army officer. He served with the Royal Artillery in the South African War (1900) and in World War I (1914–18), retiring in 1919 as an honorary brigadier general. Charles David (1869–1954), son of Joseph's brother Isaac, succeeded his father at the British branch of the Seligman banking firm.

Eustace Seligman (1889–1976), son of the economist Edwin Robert Anderson Seligman, became a highly regarded lawyer. He also served with the American Jewish Committee, continuing the family tradition of professional success coupled with community leadership.

Joseph Seligman

FOUNDER OF J. AND W. SELIGMAN AND COMPANY

Joseph Seligman founded the famous international banking house of J. and W. Seligman and Company. He also provided valuable aid to the Union during the Civil War, served after the war as a financial adviser to the United States government, and was active in many civic, cultural, and philanthropic causes.

Joseph was born in Baiersdorf, Bavaria, on November 22, 1819. He was the eldest child in the family of eight sons and three daughters born to David and Fanny (Steinhardt) Seligman. As a youngster, Joseph helped out in the family's dry-goods shop and earned extra income as a moneychanger. But life was hard in Bavaria because of the political, economic, and social restrictions imposed on Jews. Shortly after graduating from secondary school, he immigrated to the United States in 1837.

During his first year in America, Joseph worked as an assistant to the Pennsylvania businessman Asa Packer. Joseph then struck out on his own as a peddler. He did well enough so that over the next several years he gradually sent for the other members of his family.

As his brothers reached America, they joined him in his peddling business. In 1840 they opened a dry-goods shop in Lancaster, Pennsylvania; in 1841 moved their operations to Alabama, where they set up three stores; and then extended their chain with shops in other cities, including, in 1846, New York City.

In 1848 Joseph married Babet Steinhardt, a first cousin whom he had met during a return visit to Baiersdorf. They had four daughters and five sons.

In 1850 Joseph sent his brothers Jesse and Leopold, soon followed by Henry, to San Francisco, California, to set up a store near the booming gold rush. The store made so much money that throughout the 1850s the Seligmans gradually became heavily involved in buying and selling gold bullion, thus moving ever closer to the banking business.

During the Civil War Joseph, now headquartered in New York City, supported the North. Under his leadership, the Seligmans made personal contributions to the Union cause, attained contracts to supply clothing to the Northern army, and sold millions of dollars' worth of United States government bonds to help finance the war effort.

In 1865, shortly after the end of the Civil War, Joseph officially created J. and W. (for William, the second oldest brother) Seligman and Company as an international investment banking firm. He, James, and Jesse remained in New York City, while eventually the other brothers opened branches of the family firm in

Europe—William in Paris, Henry and Abraham in Frankfurt, and Isaac and Leopold in London. A San Francisco office was run by different brothers at various times. The firm prospered through many kinds of investments, but it played an especially prominent role in government finance and in railroad development.

Joseph became one of the most trusted confidential financial advisers to President Ulysses S. Grant, a family friend since the 1840s. Grant, in fact, offered him the post of secretary of the treasury in 1873, but Joseph declined.

For many years Joseph participated in New York City civic affairs. In 1871 he was an active member

American Jewish Archives, Cincinnati Campus, Hebrew Union College-Jewish Institute of Religion.

Joseph Seligman

of the Committee of Seventy, which rooted out the corrupt Tweed Ring from control of the city. During 1873–75 he served on the New York Board of Education. And he was chairman of the rapid-transit commission that laid out the New York City elevated railroad system in its report of 1875.

In 1876 Joseph helped to organize the Society for Ethical Culture. The group's leader was Felix Adler, a German rabbi's son who wanted to encourage the development of a world based on ethics rather than religious piety. Joseph found this philosophy intriguing and assisted especially in the society's industrial school. Earlier he had for many years been a member in good standing of Temple Emanu-El, but late in life he called himself a "freethinker."

Joseph contributed time and funds to many philanthropic causes. He served as president of the German Hebrew Orphan Asylum and gave money to Jewish and non-Jewish charities. To honor the memory of President Abraham Lincoln, he gave money to Lincoln's widow for several years and pressured President Grant and Congress to pass a pension bill in 1870 for her benefit.

Joseph Seligman, principal founder of the House of Seligman, died in New Orleans, Louisiana, on April 25, 1880.

Jesse Seligman

SUCCESSOR TO JOSEPH SELIGMAN

Jesse Seligman was one of the most productive members of the family. His excellent business judgment and his friendship with Ulysses S. Grant were major factors in the success of J. and W. Seligman and Company, which he headed after the death of the company's founder, his brother Joseph. Jesse was also a noted philanthropist.

He was born in Baiersdorf, Bavaria, on August 11, 1827. Jesse was the fourth of the eight sons of David and Fanny (Steinhardt) Seligman.

After graduating from secondary school, Jesse joined his older brothers in their dry-goods business in the United States in 1841. After some time in Pennsylvania and Alabama, he and his younger brother Henry opened a dry-goods store in 1848 in Watertown, New York, where Jesse became friends with a young army officer named Ulysses S. Grant.

In 1850 Jesse and another younger brother, Leopold, moved across the continent and opened a store in San Francisco, California. The area was booming because of the gold rush, and soon the shop became very profitable. Jesse wisely had rented for his place of business one of the few brick buildings in San Francisco, so that after a May 1851 fire in the city, he found himself with the only general store left standing. His profits soared.

During his California years, he renewed his friendship with Grant, whose military duties took him there. Jesse became a member of the famous San Francisco Committee of Twenty-one, which in 1857 aided the election of municipal and state candidates pledged to honest government.

It was through Jesse's huge profits and local contacts in California that the Seligmans began buying and selling large quantities of gold bullion and thus gradually entering the banking business. In 1857 he moved to New York City and became an important player in the family's shift from dry-goods importing and retailing to international investment banking. Their efforts during the Civil War reflected this shift. Early in the war they supplied clothing to the Northern army, but later they sold millions of dollars' worth of Union bonds in America and in Europe.

In 1865, shortly after the end of the war, the brothers officially created J. and W. Seligman and Company, World Bankers, headed by Joseph. During the presidency of Ulysses S. Grant, 1869–77, Jesse, and through him Joseph, enjoyed the confidence of the president, and the brothers' firm was granted many projects as a fiscal agent for the United States government.

After Joseph died in 1880, Jesse became head of the firm and held that office till his own death. During his years at the helm the company was active in flotations of railroad securities, headed the American syndicate that sold shares in the Panama Canal, and continued to serve as a fiscal agent for the United States government.

Jesse was influential in the civic and philanthropic life of New York City. He helped to found the Hebrew Benevolent and Orphan Asylum and served for several decades as its president. He was also a founder of the Montefiore Home and the United Hebrew Charities, and in 1891 Baron de Hirsch selected him as an original member of the board of trustees of the Baron de Hirsch Fund. Jesse was a patron of the Metropolitan Museum of Art and of the American Museum of Natural History.

He was a vice president of the Union League Club of New York City for many years, but in 1893 his son Theodore was rejected by the club. The membership committee explained that the rejection was "not a personal matter in any way, either as to father or son. The objection is purely racial." Jesse immediately quit the club.

He married a German woman, Henrietta Hellman, in 1854. They had seven children. Max and Theodore Hellman, Henrietta's brothers, entered the Seligman business.

During a vacation in California, Jesse Seligman died at Coronado Beach on April 23, 1894.

Isaac Newton Seligman

SUCCESSOR TO JESSE SELIGMAN

Isaac Newton Seligman succeeded his uncle Jesse as head of the famed international investment banking firm of J. and W. Seligman and Company. While running the company, Isaac also found time to become one of the most important civic leaders of his era, taking an active role in reform movements and in philanthropy.

Isaac was born in Staten Island, New York City, on July 10, 1855. He was the second son and second oldest of the five sons and four daughters of Joseph and Babet (Steinhardt) Seligman. As a child Isaac was tutored by the well-known author Horatio Alger. Later Isaac attended Columbia College, from which he graduated in 1876.

His business career began in the New Orleans, Louisiana, branch of J. and W. Seligman and Company, which his father had founded in 1865. In 1878 Isaac moved to the New York City office, and in 1894 he became head of the company after the death of his father's brother Jesse, who had run it since Joseph's death in 1880. Under Isaac's leadership, the firm maintained its United States government connections and had charge of the reorganization of many important American businesses, including the Pere Marquette railroad and the American Steel and Wire Company.

Isaac was active in New York City civic affairs, especially in reform movements. He served as treasurer of the Citizens' Union for many years, became involved in civil service reform, was vice president of the New York Chamber of Commerce, helped to found the Child Labor Association, headed the Civic Forum, was vice president of the People's Institute, and served as treasurer of the City and Suburban Homes Company, the principal model tenement-house enterprise of the city.

Isaac was a vice president of the United Hebrew Charities, a trustee of Temple Emanu-El, and the treasurer of innumerable enterprises involving the raising of funds for important New York civic and charitable causes. A music lover, he served as a trustee of the New York Symphony Society and of the New York Oratorio Society, and in 1905 he helped to found the Institute of Musical Art (later the Juilliard School of Music).

In 1883 he married Guta Loeb, daughter of Solomon Loeb of the banking firm of Kuhn, Loeb and Company. They had two daughters who died young and a son and a daughter who lived to adulthood.

Isaac Newton Seligman fell from his horse and died of a fractured skull in New York City on September 30, 1917.

EDWIN ROBERT ANDERSON SELIGMAN

RENOWNED ECONOMIST

Edwin Robert Anderson Seligman was a rare combination of scholar and public figure. One of the most influential professors and authors of economics in his time, he also pioneered the field of public finance, writing about the subject and serving as a widely sought government adviser. In addition, he was a prominent activist in most of the economic and social reforms of his day.

Edwin was born in New York City on April 25, 1861. He was the fourth of the five sons and the eighth of the nine children of Joseph and Babet (Steinhardt) Seligman, who gave him his two middle names in honor of the Union defender of Fort Sumter at the outset of the Civil War. Joseph founded the international banking firm of J. and W. Seligman and Company, which was joined by all of his sons except Edwin.

Edwin graduated from Columbia College in 1879, spent three years studying in Europe, and returned to Columbia, where he earned an LL.B. degree and an M.A. degree in 1884 and a Ph.D. in 1885. He then began teaching at Columbia as a lecturer, became an adjunct professor in 1888, and was promoted to full professor three years later. In 1904 he became the first incumbent of the McVickar Professorship of Political Economy, a position he held till his retirement in 1931.

His scholarly pursuits in economics were aided by his knowledge of many languages, including German, Italian, and Russian. He accumulated the world's most complete private collection of books, broadsides, letters, and manuscripts on economic history. Among his important writings on the subject were *The Economic Interpretation of History* (1902) and *Principles of Economics, with Special Reference to American Conditions* (1905).

He organized many scholarly projects. In 1885 he helped to form the American Economic Association and became its first treasurer; during 1902 and 1903 he served as its president. He was the principal fund-raiser for, and the editor in chief of, the *Encyclopedia of the Social Sciences* (fifteen volumes, 1930–35). His other professional activities included initiating the publication of a series of doctoral dissertations and serving as chairman of committees on academic freedom.

Edwin made major contributions in the field of public finance. Opposing the single-tax scheme promoted in his day, he believed in taxation acording to ability to pay. His advocacy of the principle of progression in inheritance taxes led to the application of the same principle to income taxation. He greatly influenced tax laws in the United States and elsewhere through a series of books, including *Progressive Taxation in Theory and Practice* (1894) and *The Income Tax* (1911).

Governments often called on him as a tax adviser. He helped to frame a New York State income tax that took effect in 1919. During 1922–23 he served as an expert with the League of Nations Committee on Economics and Finance, an experience that led to his writing the book *Double Taxation and International Fiscal Cooperation* (1928). In 1931 he acted as adviser to the Cuban government.

His efforts as a reformer were wide-ranging. He organized a company to build model New York City tenements (1885); became probably the first prominent American economist to advocate a living wage (1898); served as secretary of the Committee of Fifteen (1900–1902) that exposed the link between the Tammany-controlled New York City police force and organized prostitution; helped to establish the Greenwich House settlement (1902) and served as its chairman of the board of managers (1906–1911); helped to set up the Bureau of Municipal Research in New York City and served as the first chairman of its board of trustees (1907–1910); held the presidency of the Society for Ethical Culture (1908–1921); and served as chairman (1911–14) of the National League on Urban Conditions among Negroes (later the Urban League). To improve the conditions of Russian-Jewish immigrants on the Lower East Side of New York City, he helped to create the Educational Alliance and chaired its education committee.

In 1898 he married Caroline Beer, a sister of the historian George Louis Beer. They had one son and three daughters.

Edwin Robert Anderson Seligman died at his summer home in Lake Placid, New York, on July 18, 1939.

THE
SINGERS

THE SINGER BROTHERS—Israel Joshua Singer (1893–1944) and Isaac Bashevis Singer (1904–1991)—were the greatest modern family of Yiddish writers. They united in their rebellion against the family tradition of joining the rabbinate. Both of their grandfathers were rabbis, as was their father.

Israel rejected his parents' otherworldliness, studied secular subjects, and became famous, under the name of I. J. Singer, as a Yiddish novelist. Isaac, inspired by his older brother, also turned to Yiddish literature, writing novels, short stories, and essays. He ultimately won the highest form of recognition for his work—the Nobel Prize.

I. J. SINGER

YIDDISH AUTHOR OF REALISTIC HISTORICAL NOVELS

Israel Joshua—professionally known as I. J.—Singer was an outstanding writer in Yiddish. He was noted especially for his realistic historical novels, such as *The Brothers Ashkenazi*.

Israel was born in Bilgoray, Russian-ruled Poland, on November 30, 1893. He was the second of the four children of Pinchos Menachem and Bathsheba (Silberman) Singer.

Pinchos was a Hasidic rabbi, while Bathsheba was a woman of great learning in her own right.

When Israel was three, the family moved to Leoncin, a small town near Warsaw. In 1908, after a brief stay in nearby Radzymin, they settled in Warsaw.

His parents educated Israel for the rabbinate, but he had different plans. He secretly read Hebrew, Yiddish, Russian, and Polish books on secular topics, and eventually completely rejected his religious upbringing. At the age of eighteen he left home, as he later explained, "in quest of enlightenment and worldly knowledge."

Living in Warsaw, he did odd jobs and began, in 1915, writing tales of Hasidic life. During World War I he was conscripted into the Russian army and was detained in a forced labor camp by the Germans.

In 1917, encouraged by the promise of the Russian Revolution, he immigrated to the Russian city of Kiev. There he married Genia Kupfershtock in 1918, faced starvation and pogroms, worked as a proofreader on a small Jewish newspaper, and continued his writing. Soon, however, he became disillusioned with the Bolsheviks, and in 1921 he returned to Warsaw, where his two sons were born.

During the 1920s and early 1930s, Israel, while living in Warsaw, contributed to various magazines and newspapers, including the *Jewish Daily Forward* of New York City. Besides publishing several collections of short stories during those years, he wrote longer works, notably *Yoshe Kalb*, a realistic novel about a mystic in the rabbinic courts of nineteenth-century Galicia. *Yoshe Kalb* appeared serially in the *Jewish Daily Forward* in 1932 and was then published in book form in Yiddish and English (as *The Sinner*) in 1933.

In 1934 he moved to New York City, where, over the last decade of his life, he wrote many of his best novels. In *The Brothers Ashkenazi* (1936) he depicted the rise and fall of the industrial city of Lodz, Poland, and the fortunes of the Jews whose lives parallel its history. In *East of Eden* (1939) he drew a portrait of an idealistic worker crushed by corruption in Poland and the Soviet Union. In *The Family Carnovsky* (1943) he traced the odyssey of a family of Orthodox Jews who emigrate from Poland and search for meaning for several decades till Nazis force them to leave Germany for the United States. He also continued to write plays, which had interested him throughout his career.

One of his finest books is his unfinished memoir, *Of a World That Is No More*, published posthumously in 1946 (English translation, 1970). It reveals his acceptance of his past, despite his early conflicts with his parents and his heritage.

Israel, like his brother Isaac nearly a generation later, wrote multigenerational family novels. But, unlike his brother, the older writer linked his characters with a larger historical and socioeconomic context, including some of the most difficult and complex struggles of his time, such as the alienation of people uprooted from their traditions, the disillusionment of the Soviet experiment, and the horror of the Nazi era.

One of his books, *The Brothers Ashkenazi*, found a large readership outside the Jewish community. But it was his younger brother Isaac who brought the Yiddish tradition into the mainstream of American literature.

I. J. Singer died in New York City on February 10, 1944, at the age of fifty.

ISAAC BASHEVIS SINGER

NOBEL PRIZE-WINNING YIDDISH AUTHOR

Isaac Bashevis Singer—in Yiddish, Yitskhek Bashyevis Zinger— won the 1978 Nobel Prize for literature. The most popular Yiddish writer of his era and possibly the greatest Yiddish writer of all time, he wrote novels, short stories, and essays in Yiddish and then supervised their translation into English. In his fiction he combined the mysticism of Jewish folklore with the reality of vanished shtetl life in eastern Europe and with the experience of Yiddish-speaking immigrants in America—flavored with his unique style of ironic wit and wisdom.

Isaac was born in 1904 in Leoncin (not, as often reported, Radzymin), Russian-ruled Poland. His exact birth date is uncertain and has been variously reported as July 14, November 21, and October 26. He was the third of the four children of Pinchos Menachem and Bathsheba (Silberman) Singer. Pinchos was a Hasidic rabbi, and Bathsheba was a woman of great learning. In 1908, after a brief stay at Radzymin, the family settled in Warsaw.

Coming from a family of Hasidic rabbis (both of his grandfathers were rabbis), Isaac received a

I. B. Singer

traditional Jewish education in a heder, where he studied the Torah, the Talmud, the Cabala, and other sacred Jewish books. As a child he was fascinated by the mystical Jewish folktales that his parents told him to strengthen his religious faith. Later he studied for a time at a rabbinic seminary in Warsaw. In 1917 he went to Bilgoray, the home of his maternal grandfather, where Isaac learned about the life of the shtetl, the typical small Jewish town of eastern Europe before the Holocaust.

His parents wanted him to become a rabbi and a religious scholar, but he decided to follow in the footsteps of his older brother, Israel, and become a secular writer. In the early 1920s Isaac joined Israel in Warsaw and took a job as a proofreader with a Yiddish literary journal. Soon he began to publish stories in various periodicals. At first he wrote in Hebrew to connect himself with his forefathers, but because Hebrew was at that time (before its revival in Israel) a dead language, he switched to Yiddish, the language of his childhood. During the late 1920s and early 1930s, he published short stories, Yiddish translations, and his first novel, *Satan in Goray*, in serialized form.

In 1935 he immigrated to the United States and settled in New York City, where his brother Israel had moved a year earlier. Isaac wrote fiction and nonfiction for various publications, becoming a regular contributor to the *Jewish Daily Forward* in 1943, the same year he became a naturalized United States citizen.

While steadily gaining a reputation in the Yiddish-speaking community, he remained largely unknown in the English-language world till the appearance of the English version of his novel *The Family Moskat* (1950), which had originally been serialized in the *Jewish Daily Forward* and published in Yiddish in 1945. For the rest of his career he wrote almost exclusively in Yiddish and then took part in their translation into English. From the original Yiddish manuscript, he would read aloud the material in his own idiomatic English to a translator, who then gave literary polish to the English version. His nephew Joseph (or Yosele), Israel's son, became Isaac's principal English tanslator. Isaac's works were also translated into many other languages, including Hebrew, French, German, and Dutch.

He published over thirty books in English. They include the novels *Satan in Goray* (1955, twenty years after the original Yiddish publication); *The Magician of Lublin* (1960); *The Slave* (1962); *The Manor* (1967); *The Estate* (1969); *Enemies, a Love Story* (1972); *Shosha* (1978); *The Penitent* (1983); and *Scum* (1991). Among his popular collections of short stories are *Gimpel the Fool and Other Stories* (1957), *The Spinoza of Market Street and Other Stories* (1961), *Short Friday and Other Stories* (1964), *The Seance and Other Stories* (1968), *A Crown of Feathers and Other Stories* (1973), and *The Image and Other Stories* (1985).

Isaac also won critical acclaim for his books for children. They include *Zlateh the Goat and Other Stories* (1966); *Mazel and Shlimazel; or, The Milk of a Lioness* (1966); and *When Shlemiel Went to Warsaw and Other Stories* (1968). *A Day of Pleasure: Stories of a Boy Growing Up in Warsaw* (1969) contains autobiographical stories, some of which previously appeared in *In My Father's Court* (1966), an account of his childhood experiences set against the background of his father's rabbinic court.

Some of Isaac's work was filmed. He was unhappy with Barbra Streisand's *Yentl* (1983), based on his short story of the same name. More pleasing to him was Paul Mazursky's 1989 screen adaptation of the novel *Enemies, a Love Story*.

Isaac believed that his role as a storyteller was to entertain, not to indulge in what he called the modern writer's "futile desire to teach, to explain, to change society." Nevertheless, his fiction provides a profound reflection on the Jewish condition. *The Family Moskat*, *The Manor*, and *The Estate* are large-scale works with many characters extending over several generations; the books show the unraveling of Jewish families affected by secularism and assimilation during the nineteenth and twentieth centuries. Other novels portray Jewish characters tempted in various ways by evil, such as the seventeenth-century villagers gripped by frenzied messianism in *Satan in Goray*, the philandering conjurer in *The Magician of Lublin*, and the scholar enmeshed in a tragic love affair in *The Slave*. Isaac's short stories, filled with Jewish folklore, legends, and mysticism, are brilliantly concise character portraits, especially of the weaknesses in human nature. Though he thought of himself as only an entertainer, the literary community recognized the depth of his achievement and rewarded him in 1978 with the Nobel Prize for literature.

As a young man in Europe, Isaac married his first wife, Rachel, with whom he had a son. They divorced, and Rachel and the boy lived for a time in the Soviet Union before settling in Israel. In 1940, in the United States, Isaac married Alma Haimann, a refugee from Germany.

In 1978 Isaac Bashevis Singer moved from New York City to Surfside, Florida, where he died on July 24, 1991.

THE
SOLOVEICHIKS

THE SOLOVEICHIKS WERE A GREAT rabbinic family
that originated in Lithuania and later achieved renown
in the United States.

Joseph ha-Levi Soloveichik (fl. mid-eighteenth century), a
leader of the Jewish community in Slobodka, played a major role
in the struggle to rescind the prohibition against Jews living in
Kovno. Moses and Abraham (both fl. late eighteenth century),
Joseph's grandsons, built the great synagogue of Williampol-
Slobodka (1772), where Moses was appointed rabbi.

Moses had a son, Joseph (fl. early nineteenth century), who became the son-in-law of Hayyim of Volozhin and was rabbi of
Kovno. Joseph's son Isaac Ze'ev (fl. mid-nineteenth century) served
as rabbi in the same city.

Isaac's eldest son, Joseph Baer (1820–92), was a profoundly influential teacher, talmudist, and community leader in eastern
Europe. Joseph had two sons: Hayyim (1853–1918) invented a
new method of Talmud study and became the central figure in
Orthodox Jewry of his time, and Simchah (1881–1941) earned
renown as a rabbi in Mogilev, Russia, and as a rabbi and teacher
in Brooklyn, New York.

Hayyim had three sons, including Moses (c. 1878–1941) and
Isaac Ze'ev ha-Levi (1886–1959). Moses was a noted rabbinic
scholar in eastern Europe before immigrating to the United States
and becoming a senior professor of Talmud at the Rabbi Isaac

Elchanan Theological Seminary of Yeshiva University in New York City. Isaac succeeded his father as rabbi of Brest Litovsk, Russia, and later became the supreme halakic authority for an extreme wing of Orthodox Jews in Jerusalem.

Moses had three sons, all of whom attained prominence. Joseph Dov (1903–1993) succeeded his father at Yeshiva University, shaped mainstream Orthodox Judaism in the United States through his lectures and ordinations, and created a greatly influential neo-Kantian (or existential) philosophy of Judaism. Samuel (1908–1967) became a well-known chemist. Aaron (1918–), who, like his father and older brother Joseph, has taught at Yeshiva University, is a leading rabbinic figure in American Orthodox Judaism.

Considering the Soloveichiks' outstanding scholarly attainments, they published very little. Family tradition had it that a ceaseless desire for perfection was inconsistent with publishing (that is, finalizing) works except under special circumstances.

The spelling of the family name is recorded as both *Soloveichik* and *Soloveitchik*. However, most family members have gone by the former spelling, though Joseph Dov Soloveitchik adopted the latter.

JOSEPH BAER SOLOVEICHIK

TEACHER, TALMUDIST, AND COMMUNITY LEADER

Joseph Baer Soloveichik had a profound influence on Jewish communities in eastern Europe through his yeshiva teachings, his talmudic writings, and his community leadership.

He was born in Nieswich, Russia, in 1820. Joseph studied under his father, Isaac Ze'ev Soloveichik, who became rabbi of Kovno, and under Isaac, son of Hayyim of Volozhin, who was one of Joseph's non-Soloveichik great-grandfathers.

While in Volozhin, Joseph married into a wealthy family. But shortly thereafter his father-in-law forced the dissolution of the marriage because Joseph had failed to give the correct order of recitation of some minor prayers in a festival.

Embittered, Joseph left Volozhin and studied under S. Kluger in Brody and J. N. Orenstein in Lemberg. He then won an appointment as Gershon Menahem's successor at the yeshiva in Minsk.

In 1849 Joseph returned to Volozhin to serve as joint head of the yeshiva there with Naphtali Zevi Judah Berlin, son-in-law of Joseph's old teacher Isaac of Volozhin. In both personality and approach to talmudic studies, Joseph and Berlin differed. Joseph was dynamic and preferred practical judgment in talmudic matters, while Berlin was temperate and favored erudition. They presented their dispute to four scholars, who decided in favor of Berlin.

Joseph left Volozhin and became rabbi of Slutsk. There he taught Torah and devoted himself to helping the commmunity. During the famine of 1866 he founded a society to aid the poor and personally collected donations from door to door.

However, he still had his fiery spirit, which caused tension between him and other powers in Slutsk. In 1875 he gave up his position and moved to Warsaw, where he lived in great poverty while continuing his studies and performing acts of benevolence.

In 1878 he was invited to become rabbi of Brest Litovsk. He accepted only after receiving assurances that he would be obeyed in all community matters.

Much of his talmudic thought is contained in his two-volume book *Novellae on the Talmud: 102 Responsa and Sermons* (1863–64). Other published works include sermons on Genesis and Exodus (two volumes, 1884) and halakic novellae (1891).

His sons continued the family rabbinic tradition. One, Hayyim (or Chaim), became a major figure in Orthodox Jewry, while another, Simchah, served as rabbi of Mogilev.

Joseph Baer Soloveichik died in 1892.

HAYYIM SOLOVEICHIK

INNOVATIVE TALMUDIST

Hayyim Soloveichik was the central figure of his time in Orthodox Jewry. He created a new trend in Talmud study and won wide renown for his wisdom and benevolence as rabbi of Brest Litovsk.

Hayyim (or Chaim) was born in Volozhin in 1853. His father, Joseph Baer Soloveichik, was cohead of the local yeshiva. Hayyim studied at the yeshiva and in 1880 was appointed to the staff.

He soon developed a revolutionary method of Talmud scholarship, based on analyzing the subject under discussion into its categories. Hayyim evolved terminology to describe various concepts and used the method to explain the origins of differences in the Talmud itself and among its authoritative interpreters. The method spread throughout the world, and thousands of students came to hear him in person.

After the Volozhin yeshiva closed in 1892, he went to live with his father, now the rabbi of Brest Litovsk. Later that year his father died, and Hayyim succeeded him as rabbi. His talmudic knowledge and personal kindness gave him a special leadership status in the region. Rabbis, scholars, and laymen consulted him on all matters. Even unwed mothers went to him for advice. He gave most of his salary and, in the winter, his wood to the needy. Because the name of his city, Brest Litovsk, was sometimes shortened to Brisk, he came to be known as Rabbi Hayyim Brisker.

Strict with himself in the matter of religious observances, he was always lenient when applying them to others. However, in public religious practice he was firm in opposing changes.

Hayyim left many writings that were published only after his death. They include novellae on talmudic tractates and on Maimonides' *Mishneh Torah*.

At the age of twenty Hayyim married Lipshe Spira (or Shapira), granddaughter of Naphtali Zevi Judah Berlin, who was cohead, with Hayyim's father, of the Volozhin yeshiva. They had three sons, one of whom, Moses, became a great rabbi in Europe and then a scholar at Yeshiva University in New York City, while another son, Isaac Ze'ev ha-Levi, succeeded his father as rabbi of Brest Litovsk.

Hayyim Soloveichik died in 1918.

Moses Soloveichik

MOSES SOLOVEICHIK

TALMUDIC EDUCATOR

Moses Soloveichik was one of the most renowned rabbinic scholars of his time in both the Old World and the New. He is best remembered as a senior professor of Talmud at Yeshiva University in New York City.

Moses (or Moshe) was born in Kaslovitz, Russia, in about 1878. He was the eldest son of the famed rabbinic leader Hayyim (or Chaim) Soloveichik. Moses' mother was Lipshe (Spira or Shapira) Soloveichik, daughter and granddaughter of teachers at the celebrated talmudic academy at Volozhin.

After serving as rabbi in several Lithuanian towns, Moses became the director of the rabbinic college in Warsaw, Poland. Later he immigrated to the United States and settled in New York City, where in 1929 he joined the faculty of Yeshiva University, teaching at the institution's Rabbi Isaac Elchanan Theological Seminary. Moses earned a national reputation in his new homeland as a talmudic educator, scholar, and article writer.

He married Peshie Feinstein. They had three sons and two

daughters. The sons, too, became prominent rabbinic scholars: Joseph Dov, Samuel, and Aaron.

Moses Soloveichik died in New York City on January 31, 1941.

SIMCHAH SOLOVEICHIK

RABBI IN MOGILEV AND IN BROOKLYN

As a very young man, Simchah Soloveichik became chief rabbi in Mogilev, Russia. In his later years he earned renown as a rabbi and teacher in Brooklyn, New York.

Simchah was born in Brest Litovsk, Russia, in 1881. His father, Joseph Baer Soloveichik, was at that time chief rabbi of the city.

At the tender age of twenty, Simchah won an appointment as chief rabbi of Mogilev. He remained there for over twenty years.

In 1924 he immigrated to the United States and settled in Brooklyn. For many years he served as chief rabbi of Brisker Synagogue and was also associated with Tifereth Israel Synagogue. He earned a reputation as one of the leading talmudic scholars in the United States.

In his later years he left his synagogue duties to concentrate on studying and teaching. Many of his pupils became leading rabbis in the United States and Europe.

His wife's name was Deila. They had two sons.

Simchah Soloveichik died in Brooklyn on November 16, 1941.

ISAAC ZE'EV HA-LEVI SOLOVEICHIK

RABBI AND HALAKIC AUTHORITY

Isaac Ze'ev ha-Levi Soloveichik succeeded his father as rabbi of Brest Litovsk, Russia. In his later years Isaac lived in Jerusalem, where extreme Orthodox Jews regarded him as the supreme halakic authority.

He was born in Volozhin in 1886. His parents were Hayyim (or Chaim) and Lipshe (Spira or Shapira) Soloveichik. Hayyim was a famed rabbinic leader who became rabbi of Brest Litovsk in 1892, while Lipshe was the daughter and granddaughter of teachers at the celebrated talmudic academy at Volozhin.

Isaac studied under his father. When the latter died in 1918, Isaac was appointed by the community to succeed him as rabbi of Brest Litovsk. He soon gained wide renown for his knowledge and teaching of the Torah. Isaac did not found a yeshiva, but he taught select students. Even well-known talmudists, rabbis, and heads of academies heeded his words. He became the center of communal and congregational life in the region.

During World War II he fled from Brest Litovsk with seven of his children (five sons and two daughters). His wife and four other children were murdered in their hometown.

In 1941 Isaac settled in Jerusalem. There his eldest son, Joseph Dov, established a yeshiva, while Isaac himself taught a group of exceptional young students.

His work in Jerusalem was much more private than it had been in Brest Litovsk. He held no appointed position and avoided public appearances. However, on select occasions, when he saw a threat to the foundations of religion, he broke his silence and issued halakic rulings. He exercised great influence over a large segment of Orthodox Jewry.

Isaac Ze'ev ha-Levi Soloveichik died in 1959.

JOSEPH DOV SOLOVEICHIK

INFLUENTIAL RABBI AND PHILOSOPHER

Joseph Dov Soloveitchik [*sic*] shaped mainstream Orthodox Judaism in America through his lectures and writings and through his ordination of more than two thousand rabbis. His profoundly influential philosphy has been described as both neo-Kantian and existential.

Joseph was born in Pruzhan, Poland, in 1903. His parents were Moses and Peshie (Feinstein) Soloveichik. (Joseph later adopted the spelling *Soloveitchik*.) He came from long lines of distinguished talmudic scholars on both sides of the family. Moses was a rabbi in Europe and then a talmudic professor at Yeshiva University in New York City; Moses' father, Hayyim, introduced a new method of talmudic scholarship; and Hayyim's father, Joseph Baer, was a prominent rabbi, talmudist, and community leader in eastern Europe. Joseph's maternal grandfather, Elijah Feinstein, was the rabbi in Pruzhan.

Joseph Dov Soloveitchik

Yeshiva University Public Relations Department

Joseph spent his early years in Belorussia, where his father served as a rabbi. Later, at the University of Berlin, he studied philosophy and was attracted to the neo-Kantian school. In 1931 he received his doctorate, and the following year he immigrated to the United States.

He became the rabbi of the Orthodox Jewish community of Boston, Massachusetts, and founded the Maimonides School in nearby Brookline, the first Jewish day school in New England. In 1941 he succeeded his father as professor of Talmud at the Rabbi Isaac Elchanan Theological Seminary of Yeshiva University in New York City. For many years he also taught at the school's Bernard Revel Graduate School, where he served as professor of Jewish philosophy.

Popularly known as the Rav (an affectionate Hebrew name for teacher), he became the spiritual mentor of the majority of American-trained Orthodox rabbis and was also highly regarded by other wings of Judaism. His main influence came through his university lectures and public discourses. He had a great gift for clearly explaining difficult technical problems. His annual halakic and haggadic discourses, which he delivered at Yeshiva University on the anniversary of his father's death, attracted thousands of listeners and were regarded as a major annual academic event for American Orthodox Jewry. For years he also addressed his fellow rabbis at the annual meeting of the Rabbinical Council of America. More informally, he conducted summer classes for adults on the patio of Maimonides School in Brookline.

In keeping with his family's tradition, he wrote much but published little. Up to the 1960s he published only a handful of essays, including "The Lonely Man of Faith" (1965). In the 1970s he finally released two volumes of his teachings: *Al-ha-Teshuvah* ("On Repentance," 1976) and *Be-Sod-ha-Yahid* ("Aloneness and Togetherness," 1977).

Much of his work involved reconciling traditional Judaism with the modern world. Orthodox rabbis around the globe frequently queried him about how to apply Jewish law to contemporary problems.

Joseph viewed every person not as an orderly, rational being but as a contradictory, paradoxical one. Active and passive, attracted and repelled by the mystery of divinity, the individual is lonely in his or her ambiguous relationship with God. When one lives in accordance with halakah, one's life becomes sanctified, one behaves morally and ethically toward fellow humans, and one attains a "nearness to God." But it is difficult for a mere human to understand God's language. In modern America, especially, the reality of faith is widely denied, and the believing Jew faces a painful battle to understand God's meaning in the complex context of daily life. Joseph's great achievement was to show that Orthodoxy was not just traditionalism; intellectuality could be applied to Orthodoxy to legitimize the embracing of its immutable laws.

He married Tonya Lewitt in 1931. She held a doctorate in education and assisted him in all his endeavors till her death in 1967. They had two daughters and one son, Rabbi Haym Soloveitchik of Riverdale, the Bronx, New York City.

Joseph Dov Soloveitchik died in Brookline on April 8, 1993.

Samuel Soloveichik

NOTED CHEMIST

Samuel Soloveichik taught chemistry at Yeshiva University, became an authority on the history of chemistry, and proposed the first classification of aliphatic (fatty-acid) organic chemicals.

He was born in Poland in 1908, the second of three sons of Moses and Peshie (Feinstein) Soloveichik. Moses and many other members of the family were prominent rabbinic scholars.

Samuel earned a doctorate at the University of Brussels in 1934 and immigrated to the United States in 1939. During World War II he worked as a research chemist for various federal agencies, including the Chemical Board of Warfare.

In 1953 he joined the faculty of Yeshiva University in New York City. He was perfectly suited for the academic life, being not only scholarly in nature but also devoted to the intellectual and personal welfare of his students. In 1955 he became an assistant professor and in 1959 an associate professor of chemistry.

Samuel made significant contributions to the study of the history of chemistry. In his writings he showed that many great research chemists of the nineteenth century had died or suffered mental deterioration from performing laboratory experiments with toxic materials.

In 1966 he proposed the first classification of aliphatic organic chemicals in a table similar to the periodic table, a reference chart listing all inorganic elements. The periodic table had revolutionized inorganic chemistry in the nineteenth century, and he hoped that his table would provide organic chemists with a similarly powerful research tool.

However, only four months after making his proposal, Samuel Soloveichik died in New York City on February 25, 1967.

Yeshiva University Public Relations Department

Aaron Soloveichik

AARON SOLOVEICHIK

INSPIRATIONAL ORTHODOX EDUCATOR

Through his many years of teaching and lecturing, Aaron Soloveichik became one of the leading rabbinic figures in American Orthodox Judaism. After a stroke incapacitated him, his continued teaching gave increased inspiration to his message.

Aaron (or Aharon) was born in Pruzhany (or Pruzhan), Russia (formerly Poland), in 1918. He was the youngest of the three sons of Moses and Peshie (Feinstein) Soloveichik. Moses was a renowned rabbi in eastern Europe and spent his last years teaching at the Rabbi Isaac Elchanan Theological Seminary of Yeshiva University in New York City.

Aaron immigrated to the United States with his father in 1929, earned a B.A. degree at Yeshiva University in 1940, and took a law degree at New York University in 1946. He began teaching Talmud and the philosophy of Judaism at Jewish institutions, notably the Rabbi Isaac Elchanan Theological Seminary of Yeshiva University, where he himself had studied and where both his father and his older brother Joseph had taught.

In 1966 Aaron moved to Illinois to become dean of the faculty at the Hebrew Theological College in Skokie. In 1974 he founded the Yeshiva of Brisk in Chicago.

His lectures in classrooms and before Orthodox bodies gave him a prominent position within the Orthodox community. He saw Orthodoxy as the only true form of Judaism. Only the Orthodox conception and application of halakah, he felt, could guide people out of the problems of modern society.

In 1984 Aaron suffered a stroke, after which he endured endless pain and was barely able to walk. Nevertheless, when in 1987 he was invited to teach again at the Rabbi Isaac Elchanan Theological Seminary in New York City, he agreed. The assignment required him to travel from his Chicago home to New York City weekly and then to walk a substantial distance from his quarters to the lecture hall. His eagerness to do so, in spite of his infirmity, was an inspiration to his students as well as the community at large. "I try to elevate myself through my suffering," he explained. "I'm in constant pain. But when I give a *shiur* ["class"], I don't feel it as much."

Aaron Soloveichik had six children, four of whom became rabbis.

THE
STRAUSES

THE AMERICAN STRAUSES attained great wealth through their ownership of the famed Macy's department store in New York City and then distinguished themselves in public service and philanthropy.

The family originated in Rhenish Bavaria. Jacob Lazar was a member of the assembly of Jewish notables convened by Napoléon in Paris in 1806 and of the Sanhedrin created by Napoléon to advise him when he was considering the liberation of all Jews under his authority. In 1806 the family adopted the surname of Straus to comply with Napoléon's decree that all Jews in the Rhenish Palatinate take family names.

Lazarus Straus (1809–1898), Jacob's grandson, immigrated to the United States from Bavaria in 1852. After some years in the American South, Lazarus settled in New York City, where he and two of his sons, Isidor (1845–1912) and Nathan (1848–1931), ran a crockery business called L. Straus and Sons. Isidor and Nathan later became the owners of R. H. Macy and Company, which they built into the world's largest department store. Lazarus's youngest son, Oscar Solomon Straus (1850–1926), was the first Jew to serve in a United States cabinet.

Isidor's sons continued to lead Macy's. After the firm was incorporated in 1919, Jesse Isidor (1872–1936) became its first president, serving till 1933, when he resigned to serve as ambassador to France. Percy Selden (1876–1944), the family's management genius, held the presidency from 1933 to 1939, when ill health forced him to resign. Herbert Nathan (1881–1933) was vice president of Macy's from 1922 till his death.

Nathan's sons, however, took a different direction. After Nathan's brother Isidor—his co-owner at Macy's—died in 1912, Nathan and Isidor's sons (who inherited their father's share of the firm) had a falling-out, as a result of which the nephews bought out Nathan, who left the business. Nathan's sons, Nathan (1889–1961) and Hugh Grant (1890–1961), worked only briefly at Macy's. Nathan the younger became a housing expert and a radio station owner. Hugh Grant long served as vice president of the Brooklyn merchandising firm of Abraham and Straus, in which his father and uncle Isidor had been partners with Abraham Abraham.

Oscar Solomon Straus

Oscar Solomon, the third of Lazarus's sons, also produced a notable offspring. His son, Roger Williams Straus (1891–1957), married Gladys Eleanor Guggenheim (1895–1980), daughter of Daniel Guggenheim, whose family dominated American mining and smelting for many years. Roger Williams became president of the American Smelting and Refining Company, while his wife, Gladys, achieved renown in her own right as vice president and assistant editor of *Gourmet* magazine and as chairman of the Daniel and Florence Guggenheim Foundation.

In the next generation—the fourth (including Lazarus) in America—the Strauses enlarged the range of their achievements even further. Jesse Isidor's elder son, Jack Isidor (1900–1985), headed Macy's during its years of expansion into a nationwide

Oscar S. Straus II

chain, while his younger son, Robert Kenneth (1905–1997), held important positions in President Franklin D. Roosevelt's administration and later became a successful publisher. Jesse Isidor's brother Percy Selden had three sons, one of whom, Donald Blun Straus (1916–), became a business and association executive, serving, for example, as president of the American Arbitration Association (1963–72).

Nathan the younger had four sons. One of them, Irving Lehman Straus (1921–), is a public relations executive at Straus Corporate Communications in New York City. Another, R(onald) Peter Straus (1923–), is an executive at Straus Communications, Inc., also in New York City, where he has been a leader in Jewish communal affairs. R. Peter's wife, Ellen Straus (née Sulzberger, 1925–95), founded Call for Action, the nation's first telephone help line; edited *McCall's* magazine; served as president and general manager of her father-in-law's New York City radio station (WMCA); and was active in community and Democratic political projects.

Other members of the fourth generation include the two sons of Roger Williams and Gladys (Guggenheim) Straus. Oscar Solomon Straus II (1914–), named after his grandfather, was a partner in Guggenheim Brothers enterprises and became president of the Daniel and Florence Guggenheim Foundation and the Fred L. Lavanburg Foundation. His brother, Roger Williams Straus, Jr. (1917–), founded the prestigious publishing firm of Farrar, Straus and Giroux, Inc. (originally Farrar, Straus and Company, Inc.).

In the fifth generation of American Strauses, Kenneth Hollister Straus (1925–96), son of Jack Isidor and Margaret (Hollister) Straus, became an Episcopalian and was the last of the Straus family to serve as an executive at R. H. Macy and Company. Roger Williams Straus III (1943–), son of Roger Williams Straus, Jr., worked for his father at Farrar, Straus and Giroux as director of sales and marketing (1967–75), spent some years with other publishers (1976–85), and then returned to his father's firm, where he held the position of managing director (1986–93) till he resigned from the company.

LAZARUS STRAUS

FOUNDER OF THE STRAUS
DYNASTY

Courtesy of Straus Historical Society

The founder of the fabulously successful Straus family in the United States was Lazarus Straus. The first member of the family to immigrate to America, he established a merchandising business that his sons eventually parlayed into complete ownership of the famous R. H. Macy and Company of New York City.

Lazarus was born in Otterberg, Bavaria, on April 25, 1809. His parents were Jacob and Karoline (Meyer) Straus.

In 1843 Lazarus married Sara

Lazarus Straus

Straus, his first cousin. They had three sons and a daughter.

He became a prosperous trader in farm products, such as wheat, oats, and clover. In 1848 he took part in a revolutionary movement, but after it failed he was subjected to official discrimination, which in 1852 led him to immigrate to the United States.

Sara Straus

At first he earned his living as an itinerant merchant in the South. Later he established a general store in Talbotton, Georgia, where he was joined in 1854 by his wife and children.

The business grew, and Lazarus became a leading citizen in the town. In 1862 the family moved to Columbus, Georgia, where it supported the Confederacy during the Civil War.

When the war ended in 1865, business conditions in the South were so bad that the family moved to New York City, where Lazarus and his eldest son, Isidor, opened a wholesale crockery store called L. Straus and Son. After the next-oldest son, Nathan, entered the business, it became L. Straus and Sons.

In 1874 Nathan arranged for the family to open a crockery and glassware department in the basement of the R. H. Macy and Company store in New York City. In 1888 the family purchased a part interest in the store, of which they acquired full ownership in 1896. Even after his sons began to take the leading roles in the family's progress, Lazarus remained active in the business till the end of his long life.

In the business world, he had a reputation for integrity. In his personal life, he was a devoted member of Temple Beth El, where he served as director of the Sunday school.

Lazarus Straus died in New York City on January 14, 1898, at the age of eighty-eight.

ISIDOR STRAUS

CO-OWNER OF MACY'S

Courtesy of Straus Historical Society

Isidor Straus

Isidor Straus, with his brother Nathan, built R. H. Macy and Company of New York City into the world's largest department store. Both brothers also became noted for their philanthropy.

Isidor was born in Otterberg, Bavaria, on February 6, 1845. His parents were first cousins, Lazarus and Sara (Straus) Straus. Lazarus immigrated to the United States in 1852 and settled in Talbotton, Georgia, where his wife and children (three sons and a daughter) joined him in 1854.

Isidor, the eldest son, wanted to prepare for the United States Military Academy at West Point; but when the Civil War broke out in 1861, he had to abandon that plan because his family supported the South. After working for a time as a clerk in his father's general store, he went to Europe in 1863 to purchase supplies for the Confederacy. This project failed because of the Union blockade of Southern ports. Isidor stayed in Europe for the rest of the war, working in a shipping office at Liverpool, England, dealing in Confederate bonds, and selling cotton acceptances.

When the war ended in 1865, he returned to the United States and settled in New York City. With the money (about $12,000) that he had saved from his European ventures, Isidor and his father formed the crockery firm of L. Straus and Son; after Nathan joined the company in 1866, it became L. Straus and Sons. In 1874 the firm took over the crockery and glassware department of R. H. Macy and Company. In 1888 Isidor and Nathan gained part ownership of Macy's, and in 1896 they became its sole owners. They developed Macy's into a retail giant and simultaneously, in partnership with Abraham Abraham, built up the highly successful Brooklyn department store of Abraham and Straus.

Isidor participated in many business organizations. He held executive positions with the chamber of commerce of the state of New York, with several banks, and with the New York Retail Dry Goods Association.

An active Democrat, he helped to elect his friend Grover Cleveland president of the United States in 1892 and later influenced the president into backing the gold standard. Isidor served in the United States House of Representatives (1894–95) but declined opportunities to be nominated for mayor of New York City in 1901 and 1909.

He engaged in many philanthropic works, serving as trustee and treasurer of the Montefiore Home from its inception in 1884; vice president of the J. Hood Wright Memorial Hospital; and president of the Educational Alliance, "the people's palace" of New York City's East Side, from its organization in 1893 till his death. Among his activities in behalf of the Jewish people was his membership in the American Jewish Committee.

Isidor married Ida Blun of New York City in 1871. They had four sons and three daughters.

On April 15, 1912, Isidor and his wife were aboard the S. S. *Titanic* on its first voyage across the Atlantic. When the ship was on the verge of sinking and women were ordered into the lifeboats, Ida refused to leave her husband. Isidor was urged to go with her, but he would not leave the ship ahead of the women still on the *Titanic*. As a result, both Isidor and Ida went down with the ship.

NATHAN STRAUS

CO-OWNER OF MACY'S

Nathan Straus, with his brother Isidor, built R. H. Macy and Company of New York City into the world's largest department store. Nathan gained his greatest distinction for his philanthropic efforts to improve the health and nutrition of needy children in New York City.

He was born in Otterberg, Bavaria, on January 31, 1848. His parents were first cousins, Lazarus and Sara (Straus) Straus. Lazarus immigrated to the United States in 1852 and settled in Talbotton, Georgia, where he was joined in 1854 by his wife and their three

Nathan Straus

sons and one daughter. Nathan, the middle son, studied at a log cabin school and at the Collinsworth Institute.

In 1865, after the Civil War made life in the South difficult, the family moved to New York City, where in 1866 Nathan joined his father and brother Isidor in their merchandising firm of L. Straus and Son, soon renamed L. Straus and Sons. In 1874 their company took over the crockery and glassware department of R. H. Macy and Company. In 1888 Nathan and Isidor were allowed into the partnership of Macy's, and in 1896 they became the store's sole owners.

It was Nathan who originated the ideas for Macy's rest rooms, medical care, depositors' account system, and low-cost lunchroom for employees. He helped to develop Macy's into the world's most successful department store. Nathan and Isidor also built up, in partnership with Abraham Abraham, the Brooklyn department store of Abraham and Straus.

*April 28, 1925. Golden Wedding of Lina and Nathan Straus at "Driftwood,"
Mamaroneck. Standing: companion, Flora, Grant, Sissie, Nathan, Helen, Henry
Bernheim, Merose Day. Seated: Edward Mamelsdorf, Sarah and Oscar Straus,
Lina and Nathan Straus, Lucie Mamelsdorf, Irving Lehman, Hugh and
Jerome Straus.*

After Isidor died in 1912, his three sons inherited his share of the business. At the end of 1913, as a result of differences between Isidor's sons and their uncle Nathan, the young Strauses bought Nathan out and became the sole owners. Nathan retired from business in 1914.

But his interests had always extended far beyond the business world. He was a pioneer in public health and child welfare. In the early decades of the twentieth century, no one did more for New York City's public welfare than Nathan Straus.

His philanthropic efforts began in earnest during the economic depression in the winter of 1892–93, when he distributed food and coal. In the following winter he issued over $2 million worth of tickets that could be used for coal, food, or lodging.

In 1892 he also began his campaign for the pasteurization of milk, at that time a procedure rarely done. In 1891, 241 of every 1,000 babies born in New York City died before their first birthday; but during a four-year trial period in which 20,111 babies received his pasteurized milk, only 6 died. After a long fight against public ignorance and commercial greed, Nathan ultimately succeeded in gaining the compulsory pasteurization of milk in most American cities. By 1920 he had opened, at his personal expense, 297 milk distribution depots in thirty-six cities in the United States and abroad.

In 1909 he established, in Lakewood, New Jersey, the pioneer tuberculosis preventorium for children. In 1911 President William Howard Taft appointed Nathan the sole United States delegate to the Third International Congress for the Protection of Infants, held in Berlin, Germany. During the harsh winter of 1914–15 in New York City, Nathan again provided food for the poor.

He and his wife, Lina (Gutherz), whom he had married in 1875, devoted their late years to the people of Palestine, to whom Nathan donated nearly two-thirds of his fortune. In 1912 he established there a domestic science school for girls, a factory for men, a health bureau, and a public kitchen that became a permanent foundation. Later he opened a Pasteur Institute, many child-health welfare stations (under the auspices of Hadassah, the Women's Zionist Organization), and the Nathan and Lina Straus Health Centers in Jerusalem and Tel Aviv, established for the benefit of all inhabitants—Christians, Muslims, and Jews.

The Arab rioting in Palestine in 1929 greatly disheartened both Nathan and Lina. It hastened her death in 1930, and he died soon afterward, in New York City on January 11, 1931.

Oscar Solomon Straus

DIPLOMAT AND CABINET MINISTER

Oscar Solomon Straus, brother of the co-owners of R. H. Macy and Company, was the first Jewish United States cabinet member and one of the most distinguished American diplomats of his time. He was also an important political activist, author, and Jewish advocate.

Oscar was born in Otterberg, Bavaria, on December 23, 1850. He was the youngest of the three sons of Lazarus and Sara (Straus) Straus. Lazarus immigrated to the United States in 1852, and his family followed him in 1854. They lived in Georgia till the end of the Civil War, when they moved to New York City.

Oscar studied at private schools and graduated from Columbia College (1871) and Columbia Law School (1873). After several years of working as a lawyer, he gave up his practice in 1881 and joined L. Straus and Sons, his family's china and glassware business.

In 1882 he married Sarah Lavanburg. They had two daughters and a son.

Neither law nor business fulfilled Oscar. With financial help from his father-in-law (a merchant banker) and his two older brothers, Isidor and Nathan (who in 1888 became partners in, and in 1896 sole owners of, Macy's department store), Oscar was able to devote his life to public service.

He was an active progressive Democrat in politics, and in 1887 President Grover Cleveland named him minister to Turkey. Oscar's gift for diplomacy enabled him to win an invitation by the sultan to arbitrate a business matter between the Turkish government and Baron Maurice de Hirsch.

Oscar left his post in 1889, but from 1898 to 1900 he again represented the United States in Turkey, sent this time by President William McKinley. It was another successful tour of duty, and he won great praise from the State Department.

During Theodore Roosevelt's presidency (1901–1909), the administration often asked Oscar for his advice on national and international issues. In 1902 he was appointed a member of the Permanent Court of Arbitration at The Hague, and he was reappointed in 1908, 1912, and 1920. From 1906 to 1909 he served as United States secretary of commerce and labor, the first Jew to hold a cabinet post.

In 1909 President William Howard Taft sent Oscar back to Turkey, this time as the first American ambassador to the Ottoman Empire. Again he obtained important concessions for United States interests, especially in the American exemption from the Turkish authorities' usual supervision of foreign religious, educational, and benevolent institutions.

He resigned his final mission to Turkey in 1910. Because his foreign service had come under both Democratic (Cleveland) and Republican (McKinley and Taft) administrations, Oscar Solomon Straus can be regarded as one of America's earliest career diplomats.

In 1912 he ran unsuccessfully for governor of New York on the Progressive ticket. In 1913 he traveled through North Africa and Europe. In 1915 he was appointed chairman of the New York Public Service Commission. In 1919 he was a delegate representing the League to Enforce Peace at the post-World War I Versailles Peace Conference, where he helped President Woodrow Wilson to incorporate the League of Nations into the Versailles treaty.

Oscar's writings center on American government issues. His published works include *Reform in the Consular Service* (1894), *The American Spirit* (1913), and his memoirs, *Under Four Administrations: From Cleveland to Taft* (1922).

He made many efforts to assist oppressed Jews in Europe. After the Kishinev pogroms in 1903, he helped President Theodore Roosevelt to draft the note of protest sent to the Russian government, and he aided in the collection of money for the relief of the victims. In 1905 he met with Count Sergius Witte to discuss ways of improving the circumstances of Jews in Russia. He discussed the possible role of Zionism with Theodor Herzl, founder of the modern Zionist movement. During the peace conference after

World War I, he assisted in providing for the safeguarding of Jewish minorities in Europe.

Oscar also supported American Jewish organizations. He was the first president of the American Jewish Historical Society and substantially assisted the American Jewish Committee, the Jewish Welfare Board, and many other Jewish groups.

Oscar Solomon Straus died in New York City on May 3, 1926.

Courtesy of Straus Historical Society

Jesse Isidor Straus

JESSE ISIDOR STRAUS

HEAD OF MACY'S AND
AMBASSADOR TO FRANCE

Jesse Isidor Straus was elected the first president of R. H. Macy and Company after it was incorporated in 1919. He also held important government appointments, notably as ambassador to France.

Jesse was born in New York City on June 25, 1872. He was the eldest of the seven children of Isidor and Ida (Blun) Straus, and a nephew of Nathan and Oscar Solomon Straus.

After graduating from Harvard University in 1893, Jesse worked for a time as a bank clerk in New York City. Soon, however, he joined the Brooklyn dry-goods store of Abraham and Straus, in which his father was a partner.

In 1895 Jesse married Irma Nathan. They had two sons and one daughter.

In 1896 he moved to a junior executive position at R. H. Macy and Company, a New York City department store located on

Fourteenth Street in Manhattan and owned by his father and his uncle Nathan. In 1900 Jesse and his younger brother Percy selected the site farther uptown, at Herald Square, where the huge modern version of the store opened in 1902.

After his father died in 1912, Jesse and his surviving brothers, Percy and Herbert, inherited Isidor's share of the business, and in 1913, as a result of differences with their uncle Nathan, they bought him out and became the sole owners, with Jesse at the head. When the business was incorporated in 1919, he was elected its first president. He personally devised most of the firm's policies on merchandising, advertising, and finance. By 1930 Macy's, the world's largest department store, had annual sales of nearly $100 million.

Jesse, like so many others in the Straus family, engaged in philanthropy. He served as a trustee of several hospitals and low-rent housing projects, donated money to many causes, contributed heavily to New York University, and, with his brothers, established the Isidor Straus Professorship of Business History and gave $300,000 for the construction of the Straus Hall dormitory, both at Harvard University and both in memory of their father.

Jesse was a friend of Franklin D. Roosevelt, who, as governor of New York in 1931, made him head of the state's Temporary Emergency Relief Administration. In 1932 Jesse campaigned vigorously for Roosevelt in the latter's successful bid for the presidency of the United States. Early in 1933 President Roosevelt appointed him ambassador to France. To accept the appointment, Jesse resigned the presidency of Macy's and was succeeded by his brother Percy. Jesse was a popular American representative in France, and in 1935 he negotiated an agreement that ended the double taxation of American companies with French branches.

Because of ill health, he resigned his post in August 1936 and returned to the United States. Jesse Isidor Straus died in New York City on October 4, 1936.

Percy S. Straus

PERCY SELDEN STRAUS

MACY'S MANAGEMENT
MASTERMIND

For nearly fifty years Percy Selden Straus held positions of leadership at R. H. Macy and Company, the family-owned department store in New York City. His specialty was management innovations.

Percy was born in New York City on June 27, 1876. He was the second son and the second of the seven children of Isidor and Ida (Blun) Straus. Percy graduated from Harvard University in 1897 and would have liked to devote himself to scholarly interests. But Isidor had recently become co-owner, with his brother Nathan, of Macy's and wanted his two older sons to join him in the business.

Percy joined the firm in 1897. While his older brother, Jesse Isidor, learned the financial aspects of the business, Percy specialized in systems and operations, including personnel, maintenance, and delivery. One of Percy and Isidor's earliest and most important achievements was to initiate and carry out the moving of the store from its original location on Fourteenth Street to a building on Thirty-fourth Street; Macy's thus became one of the first stores in the uptown movement of New York City retail trade. The move was completed in November 1902.

In that same year Percy married Edith Abraham. They had three sons.

After Isidor died in 1912, his three surviving sons—Jesse, Percy, and Herbert—inherited his share of the store. At the end of 1913, as a result of differences between them and their uncle Nathan, the three brothers bought out Nathan and became the sole owners.

When R. H. Macy and Company incorporated in 1919, Percy became vice president under his older brother, Jesse. After Jesse was appointed ambassador to France in 1933, Percy succeeded him as president, a position he held till 1939, when a heart attack forced him to give up the office to Jesse's son Jack Isidor. From that time till his death, Percy filled the position of chairman and elder statesman in the Macy firm.

During his years at Macy's, Percy was the family's expert at implementing management plans. Perhaps because of his early intellectual inclinations, he eagerly adopted the new scientific management techniques of his era. He was among the first in industry to use objective testing devices for the hiring and placing of employees, to introduce formal training programs for both lower ranks and executives, to standardize systems and procedures, and to use labor-saving and automatic devices in retail oper-ations. He was probably more knowledgeable about the technical aspects of store management than any other person in the world.

Percy also engaged in a wide range of business, civic, and philanthropic activities. He was a founder and a director of the National Retail Foundation and a director of the National Dry Goods Association. Percy served on the staff of the Council of National Defense during World War I, was a member of a committee formed in New York City in 1918 to investigate organized prostitution, served as vice president of the finance committee of the Democratic National Committee in 1928, and helped the mayor's committee on city planning from 1934 to 1938. With his brothers he established the Isidor Straus Professorship of Business History at Harvard University, contributed $300,000 for the construction of Harvard's Straus Hall dormitory, and gave $1 million to New York University.

Percy gave much of himself to Jewish causes. He helped Jewish immigrants to find work through the Jewish Agricultural and Industrial Aid Society, which he eventually led as president. He also served as treasurer and chairman of the board of the Federation for Support of Jewish Philanthropic Societies of New York.

Percy Selden Straus died in New York City on April 6, 1944.

Courtesy of Straus Historical Society

Herbert N. Straus

HERBERT NATHAN STRAUS

VICE PRESIDENT OF MACY'S

Herbert Nathan Straus, with his two older brothers, bought out their uncle Nathan Straus and took control of R. H. Macy and Company in 1913. Thereafter, Herbert shared in the direction of the famed department store, and from 1922 till his death he held the title of vice president.

He was born in New York City on November 2, 1881, the youngest of the three surviving sons of Isidor and Ida (Blun) Straus. Isidor and his brother Nathan were the partners chiefly responsible for building R. H. Macy and Company into a giant in the retail business.

After graduating from Harvard University (B.A., 1903), Herbert joined Macy's as a stock boy. At the end of 1913 he and his two surviving brothers, Jesse Isidor and Percy Selden, purchased their uncle Nathan's interest in Macy's and began to share control of the business.

When Macy's was incorporated in 1919, Herbert became secretary-treasurer, and beginning in 1922 he held the title of vice president in addition to his earlier titles. Under the direction of the three Straus brothers, Macy's continued to grow. Even during the early years of the Great Depression, it maintained a robust business.

Herbert interested himself mainly with the merchandising and personnel aspects of the business. But he also shared with his brothers in the large policy-making decisions of the company. As Macy's acquired interests in other stores throughout the country,

Standing: Herbert, Percy. Sitting: Jesse.
Taken in Red Bank, NJ, where Herbert and Percy had adjoining houses.

Herbert helped to direct them as well. In 1930, for example, he was elected president of L. Bamberger and Company of Newark, New Jersey.

Though he never sought public office, Herbert took a keen interest in politics. Unlike his brothers, both Democrats, he supported the Republican party. In 1926 he founded Republican Business Men, Inc., serving as its president. In 1928 this organization played a major role in electing President Herbert Hoover. Herbert Nathan Straus also held leadership positions within the New York State Republican party.

He gave generously to many charities, usually anonymously. With his brothers, he gave a dormitory hall to Harvard University in memory of their parents and founded a professorship in Harvard's graduate school of business administration.

Herbert had wide-ranging interests outside the business world. For many years he was an active leader in the Young Men's Hebrew Association and a director of Saint Mark's hospital in New York City. He appreciated all art forms, especially music, being a fine amateur cellist and collector of instruments. His other collections included books, eighteenth-century drawings, and Greek sculptures.

He married Therese Kuhn, daughter of Edward Kuhn of New York City, in 1907. They had three sons.

Herbert Nathan Straus died in New York City on April 6, 1933.

NATHAN STRAUS

HOUSING EXPERT AND RADIO STATION OWNER

Nathan Straus had a varied career. In his early years he was a newspaperman, department store executive, editor and publisher, state senator, and successful businessman. But he won his greatest renown as the administrator of the United States Housing Authority and as the owner of the New York City radio station WMCA.

He was born in New York City on May 27, 1889. His parents were Nathan and Lina (Gutherz) Straus. Nathan senior was a partner in R. H. Macy and Company, the New York City department store. Nathan junior's original name was Charles Webster Straus after an early Macy partner. He changed it to Nathan Straus when he was a young man.

Young Nathan was interested not in business but in journalism. After graduating from Princeton University (1909), he found a job with the *New York Globe*. However, in 1910 his father fell ill, and for a few years the son worked at Macy's. In 1914 he bought the humorous weekly *Puck*, which he edited and published till 1917.

In 1915 he married Helen E. Sachs. They had four sons.

In 1917 he enlisted in the United States Navy for World War I service. In 1919 he left the navy and returned to the *Globe* as assistant editor.

The following year Nathan, a Democrat, was elected to a seat in the New York Senate, where he served from 1921 to 1926.

Nathan, Jr., and his four sons: R. Peter, Irving, Barnard, and Nathan III.

There he was active on many committees and sponsored much liberal legislation.

After leaving the Senate he became president of Nathan Straus-Duparquet, Inc., the largest hotel-restaurant equipment company in the United States. While discharging his business duties, he also became interested in the problem of housing for low-income families. In 1933 he sponsored a limited-dividend housing project, Hillside Homes, in which 118 modern buildings provided 1,415 low-rent apartments. In 1935 Mayor Fiorello La Guardia appointed him special housing commissioner for New York City.

In 1937 Nathan resigned his position with the equipment company and accepted President Franklin D. Roosevelt's appointment as administrator of the new United States Housing Authority, which made funds available to qualified borrowers and grantees for public housing and slum clearance developments. By law, the responsibility for building, financing, and operating the projects lay with local authorities, many of whom opposed the housing program. Nathan traveled across the country, answered arguments, and by 1941 successfully set up nearly a billion dollars' worth of public housing. However, the powerful building-and-loan and real-estate lobbies remained opposed to public housing and especially to Nathan Straus as the administrator. When Congress refused to appropriate more funds for the agency while he was at the head of it, he resigned in January 1942. In later years he continued to write and speak in favor of public housing, notably in his books *The Seven Myths of Housing* (1944) and *Two-thirds of a Nation: A Housing Program* (1952).

In September 1943 he bought the New York City radio station WMCA. He ran it as president from 1943 to 1959, and from 1959 till his death he was chairman of the board. His wife, Helen, helped him by taking charge of all educational and children's programming.

Disdaining the pursuit of profit only, he refused to take advertisements from advertisers he did not want. He helped to lay the groundwork for modern public-service program-ming through such shows as *Halls of Congress*, a program of verbatim dramatizations of debates and speeches from the *Congressional Record*; *New World A-coming*,which dealt with the place of African-Americans in the United States; *Wake Up, America*, a talk show in which experts gave advice to listeners on a wide range of issues; and *Pro and Con*, which offered on-air discussions of both sides of controversial topics. "I don't think there is any issue you ought not to talk about," he said. "I don't know what good thing but isn't made better by giving it publicity. I don't know what bad thing but isn't killed by bringing it out into the light."

In 1954 he introduced a series of weekly editorials on local, national, and international affairs. The programs broke an existing Federal Communications Commission (FCC) rule against a station giving its opinions without providing equal time for the expression of opposing views. However, the success of the programs influenced other stations to offer similar editorials, and eventually the FCC changed its rule.

Hugh Grant Straus (seated, second from right) with his father, Nathan, Sr. (seated, third from right).

Nathan was also active in community projects. He supported the United Jewish Appeal, and from 1954 to 1958 he chaired the Mayor's Advisory Council in New York City.

Nathan Straus died in Massapequa, Long Island, on September 13, 1961.

HUGH GRANT STRAUS

VICE PRESIDENT OF ABRAHAM AND STRAUS

Hugh Grant Straus served for many years as vice president of the well-known Abraham and Straus department store in Brooklyn, New York. He also helped to direct many other stores controlled by Abraham and Straus, and he was a noted philanthropist.

Hugh was born in New York City on September 21, 1890, son

of Nathan and Lina (Gutherz) Straus. Nathan became a co-owner, with his brother Isidor, of the R. H. Macy and Company department store in New York City.

After graduating from Princeton University (Litt.B., 1910), Hugh worked for Macy's. In 1912 his uncle Isidor died, and shortly thereafter Isidor's sons had a business dispute with their uncle Nathan, Hugh's father. As a result, Nathan, at the end of 1913, sold his interest in the business to his nephews. Hugh left Macy's at the same time.

For the next year he worked at the importing firm of L. Straus and Sons, which had been founded by his grandfather Lazarus Straus. In 1914 he joined another firm in which his father was a partner, Abraham and Straus, which operated a department store in Brooklyn. In 1918 Hugh himself was admitted to partnership in the business. When it was incorporated in 1920 as Abraham and Straus, Inc., he became secretary of the company, and the following year he was elected vice president, a position he retained till his retirement in 1945.

In 1929 Federated Department Stores, Inc., was formed to act as a holding company for the department stores operated by Abraham and Straus. Hugh was named treasurer and director, serving in those capacities till his retirement. Federated came to be the holding company for stores operated by Bloomingdale Brothers of New York City, Wm. Filene's Sons Company of Boston, and other concerns throughout the country.

Like other members of the family, Hugh engaged heavily in philanthropy. As president of the Brooklyn Federation of Jewish Charities, he helped to merge that organization into the larger Federation of Jewish Philanthropies in New York City, of which he became a director. He was a member of the advisory board of the Jewish Distribution Committee, a director of the Greater New York Fund, and a director of the Welfare Council of New York City.

His other interests included Democratic politics; he served as chairman of the finance committee of the Westchester County Democratic Committee in 1949. He had a special fondness for classical music as well as active recreations, such as horseback riding.

Hugh was married twice. In 1913 he wedded Flora Stieglitz, with whom he had two sons and two daughters before divorcing in 1955. In 1958 he married Marcelle Vignette in Paris, France.

Hugh Grant Straus died in New York City on November 11, 1961.

ROGER WILLIAMS STRAUS

PRESIDENT OF ASARCO AND PHILANTHROPIST

Roger Williams Straus transformed American Smelting and Refining Company (ASARCO) from a processing specialist into a diversified mining enterprise. His philanthropies covered many fields, and he had a special interest in furthering religious tolerance.

Roger was born in New York City on December 14, 1891. His parents were Oscar Solomon and Sarah (Lavanburg) Straus. Oscar, a famed diplomat, had just begun work on a biography of the founder of Rhode Island, Roger Williams, for whom Oscar named his son. Several years later, in 1896, Oscar's brothers, Isidor and Nathan, became the owners of R. H. Macy and Company of New York City, which they built into the world's largest department store.

Roger attended a preparatory school in Lawrenceville, New Jersey. He graduated from Princeton University in 1913.

In 1914 he married Gladys Eleanor Guggenheim. They had two sons and a daughter.

His father-in-law, Daniel Guggenheim, was president of ASARCO, and from the beginning of Roger's marriage he was groomed to take a high-level position with the company. After a World War I tour of duty in Siberia as an intelligence officer for the Military Intelligence Division of the General Staff, he returned to ASARCO and became a member of its executive committee. Following his father-in-law's retirement in 1919, Roger served as assistant to the new president, Simon Guggenheim, Daniel's younger brother.

ASARCO specialized in processing ores purchased from mining companies. In the 1930s Roger's main responsibility was buying ore for ASARCO, and during that time he observed that smaller mining companies were going out of business and that most of the larger ones were developing their own processing plants. He concluded that ASARCO should have its own mines as a reliable source of ores.

In 1941 Simon Guggenheim died and Roger succeeded him as president of the company. He soon began to push forward with his idea of developing mining projects for ASARCO. Many of his board members and executives opposed the projects because of the cost and risk involved. Roger overcame the opposition, set up the mining projects, and thus developed ASARCO into a larger, more diverse minerals enterprise.

Roger had a lifelong interest in aiding the cause of religious tolerance. In 1928 he funded the establishment of, and helped to organize, the National Conference of Christians and Jews, which he served as cochairman for the rest of his life. He wrote extensively on this topic in articles and in books, such as *Religious Liberty and Democracy* (1939).

Roger was a trustee of the John Simon Guggenheim Foundation and other foundations. His activities in behalf of Jews included serving as honorary president of the National Federation of Temple Brotherhoods, a member of the executive board of the Union of American Hebrew Congregations, honorary vice chairman of the United Jewish Appeal of Greater New York, and a member of the board of governors of the American Financial and Development Corporation for Israel.

Three months after retiring from ASARCO and four months after being named chancellor of the New York State Board of Regents, Roger Williams Straus died in Liberty, New York, on July 28, 1957.

JACK ISIDOR STRAUS

LEADER OF MACY'S
NATIONWIDE EXPANSION

Jack Isidor Straus

Jack Isidor Straus served as president of R. H. Macy and Company during the years when it expanded from its position as the world's largest single department store into a huge chain of stores across the United States. He was also known for his leadership in education, civic affairs, and philanthropy.

Jack was born in New York City on January 13, 1900, the elder of the two sons of Jesse Isidor and Irma (Nathan) Straus. Jack's grandfather Isidor Straus was a co-owner of Macy's and a partner in the Brooklyn department store Abraham and Straus. Jesse also became an executive of Abraham and Straus and from 1919 to 1933 was president of Macy's.

Jack was originally named Jesse Isidor Straus II. After his grandfather was killed in the sinking of the S. S. *Titanic* in 1912, the boy was renamed Isidor Straus II. As a young man he finally changed it to Jack Isidor Straus.

After graduating from Harvard University (B.A., 1921), Jack joined Macy's. For the next several years he worked in various departments to learn as much as possible about the overall operations.

In 1926 he became executive vice president in charge of the merchandise division and in 1928 a member of the board of directors, acting as secretary of the board from 1929 to 1933. He then served as company vice president (1933–39), acting president (1939–40), president and chief executive officer (1940–56), chairman and chief executive officer (1956–68), chairman of the executive committee (1968–76), and honorary chairman and director emeritus (1977–85).

Jack presided over the development of R. H. Macy and Company into a nationwide chain, stretching from the original Macy's of New York City to outlets in California— nearly a hundred stores by the end of his career. As the stores were acquired or built, he became director of these wholly owned subsidiaries and divisions. He adhered to the Macy traditions of wide-scale advertising, low prices, and cash sales. To facilitate cash sales, Macy's had its own bank, into which customers could deposit money that they could later draw on for making their purchases.

Jack engaged in a vast range of community affairs. He served as a trustee of the Jewish Board of Guardians (1935–49), a member of the visiting committee of the Graduate School of Business Administration at Harvard University (1938–65), a member (1944–74) and the chairman (1965–74) of the board of trustees at Roosevelt Hospital in New York City, a member of the board of overseers at Harvard (1950–54), a member at large of the board of directors of the Empire State Foundation (1952–72), a director of the New York City Economic Development Council (1965–76), a director of the United Way in New York City (1969–85), and an activist in many similar organizations. In 1973 he and his brother, Robert, endowed a chair at the Harvard Business School in memory of their father.

Jack married Margaret Hollister in 1924. They had one son and two daughters before her death in 1974. In 1975 he married Virginia Fowler (née Megear), who had a son from an earlier marriage.

Jack Isidor Straus died in New York City on September 19, 1985.

Roger Williams Straus, Jr.

FOUNDER OF FARRAR, STRAUS AND GIROUX, INC.

For half a century Roger Williams Straus, Jr., has guided the course of one of America's most respected publishing companies: Farrar, Straus and Giroux (originally Farrar, Straus and Company). Like other members of his family, he has also devoted much of his time and resources to philanthropy.

Roger was born in New York City on January 3, 1917. His parents were Roger Williams and Gladys (Guggenheim) Straus. Roger headed the huge American Smelting and Refining Company, while Gladys was the daughter of Daniel Guggenheim, leader of the famed Guggenheim mining and smelting empire.

At the age of fifteen Roger had a summer job as copyboy with the *White Plains* (New York) *Daily Reporter*, an independent newspaper, where he later worked as reporter (1936) and feature writer (1939–40). Hooked on journalism, he earned a bachelor's degree in that field at the University of Missouri (1939). While there he worked as reporter and editorial writer for the *Columbia Missourian* (1937–39) and as editor and publisher of the literary magazine *Asterisk* (1939).

From 1940 to 1945 he served as associate editor of *Current History and Forum* magazine. During World War II he also headed his own book-packaging firm, called Book Ideas, Inc.; coedited a series of history books, including *War Letters from Britain* (1941); and rose to the rank of lieutenant in the navy reserve.

In November 1945, after being discharged from the navy, he joined with the respected publisher John Farrar to found the new firm of Farrar, Straus and Company, Inc. Over the ensuing years the company underwent several name changes as new partners came and went. The most important change occurred in 1964, when the firm attained its present name of Farrar, Straus and Giroux, Inc. The new partner was Robert Giroux, who had joined the company as editor in chief in 1955.

From the beginning, Roger shaped the company into one whose principal goal was not to make as much money as possible but to

Courtesy of Straus Historical Society

Roger Straus, Jr.

publish works of literary distinction. He acquired and retained a large number of Nobel Prize winners, including T. S. Eliot, Hermann Hesse, Nelly Sachs, Isaac Bashevis Singer, and Aleksandr Solzhenitsyn.

During its early years the company had to struggle to survive because of its uncompromising focus on literary merit rather than commercial appeal. However, Roger soon developed the policy of introducing one or two obvious moneymakers with each list. The firm's first big financial boost came with such a book: Gaylord Hauser's self-help best-seller *Look Younger, Live Longer* (1950). The company also acquired some small presses and expanded its publishing range to include children's books, college texts, and paperbacks.

Roger became an outspoken opponent of the modern trend toward conglomerate ownership of publishing companies. "I think that a lot of publishing houses are being run by accountants, businessmen, and lawyers who have very little concern for the books," he complained in 1978. "They could just as well be selling string, spaghetti, or rugs."

Beyond his publishing career, Roger has been active in Jewish and philanthropic affairs. He is a member of the Union of American Hebrew Congregations, and from 1955 to 1965 he served as chairman of the publications board for *American Judaism* magazine. He was vice president of the Fred L. Lavanburg Foundation (1950–80) and the Daniel and Florence Guggenheim Foundation (1960–76), and he long served as a director of the Harry Frank Guggenheim Foundation and the John Simon Guggenheim Foundation.

Roger married Dorothea Liebmann, a childhood friend and a member of the Rheingold brewing family, in 1938. They had one son, Roger Williams Straus III, who in 1986 became managing director of his father's company. However, in 1993 young Roger resigned his position, citing philosophical differences with his father.

The son's resignation left open the question of the father's successor at the firm. In 1994, under these new circumstances, Roger Williams Straus, Jr., announced that the German printing concern Holtzbrinck had bought a majority stake in Farrar, Straus and Giroux.

THE
SUKENIKS

LEAZAR (OR ELIEZER) SUKENIK (1889–1953) immigrated to Palestine from Poland in 1912. He became the first professor of archaeology at the Hebrew University and won international renown as the first expert to identify the antiquity of the famous Dead Sea Scrolls. His wife, the former Chassia (or Hasya) Feinsod (1889–1968), pioneered the kindergarten system in Palestine. After her marriage she went by the name of Chassia Sukenik-Feinsod.

All three of their sons made their marks on the history of Israel. The oldest, Yigael, hebraized his surname to *Yadin* ("He will judge") and, as Yigael Yadin (1917–84), became Israel's youngest general and then followed in his father's footsteps as an archaeologist, leading important excavations in the Holy Land and helping to decipher the Dead Sea Scrolls.

Eleazar's middle son, Joseph (or Yoseph/Yosef/Yossi) Yadin (1920–), became one of Israel's best-known actors. He cofounded the Cameri Theater of Tel Aviv and appeared in many Israeli and international films, such as *Four in a Jeep* (Swiss, 1951), *Hill 24 Doesn't Answer* (Israel's first important feature film, 1955), *Stop Train 349* (French, Italian, and German, 1964), *Lies My Father Told Me* (Canadian, 1975), *Worlds Apart* (American and Israeli, 1980), and *Remembrance of Love* (American television, 1982).

314

The youngest son, Matityahu, was a pioneer Israeli Air Force pilot. He died at the age of nineteen during Israel's War of Independence.

Eleazar Sukenik

IDENTIFIER OF THE DEAD SEA SCROLLS

Eleazar Sukenik was a Polish-born Israeli archaeologist whose excavations and investigations led to many important discoveries about ancient Palestine. He is best known for being the first to identify the antiquity of the Dead Sea Scrolls.

Eleazar (or Eliezer) Lipa Sukenik was born on August 12, 1889, in Białystok, Poland, at that time within the Russian Empire. He immigrated to Palestine in 1912 and became interested in archaeology while a student at the Hebrew Teachers Seminary and the École Biblique et Archéologique Française in Jerusalem. Later he earned degrees at the University of Berlin, Germany (A.B., 1923), and at Dropsie College in Philadelphia, Pennsylvania (Ph.D.,1926) before returning to Palestine. In 1926 he became associated with the Hebrew University as a field archaeologist, later being promoted to a lecturer (1935) and then to (the university's first) professor (1938) of the archaeology of Palestine. He also directed the Museum of Jewish Antiquities.

From early in his career he showed a gift for both field work and laboratory analysis. He found remnants of an important Hyksos fortification at Tell Jerishe and, from 1925 to 1927, directed the clearance of the Third Wall in Jerusalem. With L. A. Mayer, he coauthored a book on his discoveries, *The Third Wall of Jerusalem* (1930).

At Beth Alpha he unearthed a remarkable mosaic pavement that opened a whole new field in the history of Jewish art. He summarized his work in *The Ancient Synagogue of Beth Alpha* (1932).

Yet another field of interest for him was numismatics. His knowledge of that subject led to his identification of the oldest extant Jewish coins dating from the period of Persian domination.

He played a crucial role in understanding the importance of the Dead Sea Scrolls. In 1947 a Bedouin shepherd boy in Jordan discovered seven scrolls in a cave. No one realized their significance for some time, but Eleazar had special knowledge to apply to the scrolls. Through his study of the epitaphs of the Jewish necropolis in Jerusalem, dating from the last century (c.30 B.C.E. to 70 C.E.) of the Second Temple, he became familiar with the script of that period. When he examined the Dead Seas Scrolls, he became the first to realize that their script placed them in the same time frame. Thus it came to light that the scrolls contained Old Testament texts up to a thousand years older than any previously known; the documents also revealed the existence of an ancient Jewish sect that lived at a place now called Qumran and that provided a link between Judaism and Christianity.

On November 29, 1947—the day of the United Nations decision to partition Palestine into Jewish and Arab states—Eleazar traveled to Bethlehem and purchased three of the scrolls. He tried to buy the four other scrolls from the metropolitan of the Syrian Orthodox Monastery of Saint Mark in the Old City of Jerusalem, but his offer was rejected.

He spent much of the rest of his life studying the scrolls. His work was published posthumously in 1955 as *The Dead Sea Scrolls of the Hebrew University.*

He married Chassia (or Hasya) Feinsod, founder of the first kindergarten in Palestine. They had three sons.

Eleazar Sukenik died in Jerusalem on February 28, 1953.

YIGAEL YADIN

ISRAELI MILITARY LEADER AND ARCHAEOLOGIST

Yigael Yadin had distinguished careers in two different fields: military service and archaeology. After quickly rising to become

Israel's youngest general, he retired from protecting his country's future so that he could explore and preserve its past. As an archaeologist he helped to decipher the Dead Sea Scrolls, led important excavations at Hazor and Masada, and discovered the famous Bar Kochba letters.

He was born in Jerusalem on March 21, 1917. His parents were the famed Polish-born archaeologist Eleazar Sukenik and the educator Chassia (Feinsod) Sukenik, known as Chassia Sukenik-Feinsod. Yigael hebraized his surname to *Yadin* ("He will judge").

While in high school, he joined the Haganah, the illegal underground defense group that later formed the core of the Israeli army. For more than a decade he combined school studies with military

Yigael Yadin

duties. In 1945 he earned his M.A. degree in archaeology at Hebrew University. Two years later he was appointed chief of operations for the Haganah.

When the nation of Israel was established in 1948, the Haganah became the Israel Defense Forces, with Yigael continuing in his same position. As the Israelis fought the War of Independence against Arabs, his biblical and archaeological knowledge helped him as a military leader. For example, in December 1948 the Egyptians controlled the main road to the town of Auja, which he needed to reach; he recalled that in biblical times there existed a parallel road, traces of which he found and used to effect a surprise attack that captured a large Egyptian force.

In November 1949 Yigael was appointed army chief of staff

and promoted to the rank of brigadier. At thirty-two he was Israel's youngest general. In December 1952 he retired from the army to resume his studies at Hebrew University.

In 1954, while on a lecture tour in the United States, he successfully conducted negotiations to buy the last four of the seven original Dead Sea Scrolls. The owner, the metropolitan of the Syrian Orthodox Monastery of Saint Mark in the Old City of Jerusalem, had refused an offer several years earlier from Yigael's father, who had privately purchased the three other scrolls in Bethlehem. Yigael's efforts, with financial guarantees from his backers, completed the acquisition for Israel of all seven original Dead Sea Scrolls, which were later housed in their own building, the Shrine of the Book, in Jerusalem.

With Dr. Nachman Avigad, Yigael deciphered the seventh scroll, an amplification in Aramaic of stories from Genesis. In 1955 Yigael received his Ph.D. degree in archaeology from Hebrew University, his dissertation being on one of the scrolls obtained by his father. This scroll, known as "The War of the Sons of Light and the Sons of Darkness," provided much new information about Jewish military tactics and regulations at the end of the Second Commonwealth. His work was published as *The Scroll of the War of the Sons of Light against the Sons of Darkness* (Hebrew, 1955; English, 1962).

From 1955 to 1958 (and again in 1968) he directed archaeological excavations at Hazor, once the capital of northern Canaan. The expedition uncovered the remains of twenty-one cities, the earliest dating back about five thousand years. Yigael was convinced that his work confirmed the biblical narrative in the Book of Joshua and cast new light on the dates and importance of Joshua's deeds. He recorded his findings in a three-volume set of books called *Hazor* (1958–62).

In 1960 Yigael headed one of four teams exploring the caves along the western shore of the Dead Sea. He and his associates discovered a batch of letters written by Simon Bar Kochba, leader of the last Jewish revolt against the Roman Empire, in the second century C.E. The letters provided the most important evidence that Bar Kochba was a real person, not just a legendary character in talmudic literature.

During the mid–1960s Yigael excavated at Masada, a fortress overlooking the Dead Sea. In 73 C.E. Jewish rebels made their last stand against the Roman army at Masada. The archaeological finds there were spectacular. The diggers unearthed the earliest synagogue ever found in Palestine; relics of daily life, such as coins and clothing; a Book of Psalms scroll a thousand years older than any similar biblical manuscript previously discovered; a two-thousand-year-old copy of part of the lost Hebrew original of the Book of Ecclesiastes, the oldest of its kind yet found; and a fragment identical with the text of a Dead Sea Scroll of Sabbath

State of Israel Government Press Office

Yigael Yadin

liturgies based on the special calendar of the sect that kept the Dead Sea Scrolls at Qumran, thus confirming the ancient origin of the Qumran scrolls. Yigael summarized the Masada findings in his book *Masada: Herod's Fortress and the Zealots' Last Stand* (1966).

He taught archaeology for many years at Hebrew University and became well known in America for his guest lectures on Israel. His other writings include many scholarly articles and the books, published in both Hebrew and English, *The Message of the Scrolls* (1957; new edition, 1962) and *The Art of Warfare in Biblical Lands in Light of Archaeological Discovery* (two volumes, 1963).

In 1977 he formed a new political party in Israel, the Democratic Movement for Change. From 1977 to 1981 he served as his nation's deputy prime minister.

He was married to Carmella Ruppin in 1941. They had two daughters.

Through his archaeological discoveries, Yigael profoundly affected the course of modern biblical studies, just as his military work had greatly contributed to the course of modern Israel. His efforts in both fields were dominated by his sense of duty—a duty in military service to link his people with the future, and a duty in biblical archaeology to link his people with their past, "to uncover the relics of biblical Israel and thus make the Book of Books more understandable to all people whose lives have been shaped by its teachings."

Yigael Yadin died in Hadera, Israel, on June 28, 1984.

THE
SULZBERGERS

THE SULZBERGERS HAVE CONTRIBUTED to many fields, such as law and business. But their chief claim to fame is their control, since 1935, of one of the world's greatest newspapers, the *New York Times*.

Mayer Sulzberger (1843–1923), a German immigrant to the United States, became a well-known jurist and scholar. His first cousin Cyrus Lindauer Sulzberger (1858–1932) was a successful merchant and a leader in Jewish affairs.

Cyrus's son Arthur Hays Sulzberger (1891–1968) married Iphigene Bertha Ochs, the only child of Adolph Simon Ochs, publisher of the *New York Times*. When Adolph died in 1935, control of the newspaper passed from the Ochs family to the Sulzbergers as Arthur took over the reins as publisher. Cyrus Leo Sulzberger (1912–93), Arthur's nephew, was the *New York Times* chief foreign correspondent (1944–54) and later wrote a regular column for the publication.

Arthur Ochs Sulzberger (1926–), Arthur Hays Sulzberger's son, published the *Times* from 1963 to 1992. In the latter year he was succeeded by his own son, Arthur Ochs Sulzberger, Jr. (1951–).

Mayer Sulzberger

JURIST AND SCHOLAR

Mayer Sulzberger spent thirty years as a successful lawyer and then served over twenty years as a respected judge. During those years he was also active in Jewish welfare work and in the promotion of higher Jewish learning in America. He crowned his career with several books devoted to scholarly biblical studies.

Mayer was born in Heidelsheim, Baden, Germany, on June 22, 1843. His parents were Abraham and Sophia (Einstein) Sulzberger. The family had included many rabbinic scholars. Abraham was a minister and teacher in Heidelsheim before the Revolution of 1848 drove him to immigrate to the United States. The family settled in Philadelphia, Pennsylvania, where Leopold Sulzberger, Abraham's brother, had settled about ten years earlier.

Mayer attended a business college, worked as a bookkeeper, studied law in the office of Moses A. Dropsie, and in 1865 was admitted to the bar. For the next thirty years he practiced law.

In 1895 he was elected a judge of the court of common pleas, serving by reelection till 1916 and holding the office of president judge from 1902 till his retirement. Several of his legal and political papers and speeches were published, including the article "The Practice of Criminal Law" (*American Law Register*, June 1903) and his Temple University address *Politics in a Democracy* (1910). After he retired he served on the committee to revise the Constitution of Pennsylvania and on the Philadelphia Board of City Trusts.

Throughout his life Mayer was active in promoting Jewish welfare and education. He served, beginning in 1865, on the board of the Jewish Hospital of Philadelphia, founded by his father; was president of the Young Men's Hebrew Association of Philadelphia (1875 and 1885); was a trustee of the Baron de Hirsch Fund (1884); and headed the American Jewish Committee (1906–1912). In the field of education, he was secretary of the board of trustees of Maimonides College in Philadelphia (1867–73); chaired the publication committee of the Jewish Publication Society of America (1888–1923); was a trustee of Gratz College, Philadelphia, from its beginning in 1897; served as a director of the Jewish Theological Seminary from 1901; and, after his retirement from the bench, became an honorary lecturer on Jewish jurisprudence and institutes of government at the Dropsie College for Hebrew and Cognate Learning, of which he was an original governor.

Mayer was among the first in the United States to establish an important collection of Hebrew manuscripts and incunabula, which, with his general Jewish library, he donated to the Jewish Theological Seminary of America in 1902. He presented his Arabic, Ethiopic, and Samaritan manuscripts, as well as some Egyptian objects, to Dropsie College.

Mayer devoted his later years to biblical studies. He published four books based on those efforts: *The Am ha-Aretz, the Ancient Hebrew Parliament* (1910); *The Polity of the Ancient Hebrews* (1912); *The Ancient Hebrew Law of Homicide* (1915); and *The Status of Labor in Ancient Israel* (1923).

Mayer Sulzberger never married. He died in Philadelphia on April 20, 1923.

CYRUS LINDAUER SULZBERGER

LEADER IN JEWISH AFFAIRS

Cyrus Lindauer Sulzberger won great success in the business world, but he was best known for his work in dealing with Jewish immigration and for his activities in Jewish philanthropy.

He was born in Philadelphia, Pennsylvania, on July 11, 1858. His parents were Leopold and Sophia (Lindauer) Sulzberger. Leopold was an immigrant from Germany, as was Abraham Sulzberger, who was Leopold's brother and the father of Cyrus's first cousin Mayer Sulzberger, the noted jurist and scholar.

At the age of sixteen Cyrus helped to found the Young Men's

Hebrew Assocation of Philadelphia. In 1877 he moved to New York City to become bookkeeper for the textile manufacturing and importing firm of N. Erlanger, Blumgart and Company. In 1891 he became a member of the company, in 1902 president, and in 1929 chairman of the board.

During those years, the huge numbers of immigrants to the United States was a national problem. In 1900 Cyrus helped to organize, and from 1904 to 1909 served as chairman of, the Industrial Removal Office, an organization with branches in 108 American cities. Its purpose was to relieve the congestion of Jewish immigrants in New York City by helping them to settle in other areas. Between 1902 and 1909 the Industrial Removal Office sent 45,711 immigrants from New York City into 1,278 towns and cities.

He was also president (1903–1909 and 1919–21) of the Jewish Agricultural and Industrial Aid Society, which helped to place about eighty thousand Jews on farms in the United States. During 1910–11 he was a member of the New York State commission on congestion of population, which presented a report to the governor recommending various kinds of legislation to help spread the population and avoid pockets of unemployment. While he was active in providing for the distribution and Americanization of immigrants, he did not push to limit immigration. In fact, he spoke out for increased liberalization of the laws governing entry into the United States.

Cyrus engaged in a wide range of Jewish philanthropies. He was a member of the executive committee of the American Jewish Committee in 1907 and its secretary in 1914–15, when the organization collected large sums for the relief of Jews overseas. His other philanthropic activities including serving as president of the United Hebrew Charities of New York (1908), president of the National Conference of Jewish Charities (1912–14), and trustee of the Federation for the Support of Jewish Philanthropic Societies of New York City (1919).

He married Rachel Peizotto Hays in 1884. They had two sons and three daughters.

Cyrus Lindauer Sulzberger died in New York City on April 30, 1932.

Arthur Hays Sulzberger

PUBLISHER OF THE *NEW YORK TIMES*, 1935–61

Succeeding Adolph Simon Ochs as publisher of the *New York Times*, Arthur Hays Sulzberger not only continued his predecessor's principles of honest and impartial jouralism but also improved the publication's news coverage and financial strength.

He was born in New York City on September 12, 1891, the son of Cyrus Lindauer Sulzberger, a successful businessman and leader in Jewish affairs, and Rachel (Peixotto Hays) Sulzberger. Arthur studied engineering at Columbia University (B.S., 1913) and then went to work for N. Erlanger, Blumgart and Company, the textile firm of which his father was president and later chairman of the board.

In 1917 Arthur married Iphigene Bertha Ochs, the only child of Adolph Simon Ochs, publisher of the *New York Times*. They had four children: Marian Effie, who became Mrs. Orvil E. Dryfoos and Mrs. Andrew Heiskell; Ruth Rachel, who became Mrs. Ben Hale Golden of the *Chattanooga Times* and the *Chattanooga Post*; Judith Peixotto, who became Dr. Judith (Sulzberger) Cohen, the wife of Richard Cohen; and Arthur Ochs Sulzberger, who followed his father and Orvil E. Dryfoos as president and publisher of the *New York Times*. In her later years Iphigene (Ochs) Sulzberger (1892–1990) played an important role at the *New York Times* by serving as a director and trustee and by conveying to successive generations of executives and employees the traditions of the newspaper and its dedication to serious journalism.

In 1917–18 Arthur Hays Sulzberger served as an officer in the United States Army Reserve. In December 1918, shortly after his discharge from the army, he began to work at the *Times* as an assistant to the executive manager. His duties were unspecified,

Arthur Hays Sulzberger

so he purposely familiarized himself with all phases of the business. By the late 1920s he had become a vice president, and during the early 1930s his role in managing the newspaper increased as his father-in-law's health declined.

When Adolph Simon Ochs died in 1935, he left controlling interest in the *Times* in trust to Arthur Hays Sulzberger's children, with Iphigene, Arthur, and Julius Ochs Adler (Ochs's nephew) as trustees and executors of the estate. They chose Arthur to succeed Ochs, and the company's board of directors soon elected Arthur president of the company and publisher of the newspaper. In a May 8, 1935, editorial Arthur committed himself to adhere to Ochs's "principles of honest and impersonal journalism" and "to give the news impartially, without fear or favor."

To preserve the ideal of impartiality, he opposed a closed union shop for news and editorial employees and barred Communist party members from jobs in sensitive departments of the newspaper. He cloaked his own opinions in letters to the editor by using the pseudonym A. Aitchess (for A.H.S., his initials).

Arthur gradually changed and improved news coverage and newspaper content. He emphasized accuracy more than ever, so that the *New York Times* became an internationally renowned "paper of record." Eventually, however, he also called for more interpretation to supplement the factual accounts.

Under his leadership the *Times* saw great technical progress as well. He expanded the paper's production facilities, purchased radio station WQXR in New York City in 1944, and created an international edition in 1949.

Though his principal goal was always to report news in the best way possible, Arthur also made money for the *Times*. During World War II, for example, the amount of newsprint available was restricted, so he cut down on advertising space to make room for comprehensive war coverage. The result was a temporary loss of advertising revenue but a large growth in circulation, which, after the war, continued to climb as advertising money came back and increased.

The company's first annual public statement of finances, issued in 1958, showed a profit for the sixtieth consecutive year. During Arthur's term as publisher (1935–61) the number of *Times* employees more than doubled, advertising linage more than tripled, daily circulation increased by 40 percent, Sunday circulation nearly doubled, and gross income increased by about $100 million.

One of his prize employees was Cyrus Leo Sulzberger (born October 27, 1942, in New York City; died September 20, 1993, in Paris, France), his nephew (son of Arthur's only brother, Leo). Cyrus was the *New York Times* chief foreign correspondent from 1944 to 1954 and later a foreign affairs columnist for the paper.

In April 1957 Arthur resigned as president of the company and was replaced by his daughter Marian's husband, Orvil E. Dryfoos.

In November of that year, Arthur suffered the first of a series of strokes that increasingly incapacitated him. In 1961 he retired as publisher and was succeeded by Dryfoos. However, in 1963 Dryfoos died and Arthur's son, Arthur Ochs Sulzberger, was named president and publisher. The elder Sulzberger remained with the company during his later years as chairman of the board (1957–68).

On December 11, 1968, four days after marking his fiftieth anniversary at the *Times*, Arthur Hays Sulzberger died in New York City.

ARTHUR OCHS SULZBERGER

PUBLISHER OF THE *NEW YORK TIMES*, 1963–92

Arthur Ochs Sulzberger published the *New York Times* through an era (1963–92) in which he not only strengthened the reputation of the newspaper as one of the greatest in the world but also introduced innovations in production and editorial management.

He was born in New York City on February 5, 1926, the grandson of Adolph Simon Ochs, who published the *New York Times* from 1896 to 1935 and made it into a national institution, and the youngest child and only son of Arthur Hays Sulzberger, who published the paper from 1935 to 1961, and Iphigene (Ochs) Sulzberger. Young Arthur was nicknamed Punch by his father, who, to celebrate his son's arrival, wrote and illustrated a book in which he remarked that the boy had "come to play the Punch to Judy's endless show," referring to the father's youngest daughter, Judith. Arthur Ochs Sulzberger retained the nickname in later years.

He was educated at private schools and, after United States Marine Corps service (1944–46) in the Pacific during World War II, at Columbia University (B.A. in English and history, 1951). In 1951 he was recalled to the Marine Corps for Korean War duty; after seventeen months he was discharged with the rank of first lieutenant and made a captain of the reserve.

In 1952 he began his journalistic career as a cub reporter with the *New York Times*, covering local assignments. In February 1953 he joined the staff of the *Milwaukee Journal*, where he worked as a reporter and on the state and local news desks. He returned to the *Times* in February 1954 to work on the foreign news desk and then as a correspondent in London, Paris, and Rome. In December 1955 he came back to New York City and in the following month was named assistant to the publisher. From April 1957 to June 1963 he was assistant treasurer of the *New York Times*.

American Jewish Archives, Cincinnati Campus, Hebrew Union College–Jewish Institute of Religion.

Arthur Ochs Sulzberger

In April 1961 Arthur Hays Sulzberger went into semiretirement and appointed Orvil E. Dryfoos, his son-in-law, publisher of the *New York Times*, having already made Dryfoos president of the company in 1957. In 1963 Dryfoos died, and on June 20, 1963, Arthur Ochs Sulzberger was designated by his father to succeed Dryfoos as president and publisher. In announcing his son's appointment, the elder Sulzberger stated, "It is our intention to maintain this family operation and insure continuance of the newspaper that the *Times* has come to be under those who by sentiment and training are particularly tied to its principles and traditions." In 1973 young Arthur also became chairman and chief executive officer of the New York Times Company.

Arthur Ochs Sulzberger introduced many changes to improve the appearance and readability of the *New York Times*. In 1964 he unified the daily paper and the Sunday edition, which had previously been a separate entity, and placed the result under a single executive editor. He also enriched and enlivened the content of the paper through a series of new editorial appointments and by expanding coverage of such areas as sports, science, religion, the arts, and women's news. During the Vietnam conflict in the 1960s and 1970s, his paper was noted for its forthright and impartial coverage.

Arthur's interests and activities went beyond the *New York Times*. He was a member of the Greater New York Council of the Boy Scouts of America and sat on the boards of directors for many organizations, including the Greater New York Safety Council and the Baron de Hirsch Fund. In 1987 he became chairman of the board of trustees of the Metropolitan Museum of Art.

He married Barbara Winslow Grant in 1948; they had a son and a daughter before divorcing in 1956. By his second marriage, in 1956 to Carol J. (Fox) Fuhrman, he had a daughter; he also adopted his second wife's daughter by a previous marriage.

In 1979 he gave up the office of president, which was assumed by Walter E. Mattson. In 1992 he handed over the office of publisher to his son, Arthur Ochs Sulzberger, Jr. The elder Sulzberger retained his positions as chairman and chief executive officer.

THE
SZOLDS

F OR NEARLY ONE HUNDRED YEARS Rabbi Benjamin
Szold (1829–1902) and his daughter Henrietta (1860–
1945) made important contributions to the Jewish community.

Benjamin was a force for over forty years in Baltimore, Maryland, where he served as a rabbi, became an early Zionist, and
produced scholarly Jewish writings. His humanitarian work benefited both Jews and Gentiles, white and black.

He instructed Henrietta in Hebrew, Bible studies, and other
subjects. She, in turn, helped him in his research and literary work.
Even as a child she was indispensable to him as his secretary, writing out passages for him when his rheumatism and arthritis prevented him from holding a pen. Later they traveled together in
Europe, and she nursed him during his final illness.

After his death she carried his Zionist and humanitarian torch
onto the world stage and created one of the brightest lights among
twentieth-century Jews. Of her many outstanding achievements,
the most memorable was her founding of Hadassah, the Women's
Zionist Organization of America.

BENJAMIN SZOLD

PROMINENT BALTIMORE RABBI

Benjamin Szold served as rabbi or rabbi emeritus of the Congregation Oheb Shalom in Baltimore, Maryland, for over forty years. During that time he won renown for his religious leadership, his work in behalf of the unfortunate, and his authorship of scholarly Jewish writings.

He was born in Nemiskert, County of Neutra, Hungary, on November 15, 1829. His parents were Baruch, a farmer, and Chaile (Endler) Szold. Orphaned early in life, he was raised by his uncles.

Benjamin spent his youth in a German-speaking milieu in Austro-Hungary. He received his early training in Hebrew and rabbinics under private tutors, and later he studied in Breslau at the secular university and the theological seminary. While still a student, he officiated in synagogues at Brieg, Silesia (1857), and at Stockholm, Sweden (1858).

In August 1859 he married Sophie Schaar. They had eight daughters.

Just one month after his marriage, Benjamin immigrated to the United States to become rabbi of the Congregation Oheb Shalom in Baltimore. He steered a moderate course for his congregation, leaning neither to Orthodox rigidity nor to Reform radicalism. However, he did insist on the strict observance of the Sabbath, and he prepared for his congregation the traditional prayer book *Abodat Yisrael* ("Service of Israel," 1863, with many later editions). He served Oheb Shalom till 1892, when he retired and was elected rabbi emeritus.

His simple, genuine humanity led him to champion those in distress, Jew and Gentile alike. Disturbed by the suffering of Russian-Jewish refugees, Benjamin, unlike many other German Jews (who regarded Russian Jews as lower class), actually took Russian immigrants into his own home, which became an informal employment agency and social service center. The refugees' plight caused him to become a firm Zionist long before Theodor Herzl organized the Zionist movement.

Benjamin also took a leading role in non-Jewish charitable causes, such as the Baltimore Association for the Education and Moral Improvement of the Colored People. During the Civil War he spoke out openly against slavery despite the Southern orientation of his city. He protected human life at every opportunity; for example, when he failed to obtain a pardon for a Union deserter, he protested by holding the hand of the condemned soldier while the firing squad shot the man dead.

Benjamin was an outstanding scholar. He showed great originality of thought in his biblical study *The Book of Job with a New Commentary* (1886). He also wrote textbooks, shorter publications, and a commentary on the eleventh chapter of Daniel for G. A. Kohut's *Semitic Studies in Memory of Rev. Dr. Alexander Kohut* (1897).

Benjamin Szold died in Berkeley Springs, West Virginia, on July 31, 1902.

Henrietta Szold

FOUNDER OF HADASSAH

Zionist leader, social worker, educator, writer, editor—Henrietta Szold was one of the greatest Jewish women of her generation and helped pioneer modern Jewish culture in the United States. Her greatest achievement was the founding of Hadassah, the Women's Zionist Organization of America.

Henrietta was born in Baltimore, Maryland, on December 21, 1860. She was the eldest of the eight daughters of Benjamin and Sophia (Schaar) Szold, both recent immigrants from Europe. Benjamin was rabbi of the Congregation Oheb Shalom in Baltimore.

After graduating from Western Female High School in 1877, Henrietta received little formal education, but her father taught her Hebrew, German (the language of the Szold household), the

Bible, Jewish history, and other subjects. From her mother she acquired a sense of duty and order.

For fifteen years after her graduation, Henrietta taught a wide range of subjects at the Misses Adams' School in Baltimore. She also taught children and adults at her father's congregational school, aided him in his research and writing, and worked as Baltimore correspondent for the New York weekly *Jewish Messenger*.

During that time she became heavily involved in the plight of eastern European Jews flooding into America. After the assassination of Czar Alexander II in 1881, anti-Semitic laws and pogroms drove hundreds of thousands of Jews out of Poland, Lithuania, and other regions of the Russian Empire. Many immigrants settled in the Baltimore area, where Henrietta helped to found an evening school for teaching them English, American history, and useful trades. She served there as teacher, superintendent, and fund-raiser. Her experience with the refugees made her realize how important their Zionist hopes were to them. In 1893 she assisted a Baltimore immigrant group in establishing Hebras Zion, one of the earliest Zionist societies in America.

In that same year a family friend, Cyrus Adler, asked her to become the executive secretary to the editorial board of the Jewish Publication Society of America, founded largely by Adler in 1888. Over the next twenty-three years, Henrietta, in effect the society's editor and translator, became the dominant figure in the organization and prepared for publication many works of great importance for the preservation of the Jewish heritage, such as a revision of the five-volume English version of Heinrich Graetz's *History of the Jews*. From 1904 to 1908 she edited the *American Jewish Yearbook* for the Jewish Publication Society. She also became a member of the executive council of the Federation of American Zionists and wrote articles for its monthly *Maccabaean* as well as for the *Jewish Encyclopedia* (1901–1906).

Henrietta nursed her father through a long illness before his death in 1902. The following year she and her mother moved from Baltimore to New York City.

There, wanting to edit her father's unpublished scholarly papers but acutely feeling her lack of formal education for the purpose, she enrolled at the Jewish Theological Seminary of America. She was the first female student at that institution and was allowed to attend only on the condition that she not seek official accreditation for her studies. Henrietta studied Talmud under Louis Ginzberg, with whom she fell in love; however, he married another woman in 1909.

Henrietta Szold

To recover from that emotional shock, Henrietta, accompanied by her mother, went abroad, traveling in Europe and the Near East. In July 1909 they arrived in Turkish-ruled Palestine. Horrified at the diseases found there, including malaria and trachoma, Henrietta resolved to do something to establish a healthful Jewish national refuge in Palestine. Early in 1910 she returned to New York City and became increasingly involved in Zionist work. "I am more than ever convinced," she said, "that if not Zionism, then nothing—then extinction for the Jew."

Later in 1910 she began serving as the American-based secretary of the Jewish Agricultural Experiment Station in Palestine and became secretary of the Federation of American Zionists. She also made speeches to small groups to publicize the Zionist cause.

Since 1899 there had been many American Zionist women's groups, but all had been small and short-lived. A typical group would be called Daughters of Zion, followed by the name of a Jewish heroine, such as Deborah or Hadassah (the Hebrew form of the Persian name Esther). In 1907 Henrietta joined a women's group called the Hadassah Study Circle, which studied Zionism. During her 1909 trip to Palestine, she was encouraged by her mother to use the Hadassah group to do medical work in Palestine. Between 1909 and 1912 that idea continued to grow in Henrietta's mind. But her Hadassah group was already running out of steam. What she wanted to do was to establish a new Zionist women's organization, but this time built on a permanent national scale and dedicated not only to study but also to practical work in furthering the Zionist cause.

Early in 1912 she helped to draw up two constitutions: one for the national organization, the Daughters of Zion; and one for the first chapter, the Hadassah Chapter in New York City. On February 24, 1912, the day of Purim, the Jewish festival that celebrates Queen Esther's victory over Haman, a group of women met at Temple Emanu-El in New York City and formally created the new organization. On that occasion Henrietta addressed the audience: "If we are Zionists, as we say we are, what is the good of meeting and talking and drinking tea? Let us do something real and practical—let us organize the Jewish women of America and send nurses and doctors to Palestine." Later, at the first national convention, the parent group was renamed Hadassah, the Women's Zionist Organization of America. Henrietta was elected the first president.

Early in 1913 Hadassah sent two nurses to Palestine. However, World War I greatly hampered the organization's ability to expand its service in the region.

In 1916 two events occurred that allowed Henrietta to devote more time to her Zionist and humanitarian projects. First, a group of Zionists (including Louis D. Brandeis) established a fund to provide her with a lifetime income, enabling her to resign from her job with the Jewish Publication Society. Second, her mother died, giving Henrietta much pain but also a new-found freedom.

Also in 1916 she organized, through Hadassah, the American Zionist Medical Unit (renamed the Hadassah Medical Organization in 1922), a corps of doctors and nurses earmarked for Palestine. But World War I prevented them from sailing till June 1918.

In 1918 Henrietta helped reorganize the Federation of American Zionists, a loose collection of clubs, into the unified Zionist Organization of America. She became director of its education department.

Soon, however, she resumed her work for the Medical Unit, and in 1920 she moved to Palestine to help administer it. Shortly after arriving she founded, and became first president of, the Histadrut Nashim Ibriot (the Society of Jewish Women) in Jerusalem, a volunteer service organization. She spent most of the rest of her life in the Holy Land.

Henrietta remained president of Hadassah till 1926 and honorary president thereafter till her death. Through her efforts it grew from just a few dozen members into a large, efficiently run organization that provided crucial medical service in Palestine and, later, Israel.

In 1927 she won the great honor of being elected to the three-member commission at the head of the Palestine Zionist Executive of the World Zionist Organization. She was given responsibility for the departments of health and education in what in effect was the government of Jewish Palestine.

In 1931 she was elected to the seven-member Executive of the Vaad Leumi, the National Assembly of the Jews of Palestine. She helped transfer health and education services from international Zionist control to local communities. In 1933 she left her Vaad Leumi seat but remained till 1939 in charge of the social service department she had established during her term in office.

Late in 1933 she was appointed the Palestine bureau director of an organization called Youth Aliyah. Through it she took a leading role in efforts to settle German-Jewish children in Palestine. By the end of World War II, Youth Aliyah had rescued about thirteen thousand children from Germany and Poland.

In later years she continued to organize child and youth welfare activities in Palestine. They included a village for boys and a vocational school for girls.

Henrietta Szold, who never married, was known as the Mother of the Yishuv (the Jewish settlement in Palestine). She died at the Hadassah-Hebrew University Hospital, which she had helped to found, in Jerusalem on February 13, 1945.

THE
TISCHES

THE TISCHES ARE MAJOR FORCES in many industries. They developed a chain of hotels, built Loews Corporation into a powerful conglomerate, and revitalized the Columbia Broadcasting System (CBS).

Laurence ("Larry") Alan Tisch (1923–) entered the hotel business and was soon joined by his younger brother, Preston Robert ("Bob") Tisch (1926–). After creating a hotel empire, they gained control of the Loews Corporation and changed it from a theater operation into a huge conglomerate, including hotel, cigarette, insurance, and watchmaking divisions. In 1986 Larry took control of CBS, while Bob served as postmaster general of the United States (1986–88), returned to Loews, and became half owner of the New York Giants professional football team (1990).

The next generation of Tisches continued the family tradition of teamwork and achievement. Andrew Herbert Tisch (1949–), one of Larry's sons, has held various positions within the Loews Corporation, such as president of the watchmaking Bulova Corporation (1985–89) and chief executive officer of Lorillard Tobacco Company (1989–95). He has been active in the leadership of the American Jewish Committee and the United Jewish Appeal. Another of Larry's sons, James S. Tisch (1953–), joined Loews in 1977 and became president in 1994.

Steven E. Tisch (1949–), Bob's elder son, became a movie producer. He produced the television movie *The Burning Bed*

(1984) and was one of three producers of the theatrical hit *Forrest Gump* (1994). His brother, Jonathan Mark Tisch (1953–), is president and chief executive officer (1988–) of Loews Hotels, a division of the family's Loews Corporation.

LAURENCE ALAN TISCH

HEAD OF LOEWS AND CBS

Laurence Alan Tisch heads one of the most powerful families in the modern American business world. He built the Tisch Hotels chain, developed Loews Corporation into a major conglomerate, and gained control of the media giant Columbia Broadcasting System (CBS).

Laurence ("Larry") was born in the Bensonhurst section of Brooklyn, New York, on March 5, 1923. He was the elder of the two sons of Abraham Solomon ("Al") and Sadye (Brenner) Tisch. Al owned a garment-manufacturing business and then ran two summer resorts in New Jersey. Sadye helped her husband to operate the resorts and encouraged their sons to work together from an early age. Her efforts produced a close-knit family of achievers.

Larry earned a B.S. degree at New York University (1942) and an M.A. degree in industrial engineering from the University of Pennsylvania (1943). He then entered World War II service with the United States Army, where he prepared secret codes for the Office of Strategic Services, the precursor of the Central Intelligence Agency (CIA).

Larry left the army in 1946, studied for one semester at Harvard Law School, and then, following his father's lead, entered the hotel business. Borrowing money from his father and a family friend, he purchased a resort hotel in Lakewood, New Jersey, installed a swimming pool and a skating rink, and soon made a success of the venture.

In 1948 he married Wilma ("Billie") Stein. They had four sons.

Also in 1948 Bob joined Larry, and they began to acquire more hotels, typically taking run-down places, improving them, and turning them into moneymakers. Within a few years Tisch Hotels, Inc., with Larry as president (1946–74), had hotels in many areas, including the Catskill Mountains, Atlantic City, and New York City. The first hotel that they built themselves was the luxurious Americana (1955) in Bal Harbour, Florida, which specialized in convention catering and soon became one of the most profitable businesses in the state.

In 1959 the Tisch brothers started buying into Loews Corporation, which ran a chain of movie theaters, and by September of that year Larry was a Loews board member and the chairman of the finance committee, while Bob became head of the executive committee. In early 1961 Larry gained complete control of Loews as chairman of the board and cochief executive officer, with Bob as the other cochief.

The Tisches quickly moved the corporation into the hotel and motel business. For their initial project they replaced an old New York City movie house with the Summit, the first new hotel built in Manhattan in thirty years. The Loews Hotels division of the corporation went on to run many more hotels in New York City, including the Americana and the Howard Johnson Motor Lodge, as well as elsewhere in the United States and in other countries.

While Bob ran the hotel business, Larry kept Loews's stock portfolio and looked for new ventures. He showed a remarkable ability to turn troubled companies into profitable enterprises. In 1968 he acquired the Lorillard Tobacco Company, followed by the CNA Financial Corporation in 1974 and the Bulova Watch Company in 1979. By cutting costs, revamping management, and emphasizing each company's strengths, he developed those sluggish companies into great successes and built huge profits for Loews. Between 1970 and 1980 he raised the corporation's revenues from about $100 million to over $3 billion.

Loews's growth stemmed largely from the smooth teamwork between the Tisch brothers. Larry, known as the "private," low-key member of the team, dealt with broad outlines and handled investment strategies. Bob, the "public," gregarious one, specialized in details and ran the day-to-day operations. They socialized together, went to temple together, and even commuted to work together. One associate said they were "as close as peanut butter and jelly."

Larry's management style was described as "Spartan." He kept personnel to a bare minimum, allowed only the simplest of office furnishings, and refused limousines and executive dining rooms for himself or anybody else. His austerity was called the "Tisch touch."

In the mid-1980s the CBS communications conglomerate faced many problems. Its television ratings were falling, its advertising revenues were shrinking, and its reputation as a first-rate news network was eroding because of its alleged "show business" approach.

To prevent a hostile takeover, CBS repurchased 21 percent of its own stock and sought the aid of Larry Tisch, who by August 1986 had acquired 24.9 percent of the company. The following month the chairman and chief executive officer, Thomas H. Wyman, resigned. The company's founder, William S. Paley, became acting chairman, while Larry took over as acting chief executive officer. Larry quickly instituted staff reductions, belt-tightening in daily operations, management shakeups, and divestitures, including the selling of CBS Educational and Professional Publishing. In January 1987 he was unanimously elected president and chief executive officer of CBS.

During the next year he continued to streamline the company. He reduced budgets, sold the magazine-publishing division, and, in a controversial decision, sold the popular CBS Records subsidiary (to Sony, the Japanese electronics manufacturer).

In 1990 he became chairman of CBS, while keeping his earlier roles as president and chief executive officer. By 1993 CBS held first place in daytime, prime-time, and late-night ratings.

However, over the next two years CBS declined again, many blaming Larry's "tight-fisted" approach. In August 1995 it was announced that Westinghouse Electric Corporation had agreed to purchase CBS.

Larry continued to head Loews. The conglomerate still controlled a wide range of successful enterprises, including Diamond Offshore Drilling.

Larry has donated time, energy, and money to many civic, cultural, religious, and philanthropic organizations. He has served as a trustee of the New York Public Library, a director of the Legal Aid Society, and chairman of the board of trustees of New York University. A prominent art patron and collector, he is a trustee of the Metropolitan Museum of Art. He is a past president of the United Jewish Appeal of New York and is a trustee of the Federation of Jewish Philanthropies. The Tisch brothers gave $10 million to the Metropolitan Museum of Art for the construction of new galleries, $2 million to New York University for the building of Tisch Hall in honor of their late father, and $7.5 million to the same university for its School of the Arts.

PRESTON ROBERT TISCH

COHEAD OF LOEWS CORPORATION

With his older brother, Laurence ("Larry"), Preston Robert ("Bob") Tisch built the Tisch Hotels chain and developed Loews Corporation into a major conglomerate. Bob also entered government affairs, successfully serving as postmaster general of the United States.

He was born in Brooklyn, New York, on April 29, 1926. Bob was the younger of the two sons of Abraham Solomon ("Al") and Sadye (Brenner) Tisch. Al operated a garment-manufacturing firm and then a couple of summer resorts in New Jersey. Sadye encouraged the family to work as a unit, advice that her sons would heed to great benefit in later years.

Bob studied at Bucknell University and served with the United States Army during World War II before graduating from the University of Michigan with a B.A. degree in 1948. In that same year he married Joan Hyman. They had two sons and one daughter.

Also in 1948 Bob joined Larry at the beginning of their development of a chain of hotels, Tisch Hotels, Inc. The Tisches' usual procedure was to buy hotels that were in decline and then to improve them, turning them into moneymakers. In 1955 they built their first new hotel—the luxurious Americana in Bal Harbour, Florida, which became one of the most profitable businesses in the state.

In 1959 the brothers began buying into the Loews Corporation, which ran a chain of movie theaters. Later that year Bob became head of the Loews executive committee, while Larry took over the finance committee. Soon the brothers became cochief executive officers of the corporation, with Larry as chairman and Bob as cochairman of the board.

The brothers transformed Loews from a theater specialist into a major conglomerate. The first step in that process was to add a Loews Hotels division, which Bob ran. In 1968 Loews acquired Lorillard Tobacco Company, followed in 1974 by the CNA Financial Corporation and in 1979 by the Bulova Watch Company.

The brothers made a good team. Bob handled day-to-day operations while Larry concentrated on overall business strategies. Bob was gregarious and appeared more often in public, while Larry was low key and preferred to work in private. Together their differences added up to a successful whole in both their business and their personal lives. They even went to temple and commuted to work together.

In 1986 Bob took a leave of absence from the business to accept an appointment from President Ronald Reagan as postmaster general of the United States Postal Service. Bob ran the 700,000-person bureaucracy with the same efficiency that had characterized his work at Loews. He made important changes in the pace of automation, in the delivery of mail, and in customer service. His principal achievement was to negotiate a union contract that had eluded his predecessors for a dozen years. In 1988 he resigned his government post and returned to run Loews while Larry shifted his attention to his new role as head of CBS.

In 1990 Bob purchased half of the New York Giants professional football team, becoming partners with the previous owner, Wellington Mara. In March 1991 the sale was officially approved at a National Football League (NFL) owners meeting.

Through the years Bob participated in activities outside his regular business milieu. He had a leadership role in the national Democratic conventions of 1976 and 1980, became a trustee of New York University, was a member of the Governor's Business Advisory Council for New York State, and served as president of Citymeals on Wheels.

In the mid-1990s Lorillard, like other cigarette manufacturers, began facing tough questions from legal authorities and from the public about what the tobacco companies knew—and when they knew—about the health risks of smoking. Bob, as cohead of Loews, which still owned Lorillard, personally had to answer many of those questions. His point of view was that Lorillard was an independent subsidiary and that Loews had no control over the quality or safety of Lorillard's products.

On a more upbeat note during that same period, he was still happily involved with the New York Giants. He also continued to be active with Loews, which was as powerful as ever and now included another subsidiary, Diamond Offshore Drilling.

THE
WARBURGS

THE WARBURGS ARE ONE OF THE MOST eminent
Jewish families in history. Bankers, scholars, politicians,
scientists, artists, musicians, philanthropists, and
other members of the family have distinguished themselves since
the sixteenth century.

The Warburgs may have originated in medieval Italy. But the
first documented ancestor was a German—Simon von Cassel, who
in 1559 moved from Hesse to the Westphalian town of Warburg
(or Warburgum). In 1668 Juspa-Joseph (died 1678), Simon's great-
grandson, moved to Altona with the adopted surname of von
Warburg. Later the family dropped the *von*.

In 1773 Grumpich Marcus Warburg (1727–1801) moved
to Hamburg. He was the father of the brothers Moses Marcus
(1763–1839) and Gershon (1765–1825) Warburg, to whom he
gave his pawnbroking business. In 1798 the brothers expanded
the business into the banking firm of M. M. Warburg and Company of Hamburg.

Moses had a daughter, Sara, who married Abraham (or Aby)
Samuel Warburg, a second cousin. Their two sons, Siegmund
(1835–89) and Moritz (1838–1910), raised the firm to the first
rank of private banks in Europe and founded the two best-known
lines of Warburgs.

Siegmund had two sons. Abraham (or Aby, 1864–1933) played
a major role in developing M. M. Warburg and Company, while

Georges (or Georg) Siegmund (1871–1923), a landowner, had an only child, Siegmund George (1902–1982), who worked at M. M. Warburg and Company in Hamburg and founded S. G. Warburg and Company in London, the city's foremost merchant bank.

Moritz had five sons. Aby Moritz (1866–1929) was an art historian. Max Moritz (1867–1946) entered the family banking business and served as financial adviser to the German delegation at the Paris peace conference in 1919. Paul Moritz (1868–1932) became a partner in the Warburg firm at Hamburg, a member of Kuhn, Loeb and Company in New York City, and a member of America's first Federal Reserve Board. Felix Moritz (1871–1937) was long a member of Kuhn, Loeb and Company but became best known as a humanist and humanitarian. Fritz Moritz (1879–1964) served in the family banking firm.

Paul had a son, James Paul (1896), who became one of the family's most prominent members. James was a financier, author, and government official.

Felix, Paul's brother, married Frieda Schiff, daughter of the famed investment banker Jacob H. Schiff. Well known for her social and community activity, she gave funds to many charities, donated the building that became the Jewish Museum to the Jewish Theological Seminary, and served as president of the Young Women's Hebrew Association.

Felix and Frieda's four sons were all prominent. Frederick Marcus (1897–1973) was a partner in Kuhn, Loeb and Company and served as president of the Ninety-second Street Young Men's Hebrew Association in New York City. Gerald Felix (1901–1971) was a cellist, conductor, and patron of music. Paul Felix (1904–1965) was a financier and philanthropist. Edward Mortimer Morris (1908–1992) acquired a remarkable art collection, partonized modern art, and engaged in large-scale philanthropy.

In addition to the above Warburgs, who were based in Hamburg and later in the United States, other branches of the family produced great achievers. Simon Elias Warburg (1760–1828) founded the first Jewish community in Sweden. His grandson

Frederik Elias Warburg (1832–99) cofounded the Central London Electric Railway.

Emil Warburg (1846–1931) was a distinguished physicist who accepted baptisim, married a Christian, and had a son, Otto Heinrich Warburg (1883–1970), who won the Nobel Prize for physiology or medicine in 1931. Otto Heinrich earned the disdain of world Jewry because he worked under the Nazis in Germany throughout World War II.

Karl Johan Warburg (1852–1918) was a Swedish historian of literature and a member of Parliament. Otto Warburg (1859–1938) was a famed botanist and Zionist who served as chairman of the botanical department at Hebrew University in Palestine and headed the World Zionist Organization, strongly supporting Jewish colonization and agricultural work in the Holy Land.

PAUL MORITZ WARBURG

BANKING REFORMER

As a young man Paul Moritz Warburg was a partner in the old Hamburg, Germany, family banking firm of M. M. Warburg and Company and later a member of the New York City-based Kuhn, Loeb and Company. His greatest renown came through his advocacy of reforms in the American banking system and his membership on the first Federal Reserve Board.

Paul was born in Hamburg on August 10, 1868. He was the third of the five sons of Moritz and Charlotte (Oppenheim) Warburg.

After graduating from the Hamburg Gymnasium in 1886, Paul worked for a Hamburg exporting firm and then for shipping and banking houses in London and Paris. In 1895 he returned to Hamburg to become a partner in the family business.

In that same year, he married Nina J. Loeb, daughter of Solomon Loeb of the New York City banking firm of Kuhn, Loeb and Company. They had a son and a daughter.

Paul Moritz Warburg

In 1902 Paul moved to the United States and joined his father-in-law's company. He became an American citizen in 1911.

Paul studied the banking practices of many countries, in particular the central banking systems found in Germany, France, and England. After a financial panic erupted in America during 1907, he called for a reform in the United States banking system. His principal aim was to set up a national reserve association to function like a central bank. In 1913 Congress enacted a variation of his plan—the Federal Reserve law, which provided for regional reserve banks under the supervision of a national reserve board.

In 1914 President Woodrow Wilson nominated, and the Senate approved, Paul Warburg as one of the five members of the first Federal Reserve Board. During his four-year term he helped to guide the United States through the huge, complex financial operations of World War I.

In 1918 he retired to private life and spent his later years organizing and operating the International Acceptance Bank, which specialized in financing international trade. He gained wide notice in March 1929 by publicly warning that the unrestrained stock speculation then raging in America would lead to a financial catastrophe. "The ultimate collapse," he predicted, "is certain not only to affect the speculators themselves, but also to bring about a general depression involving the entire country." Indeed, that October the stock market crashed, ushering in the Great Depression.

Paul's other business activities included being a director of important railroads and corporations, a member of the advisory council of the Federal Reserve Board (1921–26), and chairman of the American Bankers' Association. He wrote the book *The Federal Reserve System: Its Origins and Growth* (two volumes, 1930).

However, Paul was a multidimensional man. He had considerable knowledge of art, music, history, and literature. His donations involved substantial funds to the Juilliard School of Music. He befriended the educator Booker T. Washington and served as treasurer of Tuskegee College.

Paul Moritz Warburg died in New York City on January 24, 1932.

Felix Moritz Warburg

HUMANIST AND HUMANITARIAN

Felix Moritz Warburg was a partner in the banking firm of Kuhn, Loeb and Company for forty years. But the principal focus of his life was his support of humanistic and humanitarian causes.

Felix was born in Hamburg, Germany, on January 14, 1871. He was the fourth of the five sons of Moritz and Charlotte (Oppenheim) Warburg. Moritz was a member of the Hamburg banking house of M. M. Warburg and Company, which had been founded in 1798 by the Warburg family.

Felix studied at the Hamburg Gymnasium and took violin lessons. At seventeen he moved to Frankfurt am Main, where he lived with his materal grandparents and learned his grandfather's business of selling precious stones. During these early years his love of music brought him into contact with some of Germany's musical giants, including Johannes Brahms and Clara Schumann.

In 1894 Felix met Frieda Schiff, daughter of the American investment banker Jacob H. Schiff. Later that year Felix came to the United States, and in 1895 he married Frieda, with whom he had four sons and one daughter.

Felix Moritz Warburg

In 1897 he became a partner in his father-in-law's firm of Kuhn, Loeb and Company, located in New York City. Felix stayed with the company for the rest of his life, eventually becoming its senior partner.

However, he reserved much of his energy for cultural, educational, and charitable causes. His interest in art and music led him to contribute to the new building of the Fogg Art Museum at Harvard University, to become a trustee of the Juillard School of Music, and to support the New York Symphony Society.

He made many contributions to progress in education. In 1902 he was appointed to the New York City Board of Education, where he helped to establish special classes for retarded children and to place blind children in regular schools. He also helped to finance schools and to found the Training School for Jewish Social Service (later the Graduate School for Jewish Social Work).

In the field of social work, Felix's efforts made an equally great impact. He was a director of the Educational Alliance, which aided immigrants in adjusting to America; worked closely with Lillian D. Wald of the Henry Street Settlement; and supported programs that fought juvenile delinquency, such as juvenile courts and the National Desertion Bureau (which aimed to reduce the number of broken families). In 1907 he was appointed to the first New York State Probation Commission.

In 1915 Felix helped to create the American Jewish Joint Distribution Committee, which handled the distribution of funds raised for the relief of Jews displaced by World War I. In 1917 he

helped to found the Federation for the Support of Jewish Philanthropic Societies, serving as its president (1917–20) and its chairman (1925–37); the federation unified the efforts of Jewish
charities in New York City.

Felix was never a Zionist, but World War I showed him the
need for facing the problem of Jewish refugees. Following the
Russian Revolution of 1917, he helped to relocate Russian Jews
in the Ukraine and elsewhere. Later he saw the need for Palestine as a place of settlement for dispossessed Jews, and he established the Joint Palestine Survey Commission to study the
feasibility of a large Jewish influx into that area. During 1929–
30 he served as chairman of the Jewish Agency's administrative
committee, cooperating with the British government in trying
to promote the colonization of the Holy Land by the Jews. His
link with Palestine was strengthened when he served as a trustee
of Hebrew University in Jerusalem and helped to found
the Institute for Jewish Studies.

Felix Moritz Warburg died in New York City on October 20,
1937.

James Paul Warburg

FINANCIER, AUTHOR, AND GOVERNMENT OFFICIAL

James Paul Warburg, scion of one of the world's great banking
families, became a successful banker and economist. He also took
his financial knowledge into the realm of public affairs by writing
many books and serving the federal government under two American presidents.

James was born in Hamburg, Germany, on August 18, 1896.
He was the only son of the banker Paul Moritz and Nina Jenny
(Loeb) Warburg. His parents moved with him to the United States
in 1901, and he was naturalized in 1911. In 1917 he graduated
from Harvard University.

James joined the navy in 1917 and trained as a combat pilot for

World War I service. However, after developing a new type of aero compass, he was assigned to Washington, D.C., to supervise its production.

After the war he stayed for a time in Washington, D.C., and began his banking career there with the National Metropolitan Bank. From 1919 to 1921 he was with the First National Bank of Boston, rising from bookkeeper to assistant cashier.

In 1921 he became vice president of his father's International Acceptance Corporation in New York City. The firm specialized in financing international trade. In 1928 it was amalgamated with the Bank of Manhattan Company. James served as president of International Acceptance in 1931 and 1932, and from 1932 to 1935 he was vice chairman of the board of the Bank of Manhattan Company.

In 1933 he joined President Franklin D. Roosevelt's original "brain trust" as a financial adviser. In that capacity James helped to reform the American banking system and analyzed industrial recovery proposals. However, when President Roosevelt rejected a return to the gold standard, James resigned. He criticized the president in several books, including *The Money Muddle* (1934) and *Hell Bent for Election* (1935).

In 1937 he began to work as an independent industrial financier in New York City. He found financing for Edwin H. Land, who invented the Polaroid process. James himself invested in the Polaroid company and made a fortune.

He opposed American isolationism and wrote two books, *Peace in Our Time* (1940) and *Our War and Our Peace* (1941), in support of President Roosevelt's foreign policy of actively aiding the Allies. In 1942 James was appointed deputy director of the Office of War Information in London, charged with developing propaganda aimed at the Axis powers and at occupied Europe. In 1944 he left government service, began to write books in favor of Roosevelt, and campaigned for the president's reelection.

James's later years were preoccupied with matters of foreign policy. He criticized President Harry S. Truman's use of the United States as a global police force, helped to form the United

World Federalists to promote the idea of a world government, and began a series of books on American foreign policy. In 1961 he was appointed an assistant in the new Arms Control and Disarmament Agency. He also gave President John F. Kennedy ideas for speeches on disarmament and on ways to establish peace.

James favored compromising with the Soviet Union and Communist China to preserve peace. Similarly, while he supported the need for Israel as a Jewish homeland, he called for an even-handed treatment of Israeli Arabs. In 1962 he received the Gandhi Peace Prize.

James was married three times. In 1918 he married Katharine Faulkner Swift. They had three daughters before divorcing in 1934. In 1935 he wedded Phyllis Baldwin Browne. They had no children and were divorced in 1947. In 1948 he married Joan Melber. They had two sons and two daughters.

James Paul Warburg died in Greenwich, Connecticut, on June 3, 1969.

SIEGMUND GEORGE WARBURG

FOUNDER OF S.G.WARBURG AND COMPANY

Siegmund George Warburg founded London's foremost merchant bank, S. G. Warburg and Company. He made a significant contribution to world finance by renewing international private lending out of Europe.

Siegmund was born in Urach, southern Germany, on September 30, 1902. He was the only child of Georges (or Georg) Siegmund Warburg, a landowner, and Lucie (Kaulla) Warburg, daughter of a Stuttgart lawyer.

After completing his secondary education, Siegmund joined the banking firm of M. M. Warburg and Company, established in Hamburg in 1798 by his great-great-grandfather Moses Marcus Warburg. Siegmund was invited to enter the bank by the senior partner, his father's first cousin Max Warburg. After three years as a trainee and then periods of work at London and New York City banking and trading houses with which the firm had family or business connections, Siegmund became a partner at M. M. Warburg and Company in 1930. He opened an office in Berlin and began to flourish there. But over the next few years he encountered an increasing estrangement from Max as well as growing difficulties from the rise of Nazism. When Hitler came to power in 1933, Siegmund moved to London, England.

There he soon founded a finance company, the New Trading Company, Ltd. During the next six years he gradually gathered together a small team of other bankers, mostly of German-Jewish origin, and in 1939 he reorganized his firm into a merchant bank. In that same year he became a naturalized British citizen. In 1946 the company adopted the name of S. G. Warburg and Company, Ltd., which eventually became the most prestigious merchant bank in London.

Initially he had difficulty attracting major clients, financing mostly small companies, especially those founded by German immigrants. But by traveling throughout western Europe and the United States, he remade old business connections and established new ones. His firm developed new, creative financial techniques, such as takeover bids; became involved in ever-larger financial deals; and, by recruiting carefully, outgrew its early reputation as a purely German-Jewish house.

Siegmund performed a great service for world finance by renewing the practice of international private lending out of Europe. Businesses and governments had been without such funding since 1929. One important event in that renewal came in 1963, when he initiated the Eurobond market with an issue for an Italian government borrower.

In 1973 Siegmund retired. He spent his last years in Switzerland.

His wife was Eva Maria Philipson, daughter of a Swedish banker. They had a son and a daughter.

Siegmund George Warburg died in London on October 18, 1982.

THE
WISES [I]

ISAAC MAYER WISE (1819–1900) came from a prominent family in Bohemia. His father headed a private Hebrew day school, while one of his grandfathers was a physician learned in Hebrew lore. Isaac became a rabbi and in 1846 immigrated to the United States, where he pioneered the Reform movement.

His eldest son, Leo Wise (1849–1933), published the *American Jews' Annual* (1884–92) and served as publisher and managing editor of the English-language weekly newspaper *American Israelite* (1920–28), founded by his father. Another of Isaac's sons, Jonah Bondi Wise (1881–1959), served as a rabbi, notably at Central Synagogue in New York City (1925–59), and founded and conducted the *Message of Israel* radio program (1934–59). One of Isaac's daughters, Effie Miriam Wise, married Adolph Simon Ochs, who later became publisher of the *New York Times*.

ISAAC MAYER WISE

GREATEST ORGANIZER OF AMERICAN REFORM JUDAISM

In his time, Isaac Mayer Wise was the foremost figure in Jewish religious life in the United States. His great achievement was to fuse the spirit of Judaism with the spirit of freedom in America. While doing so, he, more than anyone else, shaped the Reform

Isaac Mayer Wise

Judaism movement in his adopted homeland.

Isaac was born in Steingrub, Bohemia, on March 29, 1819. His parents were Leo and Regina (Weis) Weis. As a child he attended his father's private Hebrew day school and then, at the age of nine, went to live with his grandfather Dr. Isaiah Weis, a physician in the town of Durmaul. There he studied at another Jewish day school and learned Hebrew lore from his grandfather.

Later he attended rabbinic schools in Bohemia as well as universities in Prague and Vienna. At the age of twenty-three he appeared before a rabbinic court of three rabbis, who conferred on him the title of rabbi. From 1843 to 1846 he served as rabbi in Radnitz, Bohemia.

In 1846 he immigrated to the United States, where he changed the spelling of his surname from *Weis* to *Wise*. He served as rabbi in Albany, New York, from 1846 to 1854. His congregation there was the first in the United States to employ family pews, which became standard in Reform Judaism. In 1854 he accepted the pulpit of Bene Yeshurun in Cincinnati, Ohio, where he remained for the rest of his life.

Isaac was disturbed by the lack of religious organization among Jews in the United States. Shortly after arriving in Cincinnati, he began publishing an English-language weekly newspaper, the *Israelite* (later the *American Israelite*), through which he called for centralized Reform institutions.

Isaac had three principal goals: to form a union of congregations, to establish a theological seminary, and to found a rabbinic conference. A master organizer, he realized all three ambitions.

In 1873 his efforts led to the organization of the Union of

American Hebrew Congregations. At first it was a confederation of synagogues in the Midwest and the South, but eventually it grew into an association of Reform congregations throughout the United States and Canada.

In 1875 his second great project came to fruition with the founding of the Hebrew Union College (later Hebrew Union College-Jewish Institute of Religion), the first permanent American rabbinic college. He served as its president for the rest of his life.

In 1889 he accomplished his final great goal with the formation of the Central Conference of American Rabbis, which became the legislative body of Reform Judaism. He held the office of president of this organization till his death.

Isaac left a large body of literary work. Because of the diversity of Reform prayer books, he tried to standardize the literature by preparing *Minhag America* ("American Usage," 1857), which was superseded, largely through his instigation, in 1894 by the Union Prayer Book. Besides his editorial writings in the *Israelite*, he published many books and pamphlets, including *History of the Israelitish Nation from Abraham to the Present Time* (1854), *The Cosmic God* (1876), *History of the Hebrews' Second Commonwealth* (1880), *Pronaos to Holy Writ* (1891), and *Reminiscences* (1901).

Isaac married Therese Bloch, daughter of a Jewish merchant, in Bohemia in 1844. They had ten children before her death in 1874. In 1876 he married Selma Bondi of New York, by whom he had four more children.

Isaac Mayer Wise died in Cincinnati on March 26, 1900.

Jonah Bondi Wise

RABBI, EDITOR, AND JEWISH ACTIVIST

Jonah Bondi Wise was a highly respected rabbi of long standing at Central Synagogue in New York City. He exerted great influence in the Jewish community through his efforts as a periodical editor, radio broadcaster, and activist with Jewish organizations.

Jonah was born in Cincinnati, Ohio, on February 21, 1881. His parents were Isaac Mayer and Selma (Bondi) Wise. Isaac gained renown as the principal pioneer of Reform Judaism in America. Selma was the daughter of Jonas Bondi, who willed a large Jewish library to Jonah.

After graduating from the University of Cincinnati (1903) and Hebrew Union College (1903), Jonah spent a year studying in Europe. He then served as rabbi at Mizpah Temple (1904–1906) in Chattanooga, Tennessee, where he established the Jewish weekly newspaper *The Scribe*, and then at Beth Israel Temple (1906–1925) in Portland, Oregon, where he participated in both Jewish and non-Jewish community projects.

In 1909 he married Helen Rosenfeld. They had a son and two daughters.

In 1925 Jonah moved to New York City, where he served as rabbi of Central Synagogue for the rest of his life. He was greatly influenced by the Reform teachings of his famous father, Isaac Mayer Wise, and edited the latter's *Israelite*, a newspaper. Jonah also contributed religious articles to other Jewish periodicals.

In 1934 he founded the *Message of Israel*, a weekly radio program. Open to members of Reform, Orthodox, and Conservative groups, the show was the first and, up to 1943, the only national weekly radio broadcast of Jewish preaching. He continued the broadcasts for the rest of his life.

Jonah spent much of his time engaged in welfare work. From 1931 to 1938 he was national chairman of fund-raising for the Joint Distribution Committee, which sent a steady flow of money to Jews in Poland, Palestine, and elsewhere. In 1939 he helped to found the United Jewish Appeal, becoming its national chairman in 1958.

He was a trustee of Hebrew Union College and a director of the Union of American Hebrew Congregations; his father had been closely associated with the founding of both of those organizations. The son also held directorships in many other national and local religious and social institutions.

Jonah Bondi Wise died in New York City on February 1, 1959.

THE
WISES [II]

Aaron Wise (no relation to Isaac Mayer Wise) came from a family that had been represented in the rabbinate for over two hundred years. He was the sixth in direct succession to hold rabbinic office. Born in Hungary, he immigrated in 1874 to the United States, where he developed New York City's Temple Rodeph Sholom into an influential synagogue. He also made his mark in scholarly pursuits, engaged in charitable activities, and helped to found the Jewish Theological Seminary of New York.

Two of his sons had memorable careers. Otto Irving Wise (1871–1919) was a lawyer who became general counsel for Western States Life Insurance Company, a director of several corporations, and a member of the board of directors of the Federation of Jewish Charities. Stephen Samuel Wise (1874–1949) founded the Free Synagogue and the Jewish Institute of Religion in New York City, became a leader of the Zionist movement in the United States, and greatly influenced the development of American Reform Judaism.

James Waterman Wise (1901–1983), Stephen's son, helped to found the American students' Zionist organization Avukah (1925) and became its national secretary, founded the Jewish journal *Opinion* (1931) and became its editor, was one of the earliest to warn of Nazism even before Hitler came to power, appeared as a platform speaker and radio commentator in defense of Jewish rights and in favor of liberal causes, helped to found and lead the Council against Intolerance in the 1930s and 1940s, and spent his last years in France as an art dealer. He wrote many published works, including the books *Liberalizing Liberal Judaism* (1924), *Swastika, the Nazi Terror* (1933), and *A Jew Revisits Germany* (1950).

Justine Wise Polier (1903–1987), Stephen's daughter (and wife of Shad Polier), was a lawyer who became the first woman to rise above the office of magistrate in the New York State judicial system, presiding as a justice of the Domestic Relations Court in New York City (1935–62) and as a judge of the New York State Family Court (1962–73). Her community activities included service in executive capacities with the American Jewish Congress and the World Jewish Congress. She wrote many published works on law and child welfare, such as the books *Everyone's Children, Nobody's Child: A Judge Looks at Underprivileged Children in the United States* (1941) and *A View from the Bench: The Juvenile Court* (1964).

AARON WISE

RABBI, SCHOLAR, AND COMMUNITY ACTIVIST

Aaron Wise gained renown as rabbi of Temple Rodeph Sholom in New York City. He also left a legacy as a scholar and as an activist in Jewish affairs.

Aaron was born in Erlau, Hungary, on May 2, 1844. His parents were Joseph Hirsch and Rachel Theresa (Rosenfeld) Weisz (or Weiss). Joseph was the fifth member of his family in direct succession to hold rabbinic office.

Aaron studied under his father and later at talmudic schools in Hungary, notably under Israel Hildesheimer at the Jewish Seminary of Eisenstadt, where he graduated as a rabbi in 1867. He then attended the universities of Berlin, Leipzig, and Halle, earning a doctorate from the last institution. For several years he served as superintendent of schools in Erlau.

In 1870 he married Sabine de Fischer Farkashazy, daughter of

Moritz de Fischer Farkashazy, an industrialist. They had three sons and three daughters.

In 1874 Aaron immigrated to the United States, where he Americanized his surname to *Wise*. His first position in his new homeland was as rabbi of Beth Elohim in Brooklyn, New York.

The following year he became rabbi of Temple Rodeph Sholom in New York City, where he served for the rest of his life. Under his ministry the congregation exerted great influence in the Jewish community by exemplifying a conservative approach to liturgical reform. He modernized the temple services in some ways, as by preparing a new prayer book, while retaining many traditional practices, notably by giving a prominent place to Hebrew at a time when many congregations were beginning to omit it.

Aaron's scholarly activities included assisting in the revision of Johann Buxtorf's Hebrew lexicon, contributing articles to periodicals, and writing *Beth Aharon*, a handbook for religious schools. For some years he edited the periodicals *Jewish Herald* and *Boston Hebrew Observer*.

Aaron founded the Rodeph Sholom Sisterhood of Personal Service, which later established the Aaron Wise Industrial School in his memory. He supported local Hebrew free schools, gave liberally to charities, and helped to found the Jewish Theological Seminary of New York in 1886.

Aaron Wise died in New York City on March 30, 1896.

Stephen Samuel Wise

PREEMINENT AMERICAN JEWISH PUBLIC FIGURE

Stephen Samuel Wise founded two of America's most important Jewish institutions: the Free Synagogue and the Jewish Institute of Religion, both in New York City. He also strongly influenced the development of Reform Judaism in the United States, made major contributions to social and political causes, and helped to lead the American Zionist movement.

Stephen was born in Budapest, Hungary, on March 17, 1874. His parents were Aaron and Sabine (de Fischer Farkashazy) Weisz (or Weiss). The family soon immigrated to the United States, where they changed to spelling of their surname to *Wise* and where Aaron gained renown as rabbi of Temple Rodeph Sholom in New York City.

Stephen decided early in life to become the seventh member of his family in direct succession to enter the rabbinate. He began his Jewish studies under his father and later continued them under other private teachers, notably Adolph Jellinek, the chief rabbi of Vienna, Austria, from whom Stephen received his rabbinic ordination in 1893. Meanwhile, he also pursued general academic studies, graduating from Columbia University in 1892 and earning a Ph.D. there in 1901.

In 1900 he married Louise Waterman, who became well known as a community worker and an artist. They had a son and a daughter.

His rabbinic career began in 1893, when he was appointed assistant rabbi to Henry F. Jacobs at the Madison Avenue Synagogue in New York City. A few months later, when Jacobs died, Stephen assumed full charge. He was only nineteen. From 1900 to 1906 he served as rabbi of Temple Beth El in Portland, Oregon.

In 1906 he came to national attention when he declined an invitation to become rabbi of Temple Emanu-El in New York City, then the most prestigious Reform congregation in the United States. He rejected the offer because he had been refused his demand for free speech in the pulpit, uncontrolled by the board of trustees.

Outraged by this experience, Stephen founded the Free Synagogue (New York City, 1907), where the pulpit would be free from any form of restriction. He served as rabbi there for the rest of his life.

The pursuit of freedom led him to found another major Jewish institution in New York City. In 1922 he established the Jewish Institute of Religion (which later merged with Hebrew Union

Stephen Wise

College), a seminary that would leave "the faculty and student body free, not merely in the matter of ritual observance, but intellectually free in accordance with undogmatic liberalism, which is at the heart of the genius of Judaism." The institute trained students for all three branches of Judaism, but the majority became Reform rabbis.

Stephen influenced the American Reform Judaism movement in other ways as well. His principal forum was the Free Synagogue. Within a year of founding the original synagogue, he opened a branch on New York City's Lower East Side, where nearly a million Yiddish-speaking European immigrants had settled. At both synagogues—the original serving primarily Americanized Jews of established means, the other serving mainly struggling Jewish masses—he popularized the Reform movement through his liberal religious services, his common touch, and his personal linkage of Reform Judaism with political liberalism and Zionism.

Throughout his entire career, Stephen involved himself with

social justice and civic reform. In 1895, during a transit strike in Brooklyn, he proclaimed his prolabor sympathies from the pulpit of B'nai Jeshurun. In Portland he successfully battled the city's "two major industries," gambling and prostitution, and helped to elect a reform mayor.

On returning to New York City, Stephen steadily increased the time and energy he devoted to social and political reform. He strongly identified himself with labor, supporting demands for better pay and improved working conditions. In his fight for the rights of the individual, he helped to found the National Association for the Advancement of Colored People in 1909 and the American Civil Liberties Union in 1920. He also fought against the Ku Klux Klan and in favor of liberalized immigration laws. His declared war on the Tammany Hall corruption in New York City politics culminated in his 1930 assault on Mayor James J. ("Jimmy") Walker, who resigned and fled to Europe. Stephen became famous for making calls for social reform in his sermons, not only at the pulpit in his synagogues but also for many years to large audiences at Carnegie Hall.

He was one of the first Jewish leaders in the United States to become active in the Zionist movement. In 1897 he helped to found the New York Federation of Zionist Societies, and the following year he led the formation of the nationwide Federation of American Zionists.

At the Second Zionist Congress in Basel, Switzerland, in 1898, he met Theodor Herzl, founder of modern political Zionism. Stephen, profoundly impressed by Herzl, agreed to serve as American secretary of the world Zionist movement.

In 1913 he made his first trip to Palestine. During World War I he and Louis D. Brandeis led the fight for Zionism in America. As an acquaintance of President Woodrow Wilson and a prominent member of the Democratic party, Stephen influenced the United States government toward approval of the Balfour Declaration (1917), which called for the establishment of a Jewish national homeland in Palestine.

He played a major role in founding the American Jewish Congress, from its preliminary conference in 1916 and its first meeting in provisional form in 1918 to the first session of its permanent body in 1922. Stephen served as president of the American Jewish Congress in 1925–29 and again in 1935–49.

Meanwhile, he also kept his connection with the Federation of American Zionists, which in 1915 was renamed the Zionist Organization of America. He served as its president from 1936 to 1938.

In the 1930s he was a leader in the struggle to mobilize American public opinion against Adolf Hitler. When, in 1942, Stephen learned of Hitler's campaign of mass murder against European Jews, he continually demanded, to little avail, that the Allied governments do something to stop the Holocaust.

During the Hitler years Stephen led the creation of the World Jewish Congress (1936, after many preliminary conferences from 1920 to 1934), an expansion of the American Jewish Congress. He saw the World Jewish Congress as the political representative of world Jewry and led it as president from 1936 till the end of his life. During World War II he constantly urged that Jewish refugees be allowed to enter the United States and Palestine. He also helped to establish the American Emergency Committee for Zionist Affairs (renamed the American Zionist Emergency Council in 1943), whose aim was to convince Americans to call for a Jewish national homeland in Palestine.

After World War II, disillusioned by criticism that he should have pressed President Franklin D. Roosevelt harder to stop the Holocaust and by political bickering within the Zionist movement, Stephen withdrew from most of his Zionist activities, though he continued to serve as president of the American Jewish Congress and of the World Jewish Congress. However, he did live long enough to witness the triumph of Zionism with the birth of the modern state of Israel in 1948.

He left a body of writings noted for their readable style. His works include the books *How to Face Life* (1917), *As I See It* (1944), and *The Challenging Years: The Autobiography of Stephen Wise* (1949).

Stephen Samuel Wise died in New York City on April 19, 1949.

OTHER GREAT
JEWISH FAMILIES

ANNENBERGS

Moses Louis Annenberg (born February 11, 1878, in Kalwischen, East Prussia; died July 20, 1942, in Rochester, Minnesota) came to the United States as a child; worked as the circulation director for all Hearst periodicals (1920–26); published horse-racing news, including the *Daily Racing Form*, and general newspapers, notably the *Philadelphia Inquirer*; and established Triangle Publications, Inc., a holding company for all of the family business interests. His only son, **Walter Hubert Annenberg** (born March 13, 1908, in Milwaukee, Wisconsin), took over Triangle Publications; added radio and television stations to it; founded the extremely popular periodicals *Seventeen* and *TV Guide*; served as ambassador to Great Britain (1969–74); and headed the Annenberg Foundation.

ARISONS

Ted Arison (born February 24, 1924, in Tel Aviv, Palestine) immigrated to the United States in 1952; founded the fabulously successful Carnival Cruise Lines in Miami, Florida, in 1972; and in 1993 returned to live in Israel, where he engaged in the construction business. His son **Micky Arison** (born June 29, 1949, in Tel Aviv, Israel) succeeded his father as head of Carnival Cruise

Lines and bought the Miami Heat professional basketball team (his purchase was approved by the National Basketball Association in February 1995). The family's Arison Foundation has given millions of dollars to Jewish causes in Israel and the United States.

BARUCHS

Simon Baruch (born July 29, 1840, in Schwersen [or Schwersenz], East Prussia, Germany; died June 3, 1921, in New York City) immigrated to the United States, served as a physician with the Confederate Army in the Civil War, moved to New York City, performed what is believed to be the first successful appendectomy in the United States (1888), and became the leading American exponent of hydrotherapy. One of his sons, **Bernard Mannes Baruch** (born August 19, 1870, in Camden, South Carolina; died June 20, 1965, in New York City), made a fortune speculating in the stock market, became a noted philanthropist, and was called "the adviser to the presidents" because of his role as unofficial adviser to many Democratic and Republican presidents of the United States. Simon's son **Herman Benjamin Baruch** (born April 28, 1872, in Camden; died March 15, 1953, in Wyandanch, Long Island) followed in his father's footsteps as a physician (1895–1903), pursued the stock market (1903–1918), worked for a banking firm (1918–42), and served as American ambassador to Portugal (1945–47) and the Netherlands (1947–49).

BEN-ASHERS

Family of Masoretes (scholars and scribes who compiled the Masora, the body of rules, principles, and traditions designed to preserve the textual authenticity of the Bible). They were active in Tiberias, Palestine, for a number of generations from the eighth to the tenth century. **Asher the Elder** (fl. second half of eighth century) founded the line. **Moses Ben-Asher** (fl. second half of ninth century), who descended directly from Asher the Elder, was a prominent Masorete. Among his works is a beautiful manuscript on the prophets, which he furnished with Masoretic notes. He was the father of **Aaron ben Moses Ben-Asher** (fl. first half of tenth century), the last and most important member of this Masoretic family. Aaron's tradition is the one that came to be accepted in the Jewish Bible.

BERGSONS

Henri Bergson

Michael Bergson (originally Michal Sonnenberg; took surname Bergson, derived from Berkson ["son of Berek"], his father being named Berek Sonnenberg [née Zbitkower]; born May 20, 1820, in Warsaw, Poland; died March 9, 1898, in London, England) was a well-known pianist and composer. **Henri Bergson** (in full Henri-Louis Bergson; born October 18, 1859, in Paris, France; died January 4, 1941, in Paris), Michael's son, won the Nobel Prize for literature in 1927. He was a master literary stylist and the first to elaborate what came to be called process philosophy, which rejected static values in favor of change and evolution.

BLAUSTEINS

Louis Blaustein (born January 20, 1869, in Prussia; died July 27, 1937, in Atlantic City, New Jersey) and his only son, **Jacob Blaustein** (born September 30, 1892, in Baltimore, Maryland; died November 15, 1970, in Baltimore), founded the American

Oil Company (today Amoco) in 1910. Jacob served as president of the American Jewish Committee, became an unofficial adviser to five American presidents, and was a delegate to the 1945 conference that formed the United Nations.

BLOCHS

Family that, in 1955, founded H & R Block, Inc., America's largest preparer of income tax returns and one of the earliest franchisers in the nation. The company name was spelled *Block* to avoid common mispronunciations of *Bloch*. **Henry Wollman Bloch** (born July 30, 1922, in Kansas City, Missouri) has been head of the company from its beginning. **Richard A. Bloch** (born 1926 in Kansas City), Henry's brother, was the *R* in *H & R* till he was forced by ill health to retire in 1978. Since then, **Thomas Morton Bloch** (born March 14, 1954, in Kansas City), Henry's son, has assisted Henry in running the company.

BLOOMINGDALES

Family famous for its Bloomingdale Brothers department store in New York City, founded in 1886 by **Lyman Gustavus Bloomingdale** (born 1841 in New York City; died October 13, 1905, in Elberon, New Jersey) and his brother **Joseph Bernard Bloomingdale** (born December 22, 1842, in New York City; died November 21, 1904, in New York City). Both were active in Jewish communal affairs and philanthropy, Lyman, for example, being treasurer of Temple Beth-El and Joseph being a trustee of the Young Men's Hebrew Association. Another brother, **Emanuel Watson Bloomingdale** (born November 25, 1852, in Rome, New York; died February 6, 1928, in New York City), became a well-known lawyer, was identified with the family department store, and spent his last years as vice chairman of the New York State Bridge and Tunnel Commission, where he had a hand in the construction of the Holland Tunnel. One of Lyman's sons, **Samuel**

Joseph Bloomingdale (born June 17, 1873, in New York City; died May 10, 1968, in New York City), was an executive at the family department store, served as president of its subsidiary Bloomingdale Brothers Realty Company, and helped to lead the Federation for the Support of Jewish Philanthropic Societies and other Jewish organizations. **Alfred S. Bloomingdale** (born April 15, 1916, in New York City; died August 20, 1982, in Santa Monica, California), Lyman's grandson (through Lyman's son Hiram [1876–1953]), was briefly associated with the family business (1938), worked as a Broadway and Hollywood producer (1939–49), and then gained his greatest fame as the Diners' Club credit organization's vice president (1950–55), president (1955–70), chairman of the board (1964–70), and consultant (1970–82).

BRENTANOS

Family of booksellers. **August Brentano** (born 1831 in Austria; died 1886 in Chicago, Illinois) immigrated to the United States as a young man, opened a newspaper and magazine stand in 1853, started a book and stationery store in 1858, and in 1870 expanded it into Brentano's Literary Emporium, which became the leading bookstore in, and a popular meeting place for the literati of, New York City. In the 1870s he was joined by three nephews, to whom he sold the business in 1877. They enlarged the firm and incorporated it in 1887 as Brentano's, Inc. The eldest of the three, **August Brentano** (born about 1853 in Evansville, Indiana; died May 1899 on Long Island, New York) retired in 1894 because of ill health. The business then became a partnership between the two remaining brothers, **Arthur Brentano** (born April 20, 1858, in Hoboken, New Jersey; died January 29, 1944, in East Orange, New Jersey) and **Simon Brentano** (born 1859 in Cincinnati, Ohio; died February 15, 1915, in Orange, New Jersey). Simon headed the firm and became an authority on fire control, writing a book on the subject: *The Control of Fire* (1904). Arthur succeeded Simon as president in 1915 and eventually built the company into the world's largest retail bookselling business. **Lowell Brentano** (born April 18, 1895, in New York City; died July 8, 1950, in New York City), Simon's son, joined the firm in 1918, became editorial director of the publications department, and later rose to a vice presidency in charge of publications. In 1933 he left the business to write plays, novels, and articles.

CASTROS

Wide spread Sephardic and Marrano family that probably derived its name from that of a town in Spain. An Egyptian branch prospered in the sixteenth century. **Abraham Castro** (fl. early sixteenth century) was director of the mint in Cairo and supervisor of economic affairs in Egypt. He was said to be the grandfather of **Jacob ben Abraham Castro** (known as Maharikas, from the Hebrew initials of his name; born about 1525; died 1610), an Egyptian halakic authority and talmudic commentator. Another branch of the family consisted of Marrano physicians in Hamburg, Germany. **Rodrigo de Castro** (born 1550 in Lisbon, Portugal; died 1627 in Hamburg) served various nobles in Hamburg, including the king of Denmark, and wrote important medical treatises that laid the foundations for the fields of gynecology and medical jurisprudence. **Bendito** (or Benedict) **de Castro** (alias Baruch Nehamias de Castro; born 1597 in Hamburg; died 1684 in Hamburg), a son of Rodrigo, served as physician to the queen of Sweden and as president of the Portuguese Jewish community in Hamburg. **Andre** (or Andreas) **de Castro** (alias Daniel Nehamias de Castro; born 1599 in Hamburg; death data uncertain), another son of Rodrigo, was also a prominent physician. **Isaac de Castro Tartas** (born about 1623 in Tartas, France; died December 15, 1647, in Lisbon, Portugal) was a famed Marrano martyr. While living outwardly as a Catholic in Brazil, he was arrested in December 1644. During his trial he proclaimed himself a Jew at heart. Subsequently he was burned alive, crying out at the end, it is said, the Shema. **David de Castro**

Tartas (born about 1625 in Tartas; died about 1700) was a printer in Amsterdam, the Netherlands. He published rabbinic books in Hebrew, Spanish, and Portuguese. In 1675 he published the earliest known Spanish-language Jewish newspaper.

COHNS (i)

Alfred Einstein Cohn (born April 16, 1879, in New York City; died July 20, 1957, in New Milford, Connecticut) was a physician who, in 1909, introduced the first electrocardiograph to the Western Hemisphere and, in 1915, initiated the manufacture of the first American-made string galvanometer for use in electrocardiography. **Edwin Joseph Cohn** (born December 17, 1892, in New York City; died October 1, 1953, in Boston, Massachusetts), Alfred's brother, was a biochemist who helped to develop the methods of separating plasma proteins into fractions. His work made possible the large-scale production of human plasma fractions for the treatment of wounded military personnel in World War II. Later his methods were adopted for use in civilian medicine.

COHNS (ii)

The brothers **Jack Cohn** (born October 27, 1889, in New York City; died December 8, 1956, in New York City) and **Harry Cohn** (born July 23, 1891, in New York City; died February 27, 1958, in Phoenix, Arizona) founded, with Joe Brandt, C.B.C. Film Sales Company (1920), later renamed Columbia Pictures (1924), an important Hollywood film studio. Harry headed production, while Jack pioneered in producing newsreels and cartoons. One of Jack's sons, **Robert Cohn** (born September 6, 1920, in Avon, New Jersey; died May 27, 1996, in Los Angeles, California), formed Screen Gems (1949), the television subsidiary of Columbia Pictures. **Ralph Morris Cohn** (born May 1, 1914, in New York City; died August 1, 1959, in Pound Ridge, New York),

Robert's brother, was president of Screen Gems till 1958, when he was succeeded by Robert.

CROWNS

Henry Crown (born June 13, 1896, in Chicago, Illinois; died August 14, 1990, in Chicago), with Irving and Sol Crown, his brothers, founded Material Service Corporation (1919), a sand and gravel company that became a major distributor of construction supplies. He later invested in real estate, aerospace, and other industries. For nine years (1952–61) he owned the controlling interest in the Empire State Building in New York City. In the 1970s he gained control of General Dynamics Corporation, a military contracts giant. **Lester Crown** (born June 7, 1925, in Chicago), Henry's son, holds executive positions at Material Service Corporation and General Dynamics Corporation; owns stakes in pro-fessional basketball (Chicago Bulls) and baseball (Chicago White Sox and New York Yankees) teams; and has served as chairman of the board of overseers of the Jewish Theological Seminary. The Arie and Ida Crown Foundation, named after Henry's parents and run by Lester's daughter Susan, disburses about $5 million a year to over a hundred Jewish organizations.

DE PASSES

Family of Sephardic Jews who settled in England in the seventeenth century and then branched out in the nineteenth century to South Africa, where they helped to develop the shipping, fishing, mining, and sugar industries. The brothers **Aaron De Pass** (1815–77) and **Elias De Pass** (born 1829 in Lynn, Norfolk, England; died May 9, 1913, in Brighton, England) settled in Cape Town, South Africa, in 1846 and became merchants. In 1848 they founded De Pass Brothers and became involved in shipping. By 1857 the firm, now known as De Pass, Spence and Company, had started the whaling industry in South Africa. Both brothers were active in establishing the first Hebrew congregation in Cape Town. **Daniel De Pass** (born about 1839 in King's Lynn, Norfolk, England; died February 4, 1921), son of Aaron, joined the firm in 1860, became the first person to work a copper mine in southwest Africa, also mined diamonds, and introduced to South Africa a variety of Indian sugar that became the mainstay of the industry. **Alfred De Pass** (born 1861 in Cape Town; died December 10, 1952, in Muizenberg, near Cape Town), Daniel's son, entered the family business, further developed its sugar interests, and later won renown as a philanthropist and patron of the arts.

FARHIS (or FARCHIS)

Family of financiers and officials in the financial administration of the province of Damascus, Syria, in the eighteenth and nineteenth centuries. The first to consolidate the family's position was **Saul** (or Shihada) **Farhi** (fl. late eighteenth century), who served as minister of the treasury under the governor of Damascus. He was succeeded in his position by his sons **Raphael Farhi** (fl. c. 1800) and **Joseph Farhi** (fl. c. 1800). **Solomon** (or Salmon) **Farhi** (fl. c. 1800), their cousin, also played an important role in the financial affairs of the time. Another of Saul's sons, **Hayyim Muallim Farhi** (born c. middle of eighteenth century in Damascus; died 1820), assisted by his brother **Moses Farhi** (fl. early nineteenth century), had an important role in governing the province of Damascus for many years. After the death of the governor Suleiman Pasha in 1818, Hayyim was, in effect, the governor of the province for the next two years. But Suleiman's official successor, Abdallah Pasha, out of jealousy and ambition, ordered the assassination of Hayyim.

Sigmund Freud

Anna Freud

FREUDS

Sigmund Freud (originally Sigismund Solomon Freud; born May 6, 1856, in Freiburg, Moravia; died September 23, 1939, in London, England) founded psychoanalysis, a new school of psychology based on revolutionary and controversial views of human behavior. **Anna Freud** (born December 3, 1895, in Vienna, Austria; died October 9, 1982, in London, England), Sigmund's daughter, founded child psychoanalysis. **Edward L. Bernays** (born November 22, 1891, in Vienna, Austria; died March 9, 1995, in Cambridge, Massachusetts), Sigmund's nephew, created public relations as a profession. **Lucian Freud** (born December 8, 1922, in Berlin, Germany), Sigmund's grandson (son of the architect Ernst, Sigmund's youngest son), is a well-known London-based painter of emotionally charged portraiture.

GABBAIS

Family with many branches in the Near East and India. One important branch began with **Ezekiel ben Joseph Nissim Menahem Gabbai** (alias Yehezkel Baghdadali; born second half of eighteenth century in Baghdad; died 1826 in Adalia, Asia Minor), who became a prominent banker in Baghdad before being appointed chief banker in Constantinople, Turkey, in which position he exerted great influence in behalf of other Jews, as by helping **Ezra Gabbai** (fl. early nineteenth century), his brother, become *nasi* ("prince") of Baghdad in 1817. Ezekiel's grandson **Ezekiel Gabbai** (born 1825 in Constantinople; died 1898 in Constantinople) was the first Jew to hold office in the Ottoman Ministry of Education and later became president of the Supreme Criminal Court. In 1860 he founded a newspaper to fight for reforms in the administration of the Jewish community. He had a son, **Isaac Gabbai** (fl. early twentieth century), who continued the newspaper till 1930.

GERSHWINS

George Gershwin (originally Jacob Gershvin; born September 26, 1898, in New York City; died July 11, 1937, in Los Angeles, California) was one of America's most naturally gifted composers. For Broadway, he wrote such songs as "Swanee" (*Capitol Revue*, 1919), "Fascinating Rhythm" (*Lady, Be Good!*, 1924), "'S Wonderful" (*Funny Face*, 1927), and "I Got Rhythm" (*Girl Crazy*, 1930). His songs for films include "Love Walked In" (*The Goldwyn Follies*, 1938). But he is best remembered today for being the most influential composer in the movement to merge American popular and jazz elements with the classical tradition, notably in his *Rhapsody in Blue* for instrumental ensemble (1924) and his folk opera *Porgy and Bess* (1935). His brother **Ira Gershwin** (originally Israel Gershvin; born December 6, 1896, in New York City; died August 17, 1983, in Beverly Hills, California) was a famous popular-song lyricist. He wrote the lyrics for most of

George Gershwin (left) and Ira Gershwin (right)

George's best songs. After George's death, Ira continued to write lyrics for hit songs, such as "The Man That Got Away" (music by Harold Arlen, for the film *A Star Is Born*, 1954).

GIMBELS

Family famous for its Gimbel Brothers department store chain, headquartered in New York City. **Adam Gimbel** (born 1817 in Bavaria; died 1896 in Philadelphia, Pennsylvania) immigrated to the United States in 1835; settled in Vincennes, Indiana, in 1842; and opened a general store called the Palace of Trade. In 1865 he moved to Philadelphia and left the Vincennes store in the hands of the eldest of his seven sons, **Jacob Gimbel** (born September 26, 1850, in Vincennes; died November 7, 1922, in Atlantic City, New Jersey), assisted by Adam's second son, **Isaac Gimbel** (born April 24, 1856, in Vincennes; died April 11, 1931, in Port Chester, New York). Later Jacob and Isaac founded their own Gimbel Brothers department store chain (1889 in Milwaukee, 1894 in Philadelphia, and 1910 in New York City). They were joined by their five brothers and Jacob's adopted son. By the time of Isaac's death in 1931 the chain consisted of seven stores with twenty thousand employees, making it at that time the world's largest department store enterprise. Over the two following generations, many Gimbels made their marks in the family business and elsewhere. A notable example was **Bernard Feustman Gimbel** (born April 10, 1885, in Vincennes; died September 29, 1966, in New York City), Isaac's son, who served as company president (1927–53), chief executive officer (1953–66), and chairman of the board (1953–66). Bernard's son **Bruce A. Gimbel** (born July 28, 1913, in New York City; died October 7, 1980, in Greenwich, Connecticut) was president (1953–73) and then chief executive officer and chairman of the board (1973–75). **Peter Robin Gimbel** (born February 14, 1928, in New York City; died July 12, 1987, in New York City), another of Bernard's sons, became an explorer and a filmmaker, especially of documentaries on sharks and on the sunken Italian luxury liner *Andrea Doria*.

GRATZES

The brothers **Barnard Gratz** (born 1738 in Langensdorf, Upper Silesia; died April 20, 1801, in Baltimore, Maryland) and **Michael Gratz** (born 1740 in Langensdorf; died September 8, 1811, in Philadelphia, Pennsylvania) immigrated to the United States and settled in Philadelphia, Barnard in 1754 and Michael in 1759. They entered into a business partnership, B. and M. Gratz, and became "merchant venturers," helping to open up settlements in the territories that came to be the states of Ohio, Kentucky, Indiana, and Illinois. Both signed the Non-Importation resolutions of 1765 as a protest against England's Stamp Act (which levied stamp taxes in the American colonies), and both joined in the American Revolution. Barnard laid the cornerstone of the first synagogue erected in Philadelphia (1782) and helped to lead the fight for changing Pennsylvania and Maryland laws prohibiting Jews from holding public offices. **Rebecca Gratz** (born March 4, 1781, in Philadelphia; died August 27, 1869, in Philadephia), Michael's daughter, was the foremost Jewish-American woman of her time and was active in many Jewish social-welfare programs, earning lasting fame as the founder of the first permanent Jewish Sunday School (1838).

GÜNZBURGS (OR GUENZBURGS)

Family of Russian bankers. **Joseph** (or Yozel/Yevzel) **Günzburg** (born 1812 in Vitebsk, Russia; died January 12, 1878, in Paris, France) founded a banking firm in 1859; helped to finance Russia's railways; helped to found, and became the first president of, the Society for the Promotion of Culture among the Jews of Russia in 1863; succeeded in removing laws against Jews in the military service; and induced Russian authorities to grant greater freedom of movement to Jewish merchants and artisans. **Horace** (or Naphtali Herz) **Günzburg** (born February 8, 1833, in Zvenigorodka, Russia; died March 2, 1909, in Saint Petersburg, Russia), Joseph's son, helped his father to create the Society for the Promotion of Culture among the Jews of Russia and succeeded him as president; followed his father as head of the family bank; advised the Russian government on business matters; became chairman of the central committee for the Jewish Agricultural Society in 1893, president of the board of directors of the Jewish Agricultural Farms in Minsk in 1901, and cofounder of the Russian Jewish Historical Ethnographic Society in 1908; and, like his father, fought for the rights of Russian Jews. **David Günzburg** (born July 5, 1857, in Kamenets Podolsky, Russia; died December 22, 1910, in Saint Petersburg, Russia), Horace's son, wrote a book on Jewish art, edited a Russian-Jewish encyclopedia, and actively promoted the welfare of Jews, as by being a member of the central committee of the Jewish Colonization Association.

HAASES

Walter Abraham Haas, Sr. (born May 11, 1889, in San Francisco, California; died December 7, 1979, in San Francisco), married a grandniece of Levi Strauss, founder of Levi Strauss and Company, and joined the firm in 1919. Soon Walter saved the foundering company by convincing Levi's four nephews (who were then in charge) not to liquidate; by getting the firm out of the wholesale dry-goods business to specialize in manufacturing their best product, blue jeans; and by expanding distribution. He was president of the company from 1928 to 1956 and chairman of the board in his later years. Walter also served as president of the Jewish Welfare Federation. **Daniel Edward Koshland** (born March 16, 1892, in San Francisco; died December 10, 1979, in San Mateo, California), Walter's brother-in-law, joined Levi Strauss and Company in 1922, long served as second in command to Walter, was president from 1956 to 1958, and later chaired the executive committee. **Walter Abraham Haas, Jr.** (born January 24, 1916, in San Francisco; died September 20, 1995, in San Francisco), the elder son of Walter Abraham Haas, Sr., made the key decisions in the late 1940s and early 1950s to concentrate on blue jeans (previously only one fourth of the company business) and to focus on the teenage market. From 1958 to 1976 he was the chief executive officer, and later he served as the honorary chairman of the executive board of directors. He also became the owner of the Oakland Athletics professional baseball team. **Peter Edgar Haas, Sr.** (born December 20, 1918, in San Francisco), the younger son of Walter Abraham Haas, Sr., joined Levi Strauss and Company in 1945 and served as executive vice president (1958–70), president (1970–81), chief executive officer (1976–81), chairman of the board (1981–89), and chairman of the executive committee (1989–). From 1981 to 1984 nonfamily members ran the firm. But in 1984 **Robert Douglas Haas** (born April 3, 1942, in San Francisco), the elder son of Walter Abraham Haas, Jr., became the president and chief executive officer, and in 1989 he began serving as chief executive officer and chairman of the board. **Walter J. Haas** (born about 1945 in San Francisco), the younger son of Walter Abraham Haas, Jr., has held various executive positions with the Oakland Athletics since 1980. **Peter Edgar Haas, Jr.** (born September 21, 1947, in San Francisco), held management positons with Levi Strauss and Company till his retirement in 1989. The family runs a philanthropic empire through several foundations holding over $600 million in assets: the Walter and Elise Haas Fund specializes in culture, the Evelyn and Walter Haas, Jr., Fund aids social services, the Miriam and Peter Haas Fund supports education, and the Richard and Rhoda Goldman Fund backs environmental causes.

KIMHIS (or KIMCHIS/QIMHIS)

Family important for its Bible commentaries and Hebrew language studies. **Joseph Kimhi** (or Rikham, an acronym of Rabbi Joseph Kimhi; born c. 1105 in Spain; died c. 1170, probably in Narbonne, France) helped to make Arabic-Jewish writings available to Jews in Europe through his translations of Arabic works into Hebrew; wrote the Hebrew grammar text *Sefer ha-zikkaron* ("Book of Remembrance"); prepared a study of lexicography and exegesis, *Sefer ha-galui* ("Book of the Demonstration"); contributed commentaries on the Pentateuch, *Sefer ha-Torah* ("Book of the Torah"); and wrote poetry found in the book *Shekel ha-kodesh* ("The Holy Shekel"). His son **Moses Kimhi** (or Remak, an acronym of Rabbi Moses Kimhi; died c. 1190, probably in Narbonne) wrote the Hebrew grammar text *Mahalakh shevile ha-da'at* ("Journey on the Paths of Knowledge"), a pioneering work that presented verb conjugations in a new order and arrangement still followed. He also prepared commentaries on several books of the Bible. **David Kimhi** (or Radak, an acronym of Rabbi David Kimhi; born c. 1160, probably in Narbonne; died c. 1235, probably in Narbonne), Moses' brother, was the most illustrious member of the family. His writings on Hebrew lexicography (*Sefer ha-shorashim* ["Book of the Roots"]) and grammar (*Sefer mikhlol*

["Book of Completeness"]) were standard works throughout the Middle Ages. He was also the most important exegete of the family, preparing commentaries on Genesis, the Psalms, and other books of the Old Testament.

KIPNISES

Alexander Kipnis (born February 13, 1891, in Zhitomir, the Ukraine; died May 14, 1978, in Westport, Connecticut) was a famed bass widely regarded as one of the world's greatest singers of German opera and art song. His son, **Igor Kipnis** (born September 27, 1930, in Berlin, Germany), is the preeminent harpsichordist of his generation. Igor received early piano lessons from his maternal grandfather, **Heniot Lévy** (born July 19, 1879, in Warsaw, Poland; died June 16, 1946, in Chicago, Illinois), a well-known pianist, teacher, and composer.

KOHENS

The first major family of Hebrew printers in central Europe. The brothers **Gershom ben Solomon Kohen** (died 1544) and **Gronem Kohen** (fl. first half of sixteenth century) produced a Passover Haggadah in 1526, and in 1527 they were granted the exclusive right to do Hebrew printing in Bohemia (this right was periodically renewed by the family throughout the sixteenth century). Gershom's sons **Solomon Kohen** (fl. sixteenth century) and **Mordecai Kohen** (1502–1592) printed prayer books, Pentateuchs, and other works. Gershom's sons **Moses Kohen** (died 1549) and **Judah Kohen** (died 1593) also joined the firm. In 1566 Mordecai took charge of the business with his five sons. During 1571–77 the company did not function. It was then resumed by Mordecai's sons, notably **Bezalel Kohen** (died 1589) and **Solomon Kohen** (fl. late sixteenth and early seventeenth centuries). **Moses Kohen** (died 1659), Solomon's son, ran the business for fifty years. Later Moses' grandsons **Israel Kohen** (fl.

late seventeenth century) and **Moses Kohen** (fl. late seventeenth century) managed the firm as "the grandsons of Moses Katz" (*Katz* being short for *Kohen zedek*, "the righteous Kohen"). They were succeeded by **Aaron Kohen** (died 1701), son of the most recent Moses. From 1701 to 1735 **David Kohen** (fl. early eighteenth century), Aaron's son, led the company as the head of "the descendants of Moses Katz." In 1784 the Kohen company history as an independent printer ended when it merged with the Bak firm.

Courtesy of Ann Landers

Ann Landers

LANDERS
AND VAN BUREN

Twin sisters who write extremely popular rival syndicated advice columns. **Ann Landers** (originally Esther Pauline Friedman; born July 4, 1918, in Sioux City, Iowa) has written the "Ann Landers" column since 1955. **Abigail Van Buren** (originally Pauline Esther Friedman; born July 4, 1918, in Sioux City) has written "Dear Abby" since 1956.

LAUDERS

Estée Lauder (originally Josephine Esther Mentzer; born July 1, probably 1908, in New York City) married **Joseph Harold Lauter** (surname later Lauder, the original Austrian form; born December 26, in New York City; died January 15, 1983, in New York City) in 1930. They began making and selling her uncle's skin creams and in 1946 founded Estée Lauder, Inc., which became the world's largest family-owned beauty company. She created products and did the marketing, while he handled the finances.

Estée Lauder

Their elder son, **Leonard Alan Lauder** (born March 19, 1933, in New York City), joined the company in 1958, became executive vice president in 1962, and succeeded his mother as president in 1973, while she took the position of chairman of the board; in 1982 he became chief executive officer as well. Estée and Joseph's younger son, **Ronald Stephen Lauder** (born February 26, 1944, in New York City), joined the company in 1965, worked for many years in its European offices, was chairman of Estée Lauder International, Inc., took a leave of absence from 1980 to 1983 to serve as United States deputy secretary of defense for European and NATO policy, held the post of ambassador to Austria during 1986–87, and then returned to the family enterprises to head the Lauder Investments, Inc., division. Leonard's wife, Evelyn (Hausner) Lauder, and Ronald's wife, Jo Carole (Knoff) Lauder, also worked for the family business. Evelyn became a senior corporate vice president. Estée Lauder has long been devoted to many charities, and the Ronald S. Lauder Foundation has actively contributed to reviving Jewish life in Eastern Europe since the collapse of the Soviet Union.

LEVITTS

Abraham Levitt (born July 1, 1880, in Brooklyn, New York; died August 20, 1962, in Great Neck, New York) was a real-estate lawyer who, with his two sons, founded the construction firm of Levitt and Sons, Inc., in 1929. He was the chairman of the board, providing the company with its philosophy and with legal knowledge. His son **William Jaird Levitt** (born February 11, 1907, in Brooklyn; died January 28, 1994, in Manhasset, New York) served as president, giving the company its drive, salesmanship, and organization. **Alfred Stuart Levitt** (died February 9, 1966, in Kings Point, New York, at the age of fifty-four), Abraham's other son, designed the firm's buildings. From 1947 to 1951 Levitt and Sons, Inc., built Levittown, New York, a highly influential, geometrically planned, purely residential community. Later the company set up similar communities in Pennsylvania, New Jersey, Israel, and elsewhere.

MANDELS

Three brothers—**Jack N. Mandel** (born July 16, 1911, in Austria), **Joseph C. Mandel** (born 1913 in Austria), and **Morton Leon Mandel** (born September 19, 1921, in Cleveland, Ohio)— purchased a small auto-parts business from their uncle Jacob in Cleveland in the 1940s and formed their own Premier Industrial Corporation, which they developed into a billion-dollar family fortune by distributing hard-to-find automotive and electronic parts. The family runs seven foundations and annually disburses about $9 million, almost all of it to Jewish causes.

MANKIEWICZES

Herman Jacob Mankiewicz (born November 7, 1897, in New York City; died March 5, 1953, in Los Angeles, California) was a journalist, playwright, and screenwriter best known as the principal author of the script for the film *Citizen Kane* (1941). **Joseph Leo Mankiewicz** (born February 11, 1909, in Wilkes-Barre, Pennsylvania; died February 5, 1993, in Mount Kisco, New York), Herman's brother, won Academy Awards two years in a row for both screenwriting and directing *A Letter to Three Wives* (1949) and *All about Eve* (1950). **Donald Martin Mankiewicz** (born January 22, 1920, in Berlin, Germany), one of Herman's sons, is a novelist and screenwriter who coscripted the highly regarded film *I Want to Live!* (1958). **Frank Fabian Mankiewicz** (born May 16, 1924, in New York City), another of Herman's sons, is a journalist and lawyer who served as press secretary to Robert F. Kennedy during 1966–68, political director of George McGovern's 1972 presidential campaign, and president of National Public Radio during 1977–83. **Thomas F. Mankiewicz** (born June 1, 1942, in Los Angeles), Joseph's son, is a screenwriter and director who coscripted and directed the movie *Dragnet* (1987).

MARSHALLS

Louis Marshall (born December 14, 1856, in Syracuse, New York; died September 11, 1929, in Zurich, Switzerland) was the foremost American constitutional lawyer of his time, led the American Jewish Committee, and worked for the freedom of all minority groups. His son **James Marshall** (born May 12, 1896, in New York City; died August 11, 1986, in New York City) was a lawyer who worked at his father's law firm and elsewhere, served on the New York City Board of Education (1938–52), and held leadership positions in many organizations, including the American Jewish Committee, the Jewish Publication Society, and the American Friends of the Hebrew University. **Robert Marshall** (born 1901; died November 11, 1939, en route from New York City to Washington, D.C.), another of Louis's sons, directed the forestry division of the United States Office of Indian Affairs (1933–37) and headed the division of recreation and soil conservation of the United States Forest Service (1937–39).

MARXES

Family of comedians never equaled, by a team or an individual, in the ability to combine nonsense, slapstick, satire, pantomime, black humor, and witty dialogue. The Marx Brothers began in vaudeville, moved to Broadway, and reached their greatest popularity in the films *The Cocoanuts* (1929), *Animal Crackers* (1930), *Monkey Business* (1931), *Horse Feathers* (1932), *Duck Soup* (1933), *A Night at the Opera* (1935), *A Day at the Races* (1937), *Room Service* (1938), *At the Circus* (1939), *Go West* (1940), *The Big Store* (1941), *A Night in Casablanca* (1946), and *Love Happy* (1950). **Chico** (pronounced *chicko*, not *cheeko*; originally Leonard; born August 21, 1887, in New York City; died October 11, 1961, in Beverly Hills, California) spoke in a mock Italian accent, loved wordplay, and performed on the piano. **Harpo** (originally Adolph, later Arthur; born November 23, 1888, in New York City; died September 28, 1964, in Los Angeles, California) portrayed an uninhibited childlike mute, wore a fright wig and an overcoat stuffed with bizarre objects (such as a blowtorch, an ice-cream cone, and a ton of hardware), and played the harp. **Groucho** (originally Julius; born October 2, 1890, in New York City; died August 19, 1977, in Los Angeles) led the team, wore an ill-fitting frock coat, sported a painted-on mustache, constantly smoked and flicked a cigar, insinuatingly twitched his eyebrows, aggressively leaned forward while walking, uttered savage wisecracks at virtually everyone, and sang comic songs (he expressed the Marx Brothers spirit when he sang "Whatever It Is, I'm against It" in *Horse Feathers*). **Gummo** (originally Milton; born October 23, 1892, in New York City; died April 21, 1977, in Palm Springs, California) appeared with the team in vaudeville but left during World War I. He was replaced by the youngest brother, **Zeppo** (originally Herbert; born February 25, 1901, in New York City; died November 30, 1979, in Palm Springs), who performed with his brothers on the stage and in their first five films (leaving after *Duck Soup*), in which he played the straight man to Groucho, sang the romantic ballads, and got the girl but not the gags. Their uncle (their mother's brother) **Al**

Marx Brothers: Harpo, Chico, and Groucho (left to right).

Shean (originally Adolf Schönberg; born May 12, 1868, in Dornum, Germany; died August 12, 1949, in New York City) was a famous vaudeville comedian, especially noted for his work in the team of Gallagher and Shean.

MENUHINS

Yehudi Menuhin (born April 22, 1916, in New York City) is one of the great violinists of the twentieth century. He is especially renowned for his use of music for humanitarian purposes, such as playing for the Allied troops during World War II; performing for survivors of the death camps in July 1945; being the first American artist, in November 1945, to perform in the Soviet Union after the war; arranging cultural exchanges between the United States and India and the United States and the Soviet Union during the height of the Cold War in the 1950s; performing in Israel for a variety of causes; and giving concerts in Arab

Yehudi Menuhin

countries for the benefit of Arab refugees. His two sisters became outstanding pianists, as soloists and as chamber music players: **Hephzibah Menuhin** (born May 20, 1920, in San Francisco, California; died January 1, 1981, in London, England) and **Yaltah Menuhin** (born October 7, 1922, in San Francisco).

State of Israel Government Press Office

Henry Morgenthau, Jr. (left).

MORGENTHAUS

Henry Morgenthau (born April 26, 1856, in Mannheim, Germany; died November 25, 1946, in New York City) was a lawyer who introduced the corporate form of operation in real estate (1899), served as American ambassador to Turkey (1913–16), promoted American participation in the League of Nations (1919), and helped to form the International Red Cross (1919). He became the first president of the Free Synagogue in New York City and was among the most outspoken in warning against Adolf Hitler in the 1930s. **Henry Morgenthau, Jr.** (born May 11, 1891, in New York

City; died February 6, 1967, in Poughkeepsie, New York), Henry's son, served as the United States secretary of the treasury (1934–45) and handled three times more money than all of his predecessors combined. **Robert Morris Morgenthau** (born July 31, 1919, in New York City), son of the preceding, has served in New York City as United States attorney (1961–70) and as district attorney (since 1975). He is a trustee of the Baron de Hirsch Fund, the Federated Jewish Philanthropies, and Temple Emanu-El.

NEWHOUSES

Samuel Irving Newhouse (originally Solomon Neuhaus; born May 24, 1895, in New York City; died August 29, 1979, in New York City) founded a media empire whose value by the mid-1990s was estimated at $9 billion, making the Newhouses the wealthiest Jewish family in the United States. Among the family members who joined the business were his two brothers, Theodore and Norman Newhouse; his two sons, **Samuel Irving Newhouse, Jr.** (1927–) and **Donald Edward Newhouse** (1929–); and **Mark William Newhouse** (born October 14, 1948, in New York City), the elder Samuel's nephew (Norman's son). Family holdings at one time or another included about thirty newspapers, such as the *Cleveland Plain Dealer* and the *Newark Star-Ledger*; the magazines *Gentlemen's Quarterly*, *New Yorker*, *Vanity Fair*, and *Vogue*; several radio stations; and cable television companies, notably the Discovery Channel. The family's Samuel I. Newhouse Foundation has donated to many Jewish and non-Jewish causes, including about $1 million annually for education.

OISTRAKHS

David Oistrakh (born September 30, 1908, in Odessa, the Ukraine; died October 24, 1974, in Amsterdam, the Netherlands) was recognized worldwide as the most characteristic representative of violinists in the Soviet Union. **Igor Oistrakh** (born April

27, 1931, in Odessa, Ukrainian Republic, the Soviet Union), David's son and pupil, was also an internationally renowned violinist. Father and son often performed violin duets and double concertos together, and sometimes David conducted violin concertos with Igor as soloist.

PALEYS

Samuel Paley (born December 15, 1875, in Brovary, near Kiev, the Ukraine, Russia; died March 31, 1963, in Palm Beach, Florida) was a successful cigar manufacturer who marketed his principal brand, La Palina, through his Congress Cigar Company. He was active in Jewish charities. **William S. Paley** (he added the middle initial S. when he was twelve; born September 28, 1901, in Chicago, Illinois; died October 26, 1990, in New York City), Samuel's son, built the Columbia Broadcasting System (CBS) into a radio and television giant. In 1927 he invested in the little company that would become CBS; and the following year, with financial help from his father, he took control of the firm. He served till 1946 as company president and thereafter as chairman.

PEIXOTTOS

Moses Levi Maduro Peixotto (born 1767 on Curaçao, the Netherlands Antilles, or in Amsterdam, the Netherlands; died 1828 in New York City), a merchant, came to the United States in 1807, and from 1816 till his death he was rabbi of the Congregation Shearith Israel in New York City. **Daniel Levi Maduro Peixotto** (born 1800 in Amsterdam, the Netherlands; died 1843 in New York City), Moses' son, was a leading physician in New York City, where he served as president of the Medical Society, helped to found the Academy of Medicine, and edited *The New York Medical and Physical Journal*, the first regular quarterly medical journal in the English language. He was also a leader in the Jewish community, serving, for example, as cantor of the Congregation

Shearith Israel from 1820 till his death. **Benjamin Franklin Peixotto** (born November 13, 1834, in New York City; died September 18, 1890, in New York City), Daniel's son, became an admired newspaper editor and lawyer; headed B'nai B'rith (1863–66); served as United States consul to Bucharest, Romania (1870–76),where he successfully fought anti-Semitism, and Lyons, France (1877–85); and founded *The Menorah* (1886), for many years the only English-language Jewish monthly. **George da Madura Peixotto** (born 1859 or 1864 in Cleveland, Ohio; died October 12, 1937, in White Plains, New York), Benjamin's son, painted well-known portraits, such as those of Moses Montefiore and President William McKinley, and did murals for the New Amsterdam Theater and the Criterion Club in New York City.

PÉREIRES

Jacob Rodrigues Péreire (or, in Spanish, Jacob Rodriguez Pereira; born 1715 in Berlanga, Spain; died 1780 in Paris, France) was the first person to teach deaf-mutes with any degree of success. He also served as counsellor of the Sephardic community in Paris. The brothers **Jacob Émile Péreire** (born 1800 in Bordeaux, France; died 1875 in Paris) and **Isaac Péreire** (born 1806 in Bordeaux; died 1880 in Armanvilliers, France), Jacob's grandsons, produced important economic writings; helped to form the Crédit Mobilier, the first modern investment bank in France; served in the French legislature; and took leadership roles in Jewish affairs. **Eugène Péreire** (born 1831 in Paris; died March 1908 in Paris), Isaac's son, was trained as a civil engineer but devoted his career to the interests of his family. He helped to administer one of the railroads that his father and uncle financed, helped to organize the Spanish Crédit Mobilier, joined the older Péreires in the French legislature, emulated his great-grandfather by aiding the education of deaf-mutes, and took an active part in Jewish communal work.

REINACHS

Hermann Joseph Reinach (born 1814 in Frankfurt, Germany; died 1899 in Paris, France) was a successful banker who moved to Paris in 1843 and had three famous sons. **Joseph Reinach** (born 1856 in Paris; died 1921 in Paris), a writer and politician, was among the most vociferous in calling for a new trial for Captain Alfred Dreyfus, a Jewish army officer falsely convicted of treason, and wrote a seven-volume history of the affair (published 1901–1911). **Salomon** (or Solomon) **Reinach** (born 1858 in Saint-Germain-en-Laye, near Paris; died 1932 in Paris) wrote many valuable works on philology, archaeology, and the history of religion and the arts. **Théodore Reinach** (born 1860 in Saint-Germain-en-Laye; died 1928 in Paris), was a jurist, politician, philologist, and historian in several fields, including Jewish studies.

ROSENWALDS

Julius Rosenwald (born August 12, 1862, in Springfield, Illinois; died January 6, 1932, in Chicago, Illinois) played a major role in developing the mail-order giant Sears, Roebuck and Company, serving as its vice president and treasurer (1895–1910), president (1910–25), and chairman of the board of directors (1925–32). He created the Julius Rosenwald Fund (1917) to further interracial understanding, and he helped to found the Federation of Jewish Charities in Chicago (1923). His elder son, **Lessing Julius Rosenwald** (born February 10, 1891, in Chicago; died June 25, 1979, in Jenkintown, Pennsylvania), held managerial positions at Sears, Roebuck and Company before succeeding his father as chairman (1932–39). He also headed the trustees of the Julius Rosenwald Fund and organized the non-Zionist American Council for Judaism (1943). Julius's younger son, **William Rosenwald** (born August 19, 1903, in Chicago; died October 31, 1996, in New York City), was a director at Sears, Roebuck and Company (1934–38), became a private investor, and engaged in extensive philanthropic activities, serving as honorary president of the

United Jewish Appeal–Federation of Jewish Philanthropies in New York City, a life trustee and honorary national chairman of the United Jewish Appeal, and a life member of the board of directors of the Council of Jewish Federations.

RUBINSTEINS

Anton Rubinstein (born November 28, 1829, in Vikhvatinetz, Russia; died November 20, 1894, in Peterhof, Russia) was, with Franz Liszt, one of the two most lionized pianists of his time. Rubinstein's *Ocean Symphony* (1951, revised 1863 and 1880) was the most popular orchestral work in Europe during the second half of the nineteenth century. In 1862 he helped to establish the Saint Petersburg Conservatory and became its first director (1862–67, again in 1887–91); one of his pupils was Peter Tchaikovsky. **Nikolay Rubinstein** (born June 14, 1835, in Moscow, Russia; died March 23, 1881, in Paris, France), Anton's brother, was an outstanding pianist and conductor, and in 1866 he founded the Moscow Conservatory, which he headed till his death. Their parents had Anton and Nikolay baptized into the Russian Orthodox church, not out of religious conviction but for the practical purpose of opening doors of opportunity in pogrom-prone Russia.

SCHNEERSOHNS

Family of religious leaders who headed the Habad (or Chabad) Hasidism movement for two hundred years. The founder of the movement was **Shneur Zalman of Lyady** (known as *Alter Rebbe* ["Old Rabbi"] and *Ba'al ha-Tanya* ["Author of the Tanya"]; born 1745 in Liozno, near Vitebsk, Russia; died 1813 in the Ukraine), whose *Likkutei amarim* ("Collected Sayings," 1797), which became known as the *Tanya* (1814), is the principal source of doctrine for Habad Hasidism. The family name of Shneur Zalman's descendants came to be *Schneersohn* ("son of Shneur"). He was succeeded as head of the sect by his eldest son, **Dov Baer** (in full, Baer

Menachem Mendel Schneerson

ben Shneur Zalman, or Baer of Lubavitch; 1773–1827), who settled in the little town of Luba-vitch, where for generations the main leaders of Habad lived, each called the *Lubavitcher Rebbe* ("Lubavitch Rabbi"). The third Habad leader was **Menahem Mendel** (1789–1866), Dov Baer's nephew and son-in-law. After Menahem's death, the sect could not agree on a successor, and three of his sons broke away to set up new branches of Habad (eventually, however, these branches reunited with the original group): **Judah Leib** (1811–66) founded a branch in Kopys; **Hayyim Shneur Zalman** (1814–80), in Lyady; and **Israel Noah** (1816–83), in Nezhin. **Samuel** (1834–82), Menahem's youngest son, succeeded his father at Lubavitch, becoming the fourth head of the original dynasty. **Shalom Dov Baer** (1866–1920), Samuel's son, was the fifth of the line and founded the first Hasidic yeshiva (1897). Next in succession was **Joseph Isaac** (born 1880; died January 28, 1950, in New York City), Shalom's son, who became the foremost religious leader of Russian Jewry during the civil war that followed the 1917 Revolution, left Russia in 1927 to live in Europe, fled the Nazis in 1940 and immigrated to the United States, and founded the Lubavitcher Yeshiva in Brooklyn and the Kefar Habad in Israel. Arguably the most successful member of the clan was the seventh leader, **Menachem Mendel**, who spelled his surname *Schneerson* (born April 18, 1902, in Nikolayev, the Ukraine; died June 12, 1994, in New York City), a son-in-law of Joseph and, on his father's side, a direct descendant of Shneur Zalman of Lyady. Menahem transformed the Lubavitch Habad from a provincial Hasidic sect into the fastest-growing segment of Orthodox Judaism.

SELZNICKS

One of the most important early families in the motion-picture industry. The founder was **Lewis Joseph Selznick** (original surname, Seleznick; unrecorded birth reported by Selznick himself on one occasion as May 2, 1872, in Kiev, the Ukraine, Russia, and on another as May 5, 1871, in Poland; elsewhere given as May 2, 1870, in Kiev; but circumstantial evidence points to 1869 in or near Kovno [or Kaunas], Lithuania; died January 25, 1933, in Los Angeles, California). He immigrated to the United States and built a prosperous jewelry business in Pittsburgh, Pennsylvania. Later he moved to New York City and became one of the earliest producers of silent films. One of his sons, **Myron Charles Selznick** (born October 8, 1898, in Pittsburgh; died March 23, 1944, in Santa Monica, California), became the industry's youngest producer, rose to the presidency of one of his father's motion-picture companies, and spent his later years as Hollywood's leading talent agent, representing over three hundred actors and directors. Another of Lewis's sons, **David Oliver Selznick** (originally without the middle name, which he adopted as a young man; born May 10, 1902, in Pittsburgh; died June 22, 1965, in Los Angeles), was the prototype of the creative, independent Hollywood producer. His films include *Gone with the Wind* (1939), *Spellbound* (1945), and *The Third Man* (1949).

SONCINOS

Family of Hebrew printers active in Italy, Turkey, and Egypt in the fifteenth and sixteenth centuries. **Moses** (fl. mid-fifteenth century) of Fuerth, Germany, succeeded in driving the Franciscan monk and troublemaker John of Capistrano out of Fuerth. **Samuel** (died 1485) and **Simon** (fl. late fifteenth century), Moses' sons, went to Italy and in 1454 received permission to settle in Soncino, near Cremona—thus the family surname. **Israel Nathan** (died c. 1492 in Brescia, Italy), Samuel's son, was a physician and talmudic scholar. **Joshua Solomon** (died 1493), one of Israel's sons, set up a

Hebrew printing press and published a talmudic tractate (1484, his first book), a complete voweled Hebrew Bible (1488), and other works. His books were the first printed editions of Talmud tractates and the Hebrew Bible. He published about forty works in his career. Joining him in the business were his brothers, notably **Moses** (died 1489). Moses' son **Solomon** (died probably 1499) also worked in the family business, as did **Gershom ben Moses** (died 1534 in Salonika, Greece), Solomon's brother. Gershom, one of the greatest printing artists in history, issued works in Hebrew, Latin, Greek, and Italian—about two hundred books in all. He made extensive travels to uncover valuable manuscripts, such as Moses Maimonides' *Mishneh Torah* and the tosaphoth of Eliezer of Touques. Gershom, famed for his brilliant lettering and overall execution, was the first to produce secular Hebrew literature and the first to use woodcut illustrations in Hebrew books. His sons **Moses** (died c. 1530) and **Eliezer** (died 1547) became printers, while the third son, **Joshua** (died 1569), served as rabbi of the Sephardi Great Synagogue in Constantinople. The last known Soncino printer was **Gershom** (died 1562), Eliezer's son, who printed in Cairo, Egypt, in 1557.

SPEYERS

Family of German and American international bankers and philanthropists. **Michael Isaac Speyer** (died 1692) settled in 1644 in the Frankfurt am Main, Germany, ghetto, where he became community head. **Isaac Michael Speyer** (died 1807), Michael's great-grandson, was an Imperial Court Jew. **Joseph Lazarus Speyer** (1783–1846), Isaac's nephew, married into the Frankfurt banking family of Ellissen. **Lazarus Joseph Speyer** (1810–76), Joseph's son, carried on the banking business from 1836 under the company name of Lazard Speyer-Ellissen. One branch of the family immigrated to the United States. The first to move was **Philip Speyer** (1815–76), who settled in New York City in 1837 and founded the banking firm of Philip Speyer and Company, which retained an affliation with the Frankfurt office. In 1845 he was joined by his brother, **Gustavus Speyer** (1825–83). Eventually the firm's name was simplified to Speyer and Company. The Speyers placed the first American Civil War loan in Germany. Gustavus had two sons, both of whom entered banking. The elder, **James Joseph Speyer** (born July 22, 1861, in New York City; died October 31, 1941, in New York City), headed the American office during the early 1900s, when it became one of the great international banking houses, especially in the financing of railroads. **Edgar Speyer** (born September 7, 1862, in New York City; died February 16, 1932, in Berlin, Germany), James's younger brother, moved to London, England, where he directed another branch of the family banking business, Speyer Brothers. It, too, had great success with railways. The worldwide business crisis during the Great Depression took its toll on the Speyers, and in the 1930s both the German and the American houses were liquidated. The last head of the Frankfurt office was **Eduard Beit von Speyer** (1860–1933), originally named Eduard Beit, a brother-in-law of James and Edgar Speyer. Kaiser Wilhelm conferred the title of *von Speyer* on Beit to ensure the continuance of the great banking name in Frankfurt. The family's philanthropic gifts benefited many institutions, including Frankfurt University, the Museum of the City of New York, and Mount Sinai Hospital of New York City.

STROOCKS

American family of businessmen, lawyers, philanthropists, and Jewish community leaders. In 1870 the German immigrant **Samuel Stroock** (fl. late nineteenth century) founded S. Stroock and Company, a manufacturer of woolen goods. He had five well-known sons: **Louis S. Stroock** (born 1855; died March 28, 1925, in Atlantic City, New Jersey), **Mark E. Stroock** (born 1863; died February 28, 1926, in New York City), **Moses J. Stroock** (born 1866 in New York City; died October 1931 in New York City), **Joseph Stroock** (born 1869 in New York City; died August 26, 1946, in Deal, New Jersey), and **Solomon Marcuse Stroock** (born September 22, 1873, in New York City; died September 11, 1941, in

White Sulphur Springs, West Virginia). Louis became president of S. Stroock and Company, headed the board of trustees at Congregation B'nai Jeshurun, and was a noted philanthropist. Mark served as a director and officer at the family firm. Moses, a lawyer who specialized in corporate law, formed a law partnership in 1907 with his brother Solomon; served as chairman of the board of education for New York City; and was active in Jewish organizations, especially the Federation for the Support of Jewish Philanthropic Societies. Joseph became president of S. Stroock and Company and financially helped Stephen S. Wise to set up the Free Synagogue and the Jewish Institute of Religion in New York City. Solomon, a lawyer who specialized in constitutional law, worked with Moses at their law firm; held positions of leadership with many Jewish organizations, such as president of the American Jewish Committee; and played a prominent role in Democratic politics. **Alan Maxwell Stroock** (born November 12, 1907, in New York City; died March 29, 1985, in New York City), Solomon's son, followed his father as a lawyer; became a partner in the family law firm; and was active in Jewish communal affairs, supporting the Jewish Theological Seminary of America, acting as vice president of the American Jewish Committee, and performing many related services. **Daniel Wyler Stroock** (born March 20, 1940, in New York City), Alan's son, is a renowned mathematician, educator, and scholarly writer-editor.

WARNERS

Four Warner brothers founded Warner Bros., one of the major film studios in Hollywood history. (The original family name is obscure. Some sources record the brothers' father as Benjamin Eichelbaum, while others record it as Benjamin Warner, with their mother, Benjamin's wife, as Pearl Eichelbaum.) **Harry Morris Warner** (originally Hirsch Warner; born December 12, 1881, in Krasnashiltz, Poland; died July 25, 1958, in Los Angeles, California) was in charge of the company's New York City business headquarters. **Albert** ("Abe," originally Abraham) **Warner** (born

July 23, 1884, in Baltimore, Maryland; died November 26, 1867, in Miami Beach, Florida) served as treasurer and head of sales and distribution. **Samuel Louis Warner** (born August 10, 1887, in Baltimore; died October 5, 1927, in Los Angeles) managed the Hollywood production studios. **Jack Leonard Warner** (originally Jacob Warner; born August 2, 1892, in London, Ontario, Canada; died September 9, 1978, in Los Angeles) took over the Hollywood studios after Sam's death. Jack's only son, **Jack Warner, Jr.** (originally Jack M. Warner; born March 27, 1916, in San Francisco, California; died April 1, 1995, in Los Angeles), worked in executive positions for Warner Bros. till 1959, when he became an independent film producer. Warner Bros. produced *Don Juan* (1926), the first motion picture with a completely synchronized music track; *The Jazz Singer* (1927), the first commercially important film with synchronized music and dialogue; *Lights of New York* (1928), the first full-length all-talking film; *On with the Show* (1929), the first all-talking color film; *Little Caesar* (1930), the motion picture that began the gangster-film craze; and such classics as *The Adventures of Robin Hood* (1938), *The Maltese Falcon* (1941), *Casablanca* (1943), *A Streetcar Named Desire* (1951), and *My Fair Lady* (1964).

WEIZMANNS

Chaim Azriel Weizmann (born November 27, 1874, in Motol, near Pinsk, Russian-ruled Poland; died November 9, 1952, in Rehovot, Israel) was for decades the guiding spirit of the World Zionist Organization and served as the first president of the state of Israel (1949–52). **Ezer Weizman** (original surname, Weizmann; born June 15, 1924, in Tel Aviv, Palestine), Chaim's nephew, headed Israel's air force (1958–66), was chief of opera-

State of Israel Government Press Office

Chaim Weizmann

tions of the General Staff Branch of General Headquarters (1966–69), and then entered Israeli politics. In 1993 he was elected president of Israel.

ZIFFS

William Bernard Ziff (born August 1, 1898, in Chicago, Illinois; died December 20, 1953, in New York City) began writing, editing, and publishing the humorous *Ziff's Magazine* (later *America's Humor*) in 1923; founded, with Bernard Davis, the Popular Aviation Corporation publishing company in 1933; changed its name to Ziff-Davis Publishing Company in 1935; published a wide range of periodicals, including *Amazing Stories*, *Flying*, *Popular Photography*, and *Radio News*; and wrote several nonfiction books on contemporary events, such as *The Rape of Palestine* (1938). His son **William Bernard Ziff, Jr.** (1930–), succeeded him at the company, bought out Bernard Davis, and added more magazines to the group, such as *Car and Driver*, *PC Magazine*, and *Stereo Review*; the son also acquired television stations. In the mid-1980s the second William, because of ill health, sold the magazines, except for a few dealing with personal computing, and continued the business as Ziff Communication Company. In 1993, on the verge of retiring, he offered the business to his sons: **Dirk Edward Ziff** (1964–), **Robert David Ziff** (1967–), and **Daniel Morton Ziff** (1972–). In 1994 the sons opted to sell the magazines for $1.4 billion and establish their own Ziff Brothers Investments company.

INDEX